Taiwan in World Affairs

*Published in cooperation with
The Gaston Sigur Center for East Asian Studies,
The George Washington University,
Washington, DC*

Taiwan in World Affairs

EDITED BY

Robert G. Sutter
and William R. Johnson

Westview Press

BOULDER • SAN FRANCISCO • OXFORD

Copyright © 1994 by Westview Press, Inc.

Published in 1994 in the United States of America by Westview Press, Inc., 5500 Central Avenue, Boulder, Colorado 80301-2877, and in the United Kingdom by Westview Press, 36 Lonsdale Road, Summertown, Oxford OX2 7EW

Library of Congress Cataloging-in-Publication Data
Taiwan in world affairs / edited by Robert G. Sutter and William R. Johnson
    p.   cm.
  Includes bibliographical references.
  ISBN 0-8133-1895-5
  1. Taiwan—Foreign relations—1945– 2. Taiwan—Politics and government—1988– 3. Taiwan—Economic conditions—1975–
I. Sutter, Robert G.   II. Johnson, William R., 1929–
DS799.848.T35   1994
327.5124'9—dc20   94-10740
                                                                                CIP

Printed and bound in the United States of America

The paper used in this publication meets the requirements
of the American National Standard for Permanence of Paper
for Printed Library Materials Z39.48-1984.

10   9   8   7   6   5   4   3   2   1

Contents

Preface

From the early 1970s until the late 1980s, Taiwan's status on the international diplomatic scene and its role in relations between the United States and the People's Republic of China (PRC) appeared to be defined by the well-known 1972 Shanghai Communiqué, the 1979 U.S. recognition of the PRC, the Taiwan Relations Act, and the Communiqué of 1982 relating to arms sales to Taiwan. However, Taiwan's burgeoning economy combined with dramatic sociopolitical changes, most noticeably since 1986-1987, have brought a more confident, diplomatically creative, influential, and assertive Taiwan to the fore. Democratization, "Taiwanization," and "sub-ethnic political competition" recently led, in the case of the opposition Democratic Progressive Party, to a call for the independence of Taiwan. Economic ministers and trade representatives from Western countries began to appear in Taipei. Some informed observers in the United States even began—rather quietly—to inquire whether the "three communiqués" were still effective operational guidelines for U.S. policy. These stunning political developments together with unmistakable economic power combined once again to thrust Taiwan onto the agendas of policymakers in Washington and Beijing.

To assess the impact of these changes for Taiwan in world affairs and their implications for the foreign policies of the United States and for U.S.-PRC relations, The George Washington University's Gaston Sigur Center for East Asian Studies decided in the fall of 1992 to form a "Taiwan study group." Robert Sutter graciously agreed to chair the study group and thereafter he provided the substantive intellectual focus and direction for the study over the entire life of the project.

A distinguished group of specialists from universities and research institutions from throughout the country was invited to write the papers that eventually became the chapters of this book. The papers were then submitted to a larger "core group" of scholars and practitioners who met in a series of eight dinner meetings at The George Washington University throughout the late fall and spring of 1992-1993 for a full discussion of the papers. In addition, formally designated discussants presented prepared written comments at the outset of each dinner meeting. The very lively dinner discussions saw a group with many diverse views who subjected the papers to thorough critical analysis. I am confident that the authors of this volume share my view that the "core group" of critics, led by the discussant, played a very important role in producing the high quality of the chapters found in this work and would wish to join me in expressing appreciation for their help. Those who attended the dinner meetings and contributed significantly to the finished product while bearing no responsibility for it included: A. Doak Barnett, Natale Ballochi, David Laux, Zhiling Lin, Mark Pratt, Lucian Pye, Thomas Robinson, Cliff Tan, David Tsai, Alfred Wilhelm, Mary Brown Bullock, James R. Lilley, and Douglas Paal.

The question inevitably arises as to whether or not to include the formal discussants' comments in the final product. In this instance, the coauthors found the decision to be an easy one. In some cases, as the reader will readily discern, the discussant's comments provide a significantly different interpretation than the chapter that they follow. In other instances, the basic interpretation found in the chapter and in the discussant's remarks are largely similar but the tone and flavor are notably and tellingly different. In still other cases, the discussant's comments will be found to add important new information that was not included in the preceding chapter. For all of those reasons, and particularly because the Sigur Center is committed above all to presenting as wide and disparate a set of views and interpretations as possible, we are most pleased to include the discussants' papers in this volume.

While the Sigur Center does not necessarily endorse any of the specific interpretations or policy prescriptions found in this volume, it does hope that the publication of these materials will contribute significantly to a fuller understanding of the many complex issues involved. Volumes produced through large "study groups" and edited in a timely manner require the assistance of many persons. The coeditors wish to express our deepest thanks and respect for Ms. Leila Hertzberg, who expertly edited all of the copy, and to Ms. Mary Evelyn (Mamie) Barrett who, as a graduate assistant at the Sigur Center, arranged all the dinner meetings and, in general, oversaw administrative arrangements for the entire project.

William R. Johnson
The Gaston Sigur Center
for East Asian Studies
The George Washington University

1

Taiwan's Role in World Affairs: Background, Status, and Prospects

Robert G. Sutter

Introduction

Backed by a vibrant economy and increasingly internationalized political and social atmosphere, Taiwan in recent years has emerged as an increasingly important actor in world affairs. As in the past, the main obstacle to Taiwan playing a greater role has to do with Beijing's strong opposition to Taiwan gaining official status as a separate entity in international affairs. Recent trends in Taiwan, in Taiwan-mainland relations, and in international developments on balance suggest that Taiwan will make greater progress in establishing itself as an important force in world economic, social, and political affairs in the years to come.[1]

Beijing is not without influence in this situation, particularly as its vast and rapidly growing economy exerts extraordinary influence on decision makers throughout Asia and the world, including Taiwan. The wider range of political forces influencing government decision makers in Taipei contains those who advocate extreme positions on self determination and independence that could jeopardize Taiwan-mainland stability and promote conflict across the Taiwan Strait. Nonetheless, the economic and political changes on the mainland seem to reinforce a moderate stance toward Taiwan based on growing economic interdependence. And, despite the existence of extreme views in Taiwan, voters and politicians there have had several opportunities in recent years to stake out extreme political positions, but have invariably chosen a moderate course designed to avoid unnecessary tension while sustaining and strengthening Taipei's *de facto* independent stature.

Historical Experience

Historically, Taiwan's importance in world affairs was more as an area acted upon by others, rather than as a significant force in its own right.[2] In the latter nineteenth century, disputes over sovereignty and control concerning Taiwan exacerbated tensions between the newly established government of Meiji Japan and the declining Manchu dynasty in China. A Sino-Japanese war in 1894-1895 ended with a settlement that passed Taiwan from Chinese to Japanese rule. For the next fifty years, Taiwan was integrated by Japanese officials into the growing Japanese empire in East Asia. Taiwan was not a significant battleground in the allied war against Japan in the 1940s, but the allied powers agreed to return the island to Chinese rule in 1945. Chinese nationalist (also known as Kuomintang or KMT) authorities sent troops and administrators to the island but their mismanagement and corruption led to a wave of dissidence and a bloody crackdown in 1947 that has soured the relationship between the nationalist "mainlanders" and indigenous "Taiwanese" to this day.

With the defeat of the nationalists by the communists on the Chinese mainland, Chiang Kai-shek and about two million other mainlanders sought refuge in Taiwan where they established the new base of their Republic of China. They appealed for additional U.S. aid but the United States seemed prepared to await the expected communist assault and victory against the disorganized nationalists, and to "let the dust settle" before moving to switch U.S. recognition as the government of China from Chiang's nationalists to the communists in Beijing.

North Korea's attack on South Korea in June 1950 saw the United States shift its stance on Taiwan, send naval forces to intervene between communists and nationalists in the Taiwan Strait, and thereby assure that Taiwan's future would be different from the mainland's. From that time forward, the United States has maintained some form of defense commitment or interest in Taiwan. During the 1950s and 1960s, the United States endeavored to strengthen Taiwan's position as a key link in the ring of "containment" the United States constructed and maintained around China's periphery in Asia. This involved the deployment of U.S. forces, the establishment of a formal defense treaty, and large amounts of U.S. military and economic aid. The United States also endeavored to encourage economic development policies that would allow Taiwan to be more economically prosperous and less dependent on U.S. aid. It notably encouraged Taiwan to break out of its past practices and employ means such as land reform, broadened international investment and trade and other means to help integrate Taiwan more closely with the world economy. In world politics, the United States was in the lead in supporting the position of the Republic of China as the sole legitimate government of China and the holder of the China seat at the United Nations (UN) Security Council.

The communists in Beijing chafed under the U.S. containment, which they viewed as their most important security threat and a major affront to their legitimacy as the government of China. From time to time, Mao Zedong employed Chinese military force along the Taiwan Strait to test the resolve of the nationalists and their American backers and to seek openings for Beijing to reassert control over nationalist-held territories. On occasion, such actions precipitated major world crises involving the United States and the Soviet Union, their allies and associates. Beijing also sometimes employed softer tactics in dealing with the nationalists, encouraging their leaders to heed the call of Chinese patriotism and work with Beijing for the cause of the reunification of China.

During the 1960s, the communists on the mainland confronted major internal problems caused by the mass starvation and deprivation resulting from the economically disastrous Great Leap Forward and the destruction of much of the Chinese Communist Party and government structure during the Cultural Revolution. In Taiwan, the nationalists were successfully laying the groundwork for the foreign investment and export-led growth that was to become a trademark of Taiwan's development in later years. Authoritarian political rule maintained social order and economic conditions attractive to outside investors. The government placed strong emphasis on developing education and material infrastructure needed for more rapid economic modernization. The United States followed economic policies that facilitated investment for export from Taiwan to the U.S. market.

U.S.-PRC Rapprochement

Taiwan's continued strong dependence on the United States was nonetheless underlined at the time of the shift in U.S. policy in Asia beginning in the late 1960s.[3] At this time a convergence of strategic needs drove Beijing and Washington closer together, leading to the Sino-American rapprochement seen during President Nixon's 1972 visit to China. The United States needed a means to sustain a favorable balance of power in Asia while withdrawing over 600,000 troops from Indochina and elsewhere in Asia under the terms of the Nixon Doctrine, and a means to balance the growing power and assertiveness of the Soviet Union. The People's Republic of China (PRC) in Beijing faced a new and growing Soviet military threat along its northern border and needed the relationship with Washington to counter Soviet threats and intimidation.

In the interest of solidifying U.S. relations with Beijing in the so-called great power triangular relationship (i.e., U.S.-PRC-USSR), U.S. leaders increasingly accommodated Beijing's demands regarding U.S. policy in the U.S.-PRC-Taiwan triangular relationship. Throughout the 1970s, the United States gradually cut back its military presence in Taiwan and in 1979 it ended official relations, including the U.S.-Taiwan defense treaty, in order to establish formal relations with Beijing as the sole, legal government of China.[4] The U.S. shift was accompanied by a massive decline in Taiwan's international standing as scores of countries switched diplomatic relations to Beijing and Taiwan was excluded or withdrew from the UN and other international organizations.

Beijing endeavored to capitalize on its enhanced stature and Taipei's growing international political (but not economic) isolation. It followed a carrot- and-stick policy of concurrent gestures and pressures designed to bring Taipei into formal negotiations on reunification. Carrots included ceasing the largely symbolic PRC artillery barrages against the nationalist-held offshore islands of Quemoy and Matsu, launching a series of official statements underlining Beijing's flexibility regarding conditions for Taiwan's return to the mainland, and gestures designed to encourage the so-called "three communications" (i.e., direct mail, trade, and transportation) between Taiwan and the mainland.[5]

The PRC's success in negotiating an agreement with Great Britain in 1984 calling for Hong Kong's return to the mainland in 1997 prompted Deng Xiaoping and other senior PRC leaders to hold up the "one country-two systems" approach used in that accord as a model for Taiwan's reunification. Deng and others promised that not only would the political, economic, and social system in Taiwan be guaranteed, as in the case of Hong Kong, but Taiwan would be able to maintain its separate defense forces.

The PRC "stick" took various forms. Taipei leaders were warned—sometimes with allusions to possible PRC use of force—against undue delay, with PRC leaders repeatedly asserting that the settlement of the so-called Taiwan issue must be given a high priority in the 1980s. America and others with unofficial contacts with Taiwan were repeatedly pressed to cut back those ties in sensitive areas, especially the sale of weapons. They were also warned against efforts to boost Taiwan's international standing through membership in international governmental organizations.

The Challenge to Taipei's Legitimacy and Taipei's Response

These developments posed the most serious challenge for the nationalist administration in Taiwan since the retreat from the mainland in 1949. Taipei's officials were loath to enter talks with the PRC on reunification. In part, this reflected their sense that they would be the decidedly weaker party in the talks and that Beijing would likely use the negotiations to further undermine U.S. and other backing for Taiwan as a separate entity,[6] thereby leaving little alternative other than acceptance of PRC terms. In part, it reflected Taipei's awareness that the vast majority of people in Taiwan had little attachment to the mainland regime. They might interpret nationalist-communist talks on reunification as a thinly disguised effort by nationalist officials to "sell out" local interests for the sake of their personal gain or patriotic instincts. They might take to the streets to register their opposition.

At the same time, the international developments undercut an important political rationale for the nationalist administration on Taiwan. The government of the "Republic of China (ROC)" in Taipei was dominated at senior levels by refugees from the main- land—"mainlanders"—who represented only about 15 percent of Taiwan's total population. It was an authoritarian, one-party state that gave little voice at the national level to the 85 percent of the population whose roots in Taiwan went back centuries before 1949 and whose identity with the mainland was blurred—"Taiwanese."[7] Nevertheless, all in Taiwan paid taxes, military service, and other means to support the nationalist government. The fact that Chiang Kai-shek was able to point to U.S., UN, and other international recognition of the ROC as the legitimate government of China helped to justify his demand that citizens of Taiwan support the regime. As U.S. and other world backing declined rapidly, Taipei had to find new sources of political legitimacy.

Under the leadership of Chiang Kai-shek's son, Chiang Ching-kuo, who ruled as premier prior to the elder Chiang's death in 1975 and then served as president from 1978 until his death in 1988, the nationalist administration adopted a multifaceted reform program designed to build a strong political, economic, and social base of support for the regime on the island. Critical elements included:

- The government-fostered rapid economic development and modernization of Taiwan in the 1970s and 1980s—development accomplished with a relatively egalitarian distribution of wealth and social-educational benefits throughout the society;[8]
- A major affirmative action program designed to bring native Taiwanese into the ruling nationalist party and into the national government, including the military, at senior as well as other levels; and
- A gradual political liberalization encouraging local, provincial, and national elections, which selected some top decision makers in government and served as indirect referenda on the state of nationalist party rule.

By the 1980s, the nationalist regime under the leadership of Chiang Ching-kuo and his successor, Lee Teng-hui (a Taiwanese), had initiated a series of reforms that put the government's legitimacy more firmly into the hands of the people on Taiwan and reflected more closely the interests of the people there. In particular:

- Martial law was lifted;
- Opposition parties were allowed to organize and their candidates to run for elections;
- Censorship and sedition regulations were eased; and
- Political prisoners were released.

In the 1990s, President Lee and the nationalist leadership undertook major reforms of national government bodies. By December 1991, all legislators and National Assembly members elected on the mainland over forty years earlier were retired.[9] A newly elected National Assembly representing predominantly people from Taiwan undertook to amend the constitution; an election to make the National Legislature predominantly representative of the people in Taiwan took place in late 1992, and an election of a new president under terms of the revised constitution was slated for 1996.[10]

Loosened governmental control and greater concern for popular opinion in Taiwan meant that nationalist leaders could no longer block residents of Taiwan from traveling to or doing business with the mainland. Although few in Taiwan showed any interest in accommodating the PRC politically, business interests backed by press and popular opinion showed great interest in economic opportunities on the mainland where labor, land, and other costs were often much lower than in Taiwan. Moreover, many in Taiwan wished to visit long-separated family members or to travel around the mainland as tourists. PRC leaders strove to facilitate such trade, travel, and other exchanges.[11]

Faced with popular pressure to increase contacts with the PRC, the nationalists took a series of measures to regulate the strong flow of contacts and control their policy implications. President Lee Teng-hui convened a National Unification Council in October 1990 to advise on these matters, and later that year, a Mainland Affairs Council was set up under the vice premier to direct cabinet level policy on Taiwan-mainland relations. As part of his political reform program, President Lee in May 1991 ended the state of civil war with the PRC and opened the way to official contacts under "one country-two governments" or "one country-two areas" formulas—formulas known to be unacceptable to Beijing.[12] To deal with the many practical issues that arise given extensive exchanges across the Strait, an ostensibly unofficial body, the Straits Exchanges Foundation, was established and after some uncertainty proved able to deal with important practical issues. The PRC set up a counterpart body, known as the Association for Relations Across the Taiwan Straits, in December 1991. On July 16, 1992, Taiwan passed a law to govern the growing exchanges with the mainland.[13]

In April 1993, relations reached a point where senior delegates from the respective mainland and Taiwan offices held formal talks in Singapore in order to reach agreement on several practical issues involved in growing mainland-Taiwan relations. By that time, Taiwan's trade with the mainland was running heavily in Taiwan's favor at an annual rate estimated at $10 billion and growing rapidly.

The main opposition party in Taiwan, the Democratic Progressive Party (DPP), viewed the progress in PRC-Taiwan relations with some concern. Party leaders were careful not to stand against the popular support for greater Taiwan trade, investment, and other unofficial exchanges with the mainland; but they opposed the nationalists' repeated calls for eventual reunification, and recently have argued that a plebiscite should be held in Taiwan to determine Taiwan's future status. DPP calls for self-determination were followed by calls for independence[14] and sometimes prompted harsh warnings from Beijing that it would resort to force to prevent moves toward formal separation of Taiwan from the mainland. In elections during late 1991, nationalist leaders were effective in referring to the PRC "threat" to encourage voters in Taiwan to steer away from "radical" DPP candidates and support the nationalists and the status quo.

Over the past year, DPP leaders have endeavored to strike a more balanced stance on Taiwan's self-determination. Party leader Hsu Hsin-liang has said that the party needs to consider views of people in Taiwan and possible actions by Beijing before moving ahead toward self-determination and independence. DPP politicians were notably more moderate in dealing with the issue during the December 1992 legislative elections than they had been during island-wide elections a year earlier. At the same time, DPP leaders capitalized on Beijing's relentless diplomatic competition against Taipei to argue that Taiwan would be better off internationally as a *de jure* separate state than in its current claimed status as the government, or at least one government, in China.

Partly in response to this challenge, nationalist leaders have pursued more pragmatic or so-called "flexible" diplomacy.[15] In particular, Taipei has been willing in recent years to establish official relations with countries, even though they may also have relations with Beijing. Meanwhile, Taipei's leaders have reached a working consensus to seek upgrading of Taiwan's membership in world political bodies, including UN affiliated agencies. The impetus for the UN related effort came from the political opposition but the policy now has been firmly endorsed by the ROC administration as well. Beijing has rejected what it sees as Taipei's "one China-two governments" approach. Up to now, Taipei's efforts, backed by a generous foreign aid program, have won diplomatic recognition from a handful of small states. More important results have been achieved through Taipei's efforts to upgrade ostensibly unofficial representative offices and other relations in a number of important developed and developing countries.[16]

In sum, the crises to Taipei's legitimacy caused by the U.S.-PRC reconciliation and related international trends resulted in several substantial adjustments in Taiwan's international and internal policies.

1. Taiwan began to break new ground in the field of "substantive diplomacy." This involved establishing increasingly close, albeit ostensibly unofficial, relations with countries that switched official recognition to Beijing. Taiwan's relations with Japan after 1972, and the United States after 1979, provided models for these kinds of extensive unofficial ties.

2. Taiwan began to show flexibility over its claim to be the sole legitimate government of China, and moved by the late 1980s to establish official ties with some governments that continued to officially recognize the PRC. Taipei was also markedly more flexible in seeking membership in official international

organizations that recognized the PRC as the legitimate government of China.

3. While continuing to promote close interchange with the United States, Taiwan used its growing economic stature to broaden relations with a wide range of other developed and developing countries.

4. Internal reforms were strongly emphasized in Taiwan both to build political legitimacy at home through even more stress on economic performance, political liberalization, and eventually democracy; and to enhance Taiwan's image abroad as a more politically attractive partner to a number of democratic developed states, notably the United States. The reforms also opened the way to greatly increased Taiwanese contacts with the mainland—a trend that served to help Taiwan ease tensions, promote understanding, and buy time to come up with a viable approach for dealing with the mainland over the longer term. At the same time, they served to build Taiwan's economic power and influence, which support a trend whereby Taiwan was no longer largely an entity acted upon by others but was increasingly using its economic and other influence in world affairs to promote its interests and concerns.

Taiwan in the World Today: Mixed Results

By 1990, Taiwan had made some substantial progress in dealing with the problems associated with the withdrawal of U.S. recognition and rapprochement with Beijing. Taiwan had diplomatic relations with twenty-eight countries, concentrated among the nations of Central and South America, and the small states of the South Pacific. Nearly all of Taiwan's diplomatic partners were not major actors in international affairs. Maintaining diplomatic relations with these countries nonetheless was a psychological boost for Taiwan in its competition with the PRC.

After Taiwan lost its UN seat and the United States switched recognition from Taiwan to the PRC, Taiwan began to work seriously to overcome its diplomatic isolation, especially with world economic powers. By mid-1993 Taiwan claimed to have unofficial relations with close to 150 countries, and established ninety unofficial offices in sixty countries that did not maintain diplomatic relations with Taiwan. Furthermore, thirty-seven countries that did not have diplomatic ties with Taipei had established unofficial instrumentalities in Taiwan and more were expected to follow suit. Taiwan's two most important unofficial relationships, politically as well as economically, were with the United States and Japan.[17]

The prospect of economic benefits through trade and investment ties with Taiwan encouraged several countries to expand their unofficial ties with Taipei. Taiwan's achievements in this area represented an impressive comeback after the heavy diplomatic losses to the PRC in the 1970s. Taiwan also recently succeeded in maintaining or reestablishing its profile in nongovernmental international organizations, attending the 1989 and 1990 Asian Development Bank conferences in Beijing and New Delhi, the 1988 Olympics in Seoul, the 1990 Asian Games in Beijing, and the 1992 Olympics in Barcelona. Taiwan entered the Asia-Pacific Economic Cooperation (APEC) along with the PRC and Hong Kong in 1991, and was pressing to gain entry into the General Agreement on Tariffs and Trade (GATT).

President Lee publicly called for Taiwan to adopt "more practical, flexible and forward-looking" approaches to expand substantive foreign relations and to make eventual breakthroughs on the diplomatic front. To facilitate this effort, Taiwan in 1988 established an International Economic Cooperation Development Fund to assist "friendly" countries develop their economies. Also very active in the spread of Taiwan's international power was the China External Trade Development Council (CETDC) established in 1970 and co-sponsored by the ROC government, which has major responsibility for building Taiwan's trade ties abroad.

Beginning in late 1988, the nationalist government appeared more willing to maintain or develop official government relations with other governments or entities, even when those governments maintained or developed official ties with the PRC government on the mainland. Nationalist officials also talked in terms of Taiwan following a "one China, two governments" policy as part of this new "pragmatic" or "flexible" diplomacy. Significant developments in this trend included:

- The nationalist government's announcement in January 1989 that, contrary to past practice, it would not suspend official relations with South Korea if Seoul decided to establish diplomatic relations with Beijing;[18]
- President Lee's trip to Singapore in March 1989 where he was treated as "President Lee from Taiwan" rather than as the head of state of China;
- Premier Yu Kuo-hua's disclosure in March 1989 that the

nationalist government was considering a "one China, two governments" policy in its foreign affairs; and

- The Foreign Ministry's successful efforts to establish formal government relations with Grenada, Liberia, Belize, and other countries, even though those states recognized the PRC as the government of China and had official relations with Beijing.

President Lee said in May 1989 that Taipei was not following a "one China, two governments" policy, and subsequent policy statements referred to formulas like "one country, two areas" and "one country, two entities." However, the actions noted above seemed to underline the trend of diplomatic flexibility.[19]

The nationalist government appeared to have a wide range of motives in pursuing this more assertive and flexible international approach:

- It served to complicate Beijing's continued efforts to isolate Taiwan internationally in order eventually to pressure Taipei to come to terms on reunification with the PRC.
- It played upon Taiwan's growing economic prominence as the fourteenth most important international trader and possessor of the world's largest foreign exchange reserves (around $80 billion).
- It allowed the nationalist authorities to stake out a more prominent international identity in order to deal with domestic pressure in Taiwan. Some of this pressure comes from Taiwanese business people and others who travel abroad and find the absence of official relations or diplomatic support a major irritant in their efforts. More importantly, oppositionists in Taiwan have pressed for Taiwan to solve its international identity problem by declaring itself formally independent of the mainland. The nationalist authorities see such a policy as likely to provoke a hostile PRC response. Such a policy would also represent a fundamental challenge to the existing constitutional order that undergirds the nationalist government in Taipei and the Nationalist Party's dominance of that government.

The nationalist authorities were aware that Beijing might be as likely to oppose their efforts at "pragmatic diplomacy" and "one China, two governments" as it was to oppose the oppositionists demands for a *de jure* "independent Taiwan." But they seemed to judge that Beijing's opposition might be softened by allowing greater Taiwanese economic, personal, and other contacts with the mainland—a policy the nationalists have followed in recent years. From Beijing's perspective, these recent contacts could be seen as offsetting the trend toward Taiwan's more independent identity in international affairs. From one perspective, Taipei presumably could use the prospect of Taiwan's greater trade and investment, which is clearly advantageous to the PRC, as a means to quiet Beijing's opposition to Taipei's more active flexible diplomacy.

In any event, Taiwan's pragmatic or flexible diplomacy is not without its possible disadvantages for the nationalist government. These may explain why nationalist leaders have been less than clear in pursuing their new approach to foreign affairs. Potential disadvantages of the "one country/two governments" and "pragmatic diplomacy" efforts could include:

- A very strong PRC reaction, especially during conditions when "hardline" leaders may become active in Beijing. Beijing in turn could increase pressure on the United States and others to choose between relations with the PRC or support for Taiwan's greater role in world affairs. Although it is unclear that the United States or others would side with the PRC under these circumstances, some nationalist officials are cautious in facing this possible risk.
- Possible resistance, from conservatives within the Nationalist Party who still feel strongly about a reunified China, to efforts that would implicitly reduce Taipei's status as the government of all of China.
- Efforts on the part of Taiwanese oppositionists to use the government's pragmatic diplomacy as an opening to press their demands for *de jure* independence—a policy seen as having dangerous consequences as far as PRC reaction and continued Nationalist Party rule in Taiwan are concerned.

Beijing, meanwhile, has succeeded in recent years in winning over a number of international actors also important to Taiwan. Saudi Arabia and South Korea have switched official relations from Taipei to Beijing. South Africa and the Vatican are also reportedly seeking to establish official ties. Indonesia and Singapore now have diplomatic ties with Beijing, and virtually all of the new governments coming from the former Soviet empire in Europe and Asia have opted for official diplomatic relations with Beijing rather than Taipei. China is seen as critical to the future of most international organizations and so these groups too generally endeavor to accommodate Beijing's insistence that Taiwan not be accorded official status in official international organizations.

The mainland government also pursues economic development policies that increase its standing and led it to surpass Taiwan among world traders, and it has acquired enough foreign exchange reserves (around $40 billion) to rank fifth in the world. Progress toward the reunification of Hong Kong with the mainland and greater Taiwan-mainland contacts are cited as evidence of the PRC-backed view that Taiwan's reunion under Beijing's rule is "inevitable."[20]

Prospects

The mixed results and complex variables affecting Taiwan's recent greater role in world affairs may mask some basic factors that appear to argue on balance for optimism when assessing Taiwan's international prospects. These include a generally effective and attractive political, economic, and social situation in Taiwan. As Thomas Gold explains in his chapter on the domestic roots of Taiwan's role in world affairs, Taiwan's administration has been buffeted by a variety of competing interests and has shown plenty of evidence of the rough-and-tumble political process of a new democracy. The fact remains that the net result of recent policies has been to strengthen the legitimacy and resolve of the authorities in charge. They have proven capable of charting economic, social, and political reforms and other policies that add to Taiwan's strength and influence in world affairs. Gold gives ample consideration to things that could go wrong and undermine positive trends; but a review of Taipei's success in using economic leverage and political-social attractiveness to upgrade numerous international relationships with governments and organizations in the developed world (especially Western Europe), and the newly developed and developing world (especially Southeast Asia) is a source of optimism about the future.

Erland Heginbotham in his chapter provides a comprehensive review of Taiwan's economic position in the thriving East Asian region, seeing Taiwan's entrepreneurs serving as important catalysts for East Asian growth and Taiwan in general providing a model for development attractive to many developing countries. Taiwan's business people seem to be uniquely efficient and effective in promoting growth and making deals in East Asia. They and their government are not passive, but are seen as aggressive and constructive actors promoting trade and investment in areas where others might fear to go. Taiwan's business people were among the first to see and develop the international economic opportunities in Vietnam, for example. Unlike the case of Japanese investment, which is often seen as heavily dependent on government support and foreign assistance, Taiwanese investment and entrepreneurial work is seen to provide immediate and reciprocal benefit to the recipient country, and to be welcomed accordingly.

In the realm of international arms sales, Harlan Jencks in his chapter points out how Taipei has adroitly exploited a combination of factors to greatly improve its military capabilities while undermining the PRC-backed international arms embargo against it. The post-Cold War environment has led to a massive arms glut and a decided "buyers market" favorable to those like Taipei who have the cash to buy what they want from hard-pressed world arms merchants. Taipei's democratic progress has also contrasted with Beijing's continued authoritarianism to improve Taipei's political image among Western decision makers in the United States and Western Europe who hold the key to access to the more modern military equipment and defense technology desired by Taiwan.

June Teufel Dreyer's chapter on important transnational issues plows new research ground in demonstrating how Taipei's leaders have been adept in adjusting their policies on sensitive global issues in order to substantiate their argument that Taiwan is a responsible actor in world affairs deserving of respectful political treatment commensurate with its size and influence. Thus, Taipei's efforts to conform to world trading practices on difficult issues like intellectual property rights, market access, and reevaluating Taiwan's currency are not only designed to avoid retaliation from major trading partners, notably the United States, but Taiwan leaders consciously accommodate these trends in order to build their case for Taiwan's entry into the GATT and other world economic bodies. Similarly, Taipei's leaders are well aware that striking a cooperative posture on other transnational issues, including crime, drugs, terrorism, refugee support, and environmental issues, builds goodwill among world leaders increasingly focused on these questions, and thereby indirectly boosts Taiwan's standing among these politicians. In particular, Taiwan's leaders have been generally prompt to limit the damage and adjust policies in the face of foreign criticism of Taiwan's practices involving driftnet fishing or Taiwan's importation of ivory or other materials from endangered species. They also are generally careful to offer help in the form of monetary and/or other assistance in response to serious international crises or disasters. Dreyer is careful to point to areas where Taiwan's record is less than exemplary and notes in particular that past development strategies have created very serious environmental problems on the island.

Although the sophisticated, often technocratic ROC leadership has been instrumental in steering Taipei's course in world affairs, the roots of Taiwan's success go deeper than that. In particular, the rising educational, social, and economic standards on the island have accompanied the trend toward democracy in recent years. Taiwan's government decision makers now are required to reflect the increasingly sophisticated middle class values of the people on the island. These popular attitudes are also more international as a result of the relatively free flow of information and frequent travel of many in Taiwan. The results are more sophisticated Taiwanese popular attitudes toward world politics and especially toward relations with the mainland.

Samuel Kim's chapter on the challenge of legitimation Taiwan faces in the international system highlights the fact that there is a broad and ever widening web of international contacts that gives citizens in Taiwan a varied way to look at their place in world politics. On the one hand, this often prompts the citizens to press their government to increase Taiwan's official stature in world affairs. For some in Taiwan, this requires Taiwan to move toward *de jure* independence. Faced with continued strong PRC opposition, however, people in Taiwan have pragmatically sought their sense of international identity through their ever widening web of international contacts in business, culture, and education, as well as politics. Under these circumstances, Taiwan's citizens may be less likely to press for *de jure* independence, but will almost certainly be more likely to choose to assert their identity and sense of legitimacy through other avenues short of a total break with mainland China.

Ralph Clough's chapter on the implications of Taiwan's role in world affairs for Taiwan-PRC relations brings us up-to-date on the seemingly odd mix of contention and cooperation that has characterized the bilateral relationship in recent years. He reminds us that this all-important relationship for Taiwan's future has several elements that remain basically contentious because the two governments disagree on crucial points: Taiwan's identity, the method of bringing about Taiwan's reunification with the mainland, and the channel to be used for negotiations between the two sides. Moreover, the PRC threatens Taiwan with the use of military force if the government should declare independence or under other conditions. Nevertheless, Clough carefully enumerates the seemingly contrary trend of rapidly growing trade and other people-to-people exchanges across the Taiwan Strait—developments that appear to reinforce more moderate policies on both sides of the bilateral relationship.

Against this backdrop, Harry Harding in his chapter on Taiwan and Greater China presents a clear definition of this often used concept along with a careful analysis of its respective economic, cultural, and political elements and how they would likely affect Taiwan-mainland integration. Finding strong economic complementarities reinforced by cultural ties across the Strait, Harding cautions that this is only one side of the ledger. He enumerates the elements of the wide gap in economic and political conditions across the Strait, deep political distrust, and other factors that block integration and in some cases push Taiwan and the mainland further apart.

In his chapter on Taiwan's international role and the implications for U.S. policy, Richard Bush points out that Taiwan's search for a new international role did not initially create problems for U.S. policy. The search came in his view partly as an outcome of U.S. actions; while the opening to the mainland authorities with whom Taiwan balanced its flexible and pragmatic diplomacy worked to Washington's indirect benefit. Looking to the future, Bush warns that demands for Taiwanese nationhood may provoke a crisis, which the United States has long tried to avoid. A more benign scenario would see Taiwan adopting an increasingly prominent international role of its own choosing—a more satisfactory outcome for U.S. interests provided it avoids crisis and confrontation with Beijing.

The authors are uniform in warning that any sanguine assessment of Taipei's growing role in world affairs is based on a number of variables that could change and therefore bear watching. Heginbotham and other economic specialists suggest that Taiwan remains well positioned to continue its recent growth and to continue to play an important role in the development of several world economics, especially those in Asia and the Pacific. Nonetheless, the recent rapid expansion of the much larger mainland China economy suggests that Taiwan could find itself overshadowed by the mainland market and heavily dependent on it as a result of the ever-increasing Taiwanese investment and trade there. Already the mainland has overtaken Taiwan in world trade, and its size and growth rate point to world attention to the "China market" being much greater than to that of Taiwan. It can be anticipated that Beijing will endeavor to use this economic influence for the sake of its political objective in striving to reunify Taiwan with the mainland.

Taiwan's economic development, meanwhile, has been closely associated with pragmatic efforts by the government elite to foster growth and economic progress. As Thomas Gold and others note, it is logical to ask whether the more complicated and unpredictable democratic decision making in Taiwan today will allow for the same level of economic competence on the part of the government leadership as in the past. The recent heated debate in Taipei over the $300 billion six year development program is seen to illustrate this danger in the view of those observers who prefer an orderly, technocratic approach to government intervention in economic development.

Harlan Jencks, Thomas Gold, and others find that democratic tendencies could also complicate Taipei government efforts to secure advanced military equipment. There is a danger in the minds of some that politicians in Taiwan will refuse to go along with the heavy tax burden associated with foreign arms purchases, or that they will place so many conditions on the sales as to make them impossible to carry out.

Of course, several of the authors, notably Ralph Clough, Harry Harding, and Richard Bush, see that a major perceived danger coming from democratic tendencies in Taiwan is that decision makers there will assert their claim as an independent country, thereby precipitating a major confrontation with Beijing. Although Taipei's leaders and voters in Taiwan have shown a pragmatic bent in dealing with this issue over the past few years, there is no guarantee that conditions might not change, prompting Taipei to move forthrightly toward self determination and independence.

There is little question that Taiwan's prestige and image in the West improved markedly as a result of its own democratization and Beijing's concurrent political crackdown after the 1989 Tiananmen incident. More recently, however, the importance of these political differences has blurred as Western countries have been attracted by Beijing's economic vitality, and by their political and security need to engage China in helping to solve important issues in Asia (North Korea, Cambodia) and in world affairs (arms proliferation, the UN Security Council). Up to this point, Taipei's leaders have been reasonably effective in incrementally improving Taiwan's international position during the post-Mao period when mainland China has put heavy emphasis on domestic economic development, a foreign policy of peace, and a strategy toward Taiwan emphasizing the carrots of greater cross-Strait exchanges rather than the stick of military pressure and force. Harry Harding, Ralph Clough, and others note that some believe that the mainland government will continue and enhance this general policy in the coming years, giving rise to a process of eventual political reform and leadership generational change that will increase Taiwan's sense of security and allow it to play an ever greater role in official world politics. But they are careful to add that prudence requires acknowledging that contrary courses are possible. Economic reverses or political struggles could give rise to a mainland regime taking a much harder line on sensitive nationalistic issues like Taiwan. Alternatively, economic success and political reform could see the unleashing of popular nationalistic feelings that would require a tougher PRC posture on Taiwan.

Taipei's leaders doubtlessly spend time assessing these variables and drawing up contingency plans to deal with possible outcomes. Nevertheless, a sober and balanced assessment can reasonably conclude that few changes are likely to be so extreme as to substantially impact the recent trend of Taiwan expanding its influence in world affairs. Thus, in the years ahead, one can expect to see a considerable advance as Taipei shows the increased self confidence, strength, and will to attract support and play a role in world politics commensurate with its importance and power.

This sanguine view should not lull U.S. policymakers into a passive position. As Richard Bush points out, U.S. policy for decades has striven to manage the multifaceted problems and complications associated with its relationship with Taiwan in the face of its relationship with Beijing. Experienced American policymakers long ago gave up any effort to "solve" the "Taiwan problem." Rather, they have focused for years on trying to preserve peace, stability, and balance between Taiwan and the mainland—conditions seen as allowing the United States to continue its advantageous policy of sustaining and developing good relations with both mainland China and Taiwan. In particular, ever since the United States began in the early 1970s the process of normalizing relations with Beijing, U.S. policymakers have been sensitive of the need to reassure Taiwan of continued U.S. support. Otherwise, it was feared, anxiety in Taipei over improvements in U.S.-PRC relations and U.S. withdrawal from official ties with Taiwan might prompt precipitous actions contrary to U.S. interests in peace and stability.

The change in international forces and domestic trends in Taiwan since the end of the Cold War have not only reinforced Taiwan's more prominent role in world affairs. In the minds of some observers, it has increased the likelihood that Taipei may feel it now has enough incentive, support, and leverage, especially vis-à-vis the PRC, to pursue a *de jure* independent posture from mainland China. As noted above, trends supporting this argument include Taiwan's success in recent arms purchases, its attractiveness to international investors and entrepreneurs, and, most importantly, the rising strength of opposition politicians on the island who adhere to a Taiwan independence platform.

Under these circumstances, it may be prudent for U.S. policymakers to exert their traditional balancing role in a somewhat different direction. This U.S. role in the past focused heavily on reassuring Taiwan of U.S. support in the face of PRC pressure. Today, perhaps some effort needs to be directed at warning forces in Taiwan against precipitous action that might prompt PRC use of force and a conflict in the Taiwan Strait. Such warnings could be done in various ways—publicly and privately. Their thrust should be to underline American interest in peace in the Taiwan Strait, along with a desire to promote greater economic and political progress and reform in both mainland China and Taiwan. Taiwan pro-independence advocates should be advised that American interests are not well served by a *de jure* declaration of independence at this time, and that a strong case can be made that it is not in the interests of the people on Taiwan. These advocates should be informed as well that if Taiwan pro-independence advocates persist in a head-long drive toward independence, U.S. officials will take steps to educate the American public about the nature of U.S. interests in Taiwan that might be jeopardized if conflict arose in the Taiwan Strait. Such actions could move concurrently with U.S. steps to draw back from past emphasis on strong support for Taiwan in the face of PRC pressure, to a more even-handed position allowing the United States to deal with a contingency where Taipei appeared to be the main threat to peace.

It seems clear that the push in Taiwan toward *de jure* independence is growing and may already have reached a point where private U.S. admonitions along the lines noted above may be in order. At the same time, U.S. policymakers need to be prepared to address directly other issues posed by Taipei's current international efforts. Most notably, should the United States support Taipei's efforts to gain entry into UN affiliated or other official agencies? Should the United States formally abandon the understanding reached with Beijing in the August 17, 1982, U.S.-PRC communiqué establishing limits on U.S. arms sales to Taiwan? And should U.S. policymakers adopt a more direct role in trying to solve the Taiwan issue before developments there reach a point where American control and influence are more limited and unable to check trends that could jeopardize U.S. interest in stability in the Taiwan Strait?

It appears obvious that the previous ambiguous U.S. policy stance under the broad rubric of "one China" and "peaceful settlement" may not be sufficient to guide American policymakers as time goes on. Nevertheless, it can be argued that there is precedent within the framework of the Taiwan Relations Act to support Taiwan's role in official international organizations and to allow for the transfer of sufficient American arms to Taiwan, without necessitating additional formal action by U.S. officials. And past U.S. promises to Taiwan leaders have appeared to produce a workable policy that keeps the United States one level removed from the complicated and sensitive PRC-Taiwan maneuverings over the issue of reunification.

Notes

The views expressed in this chapter are the author's and not necessarily those of the Congressional Research Service, the Library of Congress.

1. For background, see among others, Ralph Clough, *Island China*, (Boston, MA: Harvard University Press, 1978); John Copper, *Taiwan: National State or Province?*, (Boulder, CO: Westview Press, 1990); and Tien Hung-mao, *The Great Transition*, (Stanford, CA: Hoover Institution, 1989).

2. In general, the term "Taiwanese" refers to island residents whose roots go back many generations. They represent about 85 percent of the current population of the island. "Mainlanders" refers to island residents who came from mainland China in the 1940s or who are descendants of such migrants.

3. For useful background, see among others, A. Doak Barnett, *China and the Major Powers in East Asia*, (Washington, DC: The Brookings Institution, 1977), and Harry Harding, *A Fragile Relationship*, (Washington, DC: The Brookings Institution, 1992).

4. In the process, the United States put aside its stance of the 1950s and 1960s that Taiwan's official status remained to be determined, in favor of a position that did not quarrel with the stance of Chinese on both sides of the Taiwan Strait that Taiwan was part of China. The most important U.S. positions included those taken in the February 28, 1972, Shanghai communiqué, and statements at the time of U.S.-PRC diplomatic normalization in December 1978. See Harding, *A Fragile Relationship*.

5. Beijing's approach is reviewed in Ralph Clough's chapter in this book.

6. Most notably after recognition of Taipei, the United States in 1979 passed the Taiwan Relations Act, which gave a legal framework for continued U.S. "unofficial" relations, including arms sales and other sensitive exchanges, with Taiwan as an entity separate from PRC control. Beijing at times pressed the United States to "revise" the act.

7. In the minds of many Taiwanese, the nationalist rule was a pseudo-colonial rule of the island following 50 years of Japanese colonial rule. See Tien, *The Great Transition.*

8. This growth was especially favorable to the indigenous Taiwanese who tended to dominate the economy of the island.

9. Many such legislators had died in the 40-year period, posing a challenge for the government, which remained interested in showing some representation from regions throughout China.

10. In the past, the National Assembly generally served to amend the constitution and to act as an electoral college in choosing the president. The National Legislature was the main law making body. The National Assembly broadened its responsibilities in passing constitutional amendments in 1992. See *Free China Journal*, June 23, 1992.

11. See discussion in chapters by Ralph Clough, Harry Harding, and Erland Heginbotham.

12. Taiwan's officials have sometimes used formulas other than "one country-two governments" to describe their position. The law governing relations with the mainland, passed July 16, 1992, referred to "one country and two areas." See *Free China Journal*, July 21, 1992. PRC officials have refused to endorse formulas that give official status to Taipei as an independent political entity.

13. See discussion in Ralph Clough's chapter.

14. Supporters of a plebescite for self-determination often assumed it would lead to results favoring independence.

15. This concept is discussed in various ways in each of the subsequent chapters.

16. See discussion most notably in Samuel Kim's chapter.

17. Coordination Council for North American Affairs, July 26, 1993.

18. As it turned out, Taipei suspended ties once Seoul and Beijing established formal diplomatic relations in August 1992.

19. For background, see the Appendix on Taiwan's Pragmatic Diplomacy contained in CRS Report 90-11 F, *Taiwan's Elections: Implications For Taiwan's Development and U.S. Interests*, by Robert Sutter, December 7, 1989.

20. For background on Beijing's approach, see chapters by Ralph Clough and Harry Harding.

2

Taiwan's Economic Role in East Asian Development

Erland Heginbotham

Introduction and Origins

To appreciate fully Taiwan's economic role in East Asia requires consideration of:

- its achievements in its own economic development;
- its responses to external stimulus—foreign aid and direct investment; and
- its active role as exporter and emergence as major foreign investor.

We will want to understand how Taiwan, from an isolated, low-wage agricultural economy in the 1950s, has by the 1990s become Asia's third most dynamic, influential, and effective agent of regional economic change. It has even come to have dominant global positions in some electronic and other advanced technology niches. In so doing, Taiwan has evolved some ten distinctive aspects that have all contributed to its regional economic status and role:

1. *Development model*: A successful and distinctive model of economic development with important and expanding capabilities for participating in and influencing the Asian regional economy;
2. *Market economy*: A semi-open economy, generally market-driven

and receptive to foreign trade and investment flows, but with extensive government intervention in both the domestic economy and international transactions and extensive, persistent import barriers;

3. *Export-led growth*: An outwardly oriented economy pursuing aggressive export-led growth strategies;

4. *Trade triangulation*: A major participant in Asia's triangular trade flows, being heavily dependent on Japan and other Asian sources for its imports, but even more so on the U.S. market for most of its export expansion in the 1980s. The resultant accumulation of trade surpluses and foreign exchange reserves is a major source of its ability to project economic influence;

5. *NIC (ANIE) status*: Success as a NIC ("newly industrialized country") or ANIE ("Asian newly industrialized economy"). Taiwan is distinctive as one of Asia's four economic "tigers" or "mini-dragons." In effect Taiwan has become third most influential after Japan and China as a major agent of Asian regional economic expansion and change;

6. *Foreign investor*: Following a pattern made familiar by Japan and other Asian NICs, Taiwan experienced dramatic increases in output, wages, land prices, and other cost pressures in the 1960s and 1970s that stimulated outward investment in search of lower-cost production and export platforms, mainly in Asia. High economic savings, trade, and foreign exchange surpluses undergird growing capabilities as a regional investor;

7. *Agile entrepreneurship*: A hothouse of small- and medium-scale enterprises, with short-to-medium term time horizons, driven to capitalize on emerging financial, property, and industrial opportunities, and quick to shift from declining activities. This differs markedly from Japanese and Korean styles prone to elaboration of diversified, conglomerated enterprises with longer-term business horizons, strongly influenced by government efforts to direct investments into promising sectors;

8. *Member of the tribe*: Maintenance of close ties with Hong Kong, Singapore, and local overseas Chinese minorities in the Philippines, Thailand, Malaysia, Indonesia, and elsewhere in East Asia. Taiwan is increasingly the regional leader in this ethnic Chinese network of trade and investment flows, particularly in industrial development;

9. *Agent of integration*: Economic complementarities between Taiwan and neighboring Asian economies combine with its

emergence as a capital exporter and foreign investor in expanding the relative importance of its intra-Asian trade, investment, financial, and other economic relationships; and

10. *An alternative to Japanese economic dominance*: Challenger to Japan in certain technologically advanced sectors by elevating its technology capabilities and competing for niche markets. In so doing, Taiwan, in coordination with other overseas Chinese traders and investors throughout Asia, may offer an alternative to increased dependence on Japanese trade, finance, and investment.

Before judging the significance of various functional roles that Taiwan has come to play in the region, it is useful to consider the general economic dynamics of East Asia that create the unique opportunities and environment on which Taiwan has capitalized so effectively. Encapsulated, the main ingredients are:

- A motive development force was initially imparted by Japan's rapid economic growth in the 1950s-1970s;
- As a resource-scarce economy, Japan was strongly motivated to invest abroad to acquire industrial materials and energy;
- Available nearby in Southeast Asia were abundant natural resources, tropical products, and energy sources, which stimulated initial foreign investments and in turn spurred economic growth in Southeast Asia; supported and abetted by bilateral and multilateral economic assistance programs;
- A recurrent dynamic developed in which fast growth led to productivity gains, wage increases, labor and land shortages, increased rent and land costs, and sometimes higher interest rates and exchange rate increases as well. This cost-push dynamic eroded labor and other competitive advantages, spurring relocation of marginalized industries to lower-cost economies;
- The existence of multiple layers of progressively lower-cost labor-rich economies scattered throughout East Asia has provided a progression of lower-wage options for relocating marginalized industries. A scaled series of options has existed because various groups of economies were in different stages of policy formulation and economic development, and of opening their economies to international trade and investment flows; and
- As both resource and relocational investments accelerated with

spreading rapid growth, increasingly wealthy local and subregional markets became a further attraction for foreign investors who in turn came increasingly from capital-surplus economies located dominantly in East Asia.

Broadly speaking, East Asia divides economically into five tiers defined by their different stages of development and relative labor and land costs:

- Japan;
- the four newly Asian industrialized economies (ANIEs) of which Taiwan is one;
- the aspirant tigers: Thailand, Malaysia, Indonesia, and the Philippines (the ASEAN-4), to which must now be added such high-investment coastal provinces of China as Guangdong, Fujian, and Jiangsu;
- the emerging market industrial economies, which have begun open-market-oriented reforms; Vietnam and the rest of China, are the most notable, but India should also be mentioned because of its clear effort to piggyback on East Asia's economic dynamism; and
- pre-emergent economies—Burma, Cambodia, Laos, Mongolia, and parts of South Asia not yet participating in East Asia's intra-regional economic integration except in very marginal ways.

This schematic underscores the unusual multi-layered structure of economic complementarities that have given East Asia its unique potential for progressive stages of interactive regional growth and dynamism. It also permits us to consider Taiwan's role relative to groups of nations within the region, and understand how Taiwan's economic evolution fits into a broader pattern of regional economic development and change.

Development Model

Taiwan has had unusually compelling reasons to take its economic development seriously. Its essentially agrarian 1949 population was augmented roughly 20 percent by some 2 million refugees of the Kuomintang (KMT) government, army, and followers who fled the mainland in that year. It was confronted by hostile forces and threat of attack and invasion from only one hundred-twenty miles across the

Taiwan Strait. Understandably, it was in a hurry to strengthen the economic base for its defense. Taiwan proved exceptionally effective in using foreign aid, mainly from the United States, to accelerate its agricultural development and to create and expand an industrial base.

Taiwan's early development was particularly dependent on the United States. U.S. economic aid was equivalent to 6 percent of its GNP over most of the 1950s, and accounted for nearly 40 percent of its gross investment. "Military aid was bigger still."[1] U.S. aid financed imports of energy, primary and intermediate inputs required by industry, and equipment to establish and expand production. The United States also exerted important influences on policy, including the shape and scope of land reform. At least as important as this aid, however, was the skill and determination of Taiwan's government and people. A facetious assertion of contemporaneous aid commentators was that Taiwan achieved agricultural success in spite of U.S. aid. Finally, the United States gave a fortuitously timed boost to Taiwan's industrial development at its earliest stages: to satisfy the tremendous demands for consumable goods and combat material generated by the Korean War, and to keep transportation and supply costs down through procurement in East Asia, the United States encouraged and assisted production in Taiwan. To qualify, Taiwanese firms had to produce to U.S. military specification—the functional equivalent of international standards.

Despite many constraints, Taiwan achieved exceptionally rapid expansion of output and productivity in agriculture, spurred by a drive to increase food self-sufficiency for its inflated population. Rapid productivity gains in agriculture in turn permitted rapid transfer of labor to support industrial growth.

Two pivotal factors influential in shaping Taiwan's economic development strategies and policies were (1) a socialist philosophy of government brought over from the mainland, and (2) mistrust and frictions between the minority Kuomintang (KMT) supporters who controlled the government, and the numerically dominant Taiwanese population. These influences go far toward explaining the unusually heavy dependence on state enterprise as the leading and major initial agent of industrial development. As it became important for Taiwan to develop more technologically advanced industries, the dominant position of state enterprise in the industrial sector reportedly has given Taiwan special leverage in its efforts to expand acquisition of foreign technology on favorable terms. State enterprise is also Taiwan's mechanism for achieving economies of scale, where needed for global competitiveness, in an economy of medium and small enterprises and its substitute for developing *keiretsu* (Japanese-style) or *chaebol* (Korean-style) conglomerates for that purpose.

Taiwan's ability to achieve double-digit rates of overall and industrial growth, matched only by Korea and recently by China, is testimony to the power of its development strategies and efforts. Inward foreign investment has been substantial but has contributed only a small fraction of Taiwan's gross capital formation (3.5 percent in 1985-1987, rising to 6 percent in 1989-1990).

Market Economy

Taiwan shared with Japan and Korea (to say nothing of the island economies Hong Kong and Singapore) a severe paucity of energy and other natural resources. Like them, in order to industrialize, it was exceptionally dependent on imports of energy and industrial materials, and, as a result, on expanding its own exports in order to finance imports essential to its development. Beginning in the 1950s with very low per capita income, and domestic savings inadequate to finance development needs, Taiwan opened its economy to foreign investment as well as aid. Taiwan cautiously engaged investment even from its former colonial overlord, Japan. By 1991, in fact, the cumulative value of Japanese investment finally came to exceed that from the United States.

Important complementarities developed between Japan, on one hand, and Korea and Taiwan on the other. Japan's rapid and sustained growth in the 1950s and 1960s resulted in similarly rapid increases in wages, land prices and rents, infrastructure, and environmental costs. In spite of accompanying productivity increases, labor-intensive Japanese industries increasingly faced declining competitiveness. Taiwan, along with Korea, offered unique advantages of substantial underemployed labor, much lower wages and land costs, and extensive familiarity stemming from a fifty-year occupation by Japan (1895-1945).

From 1950 to 1991 Japanese direct investment, totalling $3.7 billion, accounted for roughly one-third of Taiwan's total inward foreign direct investment—this in spite of numerous restrictions on contacts between the two economies, and the chilling effect on relations after Japan recognized China in 1972. Even so, Japan's economic relations with Taiwan have consistently and significantly exceeded its economic relations with China. As late as 1991, Taiwan was Japan's fourth-largest market and sixth-largest source of imports. Japan-Taiwan bilateral trade in 1990, at US$23.9 billion, exceeded by US$5.7 billion Japan's bilateral trade with China. To Taiwan's frustration, its trade with Japan has showed a persistent deficit since the 1970s. This stems partly from Taiwan's heavy dependence on Japan for capital equipment and for components to supply plants built with Japanese investment, and partly from problems in exporting to Japan.

Despite ostensible allegiance to market forces, in practice Taiwan maintains a heavily protected domestic economy. In appearance, it has liberalized the economy considerably since the 1950s. Riedel finds three distinct phases of trade liberalization: (1) 1958: 250 percent nominal NT dollar devaluation and removal of quantitative restrictions on permissible imports (roughly 50 percent of importable items); (2) 1970s: cut the number of prohibited and controlled imports, while retaining licensing requirements that were exercised for "purely protectionist purposes"; (3) late 1970s, accelerated in the 1980s: in response to growing trade surpluses reduced the average tariff rate by about 84 percent.[2] Of potentially greatest significance, however, is Taiwan's continued pursuit of its January 1990 application for membership in the General Agreement on Tariffs and Trade (GATT) in which it offered as a formal concession to bring its tariff schedule into line with those of OECD countries within six years.

Some respects in which Taiwan restricts trade and investment relate closely to its concerns to avoid excessive dependence on China and undue Japanese economic influence or dominance, but to little avail. For example, Japanese investments in Taiwan are activated much more by cost-push in Japan—and Japan's need to move production of more labor-intensive components and products to lower-wage economies—than by demand-pull (to supply the needs of Taiwan's economy). As cost pressures on Japan's economy grew after the sharp yen appreciation following the Plaza Accord of September 1985, Japanese investment assumed growing importance in Taiwan.

In some Taiwanese circles, concern has grown that Taiwan increasingly has come to produce "things that fit the global strategies of those big Japanese multinationals" and that "Japanese multinationals are swallowing up Taiwan little by little."[3] The prospect of Taiwan's accession to the GATT raises further apprehension that Japan may be the primary beneficiary since it is in practice the most affected by Taiwan's restrictions on trade and investment.

Considered broadly, however, Taiwan's decision to pursue an open economic policy subjected its own economy to the stimulus of trade competition and the challenges of foreign markets, and promoted inflows of foreign capital to supplement domestic sources of growth. The result has been to accelerate Taiwan's economic growth.

Export-led Development

"Throughout the 1950s until about 1958 the government operated an import substitution policy.... the years from 1958 to 1962 saw a decisive policy shift toward an `outward orientation.'"[4] Thus Taiwan began to shift toward an export-led growth strategy and to sharpen the competitiveness of its export-oriented industries. By one definition, this strategy would involve a shift from import substitution to trade liberalization in order to expose Taiwan's export industries directly to global competition, requiring managers to maintain product competitiveness. However, Wade finds that instead "a large part" of Taiwan's export success may be attributable to export incentives: export-processing zones, tariff rebates, export tax incentives, export credit, and export cartels, along with government imposition of quality controls and assistance with export marketing.

In theory this strategy would have several important implications for Taiwan's economy. It would increase its vulnerability to cost-push erosion of product competitiveness and to competition from lower-wage economies. It would also increase pressure for shifting toward more technologically advanced industries, and for acquiring more foreign technologies.

In practice, however, Taiwan's was not a pure export-led strategy. Clearly wanting to have things both ways, Taiwan still retains a strong mix of import-substitution policy devices as well. The resulting mix includes relatively high barriers on goods produced in Taiwan that are for the domestic market but not usually export-competitive. By contrast, barriers on raw and intermediate goods required to be incorporated in exports from Taiwan are generally low or nil. Indications are that as its labor-intensive industries faced increased foreign competition, the government managed to reduce and delay their decline through protective measures, even as it promoted higher value-added industries through export incentives and market liberalization.[5] Wade details extensive and complex mechanisms by which Taiwan maintained a level of effective protection in many respects higher than average for developing economies, even up to the mid-1980s. He concludes, contrary to broadly held views:

> The state has interfered in trade not less, but differently, than in many other developing countries.... It has balanced the need to bring international market pressures to bear on domestic producers with the need to build up supply capacity in an increasing range of industries. It has accomplished this feat by avoiding both free trade and high,

unselective, and unconditional protection, and by welcoming foreign investment while placing constraints on its role in the domestic economy.[6]

Trade Triangulation

An export-lead growth strategy ties overall economic growth to success in expanding exports. Problems of gaining market access in Japan have severely limited growth prospects in Taiwan's most obvious regional market. Only gradually has diversification among the ANIEs encouraged growth of intra-sectoral trade within that group. ASEAN country consumer markets have become important only in the late 1980s; ASEAN has previously been most attractive for investment and sales of equipment and infrastructure supplies. Thus, to achieve and maintain high rates of export growth Taiwan had to depend mainly on sales to the United States and Europe, and only secondarily to Asian destinations. This triangular pattern is not unique to Taiwan but is generally typical of Asia's import, export, and economic growth patterns over the past three decades.

Because of Taiwan's early reliance on U.S. aid and political support, it was more dependent on imports from the United States than on exports to it up until 1968. By 1964, its dependence on imports from Japan exceeded that from the United States, as it has ever since. The U.S. share of Taiwan's exports showed rather consistent growth from 5 percent in 1957 to 42 percent 1972, and again in 1980-1984, when it peaked at 49 percent. By that year Taiwan was more than twice as dependent on exports to the United States as it was on imports from it.[7] The increase in export dependence "was closely associated with the real appreciation of the US dollar against all the major currencies as well as the NT dollar."[8] The residence of approximately 15 percent of all Taiwanese in the United States reinforces a persistence of these economic relationships. In the late 1980s Taiwan's unusual degree of dependence on the U.S. market began to change, as Asian markets rapidly achieved higher personal income levels and as China's economic reform has begun to generate mass market potentials on the mainland.

NIC/ANIE Status

With its rapid progression to ANIE status via annual growth averaging nearly 9 percent during the 1980s, Taiwan experienced the same forces eroding competitiveness in its low-end industries as had

Japan before it, in common with Korea, Singapore, and Hong Kong: rapidly rising wage, land, rent, infrastructure, and environmental costs. In spite of progressive erosion of its labor-intensive industries, it has continued to accumulate trade and foreign exchange surpluses, and has come under increasing pressure from the United States to moderate these surpluses through expanded imports and exchange rate adjustments. As it became a visible capital-surplus economy, it has also faced the necessity of becoming an actor in regional economic change rather than merely the stage on which change was enacted. It has become both a source of technical assistance and of direct as well as portfolio investment to numerous Asian neighbors.

Foreign Investor

With regard to endangered industries, by the 1980s Taiwan faced three external options: (1) to relinquish production to lower-cost foreign producers, (2) to invest offshore to reduce its intermediate material or component costs, or (3) to invest to relocate production in lower or lowest cost economies offshore. Generally it has avoided option (1) and pursued options (2) and (3). A further Taiwanese response to cost-push forces has been to emphasize domestic investment in more advanced technology, higher value-added industries. Corollary efforts involve greatly intensified efforts to acquire advanced technologies from abroad and to expand domestic R&D investments.

Thus Taiwan's choice of an open economy and export-led growth strategy spurred growth, accelerated its industrialization, and made inevitable its transition from a reactive capital-importing economy to a pro-active capital exporting economy, driven to look for offshore production and investment opportunities. Data on its role in this arena follows later in this chapter.

Agile Entrepreneurship

The small-scale, quick-response agility of Taiwanese entrepreneurship seems to have at least four main origins. During exposure to Western imperialism and mercantilism, many southern Chinese had the opportunity to act as middlemen or agents to Western enterprises; as a "comprador" the Chinese served variously as their agent in employing local labor, as their advisor, "guarantor," or as go-between with local businesses; their focus was the immediate transaction or opportunity. An intensely strong family orientation tends to keep business "within the family," albeit one that may extend to family across oceans and boundaries. Japanese occupation upset the traditional Chinese social hierarchy that relegated commercial pursuits toward the bottom of the social order. Finally, after 1949, land reform prodded an entire landed class, which was traditionally family-based and self-reliant, grudgingly to shift into the commercial and industrial world. At least these four factors (and doubtless many others) engendered a new class of entrepreneurs with a keen eye to quick returns, a keen awareness of emerging and changing opportunities, a proclivity for smaller-scale, usually family-oriented businesses, and a general absence of broad, long-term, or far-reaching economic agendas or strategies. One modern ramification of these characteristics is to avoid locking into products or technologies for their own values or attractions, but rather to shift quickly as new products and opportunities appear more attractive. A Taiwanese tendency to produce generic items for Original Equipment Manufacturers (OEMs), generally avoiding production of their own brand-name products, is also attributed to these characteristics.

Member of the Tribe

An exceptionally important feature of East Asian economic development has been the role of overseas Chinese. Estimated to number 50-55 million, they range from preponderant majorities in Taiwan, Singapore, and Hong Kong to economically powerful minorities in the Philippines, Malaysia, Thailand, Indonesia, and Vietnam. Taiwan alone accounts for some 40 percent of the total of that number. Those in Southeast Asia are estimated to number roughly 20 million. Linked by strong kinship, linguistic and cultural ties, reinforced by their predominant provenance from Guangdong, Fujian, and other southeast China provinces, the overseas Chinese have been influential, and in some countries dominant, in the conduct of national and especially intraregional trade, finance, and investment. One recent study credits this overseas Chinese network with accounting for the extent to which intraregional trade in East Asia exceeds what can be explained by proximity, market size, and normal trade growth.[9] (Also see discussion of this issue in the chapter by Harry Harding.)

Taiwan, with roughly two-thirds of its population said to originate in Fujian province, some 120 miles across the Strait, has had strong interests and ties in China. During the decades when hostilities and political conflicts prevented direct relations, the next best alternatives for Taiwan were dealings with Hong Kong, Singapore, and overseas Chinese communities elsewhere in Southeast Asia. These ties provided ready-made marketing and financing networks, as well as natural investment partners—often literally with family or close kin. In many families it became common practice for brothers and other family members to scatter to differing East Asian locales so as to create a widely dispersed family base for taking advantage of commercial opportunities throughout the region. For a brief time after the outbreak of political repression in China following the Tiananman Square massacre of 1989, Taiwanese sharply curtailed their new foreign direct investment in southeastern China and quickly became a major source of new direct investment in Malaysia, Thailand, Vietnam, and other Southeast Asian countries until conditions stabilized in China.

Agent of Regional Economic Integration

Widely noted has been a growing "Asianization" of East Asian economic relationships, particularly since 1985. In part, the growing percentage shares of trade among East Asian countries is a direct function of the rapid growth of the region; if most of a country's trade partners in the region are growing faster than those in other regions, its trade and in turn their shares in its trade are naturally going to increase. Proximity, kinship, and Chinese networks are other factors, increasing the advantages of and preferences for intra-Asian transactions.

Another significant factor is Taiwan's political motivation. By offering and in some cases subsidizing attractive trade and outward investment terms, as well as loans and bilateral agricultural and industrial technical aid programs to expand intra-Asian economic transactions, Taiwan has reduced its political isolation and built support vis-á-vis China. In 1992, "Taiwan continued to make progress in leveraging its commercial advantages to ease the political isolation imposed by the mainland. Breakthroughs in relations with Russia and upgrades in relations with its major trading partners have given the Taipei government a larger measure of international recognition than before."[10]

Least of all should one overlook the unique and extensive complementarities that have demonstrably put Asian neighbors at the forefront of logical partnerships in trade, finance, and investment. In addition to its abundant natural resources and labor, the region was also newly stabilized politically and strongly devoted to economic development and generally open market systems. Japan's lead as investor in major resource development projects assured rapid expansion of supplies at favorable prices.

As domestic production-cost pressures initially forced Japan to seek lower-cost economies to base production offshore in the 1970s, special considerations elevated the attractions of Asian neighbors.

- historic relations, cultural ties, and familiarity: having occupied both Korea and Taiwan for five decades, Japan had natural advantages (as well as disadvantages) in both;
- availability particularly in Korea and Taiwan of abundant, low-cost, but well educated and disciplined labor (and weak labor movements);
- stable, rapidly developing economies with favorable infrastructure; and
- emerging national markets with growing potential for economies of scale by combining exports and local sales.

Singapore and particularly Hong Kong also offered the advantages of strong financial, transportation, and entrepot services while serving as excellent production platforms for exports around the world.

As Taiwan and other ANIEs in turn encountered the same rapid growth-induced cost-push pressures that Japan earlier experienced, they in turn found highly competitive attractions for relocating and expanding their investment presence in other East Asian countries. By the late 1970s and early 1980s, the ANIEs were no longer low-wage economies; four ASEAN countries, particularly Thailand, Malaysia, and Indonesia, by that time lay claim to abundant low-wage labor supplies, supported by stable, progressive economic policies and generally favorable infrastructure. In addition, the industrial diversification of the ANIEs had also created opportunities for niche trading and investments to be made by economies like Taiwan's, as well as to take advantage of qualified managerial and technical personnel.

Mexico was also an attractive competitor for Asian trade and investment, with the added advantage of proximity to Taiwan's U.S. markets. Investment for production and distribution directly in U.S. markets was another option. However, increasingly in the 1980s East Asia's advantages carried the day, particularly as China became the dominant magnet for Taiwanese investors.[11]

Entrepreneur and Financier for China

Taiwan's success in capitalizing upon exports to catalyze its economy not only produced dramatic and sustained economic growth, it also showed up in rising balance of payments surpluses. In part because Taiwan has recognized that its economy remains highly vulnerable to China's power to disrupt not only trade with the mainland but with Hong Kong and elsewhere, it has thus sought to build up its foreign exchange reserves as a cushion against possible disruption. It has managed its foreign exchange rate so as generally to undervalue its currency, with the parallel effect of heightening its export competitiveness. Reinforcing this objective, Taiwan has achieved an exceptionally high national savings rate—roughly 33 percent of GDP—which for long periods has been the highest or among the highest in the world.[12]

The current result is that Taiwan has now accumulated $88 billion, the world's second largest foreign exchange reserve. A current account surplus at a current annual rate of $8-10 billion in recent years brings substantial annual additions to this exchange reserve. While this reserve may in part also serve as backing for Taiwan's ambitious US$300 billion six-year infrastructure plans, it also puts Taiwan under considerable pressure, especially from the United States, to reduce trade restrictions and to appreciate its currency; its conspicuous magnitude is also a powerful spur for Taiwan to deploy its financial assets for other uses.

Taiwan's evolution as a financial power has roughly coincided with the progressive reform and liberalization of China's economy, begun in 1979 on a limited and halting basis, and gradually accompanied by a relaxation of political tensions. As China extended its economic reforms by expanding their geographic scope and by liberalizing terms for foreign investment, the Taiwanese have emerged as leading investors, contributing possibly half or more of the roughly $16 billion in myriad small-scale foreign investments that have propelled Guangdong and Fujian, the provinces nearest Taiwan in southeastern China, to unprecedented annual growth rates exceeding 18 percent by 1992.

Counterweight to Japanese Regional Economic Domination

In the first half of the 1980s, Japan came increasingly to dominate foreign direct investment flows in the rest of East Asia. It was logical to expect that, as the dominant economy in the region by far, Japan would become an even more dominant investor in the region after the Plaza Accord of 1985, which led to a sharp yen appreciation. Propelled to accelerate and expand its industrial restructuring and to relocate its marginal industries much more extensively offshore, particularly in East Asia, indeed it did virtually triple its level of investment in the ASEAN countries comparing the first half of the 1980s with 1986-1992.

Amazingly, however, the ANIEs combined virtually matched Japanese foreign direct investment levels in Southeast Asia in that period, actually exceeding it in Malaysia and Indonesia in the latest years. Taiwan led the group in volume of investment, followed by Singapore and Hong Kong (with Korea a distant fourth)—in effect constituting an overseas Chinese response to Japan's growing economic dominance in the region.[13]

Several prevalent features of Taiwanese investment distinguish it from non-Chinese Asian investment and make it in some respects an antidote or alternative to excessive dependence on Japanese investment:

- It is undertaken predominantly by relatively small, independent enterprises rather than by *keiretsu-* or *chaebol*-type conglomerates;
- It rarely entails the great power and reach of these large conglomerates;
- It generally involves much smaller, more numerous, more labor-intensive individual investments than is typical of Japanese investments;
- It rarely brings its own domestic suppliers; rather it depends much more on local suppliers;
- It is more often structured in joint venture with local firms than is Japanese investment; most often it favors joint ventures with local Chinese entrepreneurs; and
- It creates plants usually oriented more toward supplying domestic rather than export markets.

These features in general give Taiwanese and other overseas Chinese investments in Southeast Asia the advantages of seeming:

- less overpowering and threatening to local enterprises; and
- more closely tied into the local economy both through joint venture partners and local suppliers, and thus more beneficial.

At the same time Taiwanese investments also have the potential to aggravate local concerns where a local Chinese minority dominates particular sectors or local economic life in general. In addition, reflecting the "follower" status of its domestic economy, Taiwanese investments involve low- to medium-technology products, which entail limited technology transfer. This may make Taiwanese investment comparatively less attractive than some Japanese investments. Apparently also there are instances of joint Japanese-Taiwanese ventures in which the Taiwanese partner substitutes for what would otherwise be a Japanese parts or component supplier in the local economy, in effect participating in Japanese dominance.

Relative Status in East Asia's Regional Economy

Benchmarks: Taiwan's Economic Significance in East Asia

Measured by its economic size, Taiwan is hardly a towering force in East Asia, accounting for barely 3.5 percent of the region's GNP. Even so, it has used its small size to such excellent effect that it has proven capable, collaborating with other overseas Chinese, of challenging and equalling Japan within East Asia as a foreign investor and successful competitor in niches of some of the fastest-growing advanced technology sectors.

Although only ninth in population among Asian economies (after Burma) with only 2 percent of the region's people, Taiwan ranks fourth in both total GNP and GNP per capita (sixth in both cases if Australia and Brunei are included in the comparison).

During the 1982-1991, Taiwan followed Thailand and South Korea in GNP growth in the region. Taiwan ranks third among exporters in the region, fourth in two-way trade, and fifth among importers by value. Amazingly, it achieved this high growth rate with a markedly lower ratio of gross capital formation to GDP—only 22 percent compared to rates

Table 2.1 Taiwan in East Asia, Population Compared (in millions)

	1992
China	1,158
Indonesia	185
Japan	124
Vietnam	71
Philippines	61
Thailand	58
South Korea	44
Burma	42
Taiwan	21

Source: Michael Malik, ed., Asia 1993 Yearbook, December 1992, pp. 6-7.

Table 2.2 Taiwan in East Asia, GNP Compared (in billions of U.S. dollars)

	1991
Japan	3,374
China	452
[Australia]	[385]
South Korea	283
Taiwan	183
Indonesia	116

Source: Asia 1993 Yearbook.

Table 2.3 Taiwan in East Asia, GNP Per Capita Compared (in U.S. dollars)

	1990
Japan	27,200
Brunei	18,500
[Australia]	[21,900]
Hong Kong	14,300
Singapore	11,800
Taiwan	8,100
South Korea	6,500
Malaysia	2,400

Source: Asia 1993 Yearbook.

of 34-39 percent for leaders Singapore, South Korea, Thailand, and Japan, suggesting an exceptionally high level of efficiency in use of investment funds.

Because of this exceptionally high rate of net national savings, Taiwan has achieved its development with comparatively little reliance on foreign borrowing and with a much lower rate of interest and inflation than other countries. Taiwan's political isolation and limited sources of aid put a very high premium on self-financing of economic development efforts.

As might be imagined for an economy largely deprived of industrial resources, Taiwan is heavily dependent on exports—second in the region only to Malaysia—measured by the importance of exports as a percent of Gross Domestic Product.[14] In 1990, Taiwan's exports accounted for 48 percent of its GDP. This percentage has increased steadily as Taiwan's export growth has greatly outpaced growth of GDP. The exceptional importance exports play in its economy has to do with Taiwan's heavy reliance on an export-led growth strategy of economic development.

While Taiwan is among the three fastest-growing economies in the region, averaging 7.8 percent real growth in the last half of the 1980s, its exports expanded at a 16 percent annual rate from 1985 to 1992.

Economic Structure and Policies

Taiwan is widely reputed for the enterprise and commercial talents and skills of its people in both the home and international marketplace, and for its strongly market-oriented economy. However, below this surface appearance is a history of extensive government participation, intervention, and direction. Interpretation of Taiwan's economic role in East Asia is best accomplished with an understanding of the extent and nature of this government role.[15]

Adding to the challenge of interpretation is political intervention in the presentation of economic data. Most notable has been the extent to which the government has, in recent years, permitted Taiwanese enterprises to conduct foreign trade and direct investment activities with mainland China, indirectly through Hong Kong, and to a growing extent now directly with China, while omitting data on these transactions from trade and investment accounts. Further compounding the difficulty of evaluation and interpretation is the absence of data on Taiwan from accounts of major international organizations, which are the best source of comparable data for international comparisons and transactions. Recourse to data from Taiwan's trade and investment partners is often necessary to fill in important gaps in data and analysis.

Typical of developing economies, Taiwan began its development efforts with inadequate domestic savings, capital accumulation, and export earnings to finance development from within. It had few external sources to look to for assistance. Internally, mistrust and contention for power between native Taiwanese and KMT supporters shaped a strategy

Table 2.4 GNP Average Annual Percent Growth

	1987-1991
Thailand	10.4
South Korea	9.5
Taiwan	7.9
China	9.8
Hong Kong	4.6
Indonesia	6.1
Japan	4.9

Source: Asia 1993 Yearbook.

of KMT governance that involved extensive intervention in economic management aimed at leveraging trade, investment, and aid to maximize development benefits. Over time, the government developed and employed a wide range of policies and interventions for that purpose.

Government agricultural and financial policies were seminal in generating economic surpluses and entrepreneurship. By 1950 it instituted land reform, first redistributing Japanese lands and later private holdings exceeding three hectares. Sale of Japanese lands generated funds used to compensate large landholders, who in effect had to look to industry to win their future. Fearful of recreating the devastating inflation that racked the mainland, KMT officials followed highly conservative fiscal policies to keep a tight lid on prices. The combined result was to shift entrepreneurship from agriculture to industry and to provide a stable economic climate effective in keeping money at home. The economic effect of the land reform "was to make an agricultural sector able to produce a sizable volume of exports and generate linkages with other sectors;... *the surge of agricultural growth checked discontent with the Nationalist regime in the countryside*, helping in turn to stabilize the industrial investment climate."[16] Evidence of industrial progress became visible as early as 1958 when the industrial composition of Taiwan's exports began to rise at a dramatic rate.

Policy instruments also came to include a mix of protection for selected industrial sectors combined with reduction of barriers mainly to those imports required to supply export-oriented industries. "The government was trying to promote both exports and, in different industries, import substitution (and hence discrimination against exports in those industries)."[17]

Authorities also exerted influence, control, and stimulus vis-á-vis native Taiwanese and other domestic private sector enterprises in large part through creation and deployment of government enterprises. These were engaged as pace-setters, stimulators of competition, and often as chosen instruments for attracting, acquiring, and controlling foreign investments and technologies.

> In many sectors, public enterprises have been used as the chosen instrument for a big push. This is true for the early years of fuels, chemicals, mining, metals, fertilizer, and food processing; but even in sectors where public enterprises did not dominate, such as textiles and plastics, the state aggressively led private producers in the early years. Later, during the late 1950s and 1960s, public enterprises accounted for a large part of total investment in synthetic fibers, metals, shipbuilding, and other industries.[18]

Government enterprises were considered better able to hold out for and extract more extensive technology transfers and foreign investment benefits on better terms than private firms.[19] The government has also required its approval of foreign investments, both inward and outward, and exercised controls over allocation of foreign exchange and exchange rates to achieve its objectives, both political and developmental.

Participation in Regional Economic Development

It can reasonably be said that the Taiwanese economy has participated in East Asian regional economic development in a very conscious, calculated, and directed way. In that sense Taiwan set the stage for its current exceptional economic influence on the region by the way it shaped its development strategy, and by coordinating the interactions of its economy with other economies of the region at the trade, investment, and foreign assistance levels.

As we examine patterns in Taiwan's economic relationships during the 1980s, the following highlights emerge:

Magnet for Foreign Investment. Inward foreign direct investment languished in a range between $100-200 million annually in 1980-1984, before enjoying a five-fold expansion through 1985-1989, bringing the average annual rate of increase to 28 percent for 1980-1989. The peak was US$1.6 billion in 1989, declining to roughly $1.2 billion in 1990. While the United States accounted for nearly half of the inflow in 1987, the flow became predominantly Asianized by 1990 (as percent of inward FDI from all sources) (see Table 2.5).

At its peak in 1989-1990, foreign direct investment inflows represented only about 6 percent of Taiwan's gross domestic capital formation. However, it had a relative importance greater than its size because it represented a principle means by which the economy acquired advanced technology. Consequently, inflows from more advanced countries such as the United States and Japan were particularly significant. Among manufacturing investments, top billing went to chemicals, electric equipment, metals, mechanical equipment, food and beverages (by receiving industry, as percent of total recorded) (see Table 2.6).

Emergence as Capital Exporter. By the late 1970s Taiwan achieved a near balance in its foreign trade and began in the early 1980s to emerge as a capital exporter. Its current account balance began to expand steady from 1981 through 1987 when it peaked at US$18.2 billion. However, with the 20 percent appreciation of the NT dollar 1987, followed by a

Table 2.5 Foreign Direct Investment Inflows

Source (percent of inward FDI)	1987	1990
Japan	20.8	37.9
Hong Kong	4.2	13.3
United States	48.5	13.6
Singapore & Philippines	2.7	2.6
Other Asian	--	2.1
Total Asian	27.7	83.6

Source: Investment Commission, Ministry of Economic Affairs.

Table 2.6 Foreign Direct Inflows By Manufacturing Sector

Industry Sector	1987	1990
Chemicals	12.1	22.2
Electrical equipment	26.6	16.4
Metals	8.5	8.1
Mechanical Equipment	26.6	16.4
Food, beverages, tobacco	5.4	4.8
Total	58.0	57.1

Source: Investment Commission, Ministry of Economic Affairs.

Table 2.7 Taiwan's Direct Investment Outflows (As percent of total recorded)

	1987	1990
United States	86.0	56.0
Philippines	--	16.6
Thailand	6.3	5.4
Singapore	0.6	2.9
Indonesia and Malaysia	2.4	2.1
Total of Selected Asian	9.3	27.0

Source: United Nations, World Investment Directory, 1992.

further gradual 12 percent appreciation by 1992, the current account surplus began to decline.

The year 1987 marked a dramatic shift in Taiwan's investment role. That year it registered a ten-fold increase in its foreign direct investment outflows as reported on a balance of payments basis in UN data. This was followed by a further five-fold increase in 1988, and a 60 percent increase in 1989. These outflows rose to US$4.2 billion in 1988 and US$6.6 billion in 1989. (Taiwan government figures on approvals are far

Table 2.8   Direct Investment Outflows By Region

	Amount	Percent of Global	Percent of Asian
Global	4,116	100.0	
To United States	1,594	38.7	
All Asia	2,158	52.4	100.0
ASEAN-4	1,739	42.3	80.6
ANIEs (3)	406	9.9	18.8
ASEAN	1,739	42.3	
Malaysia	906	22.0	42.0
Thailand	346	8.4	16.1
Indonesia	255	6.2	13.5
Philippines	231	5.6	10.7
ANIEs	406	9.9	18.8
Hong Kong	292	7.1	13.5
Singapore	76	1.8	3.5
South Korea	38	0.9	1.8

Source: United Nations, World Investment Directory, 1992.

lower at US$219 million in 1988, US$931 million in 1989, and $1.6 billion in 1990.)

Although government approval statistics show the United States as the destination of over half of the total, its share declined sharply and steadily from 86 percent in 1987 to 56 percent in 1990. The leading Asian recipients of Taiwanese direct investment, to the extent acknowledged in government statistics, are shown in Table 2.7.

These percentages tell only a small part of the story because they exclude direct investments in Hong Kong, China, and Vietnam. Taiwan became the dominant foreign investor in Hong Kong and Vietnam in those years, as it did also in the Philippines. No investments were acknowledged by government reports in either of these three countries through 1990 data. For example, compared with US$900 million of acknowledged Taiwanese investments in the United States in 1990, unrecorded investments in China may well have been US$2-3 billion of the US$6.6 billion of total outflows.

Of the total of approved direct investment outflows, by geographic destination as actually reported, Taiwan's data indicate geographic distribution for the entire period 1987 through August 1992 (in millions of U.S. dollars and percent) as shown in Table 2.8.

Much more informative are UN data that show the relative importance of Taiwanese and other ANIE investment to individual host countries in Southeast Asia for the latest available four-year periods (Table 2.9). The annual data on Taiwan and ANIE investment show year-to-year increases

Table 2.9 Relative Direct Investment Outflows

	Japan's percent of Total	ANIEs percent of Total	Taiwan's percent of Total
Malaysia			
1987	34.7	28.8	11.8
1990	23.9	46.8	36.0
Average	25.6	40.8	27.7
Thailand			
1985	34.5	-6.9	3.8
1988	51.7	28.4	11.2
Average	46.1	23.2	8.5
Indonesia			
1987	36.5	11.8	0.5
1990	25.6	29.7	7.1
Average	19.6	28.7	8.7
Philippines			
1985	7.6	2.5	0.1
1988	25.5	17.9	7.2
Average	17.2	15.8	3.2

Source: United Nations, *World Investment Directory*, 1992.

throughout the periods with the exception of a jump to 20 percent for Taiwan's share of direct investment in Indonesia in 1988. These data show that by the latest year the ANIEs out-invested Japan in both Malaysia and Indonesia, and that Taiwan alone did so in Malaysia in 1990.[20] In both Malaysia and Indonesia ANIE investment also exceeded that of Japan for the period as a whole.

Unfortunately, more interesting numbers for 1989-1991 are not available. From anecdotal evidence, the rising importance of ANIE and Taiwanese investment probably continued through 1991 for all the ASEAN countries with the possible exception of the Philippines. According to one source, by 1990 the four ANIEs accounted for 35 percent of total new foreign investment in the four ASEAN countries compared with a 27 percent share for Japan. [21]

Asianization of Taiwan Trade. IMF figures on Taiwan's trade are available from 1985 through 1991 by derivation from trading partner data. Since the Plaza Accord of September 1985 represents a major economic watershed of the 1980s, the changes from 1985 to the present are particularly significant. Table 2.10 shows the remarkable shifts over the 1985-1991 period.

Clearly Asia has come increasingly to dominate Taiwan's overall

Table 2.10   Taiwan's Trade Patterns (In billions of U.S. dollars)

Taiwan's Trade with:	Exports		Imports		2-way Balance	
	1985	1991	1985	1991	1985	1991
GLOBAL	30.7	75.7	20.1	64.0	50.8	139.7
U.S.A.	17.8	24.2	4.7	13.2	22.5	37.4
ASIA (9)	8.4	29.4	7.3	28.6	15.7	57.9
ANIES (3)	3.9	13.8	1.3	7.6	5.2	21.4
ASEAN	1.1	6.1	0.9	2.7	2.0	8.8
Japan	3.4	9.5	5.1	18.3	8.5	27.8
Hong Kong	2.7	9.6	0.7	4.0	3.4	13.6
Singapore	0.8	2.7	0.4	2.1	1.3	4.8
Korea	0.3	1.5	0.2	1.5	0.5	3.0
Malaysia	0.3	2.0	0.2	0.9	0.7	2.9
Thailand	0.3	1.9	0.1	0.5	0.4	2.4
Indonesia	0.3	1.3	0.4	1.1	0.7	2.4
Philippines	0.2	0.9	0.1	0.2	0.3	1.1

Source: IMF, Directions of Trade, 1992.

international trade.   By 1991, Taiwan's major Asian trade partners accounted for 42 percent of its two-way trade, compared with 27 percent for the United States. Taiwan's trade with East Asia grew roughly one-third faster that its two-way trade with the United States from 1985 to 1991. In exports, Taiwan's dependence on the U.S. market has declined from 44 percent in 1985 to 27 percent in 1991, and its dependence on Asian markets has increased from 31 percent to 42 percent. In spite of this trend, the United States still remains by far Taiwan's largest single market. Japan remains the single largest source of Taiwan's imports by a large margin, followed by the United States. After Japan, Taiwan's two-way trade with its three newly industrialized counterparts (the ANIEs) continues to exceed its trade with the ASEAN countries by more than 2:1, but in the late 1980s two-way trade with ASEAN gained relative to Taiwan's ANIE trade because of a boom in Taiwanese exports to ASEAN.

Taiwan's imports grew most rapidly from the other ANIEs, which have rapidly diversified their economies. Taiwan's more rapid export growth to ASEAN is almost certainly related to the great expansion in Taiwan's investments in the region in the late 1980s.

From the early 1980s, Hong Kong has been Taiwan's second largest customer in Asia. Hong Kong's share of Taiwan's exports, flat through most of the period, climbed sharply after 1987. In 1990-1991 Hong Kong nominally surpassed Japan as Taiwan's largest Asian market.   Once

Hong Kong's reexports of Taiwanese goods to China are excluded, however, it becomes clear that the real expansion was in Taiwan's indirect trade with China, and that the ANIE share of trade with Taiwan (Korea, Singapore, and Hong Kong itself) has remained fairly steady at about 12-13 percent during the 1980s. Hong Kong has consistently accounted for close to two-thirds of Taiwan-ANIE exports over the decade. ASEAN countries accounted for about half as much as the ANIEs, but gained share marginally after 1985 as Taiwan's exports to Southeast Asia grew over 30 percent annually. Strongly characteristic of Taiwan's Asian trade are the imbalances in its trade patterns, with three particular cases in point:

Japan. Taiwan has long been frustrated by an inability to close or even reduce its trade deficit with Japan. This bilateral deficit has risen every single year, from $1.6 billion in 1985 to almost $9 billion in 1991, in spite of the progressive appreciation of the yen vis-á-vis the NT dollar, from a ratio of ¥6.1/NT$ in 1985 to ¥4.9 in 1991-1992.

Other Asia. Taiwan has achieved modestly increased trade surpluses with both the ANIEs and ASEAN countries as groups. The mid-1980s marked a transition for Taiwan's trade in which it passed from a deficit or near balance in trade with a number of countries to growing trade surpluses. With the ASEAN countries this represented a transition from when Taiwan relied on ASEAN mainly for imports of raw and intermediate materials needed by its industries. In the post-1985 period, as the yen appreciated, Taiwan became more competitive with Japanese producers in electrical equipment, electronics, and a range of medium technology products imported by ASEAN countries. In addition, dramatic increases in Taiwanese direct investment beginning in 1987 coincided with increases in the percentage share of Taiwanese exports going to both the ANIEs and ASEAN countries, including components and equipment for investment projects. The annual average of Taiwan's trade balances comparing 1986-1990 with 1980-1985 illustrates that shift (see Table 2.9). Although trade with its three newly industrialized counterparts (the ANIEs) continued to dominate, Taiwan expanded its exports most rapidly during this period to the four leading ASEAN countries. It also invested significantly in these countries in 1986-1991.

China. Notable are the sharp increases in Taiwan's exports to Hong Kong from 1987 to 1989 and again in 1991. Taiwan's data do not report exports to China. Hong Kong, however, reports reexports from Hong Kong by destination and by source country (see Table 2.12).

Table 2.11   Balance of Trade By Region (in billions of U.S. dollars, noting average annual figures)

	1980-1985	1986-1990
Japan	−$1.6	−$8.8
ANIEs	+2.6	+6.2
Hong Kong	+2.0	+5.6
Singapore	+0.5	+0.6
ASEAN	+0.2	+3.4
Thailand	+0.1	+1.4
Malaysia	−0.2	+1.1
ANIEs + ASEAN	+2.8	+9.6

Source: IMF, Directions of Trade, 1992.

Table 2.12 Taiwan's Indirect Trade With China
(Hong Kong reexport data in millions of U.S. dollars)

	Exports to Hong Kong	Reexports to China	Percent of Total to China
1980	1,551	219	14.1
1984	2,087	432	20.7
1985	2,540	987	38.9
1986	2,915	810	27.8
1987	4,123	1,227	9.7
1988	5,587	2,242	40.1
1989	7,042	2,897	41.1
1990	8,556	3,278	38.3
1991	--	4,667	--
Average Growth Rate, 1980-1991	18.5%	32.0%	

Source: Hong Kong Trade Statistics.

These numbers reveal the rapid growth of indirect trade between Taiwan and China. (Taiwan still bans direct trade and investment with China.) It seems likely that much of this trade growth is related to the prominence of Taiwanese investors in the recent and ongoing multi-billion dollar foreign investments in southeast China (Guangdong and Fujian). Recent estimates are that in 1992, two-way trade with China was at least US$14 billion, roughly 10 percent of Taiwan's total two-way trade. Because it severely limits the categories of products eligible for import from China, mainly to cheap raw materials and components, Taiwan is estimated to enjoy roughly a US$5 billion surplus in its China trade.[22] (Exports to China via Hong Kong were US$6.3 billion and imports US$1.1, leaving a US$5.2 billion surplus; imports fell because of a Taiwanese crackdown on illegal imports of restricted items.)[23] It is difficult to estimate the importance of Taiwan's investment in China in recent years. Estimates of the number of Taiwanese companies that have invested either directly or through Hong Kong range from 7-12,000, and in cumulative amounts are estimated to exceed US$6 billion. While ostensibly Hong Kong dominates foreign investment in both Guangdong and China as a whole, accounting for 63 percent of the estimated US$2.7 billion of disbursed investments in 1990, these Hong Kong's numbers include investments from Taiwan and Korea, and some mainland Chinese money as well.

Continued expansion of Taiwanese investments in and exports to China should be expected over the long term as long as Chinese economic reform continues and political conditions remain stable. We can expect considerable volatility in the short term because of periodic Chinese restraints to control economic overheating, and because of periodic Taiwanese government efforts to prevent excessive dependence on the mainland in trade and investment flows.

Trade as Leverage. Singapore and Hong Kong exert relatively greater leverage for their size than Taiwan on regional economic development through trade activities since their exports, including reexports from other sources, greatly exceed their GDP in value. However, among the larger economies of the region (in GDP terms) Taiwan exerts exceptionally high leverage via merchandise exports that averaged over 40 percent of GDP.

Interestingly, despite its growing trade surpluses, Taiwan's exports have accounted for a steadily diminishing fraction of GDP since 1986, falling from over 52 percent in 1987 to an estimated 36 percent in 1992. This trend suggests that Taiwan is progressively lessening its dependence on foreign trade. Does this mean Taiwan is a declining force in regional trade? This is unlikely. Despite the declining trend, Taiwan's level of GDP dependence on exports remains high-to-moderate on the scale of world industrial nations. Second, trade data suggest that Taiwan remains an aggressive force in expansion of regional trade.

Earlier we noted an analysis by Jeffrey Sachs regarding Asianization of trade. Naturally, it is argued, if your neighbors were growing and trading faster than others, your share of trade with them should increase. In such a case, you might be a passive player with Asia's share of your trade increasing because they were expanding more rapidly than you.

However, we have noted that Taiwan's economy has grown more rapidly than all its neighbors other than China and Korea.

The following table indicates that, in addition, Taiwan demonstrated the most aggressive growth in trade as well. It shows that for 1985-1991, Taiwan's global two-way trade grew 22.4 percent (average annual rate), third-fastest of the Asian Ten after Hong Kong and Thailand. Moreover:

- Taiwan's bilateral trade with every one of the other nine grew faster than those partners' global trade grew; and
- Except for Hong Kong, Taiwan's bilateral trade with eight of the nine leading Asian economies grew much more rapidly than their global trade growth—in fact 2-3 times as fast: China (3x), Korea (2.4x), Japan (2x), and Indonesia (2x).

These comparisons suggest special growth qualities in Taiwan's Asian trade relationships; certainly investment relationships are likely to have been an important and closely linked factor in this rapid growth.

Taiwan's Regional Economic Roles: A Geographic Assessment

From the foregoing overview we can see that Taiwan has come to play economic roles in the region that are proportionately much greater than the relative size of its territory and economy. This fact is a tribute to the overall success of economic policies that have gained it this influence in spite of its political isolation in the region. However, Taiwan has achieved some of this influence through interventionist policies, which distort market behavior and conflict with international rules and practices. Ironically, it has been able to persist in some restrictive policies in part because of its political isolation; by its exclusion from the IMF and the General Agreement on Tariffs and Trade, Taiwan has escaped the commitments and pressures to realign some of its restrictive financial and trade practices with their international standards.[24]

To a significant extent the United States has substituted bilateral pressures for some of these missing international pressures in order to encourage Taiwan to liberalize market access and to adjust the NT dollar exchange rate as its foreign exchange reserves have grown conspicuously large. In these efforts, it has been inspired by Taiwan's large trade surplus with the United States.

Taiwan's Ambivalent Economic Partnership with Japan

Taiwan continues to be highly attractive for direct investments from Japan. It offers an excellent investment climate with a broad and highly qualified managerial base and a highly educated and skilled work force. It provides Japanese manufacturers a familiar environment, competitive potential for producing medium- to advanced-technology components, subsystems, and final products for reexport, particularly in electronic and automotive sectors. Metal fabrication and chemical industries have also attracted heavy investments. Japan has been the leading foreign investor in Taiwan since 1988, and has accounted for over a third of inward direct investment since 1987. As one source told the author:

> Taiwan's rapidly rising labor costs increasingly detract from its desirability as a site for textiles and other labor-intensive products. Nevertheless, other factors, such as geographical proximity to Japan, relatively low inflation rates, an increasingly developed industrial infrastructure and a large pool of skilled labor, still make Taiwan an attractive investment place for Japanese manufacturers, especially producers of medium-technology products.[25]

As a high-growth, advanced technology economy with a massive $300 billion six-year infrastructure effort underway, Taiwan remains a highly attractive marketplace for Japan's exports of production machinery, communications, power generation, and other equipment and technology. Its rapidly expanding and prospering middle class offers an increasingly attractive market for Japan's competitive consumer electronics and transportation equipment.

Growing roughly in parallel with its trade surplus with the United States is Taiwan's trade deficit with Japan. U.S. pressures on Taiwan to reduce its surplus with the United States brought to a head Taiwan's frustrations over its inability to get better access to the Japanese market. In June 1990 Taiwan introduced a number of tough trade measures designed to force Japan's hand, with rather limited results to date. Among other things, officials identified some 238 products where dependence on Japan exceeded 90 percent, and urged companies to seek non-Japanese sources. This trade imbalance will continue to irritate relations and may undermine the potential for a broader partnership. [26]

Table 2.13   Trade Growth Rates, Annual Average Growth 1985-1991

	Percent of Global Growth	Percent of Bilateral Trade with Taiwan
Taiwan	22.4	--
Japan	12.4	25.5
China	13.0	39.3
Korea	19.7	47.1
Hong Kong	43.5	37.3
Singapore	20.7	27.1
Indonesia	13.8	28.6
Malaysia	20.8	33.6
Thailand	31.8	39.6
Philippines	16.9	25.9

Source: Based on data from *UN Directions of Trade*, 1992.

Table 2.14   Average Annual Percentage Change, 1985-1992

Taiwan with:	Exports	Imports	Two-Way Balance
Global	16.2	31.3	18.4
U.S.A.	5.3	18.8	8.9
ASIA	23.2	25.6	24.4
Japan	18.6	23.8	21.8
ANIES (3)	23.5	34.2	26.6
ASEAN (4)	33.2	19.9	28.0
Korea	28.3	41.0	33.7
Hong Kong	23.7	33.0	26.0
Singapore	20.8	32.4	25.0
Thailand	37.0	26.7	34.4
Malaysia	35.3	17.9	27.8
Philippines	29.2	16.1	25.7
Indonesia	28.8	20.0	24.3

Source: Based on data from *UN Directions of Trade*, 1992.

Table 2.15   Percentage Trade Shares, 1985-1992

Taiwan's Trade with:	Exports		Imports		Two-Way Balance	
	1985	1991	1985	1991	1985	1991
U.S.A.	57.9	32.0	23.4	20.6	44.2	26.8
Japan	11.1	12.5	25.2	28.6	16.7	19.9
ANIEs	12.7	18.2	6.5	11.9	10.2	15.3
ASEAN	3.5	8.0	4.5	4.2	3.9	6.3
ANIEs + ASEAN	16.2	26.2	11.0	16.1	14.1	21.6

Source: Based on data from *UN Directions of Trade*, 1992.

Nowhere is the ambivalence in the Taiwan-Japan economic relationship more clear than with regard to their trade and foreign investment relations elsewhere in the region. By the mid-1980s Taiwanese and Korean production of semiconductors, motherboards, computer monitors and keyboards, VCRs, autos, and auto parts convinced Japanese firms of their potential to gain markets at Japan's expense. Reportedly as a result it became much harder to get access to advanced Japanese technologies, in turn forcing Taiwanese and Korean producers to look elsewhere for advanced technology. One interpretation is that the burst of ANIE investment activity in Southeast Asia in part reflects a decision to compete more directly with the Japanese for the faster-growing ASEAN markets.

Specifically, the June 1990 measures by Taiwan "conditioned new Japanese investment in the manufacturing sector on technology transfers and/or export requirements."[27] Subsequently, Taiwan exerted pressure on Japan to provide technical assistance in its economic restructuring.

> Taiwanese firms...concluded 105 technical assistance contracts with Japanese companies in 1990, a number exceeding the combined total of contracts signed with American firms (50) and European businesses (30). Much of the recent growth in Japanese technical assistance has been in the electronics and the metalworking industries. Among the reasons many Taiwanese cite for their preference for Japanese affiliations are a concern with high quality, appropriate technology, marketing prowess and after-sale service.[28]

Moreover, some Taiwanese firms have apparently decided to join, not fight Japanese firms in other Asian markets:

> Taiwanese companies increasingly are trying to become part of Japanese manufacturers' supplier networks. Their goal is to collaborate with small and mid-sized Japanese firms supplying big manufacturers in Japan. Although parts shipments from Taiwan to Japan still are fairly limited, a number of Taiwanese companies work closely with Japanese firms elsewhere in Southeast Asia. ...Taiwanese investors also fill a gap in the supply chain of less-developed Southeast Asian countries by helping provide parts to Japanese firms manufacturing there.[29]

Some see these supplier relationships in Southeast Asia as positioning Taiwan to improve its international competitiveness and possibly as helping to open the door to more exports to Japan. Some Japanese firms reportedly see advantages from alliances with Taiwanese firms in the potential for tying into the overseas Chinese business network throughout Southeast Asia and for providing helpful connections for expanding business in China.

Overall, Taiwan's economic relations and interactions with Japan within the region are destined to remain complex and ambivalent—an unstable mix of attraction and conflict. It is tempting to expect, however, that during the early 1990s Taiwan will gradually come to reduce its dependence on Japan, for several reasons:

- Japan's economic implosion in 1990-1992 has reduced its ability to export capital to and invest in the region, creating a liberating hiatus in the growth of interdependence with Taiwan;
- Taiwan's continued rapid growth and very high savings rates and foreign exchange accumulations give it increasing degrees of freedom in developing independent alternatives to dependence on Japan; and
- Taiwan's advantaged position and lead over Japan in developing trade and investments in China will reduce Japan's ability to catch up while it is preoccupied with domestic problems.

Abetting Taiwan's concern to reduce this dependence is Japan's sense that its exports of production equipment and related technology to Taiwan has backfired and created an effective competitor on its doorstep. As a result, some Japanese are also concerned to restrain equipment and technology exports to Taiwan.[30]

Taiwan and the ANIEs

The ANIEs have pioneered a development model that differs from one to another in important ways but generally incorporates the following key emphases:

- Acquisition of foreign technologies through technology purchases, alliances, and partnerships, as well as through the recruitment of technical expertise abroad, particularly in the United States, including ethnic Chinese and other Asians;
- Low-budget applied research;
- Quick applications of advanced and maturing technologies to niche markets;
- Speed, agility and flexibility moving from product design to marketing; and

- Use of strategic partnerships for access to distribution networks, capitalizing on U.S. connections, school and corporate ties, etc.

Attractions from the foreign industrial investor's viewpoint include:

- Access to low-cost R&D and engineering resources;
- Opportunity to establish low-cost, high-talent R&D laboratories;
- Low-cost local manufacture of medium technology products for regional and global markets;
- Benefits of low-cost East Asian manufacturing in more advanced technology products through transfer of relevant technologies; and
- Advancement beyond contract assembly to strategic partnerships to include design of components into locally produced consumer electronics; and
- Design and production of Original Manufacturer Equipment (OEM) for Japanese brand name producers.

It would take extensive investigation to determine which ANIE—whether Taiwan, Korea, or Singapore—led the way or had the greatest influence in defining this development model now in general use by all the ANIEs and emulated throughout the region in varying degrees. Certainly Japanese influence is evident in most of the ingredients.

In this process, along with other ANIEs, Taiwan has literally achieved world leadership in several of its selected niche markets. Taiwanese firms hold important world market shares in motherboards,[31] application-specific semiconductors (ASICs), personal computers, and such computer peripherals as monitors, keyboards, and power supplies. Taiwan's ACER computer is a brand recognized worldwide. Taiwan is said to produce nearly two-thirds of the motherboards sold globally. Taiwan is also a leader in mass-produced software and has gained prominence in microprocessor design, and with help from U.S.-trained Taiwanese with advanced U.S. degrees is vying for world-class capabilities in sophisticated semiconductor manufacture.[32]

Taiwan's government leadership has been instrumental through the creation of specialized technical institutes for research on computer, communication, information, and biotechnologies and even more narrowly on high-definition television (HDTV). The government reportedly has funded US$280 million for research into submicron semiconductor chip production, US$120 million in biotechnology and pharmaceutical research, and US$120 million for HDTV. In addition, government banks fund up to 40 percent of venture capital in eligible technologies.[33]

The relevance of this developmental framework for Taiwan's economic role in East Asia is several-fold: Taiwan has clearly established itself as:

- One of the top development role-models for the several aspirant ANIEs in East Asia, notably with mainland China in its direct line of influence;
- An important and even unique supplier of components for the consumer and computer electronics industries, which are developing as a top priority throughout the region; and
- An attractive investor or investment partner for production of niche components for local manufacturing throughout the region.

Additionally, because of both its development success and its ties to overseas Chinese, Taiwan has become an attractive investment magnet for refugee capital and flight capital when the investment climate sours in other countries in the region. In particular Taiwan has continued to attract substantial capital inflows from the Philippines over most of the 1980s. Although since 1985 overseas Chinese investment has accounted for less than ten percent of inward foreign direct investment, prior to 1980 it averaged nearly one-third, and peaked in 1980 at 48 percent.

Taiwan and China

Uncertainties Prevail. The contagion of excitement generated by China's economic reforms, the explosion of foreign and private investment in Guangdong Province following Deng Xiaoping's January 1992 visit, and his blessing of the Guangdong experiment have all greatly inflated expectations about China's economic future—and by extension, Taiwan's role in it. They have also tended to obscure one of the economic fundamentals of today's China—volatility. In earlier times when mainland authorities had the economic steering wheel more firmly in hand, China experienced repeated cycles of boom and inflation followed by application of sharp restraints, with the resulting equivalent of an economic flat tire. Since authorities are now attempting to move China forward with a mix of economic liberalization combined with continued tight political control, political events can also add greatly to the volatility of economic conditions. With China having greatly expanded its global economic interdependence, political sparks that singe its trading and investing partners can have a disproportionate harmful impact on China's economy via adverse international reactions.

Three evolving developments call forth caution flags. First is the pace of change in several coastal provinces, which have generated localized growth near or exceeding 20 percent annually. Property values, rents, wages, and other costs at locations near Hong Kong are said to rival Hong Kong's, and have sent some investors looking elsewhere. The problem is that as individual provinces overheat, few other adjacent provinces are as well suited to pick up spill-over investments. For example, Guangdong's unique proximity to a capitalist seedbed (Hong Kong), immediate adjacency to and astride transportation routes into China's rich hinterland, has no other counterpart in China. Nor do other provinces enjoy the same degree of bureaucratic flexibility and experimentation. As a result, as go the prospects for southeast China, so they go by and large for China as a whole. Even now we are seeing belated Chinese official recognition of the need for credit and other economic restraints, while overheating is also showing up in China's first two quarterly balance of payments deficits in some time.

Second, the present dust-up between Hong Kong's new governor and Beijing over political freedoms in the colony warrants another caution flag. There are two economic reasons why China might choose to hang tough against Governor Patten if its political goals warrant. To begin with, southeast China's high growth has smartly inflated its economy, wages, and prices, and has outrun infrastructure to the point that an economic cooling-off is desirable—something that continued political tensions could help accomplish. Moreover, Guangdong's success has opened doors elsewhere in China and larger foreign investments are taking shape with investments from Japan, Korea, Taiwan, Europe, and the United States that do not involve or require the intermediation of Hong Kong. Nor is it clear that the Hong Kong dispute will be seen by these large investors as necessarily reflecting adversely on the prospects for their investments since Hong Kong's involvement is not required. After all, China still enjoys one of the world's largest pools of foreign exchange reserves—the kind of credentials that is likely to loom much larger in foreign investor calculations than what may be seen as a localized political dispute essentially limited to Hong Kong.

Third, uncertainty is also posed by the Clinton administration and absence of clear indications whether it will see sufficient progress in governance and human rights to renew again next year U.S. Most-Favored-Nation treatment for China.

The point is that the pattern of China's economic development is vulnerable to forces that could easily spoil or change the unique chemistry and opportunity that the Taiwan-Hong Kong-Guangdong-Fujian axis has given Taiwanese investors for the past several years. A dampening of southeast China's growth and of Hong Kong's role could curtail the flood of small-investor, small-plant investments dependent on medium and small Taiwanese investors. That would not necessarily prevent some of Taiwan's larger investors from launching larger projects elsewhere in China, through channels independent of, or less dependent on, Hong Kong. Recalling that about two-thirds of Taiwan's residents originate in Fujian province and mainly speak Fukienese, and that increasingly the larger Taiwanese investment projects are locating in Fujian, directly across the strait from Taiwan, one can expect that transition not to be unduly challenging.

Thus the pattern of Taiwan's involvement in China will probably change by the mid-1990s and will certainly be subject to periodic retrenchments and volatility typical of China's recent development. However, it seems likely that Taiwan will continue to play a leading, if not dominant, investment role among foreign participants in the future economic reform and growth of China. This likelihood is reinforced by the persistence of Taiwan's high national savings rate, trade surpluses, and exaggerated foreign exchange reserve accumulations.

Meanwhile, at least in the early months of 1993, Taiwan's investment enthusiasm for China continues unabated, with 72 percent of 247 foreign investors indicating the mainland as their intended destination in 1993, compared with 39 percent who actually did so in 1992, with Taiwan's larger firms leading the way.[34]

Taiwan's Role and Future in Southeast Asia

As Economic Development Model. Much media ink has been devoted to debating whether Japan's, Taiwan's, or Korea's development serves as the best model for development elsewhere in Asia. At one end of the spectrum, it is argued that Taiwan's main contribution to Asia's economic development is as an economic model.[35] Important elements of Taiwan's model certainly have earlier regional prototypes, for example, in protectionist policies and extensive promotion of research in selected technologies by the Japanese government. A rather unique, effective—and perhaps even most distinctive—feature of Taiwan's "model" is the role created for government enterprise. Yet this aspect probably originated from the unique bivalence of KMT/native Taiwanese politics and might be hard to replicate elsewhere. Only Singapore has incorporated a closely similar developmental role for state enterprises, for reasons philosophical not bivalent. Nor has any other country even attempted such ambitious land reform in the context of developing a market-driven economy. Finally, the sheer scope of detail and complexity of Taiwan's interventions in import, export, foreign investment, and other transactions, as described by Wade, lend themselves poorly indeed to anything but notional emulation as a model.

Do other Asian government planners view Taiwan as Asia's best economic model? It is hard to find the evidence. One can say with much more confidence that Taiwan's economic success with government intervention to accelerate industrialization and the up-scaling of comparative advantage through education and technology certainly adds to the Asian evidence commending certain types of government interventions. Such evidence, however, can also be found in selected aspects of the Japan, Korea, and Singapore "model" as well.

As Foreign Direct Investor. As noted earlier, Taiwan became a direct investor of steadily increasing importance to the ASEAN-4 through the late 1980s up to at least 1991. According to one estimate:

> Since 1987 more than 4,000 Taiwanese companies have set up operations in Southeast Asia, pouring an estimated US$12 billion into the region and helping to turn it into an economic powerhouse. That accounts for almost half the US$25 billion capital outflow from Taiwan during that time, according to the Ministry of Economic Affairs....As these economic links grow, Taiwan is creating a more integrated regional economy.[36]

Almost certainly, the boom in ANIE growth with its pressure on production costs, combined with further pressure from ANIE exchange rate appreciation, provided some cost-push incentives to these investments. The reorientation of ASEAN country policies toward export-led growth in the early to mid 1980s stimulated their efforts to attract foreign investors in search of low-wage and lower cost economies. Because the ANIEs all faced similar cost pressures, Taiwan's role was of a piece with that of the ANIEs as a group, and emphasizes the importance and relevance of Taiwan's role as an ANIE. This group then clearly became an important and sometimes dominant source of foreign direct investment for the ASEAN countries in the late 1980s and on into the early 1990s.

Because of its continuing savings surpluses, Taiwan is almost certain to continue as an important prospective source of foreign investment in Southeast Asia. However, by 1992 familiar cost-push pressures have begun to reduce the investment attractions of ASEAN countries. The near tripling of investment inflows, combined with lively domestic investment, pushed growth rates near double digits, generated some inflation, skill shortages, and overburdened infrastructure particularly in Thailand, Malaysia, and to a degree in Indonesia. This caused governments to take a variety of measures either to restrain growth or to shift emphasis away from production projects toward infrastructure. It remains to be seen if ASEAN will succeed in attracting substantial Taiwanese capital into infrastructure investments.

Progressively through the late 1980s also China was advancing its market-oriented economic reforms, making southeast and coastal China an increasingly attractive alternative to ASEAN for offshore investors not only in labor-intensive manufacturing but even in more advanced technologies. It is clear that Taiwan by 1991-1992 had begun to shift its direct investment attentions sharply toward China (see Table 2.16).

Taiwanese investment dropped sharply in Malaysia, Thailand, and the Philippines in the past two years, and in Indonesia in 1992. A noteworthy countertrend is Vietnam, which, with a lag, followed the example of China toward economic reform and openings to foreign investors. Taiwanese are today the leading investors in Vietnam by a large margin, with approved investments of US$465 million in 1991 and US$525 in 1992. In spite of some infrastructure deficiencies, Vietnam offered an abundance of both a low-wage and a relatively highly skilled labor force.

Eager to restrain excessive investment in China, the Taiwanese government has been pushing investment seminars, business tours, and investment protection agreements in Southeast Asia. It is actively encouraging investments in Vietnam and also offers loans to improve infrastructure in some countries, including in principle a loan to finance an industrial estate at Subic Bay, Philippines.[37]

Thus, while Taiwan will certainly continue an active trade and investment role in Southeast Asia, it will do so with a keen awareness of shifts in the comparative attractions of various trade and investment options within the region as a whole. Through 1992 Taiwan seemed to enjoy a definite warming of economic relations with China and a correspondent cooling in its relations with ASEAN. This balance is highly susceptible to accentuation or to reversal. As ASEAN economics cool off and infrastructure expands, they may well regain some of theirattractions vis-á-vis China—particularly if some of the uncertainties in China cited earlier come to loom larger and more ominous. While the labor cost advantage in much of the region is now only a third to a

Table 2.16 Taiwan's Approved Indirect Investments in Mainland China, January-August, 1992, by Location (in millions of U.S. dollars)

	Number of Approvals	Value
Sharmen (Xiamen city in Fujian Province)	14	13.5
Kwangchow (Guangzhou city in Guangdong Province)	19	10.3
Kwangtung (Guangdong Province)	17	6.9
Fukien (Fujian Province)	6	4.2
Shanghai	7	3.8
Fuchow (Fuzhou, in Fujian Province)	11	3.0
Peking (Beijing)	4	2.6
Special District (Shenzhen SEZ, Guangdong Province)	24	26.3
All other areas	48	40.1
Total	150	110.6

Source: Investment Commission, Ministry of Economic Affairs, Republic of China, December 1992.

Table 2.17 Taiwan's Approved Indirect Investments in Mainland China, January-August, 1992, by Industry (in millions of U.S. dollars)

	Number of Approvals	Value
Plastic and Rubber Products	24	25.5
Food and Beverage Processing	13	15.5
Electronic and Electric Appliances	16	14.4
Basic Metals and Metal Products	22	13.2
Garments and Footwear	13	6.7
Lumber and Bamboo Products	9	5.7
Chemicals	7	5.3
Non-metallic Minerals	8	3.6
Textiles	6	3.5
Leather and Fur Products	7	1.9
Other	17	13.9
Total	150	110.6

Source: Investment Commission, Ministry of Economic Affairs, Republic of China, December 1992.

fifth lower than in Taiwan, many Taiwanese will continue to invest in Southeast Asia because it is more stable and the risks are much lower than in China. Even now, Taiwan is Thailand's second largest foreign investor, after Japan. Currently attractive regional sectors include petrochemicals, textiles, pulp and paper, and electronics. In any event Taiwan almost certainly will continue to seek and play a leading role in reintegrating Vietnam into East Asian economic life.

Emerging Changes

The foregoing sections have already indicated a number of respects in which changes already underway or in the offing are likely to modify or redirect some aspects of Taiwan's economic role in East Asia. Some other notable developments pending include the following.

Resolution of Taiwan's Entry into GATT Membership. While Taiwan's accession to GATT is far from a done deal, the outline of an arrangement for Taiwan to become a member is said to be in place. (See also discussion of this subject in chapters by Samuel Kim and Ralph Clough.) If Taiwan is finally accepted, the pressures to accelerate liberalization of its economy would quickly take effect, and would probably force it to reduce restrictions directly aimed at Japanese competitors. The flip side is that Taiwan would then also enjoy the ability to appeal to the GATT regarding its trade complaints with Japan. Either way, GATT membership is likely to enhance Taiwan's relative importance in East Asian trade.

Changing Trade Relations with Japan and the United States. Taiwan's trade deficit with Japan grew 33 percent in 1992 to US$12.9 billion, and could go to US$15 billion in 1993. Its dependence on high tech machinery, construction technology, and sophisticated electronic component imports from Japan grows in step as it expands infrastructure and shifts production into more sophisticated products such as notebook computers in which it has won 20 percent of the world market.

> From computers to consumer electronics, automobiles to paper manufacturing, the foundation of Taiwan's economic development is Japanese technology and components. It is a dependence that can become only more intimate as Taiwan competes on export markets by offering more sophisticated products and caters to a domestic market that demands the same.[38]

Taiwan has long restricted imports of a wide range of Japanese products. Because of Taiwan's interest in GATT, "the government says reducing barriers—and allowing in more Japanese imports—is inevitable in order to obtain full membership."[39] But it may also get some help from GATT in improving its access to Japanese markets.

Taiwan remains under pressure to reduce its persistent trade surplus with the United States. Accession to GATT membership would require Taiwan to liberalize trade with the United States, probably reducing its large trade surplus with the United States. Most observers doubt that Taiwan can expand its exports to Japan enough to offset its growing dependence on Japanese technology products. The potential for expanding its surplus with China, however, could provide some offset.

Economic Prospects. Taiwan's economy continues to be structured with an extraordinarily high rate of national savings and a surprising low ratio of domestic capital requirements. The resulting capital surplus gives Taiwan the important economic leverage that has created its disproportionately large economic influence in East Asia over the past decade.

Current forces working to reduce Taiwan's merchandise trade surplus may well render it difficult to sustain the high domestic savings rate and capital accumulation rates of the past. Its global 1992 trade surplus fell nearly a third—to US$9.5 billion from 1991's US$13.4 billion surplus. However, Taiwan is undergoing a marked economic restructuring from industry and into services. The latter accounted for 55 percent of GDP in 1992, up from 47 percent in 1987. Industrial output fell to 41 percent, down from 48 percent in 1986. At least 10 percent, a steadily increasing fraction of Taiwan's production, now takes place elsewhere in Asia where investors expect it to earn higher profits than at home. The income from these investments may prove to be at least a partial offset to any drag in the domestic economy. How far increased earnings from foreign investments and other service exports will go to offset lower trade balances is key to whether Taiwan is able to sustain its high net savings.

Some observers see other reasons that harder times are on the way, noting as one of these that Taiwan may be second only to Russia in damaging its environment in ways that could require many tens or hundreds of billions of dollars to remedy. Moreover, implementation of its US$300 billion infrastructure plans, which includes some funding for environmental repair, is expected to require increased taxes and government borrowing, and to reduce national savings.[40] It is not clear that the magnitude of these changes will do more than reduce in absolute terms Taiwan's large margin of advantage in economic leverage, leaving its relative strength little changed as other economies in the region face similar or even greater difficulties. As if in confirmation of such dimmed prospects, there have been recent reports that Taiwan decided to delay implementation of a number of such infrastructure projects.

Conclusion

The key qualities that emerge from this overview of Taiwan's regional economic role are its high net national savings, but particularly its entrepreneurial agility and the closely related flexibility of its economic and industrial structure. Taiwan has proven itself adept and swift in evolving from an economically and politically isolated agricultural economy through two stages of industrialization. Having first become successful as a highly competitive producer of labor-intensive products, it avoided stalling in that stage and made an equally successful transition to a niche producer of advanced technology products. In the process it achieved sustained trade surpluses and capital accumulations, which moved it into the front ranks of capital exporters in the region. In this arena it has particularly demonstrated its agility. Comprised primarily of medium and small product-oriented businesses, in contrast to the much more diversified conglomerates that constitute its main competition, Taiwanese enterprise has depended for survival and growth on its agility in spotting and pursuing product, market, and cost-advantage opportunities rather than on building and exploiting broad monopolistic market positions.

What is particularly arresting about Taiwan's outward foreign investment pattern is less its stability than its agility. Its pattern suggests the kind of sensitivity to changing cost, product, and market conditions that epitomize the role of capital in equalizing market returns. In the case of Taiwan, it is increasingly playing this role on a region-wide basis.

Given the incredible economic dynamism of East Asia today, it is difficult to foresee whether Taiwan's trade and investment will link it more closely during the 1990s with China, Japan, or Southeast Asia. Certainly if China's economic reform and political cohesion and moderation continue, a Taiwan-Hong Kong-China vector—the Greater China outcome—would seem to be the runaway favorite. One can be much more comfortable predicting, however, that Taiwanese entrepreneurs will be among the first and foremost to identify and capitalize on shifts in comparative opportunities, whether favoring China, Vietnam, ASEAN countries, India, or someplace else. The pattern of Taiwan's foreign direct investment flows in fact is certainly one of the best lead indicators available for tracking the main future directions of the East Asian economy.

Two other high probability forecasts are:

- that Taiwan's economy will continue to reduce its dependence on the United States market and move toward greater dependence on its East Asian import, export, and investment relationships, based on its highly advantageous and vast network of established economic relationships throughout the region, and
- that it will continue to play a much more active and important role in the economic evolution of the region than would be expected from its economic size.

Commentary

James Riedel

I offer here an alternative interpretation to that of Erland Heginbotham, one that differs more in emphasis than in overall direction.

Taiwan's role in East Asian development, as I see it, has three dimensions: (1) as a model for, (2) as a trade partner with, and (3) as an investor in the other countries of the region. Taiwan may assume other roles in the future, such as those of an international financial center or an exporter of higher education, as Hong Kong is doing. These comments, however, focus on the main economic roles Taiwan has played in the past.

Taiwan as a Model for Economic Development

The importance of Taiwan as a model for other developing countries, not just for those in East Asia, cannot be overstated. The export-oriented industrialization strategy in now orthodoxy, but when Taiwan pioneered this approach in the late 1950s and early 1960s it was anything but orthodoxy. The leading authorities on development economics at that time favored the inward-oriented, import-substitution strategy and accordingly predicted that the large South Asian countries would be better than the smaller East Asian countries because there was more scope for realizing scale economies in larger countries.[41] They dismissed export-oriented industrialization as a strategy for development on grounds that the demand for developing countries' exports, manufactures, as well as primary products was too inelastic. Any attempt by developing countries to expand exports rapidly, they argued, would lead to falling terms of trade.

Taiwan and the other East Asian newly industrializing countries (NICs) demonstrated—with export volume growth rates averaging around 15 percent per annum over the past three decades—that the old orthodoxy was wrong, and in the process they forged a new orthodoxy. Since then, many developing countries in East Asia and elsewhere, emboldened by Taiwan's success, have reoriented their industrialization strategies from inward- to outward-looking, and with much the same success that Taiwan experienced. If the Nobel prize in economies were given to countries instead of to individuals, Taiwan would have to be at the top of the list for its contribution as a model for developing countries around the world.

It is worth noting, however, that there is considerable debate about what the "Taiwan model" is. To some it is a validation of neo-classical economics, demonstrating the importance of "getting prices right" by pursuing liberal trade and industrial policies. Others attribute Taiwan's success more to the visible hand of government than to the invisible hand of the market. To my mind, proponents on both sides of this debate have misinterpreted the Taiwan experience and as a result have been pointlessly talking past each other.

The Taiwan experience demonstrates the crucial importance both of getting prices right and of government doing the job that only it can do. The essential duties of government, in a nutshell, are keeping the peace, establishing a system of justice, supplying public goods (social and economic infrastructure), and maintaining macroeconomic stability. Government has performed those duties better in Taiwan than in most other places, and consequently Taiwan's government deserves to be given a great deal of credit for the country's economic success, even by those who believe that market capitalism is the source of Taiwan's dynamism. The debate, however, is not about how well the Taiwan government performed its basic duties, which are routinely overlooked, but instead about how well it intervened in the market to promote industry.

The two main facts about Taiwan's industrial and trade policy are: (1) that around the 1960s Taiwan adopted a major liberalization program, which involved unifying and devaluing the exchange rate, eliminating many quantitative import restrictions, and giving exporters a system of incentives that was more or less equivalent to what would have obtained under a free-trade policy, and (2) that in spite of these measures, which collectively became the blueprint of the "export-promotion strategy," some important industrial sectors in Taiwan continued to receive generous subsidies and high levels of protection. Thus there has arisen a debate about whether the protectionism cup in Taiwan was half full or half empty, and whether Taiwan's success belongs to those who advocate liberalization or those who advocate government intervention.

I do not pretend to be a neutral party in this debate, but instead associate myself with those who see Taiwan's success stemming from liberalization rather than intervention, although I give great credit to the Taiwan government for creating an environment conducive to private sector growth by providing an adequate supply of public goods and maintaining economic stability. Beyond that, in the realm of industrial policy, it appears that Taiwan was able to have it both ways—it maintained a relatively inefficient, heavily subsidized, highly protected, capital-intensive industrial sector *side-by-side and independent of* a dynamic, labor-intensive manufacturing sector that was able to compete successfully in world markets once the obstacles to exporting inherent in the previous import-substitution regime were removed. China, since its "open door" policy, has done essentially the same thing—that is, continue to subsidize and protect a large inefficient industrial base, and at the same time promote an efficient export-oriented industrial sector.

How could they have it both ways? Two aspects of export-oriented industrialization in East Asia made it possible. The first is that the dynamic export sector is highly *footloose*; the second is that all of these countries had large reservoirs of *underutilized labor in the rural sector*, ready and willing to go to work in manufacturing at relatively low wages. The footloose nature of export-oriented manufacturing is important because it allowed this sector to avoid being saddled with the inefficiencies of the import-substituting industrial sectors, which were built up during the previous autarkic development phase. The availability of a large reservoir of low-wage labor in the rural sector was important because it allowed the export-oriented industries to expand without requiring the protected capital-intensive sectors to release labor and to contract. As long as the know-how and the material inputs for export-oriented industrialization could be obtained from abroad, and the workers (disproportionately women) could be recruited in the rural sector, Taiwan and the other successful East Asian countries could have it both ways. Of course, now that Taiwan no longer has a "surplus" of low-wage labor, it can no longer have it both ways. Accordingly, Taiwan has over the last decade undertaken fundamental reforms, which have broadened the scope of trade liberalization and begun to diminish industrial dualism. But for other countries in the region, such as China and Vietnam, which still do have a large low-wage rural work force, the original Taiwan "model" of export-oriented industrialization is highly relevant.[42]

Taiwan as a Trader in East Asia

More significance is often attached to bilateral trade flows than is generally warranted. For the most part, the geographic pattern is much less important than the level and commodity composition of trade. In Taiwan's case, the geographic pattern, dominated by imports from Japan and exports to the United States, has been important because major realignments of the *real* dollar/yen exchange rate have had a significant impact on Taiwan's terms of trade. Aside from this issue, the geographic pattern of Taiwan's trade, in particular the role of intra-Asian trade, does not appear to be a matter of much importance. True, Taiwan's trade with other East Asian countries has grown relatively rapidly in recent years, but that seems to be mainly the consequence, not a cause, of the relatively rapid growth of the economies of Taiwan and neighboring East Asian countries. When one normalizes for the relative purchasing power of different regions in world trade, there does not appear to be any bias in favor of, or against, intra-Asian trade.[43]

Taiwan as an Investor in East Asia

In developing countries pursuing the import-substitution strategy, direct foreign investment (DFI) often served as a substitution for trade, with generally negative consequences. In Taiwan, under the export-promotion strategy, direct investment has generally been a complement to trade, as foreign firms, motivated by low wages and free access to imported inputs, undertook manufacturing of labor-intensive consumer goods for export. Export-oriented DFI in Taiwan made significant positive contributions to output, employment, and export growth, but perhaps most important was its strong demonstration effect on indigenous entrepreneurs in Taiwan who followed the example of foreign firms and propelled Taiwan to unprecedented growth rates.[44]

Since the late 1970s, the relative contribution of DFI in Taiwan has been declining, no doubt because of the rapid growth in real wages. Nevertheless, it continues to play an important role and serve as a model for indigenous firms, even in the higher technology industries in which Taiwan has recently gained a comparative advantage. At the bottom end of the technology spectrum, where Taiwan is losing comparative advantage, DFI is also important, but in the opposite direction. Rising real wages have induced both foreign and domestic firms to begin relocating their more labor-intensive manufacturing activities in lower wage countries, China and the ASEAN countries being the main recipients of this investment.

These investment flows benefit Taiwan because they promote structural adjustment to changing comparative advantage at home and allow Taiwanese firms to continue to profit from the know-how they acquired over the years in manufacturing and exporting labor-intensive consumer goods. These flows are also beneficial to the host countries because Taiwan's know-how is a valuable asset that they need to successfully emulate the Taiwan model. Taiwan's firms now account for a sizable share of the dynamic export-oriented manufacturing sectors in China, Thailand, and other parts of Southeast Asia. However, perhaps more important than its direct contribution is the demonstration effect of Taiwanese DFI on indigenous, would-be entrepreneurs in East Asia.

Conclusion

Taiwan's main contribution to East Asian development was to find a strategy that works, yielding unprecedented growth rates not only in Taiwan but also in other countries in the region that adopted it. In recent years Taiwan has contributed further to regional development by helping to implement the export-oriented industrialization strategy in China and the ASEAN countries. International economic relations are often portrayed as a zero-sum game, in which one country's gain in another's loss. The fallacy of that way of thinking is evident nowhere more than in East Asia.

Notes

1. Robert Wade, *Governing the Market: Economic Theory and the Role of Government in East Asian Industrialization*, (Princeton, NJ: Princeton University Press, 1990), p. 82.

2. See James Riedel, "International Trade in Taiwan's Transition from Developing to Mature Economy," in Gustav Ranis, ed., *Taiwan, from Developing to Mature Economy*, (Boulder, CO: Westview Press, 1992), pp. 295-296.

3. Julian Baum and Louise do Rosario, "The Sumo Neighbour," in Nigel Holloway, ed., *Japan in Asia*, (Hong Kong: Review Publishing Co., Ltd., 1992), p. 57.

4. Wade, pp. 52-53.

5. Riedel, p. 270. This article illustrates that Taiwan's early dominant manufactures (textiles, footwear) were slow to decline even as exports of more advanced manufactures were rising rapidly.

6. Wade, pp. 157-158.

7. *Taiwan Statistical Data Book, 1992*, (Taipei: Council for Economic Planning and Development, Republic of China, July 1992), pp. 201-203.

8. Riedel, p. 265.

9. See Jeffrey A. Frankel, *Is Japan Creating A Yen Bloc in East Asia and the Pacific?*, NBER Working Paper Series, no. 4050, (Cambridge, MA: National Bureau of Economic Research, 1992).

10. Far Eastern Economic Review, *ASIA 1993 YEARBOOK*, (Hong Kong: National Fair Ltd, 1993), p. 280.

11. An interesting dimension of Taiwan's foreign investment is that in 1992-1993 it supplanted Japan as the largest foreign investor in U.S. treasury securities, out of need to keep its US$80+ billion of foreign exchange reserves invested in secure assets.

12. Common to Korea, Japan, and Taiwan (in varying degrees and differing time periods) in accounting for high personal savings have been: absence of social security and other safety nets for health care and old age; absence or limited availability of mortgage financing and other consumer credit; limited funding for advanced education—all necessitate much higher rates of personal saving and involve sustained, long-term effort than have been typical in Western industrial economies. Among added factors that may explain Taiwan's first-place ranking as a super-saver, two seem most compelling: a) saving to establish or buy into small businesses—the preponderant mechanism of industrial growth and opportunity in Taiwan, as contrasted with the much larger conglomerate enterprises that dominate the Korean and Japanese economies; and b) climate: Taiwan is favored by a mild, subtropical climate that does not impose heavy expenditures for clothing, shelter, and health care compelled by Korea's extremely harsh or even Japan's milder winters, as well as the higher costs of food raised in short growing seasons and poor soil.

13. For these conclusions we rely on data from the host countries as collected and processed by the United Nations Transnational Center. Unfortunately investment data are very poor for a variety of reasons. Host country figures are often based on approvals rather than transfers, so may overstate actual investment

flows at the project level. However, they often exclude reinvestment by local subsidiaries of foreign firms. Taiwan's outflow data based on balance of payments accounting are several times greater than amounts recorded in the totals and country detail for approved investments. For example Taiwan claims total direct investments in Thailand from 1959-1988 of $33 million, while Thailand reports inflows of $2,016 million from 1984 through the first three quarters of 1989.

14. We exclude Hong Kong and Singapore as special cases since their economies are very small and depend heavily on transit trade; a proper comparison would exclude transshipments.

15. Fortunately a thorough and well-documented study of this role is now available in Robert Wade's *Governing The Market: Economic Theory and the Role of Government in East Asian Industrialization*, (Princeton, NJ: Princeton University Press, 1990.)

16. Wade, op. cit. p. 76. I am indebted for this analysis to Mr. Mark Platt, a former U.S. State Department official and former U.S. Consul in China.

17. Wade, op. cit. p. 117.

18. Wade, op. cit. p. 110.

19. The Kuomintang party also controls one of the nation's largest conglomerates.

20. Data compiled from "*World Investment Directory 1992*," Volume 1: Asia and the Pacific, United Nations Center on Transnational Corporations.

21. Linda Lim, "Commentary: Explaining the Decline of U.S. Investment in Southeast Asia," *Journal of Southeast Asia Business*, vol. VII, no. 2, 1991, p. 91.

22. Julian Baum, "The Unstoppable Tide: Rapid rise in Taiwan-China trade pressures Taipei," *Far Eastern Economic Review*, May 20, 1993, p. 66.

23. "Taiwan-China trade via Hong Kong surges 28% to record US$7.4 billion," *Straits Times* (Singapore), February 23, 1993.

24. Conversely, however, Taiwan has also been unable to enlist IMF and GATT in efforts to rectify its trade complaints against Japan.

25. Telephone conversation with Dick Nanto, February 5, 1993. See also Nanto's earlier study, *Japan-Taiwan Economic Relations: Implications for the United States*, CRS Report for Congress, no. 92-583E, July 20, 1992.

26. "Japan's Economic Relations with Taiwan," *Japan Economic Institute Report*, no. 27A, July 19, 1991, p. 8. See also: Dick K. Nanto, "Japan-Taiwan Economic Relations: Implications for the United States", *CRS Report 92-583 E*, (Washington, DC: July 20, 1992).

27. *Japan Economic Institute*, op. cit., page 8.

28. Ibid, p. 10.

29. Ibid, p. 11.

30. The author is indebted on this point to Dick Nanto of the Congressional Research Service.

31. The motherboard incorporates and interconnects microprocessors, memory, controller and other computer semiconductor devices on a single board which forms the "intelligence center" of personal computers.

32. Mark Clifford, "Taiwan's Chip Blitz," *Far Eastern Economic Review*, March 25, 1993, pp. 52-53.

33. "Asia's High-Tech Quest: Can the Tigers Compete Worldwide?", *Business Week*, December 7, 1992, pp. 126-135. A much more detailed, but somewhat dated presentation is available in Wade, op. cit.

34. "Mainland picked as favored site, poll shows," *The China Post*, March 9, 1993.

35. This view is held by Professor James Riedel, of Johns Hopkins University, School for Advanced International Studies, who has written extensively on Taiwan's economy.

36. Julian Baum, "Taipei's Offshore Empire", *Far Eastern Economic Review*, March 18, 1993, p. 44.

37. Ibid, p. 27.

38. Jeremy Mark, "Trading With Japan: Deficit with Japan Gnaws at Taiwan's Trade Success," *Asian Wall Street Journal*, March 12-13, 1993, p. 1.

39. Ibid.

40. Taiwan's six-year infrastructure plans program some US$16 billion of government funds, to be matched by US$25 billion of private sector funds, for repair and prevention of environmental damage.

41. See P. Rosenstein-Rodan, "International Aid for Underdeveloped Countries," *Review of Economics and Statistics*, vol. 43, 1961, pp. 107-38.

42. This is the thrust of the argument in my paper "Viet Nam: On the Trail of the Tigers" (December 1992).

43. See James Riedel, "Intra-Asian Trade and Direct Investment," *Asian Development Review*, vol. 9, no. 1, (1991), pp. 111-46 and Jeffrey Frankel, "Is Japan Creating a Yen Bloc in East Asia and the Pacific?" Federal Reserve Bank of San Francisco, Working Paper PB92-09, 1992.

44. See James Riedel, "Factor Proportions, Linkages and the Open Developing Economy," *Review of Economics and Statistics*, vol. 57, (1975), pp. 487-94.

3

Taiwan in the International Arms Market

Harlan W. Jencks

Introduction

Until December 1979, the defense of the Republic of China on Taiwan (ROC) was based upon its Mutual Defense Treaty with the United States.[1] ROC armed forces needed to defend Taiwan against invasion by the People's Republic of China (PRC) from the mainland long enough for U.S. forces to arrive and decisively repel the invading force. Accordingly, the United States provided virtually all of the ROC's weapons and equipment under various military aid and sales programs. The significant exception was the quiet ROC relationship with Israel. Taipei copied and modified the Israeli *Gabriel* anti-shipping missile and several classes of small patrol boats in the 1970s.

In 1979, the United States shifted diplomatic recognition from the ROC to the PRC. In April 1979, the U.S. Congress passed the Taiwan Relations Act (TRA), providing that "It is the policy of the United States...to provide Taiwan with arms of a defensive character."[2] Nevertheless, ROC authorities recognized that they could no longer safely depend upon U.S. weapons supplies, so they began diversifying their overseas sources, and striving to import military technology to increase military-industrial self-sufficiency.

Initially, Taipei's emphasis in the international arms market was to replace the lost American military deterrent.[3] The ROC needed credible military forces to deter and, if necessary, resist air attack, naval blockade, or invasion. Increasingly, however, Taiwan was also adding an "outer layer" of political-economic deterrence. In 1986, the ROC government began spectacular domestic political reforms, paralleled by "flexible diplomacy." The latter refers in particular to Taipei taking advantage of Taiwan's large reserves of foreign exchange to gain recognition in various international fora.[4] The ROC has been able, in effect, to "buy" diplomatic recognition from small non-Asian countries. While it probably cannot "buy" diplomatic recognition in the industrial West, its economic clout—including weapons purchases and negotiations—has become a formidable diplomatic tool. By the late 1980s, trade and investment had created a complex web of economic interdependency with the rest of the world—including mainland China itself.[5] This web of relationships and situations constitutes a "situational deterrent," which renders military attack increasingly unlikely. An assault on Taiwan would harm the PRC economically and damage Beijing's relationships with Taiwan's global network of political and economic partners.

Reflecting the increasing importance of Taiwan's "situational deterrent," the emphasis of Taipei's activities in the international arms market has shifted from military readiness to political-strategic deterrence and to the broader goals of diplomatic legitimacy. For brevity, I will refer to these political-strategic-diplomatic goals simply as "political."

The International Arms Market

The world market for weapons and related technologies expanded spectacularly in the 1980s for several interrelated reasons. The Soviet Union, which had been engaged in an arms buildup through the 1970s, redoubled its efforts until their abrupt end in 1988-1989. In response, beginning in 1980, there was a military buildup by the United States, NATO, Japan, and the Republic of Korea (ROK). A more important factor, however, was the Iran-Iraq War of 1981-1988. It was attrition warfare on a gigantic scale, consuming weapons, ammunition, equipment, and lives at a phenomenal rate. It provided the opportunity for many firms to go into arms manufacturing and trading, some of them in countries whose previous involvement in the arms industry had been marginal. As a direct result of the Middle East war, Brazil, Argentina, Spain, Singapore, North Korea, and the PRC emerged as important weapons exporters.

Then, in August 1988, the Iran-Iraq War abruptly ended. That precipitated a collapse in the arms market that struck particularly hard at the smaller and more recent market entrants. Within a year, for example, Avibras, the state-owned aircraft manufacturer, was in the Brazilian equivalent of Chapter 11 bankruptcy.

In the summer and fall of 1989, the arms market crisis deepened when the Warsaw Pact disintegrated, and many of the newly independent East European countries undertook precipitous disarmament. In November 1990, the NATO and former-Warsaw Pact powers signed the Conventional Forces in Europe (CFE) Treaty. Under its terms, signatory states had to dispose of massive numbers of tanks, aircraft, and other conventional weapons. Demilitarization or destruction costs money, so there was a strong economic incentive to sell instead.[6] Faced with spending about US$10,000 to demilitarize each T-72 main battle tank, Czechoslovakia—which earlier proclaimed it would cease selling weapons—has sold entire regiments of T-72s to Syria. The Soviet Union reportedly had 400 surplus MiG-29 fighters in September 1991.[7]

Further cuts in military spending in all the NATO countries, including the United States, followed the 1991 collapse of the Soviet Union. Many arms manufacturers and dealers have been driven to desperation. Some have gone broke, while others have been forced to contract and/or consolidate. While some governments are taking over failing ordnance enterprises, others are trying to privatize money-losing state-run industries. To cite only two of dozens of examples, FFV Ordnance and the venerable Bofors firm were forced to consolidate into Swedish Ordnance (which subsequently changed its name back to Bofors); Matra MS2i, a subsidiary of Matra Defense of France, is currently in the process of merging with CAP Sesa Defense. International projects have also been cut back. The European Fighter Aircraft (EFA) project, which originally included most of the European NATO governments, has lost all but three participants; the multinational NATO Replacement Frigate (NRF) project may collapse altogether.

The early 1990s are witnessing the most spectacular buyer's market in arms since 1945. There is a global glut of state-of-the-art weapons. Worldwide, sellers of military equipment are cutting prices and offering unprecedented bargains. Large percentages of sale prices are routinely covered by offsets and counter-trade; many deals include coproduction arrangements and transfers of sophisticated technology to buyer countries. The latter are spawning still more competition, as new armament industries emerge in India, Egypt, Iran, and Taiwan.

The situation has created unique opportunities for the states of East Asia, especially the PRC, the ROC, and the ASEAN states. These states deferred military equipment modernization during the 1980s because of other budgetary priorities. Beginning about 1989, however, they began to take advantage of the emerging buyer's market to modernize forces that had been allowed to deteriorate over the previous decade. Thus, it is misleading to say there is an "arms race" in Southeast Asia. Military buildups are taking place—not in response to each other, but in response to market opportunities.

The same is true of the widely noted foreign arms acquisitions of the PRC. Despite their distaste for the Beijing regime in the aftermath of the Tiananmen massacre, even the United States and the West European democracies have resumed squabbling over military technology sales to China.[8] Under market pressure the weapons embargo—the last vestige of the West's post-Tiananmen sanctions—is crumbling.

An interesting example of the state of the international arms market is being played out in 1993 in Malaysia, where the United States is energetically attempting to sell the F/A-18 fighter, and to dissuade Kuala Lumpur from buying Russian MiG-29s.[9] Still another illustration is the recent Indonesian acquisition of thirty-nine naval vessels (a sizable proportion of the former-East German Navy) for an estimated cost of US$120 million—less than the cost of *one* Western-built warship.[10]

Taiwan in the Arms Market

Taiwan is now a major defence market after establishing itself as a successful economy.

—Jane's Defence Weekly

Taiwan's activities in the international arms market have begun to appear in the popular press. A casual observer might think that this has happened suddenly—as a result of market forces, the ROC's military needs, and its abundance of foreign exchange. In fact, Taiwan's market entry has been fairly gradual, largely unrecorded outside of the specialized military-industrial press. That evolution has been shaped by the internal politics of Taiwan and the PRC, and by the economic and market pressures affecting all of the world's arms sellers.

A pressing military need for Taiwan in the early 1980s was for an improved fighter aircraft to replace its already aging fleet of F-104 and F-5E fighters. Two hundred and seventy-four F-5E/Fs were license-produced in Taiwan by the Taiwan Aero Industry Development Center (AIDC, at that time under the ROC Air Force) from 1974 to 1986. In order of preference, the ROCAF hoped to purchase the (then new) General Dynamics F-16, the McDonnell-Douglas F-4C, or the

Northrup F-5G.[11] The latter, a highly advanced version of the F-5E, was so advanced that after the Reagan administration decided not to sell it to Taiwan, it was redesignated F-20. The F-20 was intended primarily to be an export fighter. Because it was not purchased by any government, the F-20 program was dropped—a severe financial blow to Northrup.

In 1980, Taipei came to an initial agreement with Israel to buy *Kfir* fighter aircraft. However, Saudi Arabia, which provided virtually all of Taiwan's oil and was one of the few major countries still recognizing Taipei diplomatically, vetoed the sale. The Saudis had acquiesced to, perhaps not even noticed, the *Gabriel* and patrol boat deals. Here is a common phenomenon: Fighter aircraft generate far more press coverage and diplomatic activity than other weapons systems.

Stymied in its efforts to purchase foreign fighters, Taipei established the Chung Shan Institute of Science and Technology (CSIST)—the Defense Ministry's primary research and development organization in Kaohsiung. By 1992, CSIST claimed to employ 6,300 scientific and technical personnel and over 8,500 technicians.[12] In Washington, Taiwan's Coordination Council of North American Affairs (CCNAA) has a director for defense procurement, currently Lieutenant General K. C. Lin.

In September 1981, Taipei succeeded in exploiting the severe under-utilization of Dutch shipyards by ordering two modified-*Zwaardvis*-class diesel-electric submarines. Although construction was somewhat delayed by the financial difficulties of the builder, the two subs were launched in late 1986 and commissioned (as *Hai Lung* and *Hai Hu*) in the ROC Navy in 1988. Owing to pressure from Beijing, however, the Dutch government decided in 1984 not to sell Taiwan any more submarines.[13]

On August 17, 1982, President Reagan signed a joint communiqué with PRC Premier Zhao Ziyang stipulating that the United States would gradually reduce arms sales to Taipei, and not increase the technological level of weapons sold. Accordingly, after 1982 the monetary value of U.S. weapons sales, valued in constant dollars, declined each year. Despite PRC protests, however, the United States licensed increased exports of military technology, which the Reagan and Bush administrations interpreted as not being covered by the 1982 communiqué.

Through the 1980s, the Chung Shan Institute introduced a series of weapons systems embodying significant inputs of American military technology. These included the AT-3 *Tzu-chiang (Self-strengthening)* trainer/attack aircraft and the *Tien Kung-I (Sky Bow)* surface-to-air missile (SAM). The latter looks like the American *Hawk* SAM and employs a phased-array radar antenna, which appears to be closely patterned after that of the Raytheon *Patriot*. According to *Flight International*, 85 percent of the *Patriot* design was passed to CSIST through a technology transfer agreement as early as 1981.[14]

Taiwan also introduced the *Tien Chien I (Sky Sword I)* air-to-air missile (AAM), which looked remarkably similar to the advanced American AIM-9L *Sidewinder*. Possibly, AIM-9L technology came via Israel—another channel via which Taiwan and the United States could contravene the 1982 communiqué.

In 1988, AIDC (by then subordinated to CSIST) unveiled the prototype of its Indigenous Defense Fighter (IDF, later named the *Ching-kuo*). The IDF looks like a cross between the F/A-18 and F-16, and has a Garrett engine. Reportedly, the design was assisted by General Dynamics (airframe) and Stiegler (avionics).[15] Also in 1988, the ROC Navy concluded a deal with Bath Iron Works of Bath, Maine, transferring complete sets of plans for the American *Oliver Hazard Perry*-class (FFG-7) missile frigate. Modified copies would be built by China Shipbuilding in Kaohsiung (see below).

Aside from specialists, few observers of the Asian scene took much note of this flow of American military technology to Taiwan in the 1980s. Then came the collapse of the international arms market, paralleled by political reforms in Taiwan and the Tiananmen massacre and crackdown in the PRC. Arms manufacturers in the United States and Western Europe began to seriously pursue sales in Taiwan to earn foreign exchange and, above all, to save jobs. In the aftermath of Tiananmen, PRC protests carried less weight. Democratic governments now can more easily justify such sales to their people and their allies—economically and ideologically. Also, governments that recognize Beijing diplomatically can rationalize most of Taiwan's purchases because they are arguably "defensive." Press and public opinion in the democratic West generally favor the sales.

Recent ROC arms purchases have been more important "politically" (e.g., improving Taiwan's international contacts and influence) than militarily. That helps explain why Taiwan is simultaneously negotiating for fighter planes from the United States, France, and Israel; frigates from the United States, France, and Germany; and submarines from Germany and Holland. In purely military terms, the training and logistical complications of military equipment from so many different countries cause inefficiency. It is strategically advantageous, however, to be purchasing state-of-the-art equipment in as many different countries as possible.

Recent Transactions

Aircraft

The PRC recognizes that the United States has a special relationship with Taiwan "left over from history," and therefore has been somewhat less outraged at American military technology transfers to Taiwan than at anyone else's.[16] It was therefore something of a milestone in Taiwan's diplomatic fortunes when, in December 1990, Italy's Aeritalia became the first European aircraft manufacturer to demonstrate a military plane in Taiwan, showing its AMX trainer/attack aircraft.[17]

For Taiwan, 1992 was the "year of the fighter." Taipei stepped up its public relations campaign in the West, pressing its need for a modern fighter to meet the threat posed by the PRC acquisition of twenty-four Russian Su-27s. In March, the Bush administration quietly gave permission to Israel to sell twenty *Kfir* fighters to Taiwan (permission was necessary because of the *Kfir*'s General Electric J-79 engine). Israeli officials claimed they had "obtained China's tacit approval for the sale. China reportedly does not regard the *Kfir*, which the Israeli Air Force is retiring, as a threat and it is said to want to avoid offending Israel, on which it depends for military technology."[18]

The *Kfir* was originally based on the French *Mirage-5*. Its initial operational capability (IOC) in the Israeli Air Force was about 1975. The current version is the *Kfir-C7*, whose IOC was 1983.[19] Even refurbished *Kfir-C7s* probably would be no match for Su-27s. Taiwan sources say they really prefer the American F-16 or the French *Mirage 2000*. Nevertheless, talks have continued between Israeli Aircraft Industries (IAI) and Taipei. IAI reportedly was in contact with Taiwan as early as 1989, and by August 1992 Israeli sources claimed they were discussing a deal worth US$400 million for forty *Kfir-Cs*. While Israel's Defense Ministry reportedly supported the sale, the Foreign Ministry opposed it, maintaining that a trade freeze by the PRC "would cost Israel billions of dollars of business."[20] The *Kfir* is a fairly old aircraft, which would cause logistical complications in Taiwan, so it is uncertain whether Taiwan will buy it. Nevertheless, a deal might be signed just for political reasons.

Negotiations to sell the French *Mirage* to Taiwan were first publicized in late March 1992 when PRC Foreign Minister Qian Qichen declared that the PRC would "react most energetically" if any such sale took place.[21] In May, Defense Minister Pierre Joxe publicly called for the sale of the new *Mirage 2000-5* to Taiwan. There were rumors in Paris that a deal for sixty *Mirages* was under discussion for a possible price of up to FFr30 billion (US$5.45 billion), plus an option for sixty additional aircraft later on.[22] The debate took on added urgency in July when Dassault Aviation announced that it would halt development of the *Mirage 2000-5* at the end of 1992 unless it got an export order. The French armed forces and Defense Ministry by this time openly advocated the sale, which the Foreign Ministry continued to resist due to concerns about relations with the PRC.[23] Beijing repeatedly stated that it was "firmly opposed to the selling of weapons to Taiwan by any country and by any means," and would "react strongly" to any such deal.[24]

On September 10, a French radio report said that "the Army staff headquarters" in Taipei had announced it was putting off the final decision to buy *Mirages* under pressure from the United States. Washington reportedly had "given the impression that it would not take a very favorable view of a contract concluded with France," at least until negotiations were concluded on the F-16 sale, which President Bush had announced eight days earlier (see below).[25]

Talks continued, focused by mid-September on the cost of the *Mirages* plus their associated air-to-air weapons. The latter were said to include the Matra *Magic II* and *Mica* AAMs. Taiwan reportedly wanted a 20 percent reduction on the *Mirage*'s $77 million-per-unit price. In early November, *Far Eastern Economic Review* (FEER) reported that Paris was "ready to sell" 120 *Mirages* rather than the sixty aircraft previously reported. The deal was also said to include FFr1.1 billion (US$211 million) worth of heavy transport helicopters and various other weapons. According to *FEER*, the announcement was being delayed until after the U.S. presidential election "at Washington's request."[26]

It appears that a deal for sixty *Mirages* for US$3.6 billion was signed in mid-November. Firms involved are Dassault, SNECMA (engines), Thomson-CSF (avionics), and Matra (missiles). Probably owing to French concern about Beijing's sensitivities, the deal was not announced until January 1993.[27] A clear indication that the deal had been signed was a November 1992 announcement by the French Air Force that it would expend FFr4.6 billion (US$830 million) to upgrade its current fleet of *Mirages* to the same standard as the 2000-5 version, a step it could not have afforded had not a substantial foreign sale brought down the unit price.[28]

Because the *Mirage* sale was not officially announced until months after it became known, Beijing was unable to orchestrate the storm of wounded outrage that met the F-16 announcement. *Xinhua* carried an interview on January 11, 1993, with Deville Le Pen, chairman of the France-China Committee, who expressed his regret over the French government's approval of the sale. Supposedly, many member enterprises of the France-China Committee had made "strong efforts to prevent this military sale. Despite strong opposition from the Chinese government, the French government perfidiously went ahead with approving this arms transaction."[29] Subsequently, Beijing ordered the closure of the French Consulate in Guangzhou and took steps to limit French commercial sales in South China (see below).

For Dassault, the only remaining high-performance aircraft manufacturer in France to be largely privately owned, the Taiwan order was literally a lifesaver. The company had not made an export fighter sale in six years, had already laid off a number of employees, and was in danger of going out of business.[30]

French domestic pressure for the *Mirage* sale was almost entirely economic. By contrast, economic pressure for the F-16 sale was reinforced by stridently anti-PRC rhetoric from both the left and right of the American political spectrum. In June 1992, the Bush administration rejected Taipei's request for the F-16, in keeping with the policy that had been in place since 1981. However, as the president's reelection campaign began to unravel, General Dynamics, maker of the F-16, announced on July 29 that it would have to lay off 5,800 workers by 1994.[31] In a radio interview the following day President Bush said he was taking "a new look" at the possibility of selling F-16s. He ordered a "complete reevaluation" of Taiwan's security situation by the U.S. military and intelligence communities.

Texas Governor Ann Richards declared, "I don't know what deals have been made between George Bush and Communist China. But when it means the loss of 5,800 workers, it is time to wake up and smell the coffee." According to Texas' influential Senator Lloyd Bentsen, it "doesn't make sense to turn a deaf ear when the cash-rich government of Taiwan expresses an interest in buying up to 150 F-16s off the shelf." The Bush administration, he continued, was "willing to stand by and allow 3,000...Texas jobs to be exported to France."[32]

On August 5, some 200 U.S. congressmen signed a petition urging President Bush to approve F-16 sales to Taiwan to save American jobs.[33] On August 13, T. Y. Wang, an assistant professor at Illinois State University, editorialized in the *Christian Science Monitor* that "it is difficult to understand why the U.S. president is willing to appease

Beijing's leaders at the expense of 6,000 American jobs when the French government is doing just the opposite." He added that "it is simply no longer in the interest of the U.S. to protect the last major communist state. It makes better sense to search out ways to restrain China's influence."[34] Taipei's *Free China Journal* reprinted Wang's editorial on August 28, but tellingly changed the headline to "Taipei Could Save 6,000 US Jobs."

On August 11, General Lin Wen-li, commander of the ROCAF, told an interviewer that he needed modern fighter planes but would insist on a fair price and a reliable logistics package. "Buying airplanes is buying weapons systems that must have a guarantee of support for the next 10 or 20 years," he said.[35] Indeed, when Taiwan buys a complex system like a fighter plane, it is also buying political and economic ties for a prolonged period. In all of its negotiations, the ROC has insisted on full logistics packages. It is instructive to recall the licensed-production deal for the F-5E, in the 1970s. If those aircraft had been produced at a normal rate, the production line would have closed down by 1980 or 1981. Instead, production was slowed to a crawl in order to keep the line open—prolonging the life of the contract and its political symbolism—until 1986.[36]

On August 24, the *Asian Wall Street Journal* editorialized that "the world's leading democracies would be wise to step in as a friend and escort" to Taiwan. The paper suggested that both the F-16 and the *Mirage* should be sold to Taiwan, and that France and the United States should sponsor Taiwan's membership in the General Agreement on Tariffs and Trade (GATT).[37]

On September 2, facing the prospect of losing Texas' thirty-five electoral votes, President Bush announced approval of the sale of 150 F-16A and F-16B aircraft to Taiwan. His military justification, according to a Pentagon spokesman, was that "a discrepancy is building" because of recent PRC acquisition of Russian weapons systems, including Su-27s. Since Beijing was bound to invoke the August 1982 joint communiqué, the Bush administration announced that, in its view, the sale did not violate any of the existing bilateral agreements with Beijing because the United States could no longer provide the logistical support necessary to keep Taiwan's F-5E and F-104 inventory flying. It was therefore necessary to supply a somewhat newer fighter or provide none at all. The Pentagon claimed that the F-16A/B variants powered by the Pratt & Whitney F-100-PW-220 engine "will meet the current diplomatic limitations."[38]

American officials who were involved have emphasized to me that the F-16 decision really was based largely on U.S. concern about Taiwan's deteriorating military situation vis-á-vis an increasingly well-armed PRC. Taipei's request for F-16s already was under consideration before Bush's reelection campaign got into trouble. Even had there been no election, the June decision not to sell might well have been reconsidered early in 1993. A large sale of *Mirage 2000-5s* would have rendered the F-16 sale *militarily* unnecessary, but the *Mirage* sale might not have happened without the American precedent. Moreover, Washington understands—as well as Beijing and Taipei do—that the sale sends an unmistakable political-strategic signal from the United States.

In statements directed toward Beijing, the Bush administration emphasized that the F-16A and the two-seat F-16B are relatively old, having been used by the U.S. Air Force for well over a decade. In Taiwan, on the other hand, they emphasized that the F-16A/Bs will be updated versions similar to those currently operated by many U.S. Air Force units. Immediately after the decision, General Lin stated that the ROCAF would be happier with more advanced F-16C/Ds, and would try to acquire them in future negotiations. Defense Minister Chen Lü-an went to the crux of the matter, however, when he called Bush's decision "a significant *political* breakthrough" in U.S.-ROC relations.[39]

Comment on the sale in Taipei was predictably upbeat. Premier Hau Pei-tsun said it was a "wise decision." The Foreign Ministry was happy to note the willingness and determination of the U.S. government to "faithfully implement the Taiwan Relations Act."[40] A Foreign Ministry spokesmen said the American decision was in keeping with "the international community's recognition of Taiwan's political and economic achievements [which] have paved the way for the latter's aquirement [sic] of the US fighters."[41]

Notwithstanding talk about international respectability and defense against the communist evil, the Taipei press did not hesitate to emphasize--even exaggerate--the economic importance of the order to the United States. An editorial in *Express News,* published by CNA in Taipei, claimed that Bush's decision could "save at least 3,000 jobs in Texas and 7,000 more elsewhere in the United States. The figures are especially significant at a time when the incumbemt [sic] president is facing an uphill struggle in the election because of the economic recession."[42]

On September 4, the ROC National Treasury announced that a "letter of intent" had been signed with the French to buy 60 *Mirage 2000-5s.*[43] The F-16 and *Mirage* deals together would cost an estimated US$9 billion and increase the defense budget by NT$40–50 billion each year over the coming five years, according to the announcement. The finance minister indicated that there was already debate within the government as to how the money should be raised.[44] That debate was nothing compared to the protests from Taiwan's political opposition over cost and terms. While all parties in Taiwan welcomed the sale, the opposition Democratic Progressive Party (DPP) led the demand for the newer F-16C/D, and protested the deal's lack of technology transfers or offsets.

The response in Taiwan and elsewhere demonstrated that the F-16 deal was important far beyond the military value of 150 fighter planes. It represented a milestone in the relationship between the United States and Taiwan, and carried the promise of additional arms supplies in the future. *The Free China Journal* claimed that the decision "lifted for all practical purposes a decade-long U.S. ban on the sale of sophisticated arms to Taiwan." Despite the emphasis in Washington on the relative obsolescence of the F-16A/B, the perception in Taiwan—and in the American arms industry—was that from now on almost anything goes as far as selling weapons to Taiwan. Reportedly, McDonnell-Douglas immediately approached the Bush administration for permission to offer Taiwan the F/A-18 multi-mission fighter.[45] With considerable justification, Taipei hoped that the F-16 sale also would decrease the inhibitions of other Western governments.[46]

The same day President Bush announced the sale, Defense Minister Chen told an interviewer, "We would never purchase outdated models."[47] Testifying before the Legislative Yuan on October 28, he said the version Taiwan would receive is the F-16 MLU (Mid-Life Upgrade), an advanced model of the F-16A and B types. The F-16A/B MLUs are brand-new airplanes, which countries in Europe and Scandinavia were also expected to incorporate into their air forces in the next few years, Chen added. Moreover, since President Bush's announcement meant only approval for negotiations, Chen did not rule out the possibility of negotiating for a more advanced version of the F-16. In response to questions, he stated that *Mirage* negotiations with France also would continue, as would construction of the IDF, the first twenty of which were expected to enter service in 1994. Chen "cautioned that the ROC cannot rely solely on American F-16s. The Ministry's purchase of high-capacity fighter planes will not be from any one source, but from various sources."[48]

Despite emphasis in the ROC press on the state-of-the-art technology embodied in the aircraft, objections by the ROCAF and the DPP about not getting C and D models would not be stilled.

Reportedly, General Dynamics also weighed in, lobbying with the U.S. government for export of the F-16C/D.[49] However, a political milestone had been passed. The technological and financial arrangements of this deal were highly concessionary to the United States, but under the political circumstances were probably the best Taiwan could get. That will not be the case in the future, however (see below).

The actual "letter of offer and acceptance" (LOA) that constituted the F-16 sale contract was signed in Washington on November 12, 1992. Despite Minister Chen's hopes, it stipulated 150 Mid-Life Upgrade versions of the F-16A and B, at a price of US$6 billion. Delivery of the first aircraft in Taiwan is scheduled for 1996. On November 13, the U.S. government and CCNAA also signed an agreement for the F-16's Pratt & Whitney engines. The order is for about 180 engines plus spare parts and support equipment, and is estimated to be worth up to an additional US$1 billion. The engines are scheduled for delivery from the last quarter of 1996 until the end of the decade. A Pratt & Whitney spokesman said the F-100-PW-220 engine "embodies state-of-the-art technology derived from our newest generation of fighter power plants."[50]

Beijing's reaction to the F-16 sale was predictable. PRC Vice-Foreign Minister Liu Huaqui summoned Ambassador J. Stapleton Roy and lodged a strong protest, primarily citing the August 17, 1982, Sino-U.S. Communiqué. The PRC press ejaculated outrage for the next several weeks.[51] Commentary denounced the Bush administration's decision with terms like "short-sighted," "perfidious," "lying," and "treacherous;" and threatened a terrible setback and cooling in Sino-American relations. In contrast to American and unofficial Taiwanese sources, the PRC press characterized the F-16A/B as highly modern and effective aircraft in service with the U.S. and NATO air forces. Far from being a purely defensive weapon system, said Beijing, it poses a grave offensive threat.

In contrast to the avalanche of hostile words, actual PRC retaliation was minimal. The PRC briefly delayed several import deals—notably for commercial aircraft—from the United States, but that was about all. Partly, this was because U.S. congressional debate on China's Most-Favored Nation (MFN) status was underway. On September 28, President Bush vetoed a congressional bill that put conditions on the renewal of China's MFN status for 1993-1994. His action was warmly and officially welcomed in Beijing.[52] Significant PRC retaliation against American interests (e.g., down-grading diplomatic relations or excluding U.S. firms from the Canton subway bidding) would have discredited the Bush administration's China policy on the eve of the election—the last thing Beijing wanted to do: Despite the F-16 sale, George Bush was still the PRC's best friend in Washington.

Although the PRC Foreign Ministry no doubt understood that the Democratic Party controlled the Congress that passed MFN conditions, it still expressed the faint hope, in several commentaries following the November 3 election, that the incoming Clinton administration would reverse the F-16 decision. This was despite Senator Bentsen's appointment as Bill Clinton's Treasury Secretary.

Meanwhile, work proceeded on the IDF program, which was initiated in 1981 in the immediate aftermath of President Reagan's decision not to sell the F-4 or the F-5G/F-20. In 1983, the United States quietly approved a cooperative venture to build an engine for the IDF. This led to the creation of ITEC (International Turbine Engine Corporation), a joint venture set up by AIDC and the Phoenix-based Garrett Engine Division of Allied Signal Aerospace Company.

In 1989, after development work on both the aircraft and the engine, Garrett received a U.S. government license for coproduction in Taiwan of the TFE 1042-70 (F-125) engine, with a rated thrust of 9,500 pounds. Meanwhile, General Dynamics won approval in 1983 to assist the ROC in designing the IDF fighter itself.[53] The IDF began flight testing in 1989. By 1990, however, amid speculation about PRC purchases of advanced Soviet aircraft, the ROCAF decided the IDF would need a much bigger engine. General Electric came forward with a scaled-down version of its F-404 engine (the GE J-101/SF) rated at 12,900 pounds thrust, which would compete with an upgraded version of ITEC's F-125. A 1990 report also referred to a more advanced TFE-1088 engine.[54] Reportedly, the IDF engine competition has been put on hold as a result of the F-16 deal, and ITEC expects to continue production of the F-125. Full-scale production of the IDF has been delayed repeatedly; the date currently given for IOC is 1996.[55]

Contrary to some foreign speculation, CSIST is quite serious about the IDF program.[56] Only a diminishing number of even the world's established aviation industries (those in the United States, France, Sweden; possibly the UK, Japan, Italy, and Russia) remain capable of designing and manufacturing "domestic" state-of-the-art warplanes. Multinational projects like NFA, the Panavia *Tornado*, and the Japanese-American FSX are increasingly common. Though the IDF has certainly been less than successful so far, it is the closest any newly industrialized country has come to producing a domestic state-of-the-art combat aircraft since the jet age began. The Israeli *Lavi* and the Indian

LCA both failed badly in the 1980s; even Sweden's *Grippen* is having a very difficult gestation.

Partly because AIDC was taken away from the ROCAF and placed under CSIST, the air force has been unenthusiastic about the IDF from the beginning. Mostly, however, differences over the IDF flow from differing institutional agendas. CSIST wants to import technology and develop military-industrial self-sufficiency for the future. The air force wants to import foreign (preferably American) fighters to provide *operational capability* to defend Taiwan *now*. For forty years or more, on the other side of the Taiwan Strait, the PLA Air Force and the PRC's research, development, and industrial organs have had the same disagreements for the same reasons.[57]

Garrett's F-124, an earlier version of the TFE 1042 with only 6,425 pounds thrust, is in the bidding to be the power plant for the U.S. Navy's new T-45 *Goshawk* trainer. If that deal materializes, about 15 percent of the F-124 engines would be produced by ITEC—the first significant military export from Taiwan to the United States.[58]

The IDF program is perhaps the most bewildering part of what Paul Beaver of *Jane's Defence Weekly* characterizes as "Taiwan's bewildering series of combat aircraft developments and procurements." In a January 1993 debate on the F-16 and other program budgets, the Legislative Yuan approved a major fighter aircraft procurement program totaling NT$318.8 billion (US$12.75 billion) as a supplement to the 1993 budget. This covered the initial year's payment for the F-16 deal. It also probably included the first year's payments on the *Mirage* deal, which had not yet been formally announced.

The budget reportedly also included $10 billion for the IDF program, which will continue, but not as originally planned. Carl Baerst, president of ITEC, said, "There will always be a requirement for a number of IDFs, as Taiwan needs a multi-aircraft capability. The F-16 purchase could affect the need for an upgraded version of the IDF but it won't affect the actual programme." According to Baerst, the ROC Air Force plans to purchase 256 IDFs, including up to fifty two-seat advanced trainers.[59] However, on the day of President Bush's F-16 announcement, ROC Defense Minister Chen Lü-an told an interviewer that production of the IDF "will go on as planned. We have decided to produce 120 to 130 of these planes....We will stop improving the engine *for the time being* because if we start developing or improving the engine, the production of engines will not be able to meet the needs of the *first batch* of 130 planes."[60]

Still more "bewildering" is the plan to upgrade the ROCAF's fleet of

298 Northrup F-5E fighters, including new power plants and avionics. Ironically, the resulting aircraft (designated F-5E-SX) "will look essentially identical" to the F-20, which Taiwan was denied in 1981, and will contain more advanced features. The latter may include the General Electric AN/APG-67(V) radar, which "has some commonality with the F-16's Westinghouse AN/APG-66 system." A Taiwan-developed version of the AN/APG-67(V) with look-down, shoot-down capability, called *Golden Dragon 53*, has been selected for the IDF.[61]

If all the current upgrade, production, and foreign purchase plans are fulfilled, the ROCAF will be operating at least 130 IDFs, plus sixty *Mirages*, plus 150 F-16s, plus about 298 upgraded F-5E-SXs—totalling at least 650 really modern fighter aircraft—by the year 2000.[62]

Air Defense Missiles

Development of the *Tien Chien I* AAM has been noted. In addition, the *Mirage* deal includes over 1,500 Matra *Mica* AAMs. Moreover, Taipei currently is said to be negotiating with the U.S. government to buy the AMRAAM (Advanced Medium-Range Air-to-Air Missile) to be used by both the F-16 and the F-5E-SX. Additionally, a *Tien Chien II*--reportedly similar to the American AIM-7 *Sparrow* radar-guided medium-range AAM--is said to be under development. Although models of it have been seen, production has been delayed until at least 1994.[63]

In purely military terms, state-of-the-art SAMs are as important—arguably more important—than fighter aircraft. Transfers of SAMs and air defense technologies to Taiwan continued though the 1980s with relatively little fanfare, as noted above. Developments in 1991-1993 have been extremely important militarily and technically, but they continue to be overshadowed by the F-16 and *Mirage* deals. On August 5, 1992, amid the F-16 debate, the U.S. Defense Department announced approval of a US$126 million sale of 207 SM-1 *Standard* naval SAMs for the ROC Navy. The sale package included full logistic support, parts, components, and technical training.[64]

MILAVIA News reported that 20 percent (US$390 million) of the ROC's 1991 defense budget was slated for missile production, including "an undisclosed sum" that was earmarked for purchase of parts and technology for the *Tien Kung* SAM.[65] Taiwan received *Hawk* and *Chapparal* SAMs from the United States in the 1960s and 1970s, and CSIST has been developing the *Tien Kung* system for at least a decade.

There are at least two *Tien Kung* variants. The *Tien Kung-I* is a low- to medium-altitude SAM that probably completed its firing trials in 1985.

It was expected to begin production in 1990, though it is not clear whether that has happened. The *Tien Kung-II* reportedly completed its first flight test in late 1988 or early 1989. There have been subsequent reports of a *Tien Kung-III* under development.[66]

As noted above, Raytheon reportedly had sold 85 percent of the early-version *Patriot* to CSIST by 1981. According to a 1991 report, the ROC hoped to "complement" the *Tien Kung-I* by purchasing the *Patriot*.[67] In January 1992, the Bush administration issued a license to Raytheon to sell the advanced *Patriot* anti-missile guidance radar and command and control systems to Taiwan for incorporation into the *Tien Kung-II*.[68] Then, last June, Raytheon announced what was apparently an additional license to provide technical assistance and some equipment—reportedly seven complete *Patriot* firing units—also for incorporation into the *Tien Kung* system. CSIST's president, Admiral Liu Shu-hsi, citing the increased danger posed by the PRC's new M-9 and M-11 missiles, said he wanted to modify the "basic" *Tien Kung-II* to "perform like a *Patriot*."[69]

In September 1992, the State Department notified Congress of a full-blown coproduction deal that, in February 1993, was still under negotiation between Raytheon and (presumably) CSIST. The joint venture, called Modified Air Defense System (MADS) will reportedly cost Taiwan US$1.3 billion. Raytheon will provide ground support equipment, training, and technical support, and will manufacture the nose end of the missile. "Taiwan will produce the rear section of the missile, including propulsion and control sections, based on a Raytheon technical data package covered under a separate $120 million agreement." The deal "extends over a four-year period, with options for Patriot-type improvements to be incorporated at a later date."[70]

In May 1991, Beijing protested to Brussels over a report that a Belgian company would sell rocket motors to Taiwan.[71] There has been no subsequent information on this transaction, which at least illustrates Taipei's continuing efforts to expand the ranks of its military suppliers.

Helicopters

The world helicopter market has been severely depressed. In 1991, the world's nine major helicopter manufacturers had "the lowest level of orders since 1960."[72] Yet, in February 1992 *Jane's Defence Weekly* characterized the Taiwan helicopter market as "sizzling." In early 1992 the ROC Army announced the purchase of forty-two AH-1W *Super Cobra* and twenty-six OH-58D *Kiowa Warrior* helicopters from the U.S. Navy, plus twelve OH-58Ds from the U.S. Army.

According to *Jane's Defence Weekly,* "The most important newcomer" to the helicopter market is AIDC, which reportedly is "interested in obtaining contracts to upgrade the Bell UH-1s currently in Taiwanese service."[73] It also is said to be negotiating with Bell Helicopter Textron for licensed production of the OH-58D/406.[74]

In October 1992, the Bush administration notified Congress of its intent to license the sale to Taiwan of twelve Kaman SH-2F LAMPS-1 (Light Airborne Multi-Purpose System) anti-submarine warfare (ASW) helicopters and twelve spare engines for US$161 million.[75] These ASW helicopters will probably be deployed on the newly leased *Knox*-class frigates and the new *Cheng Kung*-class (PFG-2) frigates. Washington earlier denied Taipei's request for a newer model LAMPS, the SH-2G.[76]

Naval Systems

The ROC Navy is in the process of replacing all twenty-four of the 1940s-vintage American destroyers currently in service by a combination of leasing, purchase, and construction. In addition to the LAMPS-1, the Navy has upgraded its aviation forces with Grumman S-2 *Tracker* maritime patrol aircraft and Sikorsky S-70C *Seahawk* ASW helicopters.[77]

An earlier attempt to upgrade the destroyer force was a proposed joint development scheme with Taipei's long-time friends in Seoul. The ROC hoped to share technology and production of the *Ulsan*-class frigates, which were under development in the ROK. After extended negotiations, however, Taipei decided in 1989 not to proceed with the purchase of eight frigates. The Legislative Yuan criticized the deal as a "futile exercise in buying friendship" because Taiwan would not get a big enough share of either the technology or production.[78]

On July 19, 1992, President Bush approved the lease of three *Knox*-class frigates to Taiwan for five years. The ROC will pay US$14.5 million to lease the frigates, plus additional expenses for maintenance and crew training. The first two ships, the ex-*USS Brewton* and ex-*USS Peary*, sailed to Taiwan in midsummer. In August, Taiwan lodged a request with the United States for approximately US$212 million worth of naval weapons and ammunition, including forty-eight ASW rockets (ASROCs), and ammunition for five-inch guns and *Phalanx* close-in weapons systems (CIWSs).[79]

A far more important transaction almost completely escaped public notice in 1987, when the state-run China Shipbuilding Corporation and Bath Ironworks of the United States signed an agreement to build a modification of the American *Oliver Hazard Perry* (FFG-7) class frigate.

This US$1.6 billion deal will result in the production of eight frigates in Kaohsiung. The first of these Taiwan-made PFG-2 frigates, the *Cheng Kung*, was launched in January 1992; IOC is expected in May 1993. The *Cheng Ho*, second of the class, was launched on October 15, 1992; IOC is expected in April 1994. Two additional ships are currently under construction. The *Cheng Kung*-class displaces 4,300 metric tons. Its weapons systems will include the *Hsiung Feng II* anti-shipping missile, *Seahawk* ASW helicopter, and SM-1 SAM.[80] Other weapons will include ASW torpedoes and the *Phalanx* CIWS.[81]

Late in 1989, Taipei announced that it would purchase six frigates from France. Following protests by Beijing, however, the French cancelled the sale in January 1990. Then, in March 1992 the French government confirmed that it had decided, after all, to sell sixteen 3000-ton *Lafayette*-class missile frigates for an estimated FFr13 billion (US$2.5 billion).[82] The deal authorized the sale of "empty hulls," which the ROC Navy would have to fit out on its own. Then, in May 1992—as speculation intensified about a *Mirage* sale—*Jane's Defence Weekly* reported a FFr300 million (US$54 million) deal with the French firm CSEE-Défense to supply decoy launchers and optronic fire control systems for the *Lafayette* frigates.[83] The first hulls are expected to be delivered by 1994.

As with fighter aircraft, the ROC is pursuing multiple foreign suppliers for combat ships. In 1991, German shipyards delivered four 500-ton MWB-50 class coastal mine-hunters. Although they were officially sold as offshore oil platform support vessels, they were converted for mine-hunting in Taiwan with a French Thomson-Sintra system.[84]

Exploiting the momentum created by the F-16 and *Mirage* sales, Taipei has been pushing to place orders in Germany. When German Post and Telecommunications Minister Christian Schwarz-Schilling visited Taiwan in May 1992, he expressed the hope to win contracts in Taiwan's new six-year development plan. He was given to understand that orders for civilian telecommunications from Germany might be considerably increased if Germany were willing to sell weapons systems as well. In October 1992, following the F-16 announcement, German Parliamentarian Ortwin Lowack visited Taiwan, saying that the outlook was "positive" for German submarine sales. The ROC Navy reportedly was particularly interested in frigates and Type-209 diesel-electric submarines.[85]

In early 1993, Germany's Federal Security Council considered selling up to ten Type-209 submarines and ten MEKO-200 frigates valued at DM12.5 billion (US$7.95 billion). The Council finally decided not to export the equipment to Taiwan in view of Germany's standing policy not to export defense equipment to less-stable areas, and also because of its fear of losing trade with the PRC. A German Foreign Ministry study concluded that "The value of lost trade with China over the years could massively exceed" the value of the proposed Taiwan deal. Northern German regional politicians had been pleading for approval, and the decision was a blow to German shipbuilders.[86]

Under economic pressure, the Netherlands may soon lift its 1984 weapons embargo on Taiwan. In February 1992, the Dutch government refused to issue an export license for ten modified-*Zwaardvis*-class submarines to Taiwan for US$4.7 billion. The Parliament immediately passed a resolution placing conditions on the ban, however. The resolution required that during 1992 there had to be a substantial increase in Dutch trade with the PRC and that no other European country would sell arms to Taiwan. Neither condition was met. A number of Dutch trade delegations traveled to the PRC but trade increased only about 30 percent, far short of expectations. That, coupled with the F-16 and *Mirage* deals, shifted opinion in the Dutch Parliament strongly in favor of selling arms to Taiwan.

Dutch naval and electronics manufacturers maintained pressure throughout 1992. Representatives from the firm Signaal reportedly are pursuing a US$555 million market for radars and combat systems in Taiwan. In early 1993, Rotterdam's RDM shipyard presented the ROC Defense Ministry with a proposal to construct submarines in Taiwan under license. This would be similar to the frigate construction arrangement with the United States. RDM hopes such technology transfer and assembly in Taiwan would not violate the Dutch government's interpretation of its 1984 agreement with China.[87]

RDM, one of the oldest shipyards in the Netherlands, may soon have to close its submarine division altogether, unless production of components for Taiwan allows it to keep operating—securing jobs for about 500 workers. The ROC, for its part, may delay response to the Dutch offer, hoping to elicit more attractive proposals from other European shipbuilders (every shipyard in Europe seems to need orders desperately). Reportedly, the ROC Navy was holding out hopes for the German Type-209s, which it regards as technically superior. However, the German decision not to sell at all has increased the odds for a deal with RDM.

Surface-to-Surface Missiles

As noted earlier, Taiwan has received assistance from the United States and Israel with missiles and missile technologies. In the 1981 National Day parade, the ROC Army first displayed its *Ching Feng (Green Bee)* ballistic missile, which appears to be closely based on the American *Lance* battlefield missile, and has a range of 130 kilometers. The *Lance* is operated by Israel, which presumably assisted CSIST with *Ching Feng* development.[88]

There have been recent unconfirmed reports of a 950-1,000 kilometer-range ballistic missile called *Tien Ma (Sky Horse)*.[89] Such reports evidently provoked American concern. According to an unconfirmed report cited in *Jane's Strategic Weapon Systems, 1992*, the United States intervened to prevent the *Ching Feng* from entering service. If so, it certainly also would be trying to prevent *Tien Ma* development. In October 1990 the United States refused to supply "critical missile booster technology" to Taiwan, causing the termination of Taiwan's plans to develop a satellite-launch capability.[90] Nevertheless, missile development in Taiwan continues. On March 11, 1991, CSIST announced that missile research and development over the next ten years had been allocated approximately NT$18 billion (approximately US$0.7 billion).[91]

The *Hsiung Feng (Male Bee)* anti-shipping missile, derived from the Israeli *Gabriel II*, has been in operation with the ROC Navy for some time. The *Hsiung Feng II* is under development, reportedly incorporating technology from the McDonnell-Douglas AGM-84 *Harpoon*. The initial version of the *Hsiung Feng II* will be surface-launched, have a range of 80-100 kilometers, and have an active radar and imaging infrared terminal guidance seeker system. An air-launched version also is expected in 1993.[92]

Taiwan as an Arms Exporter

Taiwan has exported small arms to Central American countries. It also exports computers and other electronics hardware and software, some of which may fall into the nebulous category of "dual-use" or "grey-area" technologies. Otherwise, Taiwan has not been much of an exporter. The main current possibility, ironically enough, seems to be that, "using its long-term memorandum of understanding with Eurocopter, Taiwan sees a possible market for utility and support helicopters in [mainland] China." In February 1992, the PRC's China Aviation Technical Import-Export Corporation (CATIC) announced it would cooperate with Aerospatiale of France and Singapore Aerospace on the new P120L light helicopter. The project reportedly has moved from project definition to the developmental stage, and ultimately is to lead to the production of the helicopter in all three countries. Taiwan AIDC might buy into this project as well, conceivably leading to Taiwan-PRC coproduction.[93]

The only other significant possibility for a military export sale is ITEC's 15 percent share in Garrett F-124 engines for the U.S. Navy's T-45 *Gosshawk*—if Garrett gets the contract.

The current *political* environment probably would allow Taiwan's arms industries to begin serious international marketing. Market *economic* conditions are so bad, however, that only a prospect of significant *political* payoffs could justify entering the market at this time.

Proliferation Concerns

In June 1991, the ROC government began talks with the United States on the issues of nuclear, missile, and chemical warfare proliferation.[94] The ROC is a signatory of the Nuclear Non-Proliferation Treaty (NPT). Although its anomalous diplomatic status so far has prevented Taipei from signing the Chemical Warfare Convention (CWC) or the Missile Technology Control Regime (MTCR), it has indicated its willingness to adhere to both, informally.[95]

There has been some suspicion of Taiwan importing sensitive missile technologies from South Africa, one of the only industrialized states to maintain full diplomatic relations with the ROC through the past decade. In 1991, the U.S. State Department imposed a two-year punitive embargo on the South African Arms Corporation (ARMSCOR), for having "engaged in missile proliferation activities." These unspecified activities were said to have involved possible sales to Iraq, Israel, Chile, Iran, or Taiwan.[96]

The most ominous arms control implications of Taiwan's arms purchases, however, are their influence on PRC behavior. On September 3, 1992, PRC Vice Foreign Minister Liu Huaqui stated that in light of the previous day's F-16 announcement, "China would find it difficult to stay in the meeting of the five on arms control issues" unless the United States reversed its decision. He was referring to the Arms Control in the Middle East (ACME) talks (also called the "Big Five" talks because they involve the five permanent members of the UN Security Council). The Chinese also intimated that they might withdraw, at least temporarily, from the CWC; but in January 1993 they were among the 125 initial signatories. The official *Xinhua* news agency announced on September 7 that an Iranian military team had visited Beijing to discuss arms purchases, but did not say exactly when the Iranian visit took place.[97]

The PRC has not returned to the "Big Five" talks. They never were enthusiastic participants, and the talks essentially had been at an impasse since May 1992. There is a general consensus that the Chinese were looking for an excuse to postpone or suspend their participation, and that the F-16 sale provided the excuse they were looking for.

The first meeting of the "Big Five" delegations was in July 1991 and resulted in guidelines to govern international weapons sales, including an agreement not to interfere in the internal affairs of any state with weapons deals nor to promote "destabilizing" arms sales.

This led to Beijing raising a new objection to arms sales to Taiwan by any of the Big Five: Since China regards anything involving Taiwan as its internal affair, such sales violate the "Big Five" guidelines.[98]

It may turn out that the F-16 deal has a relatively insignificant effect on PRC missile sales and adherence to MCTR guidelines. It appears that the most publicized and worrisome sales, including the reported M-11 tactical missile sale to Pakistan, were concluded well before the F-16 announcement. At this writing, there is no hard evidence that the PRC has directly violated MTCR guidelines since its commitment to adhere to them in the spring of 1992.

Political Uses of the Market

To date, Taiwan has been a somewhat atypical buyer in the international arms market, and consequently a particularly attractive one. Taipei generally has not demanded the offsets and technology transfers demanded by most countries. Moreover, it recently has been able to offer aid, loans, and "reverse offsets" in the form of access to the Taiwan market—especially to the lucrative contracts and package deals involved with its ongoing National Infrastructure Program. In part, it makes these concessions because its *primary* goals in the arms market are neither military, technological, nor economic, but political. In addition to weapons and technologies, Taiwan enters the arms market seeking friends, influence, and international legitimacy—all of which provide "situational deterrence."

This is not to say that Taipei is indifferent to technology transfers or unaware of the economic benefits of offsets and coproduction. It was asking for technology transfers and coproduction from the United States in the 1970s, when some American officials doubted whether Taiwan was technically capable of coproducing the F-5E. In large part, Taipei has gotten fewer offsets and technology transfers because it has lacked leverage: No matter how friendly and well-meaning, the United States was a monopoly supplier.

There is an interesting reversal of normal procedures in the American and French frigate deals and the proposed Dutch submarine deal. Normally, it is the *buyer* who insists upon technology transfers, and coproduction or assembly in its own shipyards and factories. That is because the buying country's leaders normally wish to save foreign exchange, preserve the maximum number of domestic jobs, and/or upgrade domestic arms industries. But when Taiwan is the buyer things often work in reverse. Taiwan has a labor shortage, so there is little concern about jobs. Indeed, jobs in Taiwan appear *never* to be a factor in negotiations. Rather, the *seller* prefers assembly or coproduction in Taiwan so as to diffuse PRC retaliation, as illustrated by the 1993 RDM submarine proposal.

But the situation is changing. Taiwan is in a strong position to demand more from sellers. Moreover, some ROC government officials and many opposition politicians now demand technology transfers as a condition of future buys. On January 14, 1993, the Legislative Yuan approved the first year's payments for the *Mirages* and F-16s, appropriating US$12.47 billion. But it placed a condition that there "should be local procurement or technology transfer valued at no less than 10 percent of the purchase price in the coming years."[99] Opposition politicians also decried the way the deal was made in secret, denying "lots of industries an opportunity to supply parts or benefit from technology transfer."[100]

Economy and efficiency in arms buying also are becoming more important. ROC Defense Minister Chen Lü-an told a Defense Ministry conference on September 23, 1992, that future purchases of weapons and military supplies would no longer be conducted in secret. "In the past," he said, "different arms purchases were handled by different military units, sometimes leading to confusions [sic] and an unnecessarily large expenditure of time."[101] He announced that most future purchases would be carried out openly, so that a wider range of experts could be involved in the decision making. A Military Supplies Review Committee would be established to review procedures, along with a program to train experts in arms purchases. The committee is expected to be composed of officials of various agencies and to be headed by a vice chief of the general staff. Minister Chen said that an official "arms purchase bureau" eventually may be created to take full charge of arms purchases.[102] These actions are in response to two developments: First, Taiwan is expecting a lot more arms purchases from overseas and is preparing to handle them. Second, the political system in Taiwan is opening up, demanding more open foreign arms purchasing procedures.

ROC participation in the international arms market is entangled with other international issues, such as Taipei's relationships with the constituent republics of the former Soviet Union (FSU). On June 26, 1992, Taiwan's Society for Strategic Studies welcomed Admiral Vladimir Sidorov, former deputy commander-in-chief of the Soviet Navy, for a six-day stay. "Fending off hordes of Taiwan reporters questioning him about possible arms sales to the ROC, Sidorov said the livelihood of some 20 million Russian citizens is dependent on Russia's defense industry and that he, personally, thought consideration should be given to selling arms to Taiwan."[103]

Although Sidorov was nominally on a "purely academic visit," he had interviews with Premier Hau Pei-tsun, Defense Minister Chen, Vice Foreign Minister John Chang, Chief of the General Staff Liu Ho-chien, and Presidential Strategic Advisor Admiral Soong Chang-chih. Sidorov urged Taiwan's entrepreneurs and industrialists to invest in and extend loans to Russian businesses. He pleaded, "Help Russia and the CIS stand up and help rescue the Russian economy that now is on the brink of collapse."[104] Several times during his visit, Sidorov repeated, almost apologetically, that the sales of Su-27s and other systems to the PRC were "purely commercial" and did not indicate any unfriendliness toward the ROC.

In the aftermath of Sidorov's visit, both the ROC and Russian Defense Ministries strongly denied that any arms deals had been made. Vice Foreign Minister John Chang said the ROC's military and defense relations with the FSU "should start with the exchange of technologies, since the time is not right for bilateral weapons sales."[105] However, Taiwan points to the fact that it is probably a better partner for Russian defense industries than the PRC, since Taiwan is so much more advanced technologically. Despite official denials, Taipei might at least want to acquire samples of the equipment being sold to Beijing just to learn more about its characteristics and potential weaknesses.[106]

Taipei has also attempted to influence or exploit sales to the PRC from the FSU. In midsummer 1992, speculation abounded that the

PRC was about to purchase the partially completed 67,500-ton aircraft carrier *Varyag* from the Nikolayev South shipyard on the Black Sea in Ukraine. Coming amid the continuing debates over the F-16, *Mirage*, and *Kfir* sales, this speculation, as well as the Su-27 sale, was used by the ROC and its friends to lobby for approval of the aircraft sales.[107]

Not only was the ROC lobbying in Washington, Paris, and Jerusalem; it may have been lobbying in Kiev as well. On July 26, a gigantic An-124 aircraft of the Ukrainian airline, loaded with US$6 million worth of donated medical supplies, left Taipei's Chiang Kai-shek Airport, bound for Kiev.[108] On August 26, the deputy chairman of Ukraine's Parliament arrived in Taipei with a government delegation and expressed "reservations" about selling the *Varyag* to the PRC. He also expressed the desire to establish relations with the ROC similar to the relations maintained by the United States, Japan, and others. In late August, ROC Vice Economics Minister Chiang Pin-kung traveled to Ukraine, Belarus, Latvia, and Russia with a sixty-member delegation. He participated in the first ever ROC-Ukraine trade and investment conference in Kiev. The two sides reportedly agreed to sign an investment guarantee pact; guidelines for promoting technology exchanges; and arranged to set up reciprocal representative offices to handle trade, visas, and tourism. They also agreed to lease jointly three satellite links for direct communications between the two capitals.[109]

In November 1992, negotiations for the *Varyag* collapsed—probably because the PLA realized it was an utterly impractical proposition.[110] While Ukraine–ROC economic links surely had little influence, it is clear that Taipei provided Kiev with incentives not to sell the carrier to Beijing.

The F-16 and *Mirage* sales may have removed most of the inhibitions, at least in the United States and France, for further arms sales to Taiwan. Although that remains to be proven, several defense contractors have already taken action on that assumption. Litton, it seems, expects to make additional sales in Taiwan. As noted earlier, shortly after the F-16 announcement, McDonnell-Douglas reportedly approached the Bush administration for permission to offer Taiwan the F/A-18 multi-mission fighter.[111] Litton Applied Technology Division has established a support center in Taipei to "support operators of Litton's threat warning, ESM [electronic support measures] and decoy systems" in Taiwan and the Far East.[112] In January 1993, representatives of France's Giat Industries reportedly were in Taiwan attempting to sell 105mm light guns. Renault-SMS representatives were trying to close a deal for 300 VAB armored personnel carriers. Thomson-CSF is offering its *Rita* field camouflage system. The French-German Euromissile combine is offering the *MILAN* antitank system. Matra is attempting to follow up its sales of air-to-air missiles with a deal for the *Mistral* SAM.

PRC reaction to the *Mirage* sale initially was considerably milder than expected. Heavy diplomatic retaliation, at least, had been expected, in light of PRC Foreign Minister Qian's statement that any French arms deal was "different" from U.S. sales to Taiwan because the three Sino-U.S. joint communiqués make U.S. weapons sales to Taiwan "permissible" within a limited period of time.[113] Beijing forced the closure of the French consulate in Canton and disqualified the Anglo-French Consortium GEC-Alsthom from bidding on construction of the Canton subway. The latter measure lacked credibility since GEC-Alsthom was widely believed to be out of the bidding already.[114] By mid-March 1993, however, the PRC had frozen several French contracts and halted most negotiations for others. *The Journal of Commerce* reported that 1993 was "shaping up to be a dismal year for [French] trade with China."[115] It remains to be seen how soon and how well French trade with the PRC recovers, and whether trade with Taiwan expands enough to compensate.

Conclusion

Taiwan's military forces are modernizing rapidly with weapons and equipment that are imported and others that are domestically manufactured using imported technology. ROC leaders are adroitly using the current international "buyer's market" to acquire these weapons and technologies, diversifying their overseas sources and increasing Taiwan's military-industrial self-sufficiency. More importantly, arms market activity is integral to Taipei's "flexible diplomacy"—the use of its economic clout as a diplomatic tool. A web of relationships and situations—including arms transactions—constitute a political-economic "situational deterrent," which renders military attack by the PRC increasingly unlikely.

Reflecting the increased capability of the ROC armed forces and the primacy of the "situational deterrent," the emphasis of Taipei's activities in the international arms market has shifted from military readiness to political-strategic deterrence and to the broader goals of diplomatic legitimacy.

This set of policies has served Taiwan well in the 1980s and early 1990s, but the current highly favorable circumstances will not last.

Taiwan's evolving democracy will complicate matters. Opposition politicians will demand still more open weapons acquisition procedures, which may increase the fairness of domestic business, but will make it much harder to manipulate the international arms market through secret negotiations. As in other industrialized democracies, opposition politicians and the free press will insist upon more technology transfers, coproduction deals, and offset arrangements—not only out of economic need, but also from nationalistic pride.

The PRC is refurbishing its image and opening its economy even wider. That will make exclusion from the PRC market increasingly costly for those who sell arms to Taipei.[116] The global "buyer's market" won't last forever either. European shipyards, American aerospace contractors, and Russian tank factories will eventually find new customers or (more likely) merge, diversify, and/or go broke. The vast surplus of modern weaponry eventually will break down or be destroyed; and all of it inevitably will become obsolete. In that not-too-distant future, a fully democratic Taiwan will not be able to exploit the international arms market as confidently as it does today, nor will it be able to go back to secretly and self-effacingly manipulating it as it did in the early and mid-1980s.

Commentary

Ronald N. Montaperto

Introduction

The Primacy of Military Deterrence

In the early 1980s, Taiwan's strategic position changed dramatically as the keystone of its defense, the military alliance with the United States, was replaced by the Taiwan Relations Act (TRA). Although the event had been anticipated for nearly ten years, Taipei seemed strangely ill-prepared to face the future. Not the least of its difficulty was bound up with uncertainty about how the TRA would weather the storms that were certain to erupt as Washington and Beijing developed the modalities of their new, official relations.

Taipei's response to the new security challenge evolved very slowly. With the passage of time, it became clear that Taiwan's emerging posture comprised a variety of diplomatic, economic, and military approaches, means, and instruments. At different times since the early 1980s, the authorities have chosen to emphasize one or more sets of approaches over others.

As the mix has evolved, the military instrument has emerged as the most important component of Taiwan's overall strategic posture. Although Taiwan's security policy has economic, political, and diplomatic components, at the core it is Taipei's ability to deter China from launching military operations against it that keeps Taiwan secure.

In this light, Taiwan's primary goals in the international arms market involve securing the weapons systems and technologies that will enable it to preserve its qualitative military edge over China. By this means, Taiwan preserves the military balance in the Taiwan Strait and also maintains deterrence. Although Taipei regularly stretches or overlooks a point or two in order to secure military gain, it is well aware that qualitative superiority in the military sphere is what makes "flexible diplomacy" possible.

Taiwan's Deterrent Force

As Taiwan's military authorities began to come to terms with the new strategic environment after passage of the TRA, they were influenced by a perception of four major problems. The effort to solve these problems and perceived ambiguities set the terms of reference and development parameters that provide Taiwan's present military forces with their unique structure and characteristics.

First, despite the reassuring language of the TRA, there was considerable doubt about the durability and reliability of the U.S. commitment to the island's defense. Accordingly, the arguments of those who had long favored diversifying Taiwan's sources of supply were strengthened. So too were the arguments of those who felt that the island needed to develop its own indigenous research and development and production capabilities. Although self-sufficiency was never considered to be within the realm of possibility, it was decided that, whenever possible, Taiwan should acquire or develop the technological knowledge and capabilities that would help to reduce its dependency on external sources. The reduction of military dependency was defined as a guiding value. Achieving this value later emerged as a main mission of the Chung Shan Institute of Science and Technology (CSIST). CSIST primacy in this regard also accounts for the major expansion of its programs and influence in the 1980s

Second, the Taiwan military establishment was deeply concerned with a number of glaring gaps and asymmetries in its capabilities and force structure. Perceived to be the result of Taipei's past reliance on U.S. military power, these asymmetries emerged as yet another incentive to reduce the regime's military dependence.

More important, dissatisfaction with the asymmetries also eventually provided direction for a new approach to force modernization. For example, during the period of alliance with Washington, the pressure and constant availability of the Seventh Fleet had resulted in a reduction in the attention paid to Taiwan's naval forces. In the same way, the U.S. military presence had undercut arguments in favor of several improvements in the capabilities of the ground and air forces. Finally, the Taiwan military was deeply concerned about what it considered to be critical deficiencies in its aid defense capabilities.

A third influence on the direction of military development in post-alliance Taiwan was the leadership's estimate of Chinese military capabilities and of the potential for successful modernization of the People's Liberation army. Concerns about these matters was very high indeed.

Taiwan's military leaders acknowledged that, owing to a combination of Taiwan's defensive strength and China's offensive weakness, Beijing lacked the overall capability to mount a successful invasion of the island. They also judged that Taipei's deterrent capability would hold through the 1980s.

Concern was expressed, however, that if developments in China's military modernization program were left unanswered, it could result in the erosion of Taipei's qualitative advantage over mainland military forces. Therefore, a major program of selective military development was considered essential to maintain Taiwan's relative advantage.

A final influence emerged in Taiwan's assessment of China's probable military intentions through the 1980s and 1990s. Here it was determined that China's priority on domestic economic development reduced the probability of military operations against Taiwan virtually to zero. Economic development required regional stability, external investment and technology transfer, and the peaceful reintegration of Hong Kong into China. All of these needs would be ill-served by emphasizing military means in dealing with cross-Strait relations. In the unlikely event that Beijing were to decide to use its military instrument against Taiwan, a naval blockade in combination with some sort of air operations—not an invasion—was most probable.

In effect Taiwan had a window within which it could take steps to develop new military capabilities that would enable it to maintain its overall deterrent. Political, economic, diplomatic, and other means would be used to garner broad external support and reduce the likelihood of military conflict. Implementing this aspect of the strategy required that Taipei immediately take all steps necessary to redress the perceived imbalances and asymmetries in its military force structure. That process began in the 1980s and continues to develop through the present day.

In response to this challenge, Taiwan's authorities immediately implemented new plans for upgrading equipment, increased the pace and scope of other programs that were already in place, and laid plans for acquiring new systems, either by outright purchase or by development in Taiwan. The ground forces focused upon improvement and modernization programs involving tanks, armored personnel carriers, and artillery. In most cases, this involved upgrading equipment already in place rather than developing or acquiring new systems. The ground forces component of the force improvement program was largely completed by the late 1980s, essentially with the United States as the major external source of support.

The naval modernization program posed a far more difficult challenge owing to the fact that Taipei had a greater distance to travel in order to achieve anything even approaching a modern naval capability. Progress has probably also been slower owing to political considerations; naval acquisitions provided considerably more scope for engaging the political and economic instruments that, by the early 1980s, had become integral aspects of Taiwan's overall strategy.

In the last ten years or so, Taipei has engaged Israel, South Korea, the Netherlands, West Germany, and the United States on matters related to acquiring both naval platforms and the armaments and other equipment necessary to develop a modern, capable naval force. Calculations related to diplomatic and political advantage almost certainly are important in accounting for the wide-ranging nature of Taipei's contacts. Taipei's desire for destroyer equivalents, frigates, patrol craft, submarines, anti-submarine warfare systems, and ship-borne air defense systems, however, is obviously rooted in pressing military necessity. New naval systems are required in order to come to terms with one of the most likely potential Chinese military actions: the threat of a naval blockade that makes use of Beijing's overwhelmingly superior submarine capability.

The naval modernization program continues to progress. Taiwan's program, however, will probably be extended as China proceeds with its own plan for constructing a modern naval force. In this area, the relationship between military and political/diplomatic motivators will probably continue to evolve with Taipei attempting to derive maximum political benefit from each transaction. The driving force, however, will continue to be perceived military necessity.

A third area of activity involves Taiwan's quest for a fighter aircraft and the missiles to arm it. As with the starting point of the naval modernization program, the military justification for a new fighter lies beyond question. That Taipei attempted an indigenous solution by means of the IDF is usually presented as a consequence of Washington's unwillingness to complicate its relations with Beijing by approving the sale of F16s to Taiwan. No doubt, this interpretation is based upon fact.

It is difficult to believe that even before the program began Taipei had failed to become aware of the longer term benefits to its overall position that accrued from its participation in what amounted to a joint development program. The IDF program provided Taiwan with a major infusion of basic aircraft developmental technology; the quality of this technological benefit certainly exceeds the levels that would have accrued from the transfer of finished systems and is probably greater than the benefit that would have been derived from participation in a program of licensed production, as was the case with the F5.

If this assessment is valid, then it follows that the military component of Taipei's overall calculus weighed at least as heavily as the political or diplomatic components in structuring Taiwan's participation in the international fighter aircraft market of the 1980s. In fact, the military component was probably decisive in this regard.

Nor do Taipei's recent achievements in the international fighter aircraft market of the 1990s negate this interpretation. That Taiwan is now able to deal with the United States, Israel, France, and Italy in its effort to acquire a modern fighter aircraft capability is more a function of developments in the relations of those nations with China than anything that Taipei has initiated.

It is natural that Taiwan will seek to use its new-found flexibility to secure the best possible terms for itself and simultaneously to do all that it can—but always within limits—to ensure that the stresses between Beijing and the four supplier nations are exacerbated. However, the acquisition plans and quantities are all readily explained by the military virtues of diversification of supply and enhancement of the military/technological base. Even the total quantity of fighters, approximately 650, including *Mirage* 2000s, F16s, and reconditioned F5s, reflects a prudent judgement taken on essentially military grounds rather than a desire to use the acquisition plan to secure political or diplomatic gain. It is difficult to accept the notion that Taipei is acquiring aircraft it does not really need.

The fourth mission area, essentially ground-based air defense, reflects a similar pattern and orientation. Since the early 1980s, most of the work that has been done has involved indigenous or joint development of various missiles and the acquisition of different types of radar, and command, control, and communications systems. In virtually every case, the United States has been the major source of external assistance and technological innovation. It is likely that this pattern will persist into the future.

Reflections on the Past, Pondering the Future

Ever since Taiwan began the process of adjusting to the new environment that emerged as its formal security ties with the United States ended, it has been most concerned about maintaining its ability to deter China from utilizing its military instrument as a means of managing cross-Strait relations. Since the early 1980s, Taipei has seen the orderly, reasonably independent development of its own military capabilities as the most effective means of achieving this goal.

This has involved a fairly objective comparative assessment of the capabilities and intentions of the two sides as well as a series of judgements about the future. In every case, Taiwan has sought to preserve the qualitative military advantages it possessed at the beginning of the Taiwan Relations Act era. This in turn has required that judgements about new programs and systems be tested against essentially military criteria.

As Taiwan has sought to acquire the new systems it has identified as being essential, that is, as Taipei has participated in the external arms market, its goals have been primarily military and strategic and only secondarily political and economic. Even when a decision involves additional expense or an exercise in production gymnastics, it can be justified by the requirements of an insistence upon military prudence.

Overall, Taipei's purpose has been to maintain the qualitative edge in military systems that facilitates continuing deterrence. By this means, competition between the two sides is in effect prevented from assuming a military character and Taiwan gains an opportunity to bring its considerable economic and political assets to bear. This nexus of the military on the one hand and the political and economic on the other is the new keystone of Taiwan's defense policy.

Whether Taiwan will continue to enjoy success in the international arms market is probably an open question. Much of what it has accomplished in the last few years is, at least in part, a result of the decline of China's international position as a result of its human rights, arms sales, and trade policies. It is also very much the result of the decline in China's relations with the United States that has occurred since 1989. As Beijing continues to progress towards regaining its international position, the Chinese government will once again be able to exert pressure against nations that continue to supply arms to Taiwan. When this will occur, or what gain Taiwan will be able to achieve in the interim, remains to be seen.

Taiwan may also become the victim of its own success. If the aircraft purchases come to fruition, this, in combination with other force improvements, will provide the island with a truly powerful military force. How the Taiwan military establishment will play in the reunification endgame is another open question. Also, when reunification is eventually accomplished, the problems involved in integrating Taiwan's military establishment into the national arms will inevitably prove to be of formidable proportions.

The strategies outlined above, and Taiwan's approach to the international arms market, are likely to endure for the next few years. The success of that strategy is also likely to gain for Taipei an increased flexibility. As that happens, Taiwan's authorities may well choose to become more adventurous in their arms acquisitions policies and give greater weight to economic and other considerations.

Notes

1. The "Mutual Defense Treaty between the United States and the Republic of China" was initialed on December 2, 1954. The complete text is in John M. Maki, ed., *Conflict and Tension in the Far East: Key Documents, 1894-1960,* (Seattle, WA: University of Washington Press, 1961, pp. 226-28).

2. Taiwan Relations Act of 1979, Sec. 2. (b). The complete text is in Dupre Jones, ed., *China: U.S. Policy since 1945*, Congressional Quarterly, 1980, pp. 343-45.

3. Much of the following was prompted by discussion of an earlier draft of this chapter by the Taiwan Study Group of The Gaston Sigur Center for East Asian Studies, The George Washington University, Washington, DC, on March 11, 1993. I am especially grateful to Ronald Montaperto, Eden Woon, and Alfred Wilhelm.

4. In July 1992, Taiwan held foreign exchange reserves of US$82 billion (US$90 billion, counting gold). *The Free China Journal (FCJ)*, July 14, 1992. The term "flexible diplomacy" is referred to in several chapters and is defined in the introduction.

5. Patrick M. Morgan. *Assessing the Republic of China's Deterrence Situation.* SCPS Paper, Kaohsiung Taiwan, ROC, Sun Yat-sen Center for Policy Studies, National Sun Yat-sen University, April 1991.

6. *Jane's Defence Weekly (JDW)*, December 1, 1990, p. 1,084.

7. Tai Ming Cheung, "A sale is in the air," *Far Eastern Economic Review (FEER)*, September 6, 1990, p. 20.

8. "COCOM Deadlocks on List Review," *Arms Control News*, December 22, 1992, p. 2.

9. "Scrambled jets," *FEER*, February 18, 1993, pp. 10-11.

10. Tai Ming Cheung, "Instant Navy," *FEER*, February 18, 1993, pp. 11-12.

11. A. Doak Barnett, *The FX Decision: "Another Crucial Moment"* in *US-China-Taiwan Relations*, (Washington, DC: The Brookings Institution, 1981).

12. Chung Kuo Shih Pao (Taipei), February 18, 1992, p. 9.

13. *Jane's Fighting Ships, 1987-88* (London), 1987, p. 497.

14. "Taiwan Puts New Missile on Display," *Flight International*, November 27-December 3, 1991, p. 12.

15. *Jane's All the World's Aircraft, 1987-89,* Jane's Publishers, 1987, pp. 145-232.

16. The transactions discussed in this section are selected because of their high international visibility or because they illustrate points in my analysis. This is not a comprehensive listing of Taiwan's arms transactions.

17. "Italian-Brazilian AMX fighters demonstrated in ROC sales pitch," *FCJ*, December 10, 1990, p. 2.

18. "Kfirs to Taiwan," *Israeli Foreign Affairs*, vol. 8, no. 4, April 28, 1992, p. 8.

19. *Jane's All the World's Aircraft, 1987-89,* Jane's Publishers, 1987, pp. 145-46.

20. "Talks on Kfir sale," *JDW*, August 15, 1992, p. 7.

21. "China warns over Mirage 2000-5s," *JDW*, April 4, 1992, p. 551.

22. "Joxe favors Taiwan sale," *JDW*, May 23, 1992, p. 870.

23. J. A. C. Lewis, "Export delay may kill 2000-5," *JDW*, July 4, 1992, p. 6.

24. *Agence France Press (AFP)* (Hong Kong), September 12, 1992, in Foreign Broadcast Information Service *Daily Report-China* FBIS-CHI-92-178, p. 1.

25. *Paris France-Inter Radio Network* in French, September 10, 1992, trans. in FBIS-CHI-92-177, p. 69.

26. *FEER*, November 5, 1992, p. 6.

27. "Paris silent on Taiwan progress," *JDW*, November 28, 1992, p. 7; and "Joxe approves $775m Mirage 2000 upgrade," *JDW*, February 13, 1993, p. 12.

28. "Mirage upgrade will total $830m," *JDW*, December 5, 1992, p. 15. Also see J. A. C. Lewis, "Air force bags Mirage exports," *JDW*, November 7, 1992, p. 8 and J. A. C. Lewis, "Paris silent on Taiwan progress," *JDW*, November 28, 1992, p. 7.

29. *Xinhua*, January 12, 1993, trans. in FBIS-CHI-93-007, pp. 15–16.

30. Paul Beaver, "Taiwan keeps fighter aircraft options open," *JDW*, January 16, 1993, pp. 14–15.

31. "USA reconsiders F-16 sale ban," *JDW*, August 8, 1992, p. 5.

32. Both quotations are in Tammy C. Peng, "US wavering: May sell ROC F-16s," *FCJ*, August 4, 1992, p. 2.

33. Tammy C. Peng, "US sells SM-1 missiles to ROC; Bush may okay F-16 fighter deal," *FCJ*, August 14, 1992, p. 2.

34. T. Y. Wang, "Why Taiwan Should Get F-16s," *Christian Science Monitor*, August 13, 1992, p. 19.

35. Tammy C. Peng, "ROC air force wants world-class fighters," *FCJ*, August 11, 1992, p. 1.

36. *Jane's All the World's Aircraft, 1987-89*, Jane's Publishers, 1987, p. 232.

37. *Asian Wall Street Journal*, August 24, 1992, cited in *FCJ*, August 28, 1992, p. 2.

38. "F-16 sale justified by 'discrepancy'," *JDW*, September 12, 1992, p. 5.

39. Quoted in Tammy C. Peng, "President Bush approves F-16 sale to ROC," *FCJ*, September 4, 1992, p. 1 (emphasis added).

40. *Central News Agency (CNA)* (Taipei), September 3, 1992, in FBIS-CHI-92-173, p. 54.

41. *CNA*, September 4, 1992, in FBIS-CHI-92-173, p. 54.

42. *CNA* (Taipei), September 3, 1992, in FBIS-CHI-92-173, p. 55.

43. A "letter of intent" is a formal agreement to negotiate in good faith. It is neither a contract nor a guarantee that there will be one.

44. *CNA*, September 4, 1992, in FBIS-CHI-92-173, p. 54.

45. "US denies F-16 sale violates communique," *FCJ*, September 8, 1993, p. 1.

46. For example, see Hamilton Huang, "Why does the mainland hate F-16 deal so much?" *FCJ*, September 8, 1992, p. 6.

47. *Taipei Radio*, September 2, 1992, trans. in FBIS-CHI-92-172, p. 42.

48. Tammy C. Peng, "US F-16 fighter planes due for delivery as early as 1995," *FCJ*, October 30, 1992, p. 2.

49. "F-16 Fracas," *Pacific Research*, November 1992, p. 17.

50. "F-16 contract finalized, delivery to begin in 1996," *FCJ*, November 17, 1992, p. 2.

51. *Xinhua*, September 3, 1992, in FBIS-CHI-92-172, p. 1. For a sampling of reaction from the PRC and the Hong Kong communist press, see FBIS-CHI-92-172 through FBIS-CHI-92-178.

52. *Xinhua*, September 29, 1992, in FBIS-CHI-92-189, p. 2.

53. *Chung-yang Jih-pao* (Central Daily) (Taipei), October 16, 1992, p. 7, trans. in FBIS-CHI-92-209, pp. 71–72.

54. *JDW*, September 22, 1990, p. 514.

55. *JDW*, September 22, 1990, p. 514, claimed that series production of the IDF had already begun, and that it would be operational by the end of 1992. However, "Peking Interested in Soviet Fighters," *China Post* (Taipei), in English, November 2, 1990, p. 4, in FBIS-CHI-90-215, p. 49, said the IDF would not be ready for mass production until 1993. At this writing, even that seems unlikely.

56. Harry Harding's perceptive questioning prompted the following discussion.

57. See Harlan W. Jencks, *Some Political and Military Implications of Soviet Warplane Sales to the PRC*. SCPS Paper, Kaohsiung Taiwan, ROC, Sun Yat-sen Center for Policy Studies, National Sun Yat-sen University, 1991, pp. 17-20.

58. Carol Reed, "The power game," *JDW*, October 17, 1992, pp. 43-46. Also see Carole Reed, "Garrett growing IDF power plant," *JDW*, March 21, 1992, p. 473.

59. Paul Beaver, "Taiwan keeps fighter aircraft options open," *JDW*, January 16, 1993, p. 14.

60. *Taipei China Broadcasting Corp. News Network*, September 2, 1992, trans. in FBIS-CHI-92-172, p. 42, emphasis added.

61. Paul Beaver, "Taiwan keeps fighter aircraft options open," *JDW*, January 16, 1993, pp. 14-15.

62. Paul Beaver, "Taiwan keeps fighter aircraft options open," *JDW*, January 16, 1993, pp. 14-15.

63. Paul Beaver, "Taiwan keeps fighter aircraft options open," *JDW*, January 16, 1993, p. 14.

64. Tammy C. Peng, "US sells SM-1 missiles to ROC; Bush may okay F-16 fighter deal," *FCJ*, August 14, 1992, p. 2.

65. *MILAVIA News*, May 5, 1991, p. 6.

66. "New Asian Missile Systems," *World Weapons Review*, July 11, 1990, pp. 1-4.

67. Paul Beaver and Raymund Cheung, "Taiwan displays new systems," *JDW*, October 26, 1991, p. 759.

68. Jim Mann, "US Clears Way for Made-In-Taiwan Missiles," *Los Angeles Times*, January 12, 1992, p. 85.

69. Barbara Opall, "Taiwan Pursues Western Missile Acumen," *Defense News*, June 1, 1992, pp. 1, and 28.

70. Barbara Opall and David Silverberg, "Taiwanese May Soon Coproduce Patriot," *Defense News*, February 22-28, 1993, pp. 1 and 21. For commercial reasons, the deal was kept confidential between September 1992 and February 1993. Hence, the muddled initial report in "Optical recorder for Patriot," *JDW*, October 24, 1992, p. 22.

71. *Xinhua*, May 18, 1991, trans. in FBIS-CHI-91-100, p. 23.

72. Paul Beaver, "Market Survey: Helicopter Airframes," *JDW*, February 29, 1992, p. 363.

73. "Further helicopter buys for Taiwan," *JDW*, February 29, 1992, p. 338.

74. Paul Beaver, "Market Survey: Helicopter Airframes," *JDW*, February 29, 1992, p. 364.

75. "Turkey plans AMRAAM buy," *JDW*, October 3, 1992, p. 17.

76. Tammy C. Peng, "Bush sells ROC helicopters to defend Taiwan," *FCJ*, September 25, 1992, p. 1.

77. Joris Janssen Lok, "Blue water navies: Flagship fleets of Asia/Pacific," *JDW*, April 11, 1992, p. 623.

78. David S. Chou, "The Prospects for Peking-Seoul Relations: A Taiwan Perspective," *Issues and Studies*, vol. 26, no. 9, September 1990, pp. 54-55.

79. *FCJ*, July 24, 1992, p. 1; and Barbara Starr and John Boatman, "USA reconsiders ban on F-16 sales to Taiwan," *JDW*, August 8, 1992, p. 5.

80. Tammy C. Peng, "Navy missile frigate program shipshape," *FCJ*, October 20, 1992, p. 1; "2nd frigate is launched," *JDW*, October 31, 1992, p. 12; and "Taiwan's First Locally Built Frigate to Join Fleet," *Executive News Service*, October 15, 1992.

81. *CNA* (Taipei), January 13, 1993, in FBIS-CHI-93-009, p. 55.

82. J. A. C. Lewis, "France takes new initiative in tricky Taiwan market," *JDW*, January 23, 1993, p. 17; *JDW*, April 4, 1992, p. 551, and *FEER*, March 19, 1992, p. 12.

83. "Taiwan contract for CSEE," *JDW*, May 9, 1992, p. 794.

84. Taipei China Broadcasting Corporation News Network, June 22, 1991, trans. in FBIS-CHI-91-124, p. 66.

85. Taipei Radio, October 21, 1992; and *CNA*, October 22, 1992, both in FBIS-CHI-92-306, p. 38; and Susan Yu, "Outlook 'positive' German submarines for ROC Navy," *FCJ*, October 23, 1992, p. 2.

86. "Taiwan submarine veto," *FEER*, February 11, 1993, p. 14; and "Germans block sale of submarines, frigates," *JDW*, February 6, 1993, p. 7.

87. "Dutch firms ready for Taiwan signal," *JDW*, February 15, 1992, p. 218; "Dutch export challenge," *JDW*, November 28, 1992, pp. 25-26; and "Germans block sale of submarines, frigates," *JDW*, February 6, 1993, p. 7.

88. *Jane's Strategic Weapon Systems, 1992,* Issue 09, n.p.; and *Jane's Weapon Systems, 1987-88,* p. 121.

89. "Assessing Ballistic Missile Proliferation and Its Control," Center for International Security and Arms Control (Stanford), June 1991; and Duncan Lennox, "Missile race continues," *JDW*, January 23, 1993, pp. 18-20.

90. *Aviation Week and Space Technology*, October 22, 1990, cited in "Taiwan," *Proliferation Watch*, November–December 1990, p. 15.

91. *Nuclear Developments*, March 19, 1991, p. 11.

92. *CNA*, October 29, 1992, in FBIS-CHI-92-210, p. 61; "Taiwan Puts New Missiles on Display," *Flight International*, November 27–December 3, 1991, p. 12; and *Jane's Strategic Weapon Systems, 1992,* Issue 09, n.p.

93. Paul Beaver, "Market Survey: Helicopter Airframes," *JDW*, February 29, 1992, p. 363 and 365; and *JDW*, February 22, 1992, p. 290.

94. Harlan W. Jencks, "F-16s to Taiwan: Proliferation Implications," *Missile Monitor*, no. 3, Spring 1993, pp. 12-15.

95. *China Post*, June 18, 1991, p. 6.

96. David Bereford, "US Ban Deals Big Blow to South African Arms Maker," *The Guardian* (UK), October 17, 1991, p. 11.

97. Paul Lewis, "Chinese Ire at US Could Prompt More Arms Sales to Iran," *Defense News*, September 14–20, 1992, p. 19.

98. David Silverberg, "Amid Arms Flurry, Nations Pursue Arms Curbs," *Defense News*, October 5-11, 1992, pp. 4, 5, and 44.

99. "Cash for jet deals," *FEER*, January 28, 1993, p. 14.

100. Taipei Voice of Free China, January 13, 1993 in FBIS-CHI-93-008, p. 58; and "F-16, Mirage jet fighter budget passed," *FCJ*, January 19, 1993, p. 2.

101. Taipei Voice of Free China, September 25, 1992, in FBIS-CHI-92-189, p. 64.

102. "Wraps removed from ROC arms deals," *FCJ*, September 25, 1992, p. 2.

103. Tammy C. Peng, "Russian admirals visit Taiwan; salute progress," *FCJ*, June 26, 1992, p. 1.

104. Quoted by Tammy C. Peng, "Admiral charts peaceful course for ROC, Russia," *FCJ*, June 28, 1992.

105. *FCJ*, July 17, 1992, p. 1.

106. Gerald Segal, "Russia and the Chinas-New Risks," *Jane's Intelligence Review*, September 1992, pp. 416 and 417.

107. For example, see "Peking carrier deal said clinched," *FCJ*, August 7, 1992, p. 2.

108. *FCJ*, July 8, 1992, p. 2.

109. "Ukraine-ROC pacts forging strong ties," *FCJ*, September 1992, p. 2.

110. Joris Janssen Lok, "Varyag doomed as sale collapses," *JDW*, November 21, 1992, p. 5.

111. US denies F-16 sale violates communiqué," *FCJ*, September 8, 1993, p. 1.

112. *JDW*, January 23, 1993, p. 13.

113. Quoted in *FEER*, January 7, 1993, p.12.

114. This and the following are from J. A. C. Lewis, "France takes new initiative in tricky Taiwan market," *JDW*, January 23, 1993, p. 17.

115. Tara Patel, "French Jet Deal Sparks Backlash In China Trade," *The Journal of Commerce*, March 11, 1993, pp. 1A and 2A. I am grateful to Ken Allen for bringing this to my attention.

116. This forecast assumes that the PRC will remain united under the control of the Chinese Communist Party. I do not regard that as an entirely safe assumption, but predicting alternative futures is impossible.

4

Taiwan's Position Regarding
Transnational Issues

June Teufel Dreyer

Introduction

In keeping with both its long-standing position as one of the world's leading trading nations and its recently formulated activist diplomacy, the Republic of China (ROC) on Taiwan has assumed an increasingly assertive role with regard to transnational issues. These have included trade practices, the environment, narcotics, human rights, and democracy. At times, especially on some environmental issues, the pattern has been that concern with an individual issue begins at the domestic level, and moves from there to the international sphere. At that level, the ROC has typically dealt with problems on a bilateral basis, while seeking to join international organizations relevant to those problems. At other times, the ROC administration is forced by international pressure to lead Taiwan to conform with accepted norms regarding sensitive transnational issues.

The government's intention is to show itself a responsible member of the international community of nations. Clearly, it is in the self-interest of the ROC to be perceived as such. At the same time, it is in the individual self-interest of certain of the ROC's citizens to behave otherwise, thus sullying the image that the government has worked so hard to create. The impressive democratization of the island's political system in recent years has heightened popular awareness of civil liberties, thus making the government's task of reining in the activities of these individuals more difficult.

Efforts to join international organizations, including the General

Agreement on Tariffs and Trade (GATT), the Organization for Economic Cooperation and Development (OECD), the United Nations (UN), and the Montreal Protocol have been hampered by the resistance of the People's Republic of China (PRC) to admit the ROC to membership. The ROC has responded by intensifying its diplomatic, economic, and other efforts to conform to international norms seen as important in these international bodies, while developing the nation's global and regional financial position to the point that it cannot be ignored, the PRC's resistance notwithstanding. Concerns have been raised, particularly within the opposition Democratic Progressive Party (DPP), about the unfairness of Taiwan being asked to conform to international norms at the same time it is denied admission to the international institutions that decide and enforce these norms. Where lack of normal diplomatic relations has meant that the legal framework for solving disputes is also lacking, ROC officials have frequently been able to work out mechanisms to deal with the problems while simultaneously enhancing their country's international *persona*.

Trade Practices

It is frequently noted that the business of Taiwan is business. The island's lack of natural resources and the limited size of its internal market have made emphasis on the import-export trade a *sine qua non* for economic development. The result of this emphasis has been a stunning success: by the early 1980s, the ROC was acknowledged as a newly industrialized country (NIC) and, with South Korea, Hong Kong, and Singapore, a respected member of the "four little dragons."

By 1987, however, trade issues had begun to accumulate. One of the most obvious was the ROC's overwhelming dependence on the U.S. market. This dependence was combined with a large imbalance of trade in Taiwan's favor, and occurred at the time of a fast-growing U.S. budget deficit. Hence, increasingly contentious American negotiators were in a position to exercise considerable leverage over the ROC. Among other demands, they pressed hard for the elimination of tariff and non-tariff barriers that made it difficult for U.S. goods to enter the Taiwan market, for an appreciation in the exchange rate of the New Taiwan (NT) dollar, and for better protection of intellectual property rights (IPR).

The ROC acceded to these requests, removing many barriers to the free entry of goods and allowing the NT dollar to gradually rise from 40 to the dollar to about 25 in barely two years. In June 1992, a revised copyright law went into effect. Expanding the previous law from five sections and fifty-two articles to eight sections and 117 articles, the new law is far more explicit in its coverage. It calls for strict criminal penalties, such as longer prison terms, heavier fines, and stricter penalties for repeat offenders. The government is now required to prosecute suits that formerly had to be initiated by the plaintiff.[1]

However, while American pressures to revalue the currency and open markets helped redress the imbalance of trade with the United States, they helped Japan even more. As tariff and non-tariff barriers were eliminated, Japanese exporters were the ones who took best advantage of the situation, particularly in areas like machinery, industrial parts, and consumer products. Taiwan's huge trade deficit with Japan has been a second major problem.

Government planners set goals to alleviate both problems. Steps were taken to:

- diversify trade patterns by becoming a global trader;
- internationalize the economy by opening the domestic market to competition from foreign products and services; and
- liberalize such areas as import and foreign exchange regulations to stimulate investment and the upgrading of local products.

Individually, each of these would be a difficult undertaking. Collectively, they constituted a formidable challenge of economic transition. Opposition from the PRC to any dealings with Taiwan that might be interpreted as recognizing its separate status has also caused problems.

Nonetheless, barely five years after the task was begun, there have been a number of successes. Several semiofficial organizations have played important roles. For example, CETRA, the China Economic Trade Development Council, has facilitated the development of business ties with foreign countries while at the same time helping domestic manufacturers develop brand names and design products for targeted markets.[2]

Another group, RSEA, the Retired Servicemen Engineering Agency, which is under the ROC Executive Yuan's Vocational Assistance Commission for Retired Servicemen, does research on the investment climate of different countries. Where prospects look good, it sets up industrial parks in the area to house Taiwan-funded projects there. RSEA, which first ventured into the overseas market in 1965, also circulates information to prospective investors on a country's business climate—its laws, general treatment of foreign capital, and popular customs. For those who decide to go ahead, the organization helps with obtaining licenses, loans, legal and financial counseling, and hiring professionals and laborers. This kind of information is extremely valuable to ROC investors who, unlike those of the huge and multi-faceted Japanese and Korean conglomerates, tend to be individuals or small groups.[3]

The government's encouragement to look outward coincided with a deterioration of the domestic investment environment, due to labor shortages, rising labor costs, high land prices, increasing concerns with pollution, and the rapid appreciation of the NT dollar.[4] The combination of these factors led to a tremendous diversification of the ROC's investment and trade patterns. In 1987, government-approved outward investment, exclusive of that which was directed toward mainland China, grew by 80 percent, to US$80 million; by 1991, it was $1.65 billion.

According to official figures, the total amount invested abroad from 1986 through 1991 exceeded $4.52 billion, of which 43 percent ($1.93 billion) went to Asian countries, 33 percent ($1.47 billion) to the United States, and 16 percent ($716.8 million) to Europe. Even these large figures underrepresent the actual totals, since medium and small-sized businesses often do not bother to register their investments in Southeast Asia. The Ministry of Economic Affairs estimates that all outward investment from the ROC during the 1986-1991 period totalled $19 billion, which would rank Taiwan as the world's ninth largest supplier of foreign investment capital—an amazing achievement for a small island whose 20 million citizens had a per capita income slightly above $8,000 in 1991.[5]

By any reckoning, Taiwan has become the largest foreign supplier of investment in Vietnam, and is a primary source of investment for Malaysia, Thailand, the Philippines, and Indonesia. Taiwan's investments in Southeast Asia are concentrated in electronics and electrical appliances, textiles, chemicals, basic metals, and metal products.

ROC investors began entering mainland China in 1987, as soon as the government began allowing citizens to visit their relatives there. Prospective investors who did not have an actual relative became creative at inventing one, and hence many people availed themselves of the opportunity to assess the investment climate on the mainland. Despite various restrictions imposed by the ROC government, by mid-1992, 2,582 mainland investment projects with a total paid-in capital of $837 million

Table 4.1 Government Approved Outward Investment
(excluding figures for mainland China)

Year	Amount in U.S. Dollars	Percent Increase
1986	56.7 million	--
1987	102 million	80
1988	218 million	114
1989	930 million	327
1990	1.55 billion	67
1991	1.65 billion	6.5

Source: Table created from data adapted from "Outward Investment Alters Taiwan's Corporate Structure," *Business Taiwan* (Taipei), December 14, 1992, p. 3.

had been registered with the Ministry of Economic Affairs. The actual figures are apt to be much higher since, as with Southeast Asia, much of the investment is unregistered. Bicycle and footwear manufacturing, metal products, electrical appliances, and restaurants were the foci of Taiwan's investment in the mainland.

By contrast with Southeast Asia and mainland China, where ROC capitalists have invested mainly in manufacturing projects in local markets, the majority of those investing in the United States and Europe do so to gain marketing channels and access to market information and advanced technology. For example, the $335 million acquisition of America's Wyndham Foods[6] by the ROC's President Enterprises in 1990 has enabled President to market its products in the United States. The company was so pleased by the results that it subsequently bought Famous Amos cookies as well. Taiwan's manufacturers have also invested in 220 companies in Silicon Valley with a total capitalization of $690 million.

Inevitably, there were concerns that moving so much capital and plant facilities to so many places may result in a "hollowing out" of the island's manufacturing industry. For example, a survey done by the Ministry of Economic Affairs found that 16 percent of those who had invested abroad had either closed down or scaled back their operations within the ROC. In some cases, however, the offshore facilities are integrated with operations at home. For example, labor-intensive parts may be manufactured abroad and assembled into a finished product in Taiwan, thereby keeping production costs down and circumventing the problem of labor shortages at home. The sporting goods division of another enterprise has chosen to manufacture its lower-priced tennis rackets in Thailand, while its Taiwan plant specializes in rackets that sell for over $150.[7] While fears of hollowing out still remain, there is no question that this diversification of trade and investment abroad has vastly expanded the influence of Taiwan's economic power and related influence in world affairs.

Government leaders have also quietly pointed out to foreign countries that these countries' access to lucrative construction contracts in upgrading the island's infrastructure may be contingent on certain actions that the PRC would construe as recognition of the ROC's separate international status. For example, the German government has been reluctant to anger the PRC by selling frigates and submarines to the ROC, despite pressure from a severely depressed domestic shipbuilding industry.[8] When a reporter for a leading German magazine queried the deputy director-general of the Government Information Office on this matter, he replied that "while military deals are not such pleasant business, they do lead to other economic relations."[9]

Additionally, Taiwan has been extending its economic influence through efforts to build its capital city into an international financial center. The island is conveniently situated geographically, and its foreign trade and domestic markets are larger than the two neighboring financial centers, Hong Kong and Singapore. However, restrictions on the participation of foreign financial institutions and on the movement of capital into and out of the ROC posed real problems.

A number of steps were taken toward financial liberalization. In 1989, banking laws were amended to permit the branches of foreign banks to set up savings departments, which could then use these deposits to make long-term loans. Foreign bank branches were also allowed to set up trust departments, and to apply for licenses as securities underwriters, brokers, and dealers.

In 1990, the government formally incorporated the goal of developing Taipei into a regional financial center into its Six-Year National Development Plan. The Central Bank of China (CBC) subsequently took several steps consonant with that goal, including the creation of a foreign exchange (forex) call market[10] to provide a convenient mechanism for raising short-term forex funds by all participating members who are strapped for hard currency. Prior to this, most forex banks in the ROC had to rely on foreign financial services like the Singapore Interbank for the supply of such funds. Restrictions were eased on foreign financial institutions setting up operations, telecommunications were improved, and preparations were made to establish a gold market.

While much has been accomplished, more remains to be done. Goals include internationalizing the NT dollar, allowing nonresidents to open NT dollar accounts and relaxing regulations on their holding and use of the currency, constructing an international financial building, and improving telecommunication facilities.[11] An Overseas Chinese financial expert notes three major obstacles to developing Taipei into a major international financial center: government regulations that are both too stringent and too conservative; the lack of an adequate banking structure; and excess capital requirements.[12]

In addition, fear of reprisals from the PRC has made many foreign banks wary of taking advantage of the opportunities created by the ROC. However, when in February 1993, two Japanese banks, Bank of Tokyo and Tokai Bank, upgraded their representative offices to branch banks, others were considered likely to follow. Meanwhile, Chang Hwa Commercial Bank became the first Taiwan bank in over 40 years to open a branch in Tokyo.[13]

On the other hand, the establishment of the ROC Export-Import Bank in Mexico has been delayed by Mexican insistence that it use the title "Chinese Taipei" instead of ROC in the title.[14] A substantial number of Taiwanese investors has been attracted to Latin American countries; Mexico, with its *maquiladoras* or export processing zones and proximity to the U.S. market, was of particular interest. This existing interest was significantly enhanced by the announcement that a North American Free Trade Agreement, including the United States, Canada, and Mexico, would be established.

Another way in which the ROC has sought to deal with transnational trade issues is by joining the leading trade organization offering a dispute settlement mechanism to its members, the General Agreement on Tariffs and Trade (GATT). Founded at U.S. initiative after World War II in order to restructure the international economic order and promote world trade, the organization has grown to include ninety-nine members and covers about 90 percent of world trade. The ROC is the last major free market economy still excluded from it.[15]

For many years, mainland China's opposition to Taiwan's participation intimidated major members of GATT from supporting the ROC's entry, even though the PRC is not itself a member. The ROC had in the late 1980s adopted a pragmatic diplomacy that no longer refused to recognize countries that recognized the PRC, and that sought to join international organizations regardless of whether the PRC was a member. Bolstered by international revulsion against the Beijing government after its brutal suppression of unarmed demonstrators in June 1989, the ROC government formally filed to join GATT on January 1, 1990.[16]

In its application, the ROC government, applying as "the Separate Customs Territory of Taiwan, Penghu, Kinmen, and Matsu," stated its willingness to accept the obligations of a developed member country. This meant that the ROC would adhere to GATT's rules for liberal trade and open its market, thereby waiving the exceptional treatment, including permission for special tariff protection, import controls, and export subsidies accorded to less-developed GATT members.

The government agreed to slash tariffs, which had been as high as 14.1 percent as recently as 1971, from the existing 5.4 percent to 3.5 percent in order to be comparable with other industrially developed countries. Nominal rates for 94 percent of the imported items were bound to 30 percent or less; the other 6 percent, including some agricultural products, were bound to 50 percent or less. Other measures taken included:

- abolishing the import restrictions on certain goods from certain areas, including the ban on Japanese-made cars and the quota on Korean-made cars that conflict with GATT's principle of equal treatment of all members;
- ending the priority status given to American-made goods in government purchasing projects;
- facilitating foreign businesses' access to Taiwan's securities and insurance sectors;
- providing better protection for copyrights and intellectual property rights; and
- extending preferential tariffs to the nineteen GATT member countries that had not already received them.[17]

The GATT application also provided impetus for a massive privatization effort. Since GATT membership necessitated Taiwan's opening its domestic markets to foreign products, state firms would have to become more competitive.[18] Efforts began in 1989, when then-Premier Lee Huan directed the Council for Economic Planning and Development to set up a special task force to promote the privatization of public companies. It drew up regulations that were passed by the Legislative Yuan in June 1991, marking one of the most revolutionary changes in the country's economic policies in decades. Twenty-two state-run enterprises with $148 billion in assets and 69,000 employees were to transfer 51 percent of shares to the private sector through listing on the open market.

Since the budgets of public firms were subject to annual review by legislators who had the habit of making demands on them of behalf of special interest groups, free market mechanisms could be thwarted. Therefore, removing these budgets from legislative scrutiny was an important step toward increasing efficiency of management. It is also anticipated that privatization will result in a more competitive work force.

The large-scale opening of domestic markets also caused problems for non-state industries: car and home appliance manufacturing suffered from a flood of imported goods. The biggest problem, however, was in the agricultural sector, with the ROC cutting the nominal tariff for agricultural products from 26 percent to 18 percent in four years. The ROC faces talks with New Zealand, Australia, Canada, and several developing nations, all of which are major exporters of agricultural goods. It must bargain for enough transition time for the country's farmers to adjust to the changes. At present, there are about seventy domestic agricultural items under administrative protection.[19] The GATT subcommittee of the ROC's Agriculture Commission is considering a plan to gradually decontrol rice imports. At first, it would permit the import of just 3 percent of annual rice consumption, while levying a tariff of 200 percent. Should the quantity of rice imported exceed 3 percent, the tariff for that portion over the quota would be 300 percent.[20]

The ROC was granted observer status at GATT meetings in September 1992, thirty-three months after first applying. In a significant victory for government planners, the "Separate Customs Territory of Taiwan, Penghu, Kinmen and Matsu," received its status under Article 33, which applies to sovereign customs territories. Beijing had insisted that it be under Article 26, under which the colonies of Hong Kong and Macao had been admitted.[21] Screening on the ROC's application for full membership began on March 25, 1993, with twenty-five GATT members raising a total of 530 questions on the country's trade practices. These centered about import regulations, protection of local agriculture, intellectual property rights, and government purchases.[22] These questions notwithstanding, Taiwan, aka "the Customs Union," is expected to be admitted to full membership by the end of 1993.

The ROC also plans to seek observer status at the Organization for

Economic Cooperation and Development (OECD). A gradual approach is envisioned, in order to mitigate interference from Beijing. Taiwan will first seek to become an observer in the OECD's trade committee before applying for observer status in the organization as a whole and, eventually, full membership. The OECD, based in Paris, promotes the economic development and social welfare of its member states. The twenty-five-country organization comprises mainly developed countries, including the United States, Japan, Canada, Britain, France, Germany, and Italy. Taiwan became an OECD dialogue partner in 1989, along with other newly industrialized Asian countries such as South Korea, Singapore, Thailand, Malaysia, and the colony of Hong Kong.[23]

The same technique of gradual association, in part involving careful adherence to international norms on important transnational issues, is to be applied to the United Nations. Present plans are for the ROC to develop relations with specialized agencies related to the UN and hope to rejoin the body as a whole at a later date. Heretofore, the PRC has successfully blocked Taiwan's efforts to join any UN-related agencies, and has even prevented the UN from including any information about the nation in its official publications.[24]

Bilateral ties, formal and informal, are also used to solve trade issues. Despite the tougher intellectual property rights law discussed above, violations continue. In mid-February 1993, the International Intellectual Property Rights Union, a nongovernmental organization based in the United States, lodged a complaint for losses to American businesses of $669 million regarding movies, records, computer programs, and books. Further negotiations are expected between the Office of the U.S. Trade Representative and the Ministry of Economic Affairs.

As a demonstration of its resolve to stamp out commercial piracy, in May 1993 the government publicly destroyed over $40 million of illegal videotapes and pirated laser disks. In a ceremony presided over by the director-general of the Government Information Office (GIO), a steamroller drove over a 50-meter-long array of tapes and disks that the GIO had confiscated from factories, video-viewing parlors, and underground cable TV stations.[25] During the same month, in a first-of-its-kind case, three men were sentenced to terms ranging from two to four years for copying software packages created by America's Microsoft corporation.[26]

Further government efforts were thwarted by the legislative branch. The Legislative Yuan held up the conclusion of an ROC-U.S. intellectual property rights accord since 1987 due to disagreement over eight controversial articles including the banning of unauthorized imports of copyrighted products; implementing retroactive patent protection of U.S. pharmaceuticals and pesticides; and barring illegal television stations from airing unauthorized copyrighted videotapes.[27] Legislative action finally came in April 1993.

It should be noted that the intellectual property rights issue is complicated, and does not separate neatly into United States versus ROC. Sophisticated pirating operations have seriously affected Taiwan's movie industry. Internationally acclaimed director Stan Lai has complained that his *Peach Blossom Land*, which won a silver medal at the Tokyo Film Festival, appeared in top-quality copy soon after it opened in theaters. The island's filmmakers have learned that, ironically, the best way to meet expenses is through foreign sales.[28] Conversely, a U.S. company based in the Kaohsiung Export Processing Zone has warned American officials that a U.S. decision to impose intellectual property rights sanctions would force the company to close its operations. The sanctions' requirement for 100 percent verification on the origin of component parts would, company officials estimate, increase its production time by an economically unacceptable thirty to sixty days.[29]

In yet another facet of its efforts to deal with trade issues, Taiwan has signed cooperation agreements with arbitration groups from 126 countries with whom it maintains trade ties. The ROC's Commercial Arbitration Association is also consulting with Hungary, New Zealand, Panama, and several other Latin American states about signing similar agreements. Successful arbitration eliminates the need for time-consuming and costly court proceedings.[30]

Environmental Issues

In common with most developing countries, the ROC paid relatively little attention to environmental issues while concentrating on efforts to strengthen its economy. As a result, the beauty of "Ilha Formosa," the "beautiful island," deteriorated badly. Taipei and Kaohsiung, as the most heavily populated cities, suffered most. An English-language documentary film, *Global Dumping Ground*, used Taiwan and Mexico as its major examples.[31]

By the early 1980s, the environment had become the focus of much concern. The mayor of Kaohsiung made cleaning up that city's Love

River a priority. Having determined that he had succeeded, the mayor underscored his achievement (as well confirming his reputation for eccentricity) by jumping into the river wearing a business suit, and emerging with a live fish in hand.[32]

In August 1987, the government established an Environmental Protection Agency (EPA) to coordinate island-wide efforts to combat pollution. A system was established that required factories to file regular, detailed reports on their pollution levels, measured according to EPA guidelines. In 1990, it became mandatory for all new cars to be equipped with catalytic converters, with standards for limiting pollution from auto exhaust emission equal to the strictest elsewhere in the world. In 1991, stringent standards on motorcycle exhaust were also imposed, with manufacturers put on notice that failure to comply would mean that they would be closed down.

Under an operation known as Flying Eagle, the EPA dispatched helicopters to find belching smokestacks; the helicopters hovered overhead until ground inspectors arrived. A related helicopter effort, Operation Rambo, had EPA officials descending batman-like on factories in the middle of the night to check for unlawful emissions of waste water and to levy fines. Inspectors reported that, although some factories *were* equipped with advanced facilities for processing waste water, they had decided to save money by not using them. Other factories were discovered to have constructed secret drainage pipes, some of them several kilometers long, to empty untreated waste water into rivers or the ocean.[33]

There has also been a major educational effort to enlighten citizens on the causes and dangers of environmental problems. The EPA has sponsored seminars for groups from elementary school on up to discuss the need for conservation. For the youngest, it produced a cartoon special starring an extraterrestrial Environmental Protection Bunny who gave suggestions on how to keep Earth clean.[34]

More concrete measures were introduced as well. Color-coded recycling bins with winsome faces were placed on urban sidewalks: yellow for aluminum cans and other metals, green for glass, red for plastic waste, and blue for paper trash. For a time the bulky "aliens," as they were called, were quite popular, especially with children. However, legislators later argued that they took up too much space on already-crowded sidewalks. In addition, large cranes were needed to hoist them in order to remove their contents. In 1992, after three years in use, the aliens were removed.[35]

Both the government and private citizens groups have made admirable efforts to improve the environment of Taiwan's overcrowded and highly industrialized territory.[36] Nonetheless, serious evasion of environmental laws persists. Concerns have also been raised that scofflaws may react to tighter government regulations by moving problem industries to countries where environmental consciousness is less well-developed. One segment of *Global Dumping Ground* dealt with a battery-recycling operation in Guangdong that was leaching lead into the soil. It had been relocated from Taiwan to the mainland to escape ROC restrictions. The mainland has also been negotiating with the ROC over a site to bury its nuclear waste in the PRC.[37]

With regard to regional and international environmental management issues, the ROC has had problems stemming from the PRC's opposition to allow it to participate in regulatory groups. The island was not invited to participate in the UN's Earth Summit in Rio de Janeiro in June 1992, though the government informed representatives to the conference that the ROC also wished to help save the Earth. It proclaimed Taiwan's determination to follow the environmental conclusions reached there in setting worldwide industrial pollutant standards. In line with this decision, the Ministry of Economic Affairs established a task force on the effect of global warming to draft standards for control over carbon dioxide emissions and the use of chlorofluorocarbons.[38]

Similarly, Taiwan was not represented at the first meeting of the Northeast Asian environmental group, which met in Seoul in February 1993. Its five participating countries, South Korea,[39] Japan, China, Mongolia, and Russia, formally adopted recommendations to negotiate energy and air pollution questions, capacity-building, and ecosystem management. The Asian Development Bank has promised to finance three projects in these areas, and more assistance is expected from the World Bank. It seems unlikely that the ROC will be invited to attend the next meeting, to be held in Beijing in September 1993.[40]

Taiwan has likewise been excluded from membership in the 81-signatory Montreal Protocol. Its inability to become a Protocol member is worrisome, since local industries could lose as much as $8 billion beginning in 1996, due to provisions calling for international trade sanctions connected with Protocol decisions on phasing out the production of ozone-depleting chlorofluorocarbons (CFCs) by that year. Despite the PRC's efforts to prevent a Taiwanese delegation from attending, an eight-person delegation was able to attend and to present the Taiwanese position at the 1992 meeting of the Montreal Protocol.

Members produced data showing that the country had reduced its use of CFCs by 30 percent, and urged that Taiwan be given a fair chance and not be placed on a trade sanction list for purely political reasons. The delegation also rejected the PRC's contention that all statements and reports on Taiwan's progress on CFC reduction should be submitted under its supervision. This kind of reckoning would have allowed the protocol authorities to tally the island's achievements as part of the PRC's baleful record on CFC reduction.[41] This would, in effect, credit the PRC for the ROC's accomplishments.

A total ban on CFCs in 1996 would be difficult for the ROC's home appliance and information industries, which often use CFCs as coolants and cleaning solvents. It is generally believed that Taiwan's chances of entering the Protocol will be better after it is admitted to GATT. Meanwhile, the EPA has suggested bilateral talks with the contracting members of the Montreal protocol to lobby for their support.[42]

Taiwan has also attempted through bilateral negotiations to defuse two other potentially explosive conservation issues, those of driftnet fishing[43] and wildlife protection. The former is an adaptation of gillnetting, wherein fish are caught by the gills using wide-meshed, nylon nets. A driftnet is a chain of gillnets, forming a continuous curtain that can stretch for as long as 50 kilometers. Driftnet fishing was introduced to Taiwan from Japan in the late 1970s, in the midst of the second global oil crisis. Since driftnetting requires much less fuel than other methods of deep-sea fishing, it was enthusiastically accepted. Fishermen also discovered that they could catch four times the fish with one-third the crew. By 1990, driftnetting accounted for 24 percent of the value of the ROC's deep-sea fishing industry, with tuna and squid being the sought-after species.

By the late 1980s, however, suspicions that the indiscriminate nature of the operation was depleting marine resources began to be voiced. The net, which is made of nylon and practically invisible, ensnares all sealife large enough to get tangled in its web. Protests came from Alaska to Australia, and included several small Pacific states that, although maintaining diplomatic relations with the ROC, are being vigorously courted by the PRC. Earthtrust, a Hawaii-based environmental group, produced a wrenching film showing a wide variety of "innocent victim" marine life—dolphins, sharks, sea birds, turtles, and seals—struggling in vain to free themselves. In short, driftnet fishing quickly evolved into an explosive issue involving complex interactions of economics, environmentalism, politics, and diplomacy.

In late 1989, the United Nations passed resolution 44/225 calling for the immediate reduction of, and eventual complete ban on, driftnetting. During the same year, the major practitioners of the art, Japan, South Korea, and the ROC, signed a North Pacific driftnet fishing agreement. In the case of the ROC, this was accompanied by sharp domestic protest on legal and environmental impact issues. The former involved charges that ROC negotiators had signed a document that violated the country's sovereignty. Among other provisions, the agreement requires driftnetters to install automatic transponders that allow U.S. authorities to monitor the locations of ROC vessels to ensure that they do not enter into North Pacific salmon grounds. U.S. officials were also authorized to board Taiwanese vessels, along with ROC officials, to observe fishing operations. And fishing boats were required to return to Taiwan before selling their catch so that they could be inspected by ROC officials to see that they did not contain illegally caught salmon.

As for environmental impact, fishery associations in all three countries argued that there is no scientific evidence to support charges that driftnetting depletes fishing resources, since the nets catch only fish above a certain size. Moreover, modifications can be made to reduce the damage to non-targeted species. For example, the length of the nets could be diminished, mesh-size could be increased, and the depth at which the nets hang could be lowered in order to reduce the chances of catching sea birds and marine mammals. Also, the fishing season could be shortened. Expert testimony was produced to back the claim that the U.S. fleet of purse seiners[44] operating in the Pacific is far more destructive of marine resources than driftnetting. Statistics were presented indicating that each of the forty 1,000-ton purse seiners in this U.S. fleet catches from 5,000 to 8,000 tons of fish, or about 320,000 tons, annually, and that 8 percent of the catch weighs under fifteen kilos, many of them juveniles.

Such arguments had no noticeable impact on what had become a highly charged emotional issue.[45] Australia, New Zealand, and several Pacific island countries banned the ROC fleet from entering their ports for supplies, and established heavy fines ($150,000 in the case of the Cook Islands) for driftnetters who entered their Exclusive Economic Zones. In 1990, U.S. canned tuna factories began boycotting tuna that had been caught through driftnetting, causing drastic losses for fishermen.

In early 1991, the ROC gave up its efforts to save at least a portion of the driftnetting industry and formally accepted the UN resolution.

Then-Premier Hau Pei-tsun instructed the ROC's Council of Agriculture (COA) to eliminate driftnet fishing operations completely by the end of 1992. The COA adopted various phaseout measures, including buying up driftnetting vessels over 15 years of age in order to get them out of the water and offering low-interest loans of up to $189,000 to help owners of newer driftnet vessels retrofit their boats for other types of fishing activities. The retrofitted boats would also be eligible for funds to promote their products in the consumer market. Adjustments were made when boat-owners complained that the eligibility criteria for being granted the incentives were too strict, and the loan ceiling too low.[46] These efforts have succeeded in putting a significant portion of the driftnetting fleet out of business. However, "rogue" trawlers continue to ply the seas in sufficient numbers to embarrass the government internationally.[47] Other fishermen have simply reregistered their vessels, and continue driftnetting while flying the PRC or Honduran flag.

With regard to wildlife conservation, organized domestic concern stretches back more than twenty years. The most important legislation has been the Enforcement Rules of the National Park Law (1972), the Cultural Assets Preservation Law (1982), and the Wildlife Conservation Law (1989). Also, several areas have been given differing levels of protection by the COA, the Ministry of the Interior, the provincial Forestry Administration, and local government agencies. Within the island's four national parks (Kenting, Yangmingshan, Taroko, and Yushan), comprising 6 percent of the total area of Taiwan, it is illegal to hunt, fish, destroy vegetation, pollute the air or water, fell trees, or pick plants. Under the Cultural Assets Preservation Law, nine nature reserves have been established around the island to protect rare flora and fauna, with several more proposed.

Conservationists exercise growing influence. Plans for the New Southern Cross-Island Highway were drawn up in 1987, but construction has yet to start, despite considerable pressure from business interests. Environmentalists claim that the highway, which passes through the island's largest wildlife preserve at Tawu Mountain, would devastate local wildlife. They also mounted an impressive effort to save at least part of the Ssutsao wetlands, near Tainan City, from the Ministry of Economic Affairs' plan to build an industrial park there.[48]

Internationally, problems have arisen because of certain animals that are regarded as culinary delicacies or are important ingredients of traditional Chinese medicines. Bowing to foreign pressure on an endangered species, the COA in 1987 banned the import and consumption of tiger meat. And, in 1989, after an international outcry over the killing of dolphins by ROC fishermen on the Penghu Islands, the government prohibited the practice.

The most recent issue has involved the import of rhinoceros horns. Practitioners of traditional medicine believe that the powdered horns are excellent treatment for fevers. Trying for a compromise between international pressure for a ban and domestic consumers who wanted continued access, the government for a time allowed the use of powdered rhino horn, but in limited amounts. Patients were required to present a legal medical prescription, which was to be given only in cases of serious illness. This was not sufficient to appease international conservation groups: in November 1992, three environmental groups[49] alleged that the ROC government was turning a blind eye to the "rampant import of rhino horn," and called for a wide-ranging boycott of "Made in Taiwan" products.[50]

The COA, nettled that so little credit had been given to its efforts to protect the rhinoceros, contended that the ROC was the sole Asian country to have taken active conservation measures to protect endangered species. It noted that the COA had destroyed 67 kilograms of rhino horns seized in crackdowns on smugglers since 1990 and that, after being alerted by a South African endangered species protection organization, the COA had assisted in the arrest of a local businessman who was involved in the case.[51] The environmental agency whose investigative report had formed the basis for the three other agencies' charges, the British-based Trade Record Analysis of Flora and Fauna in Commerce (TRAFFIC) Foundation, backed the COA's contention and pointed out that Taiwan was its only Asian member.[52]

Nonetheless, then-Premier Hau Pei-tsun issued an overall ban on the use of powdered rhinoceros horn in medical prescriptions, and the COA announced that it would stop issuing permits for importing and trading the horns. The COA also stated its intention to revise the Wildlife Conservation Law to make it more stringent: fines would be increased from a maximum of $10,000 NT to between five and ten times the market value of the banned goods.[53]

Where there is demand, however, there will be suppliers, laws notwithstanding. Barely three weeks later, police confiscated forty-three crates containing over 2,000 pounds of rhino horns and deer antlers at Chiang Kai-shek International Airport. The contraband cargo, worth millions of dollars on the black market, had been shipped from New Zealand via Hong Kong and Manila in crates labeled "glass products," which are exempt from inspection. Two main suspects and six others were charged with violating ROC laws on smuggling, forgery, quarantine, and trade in endangered species.[54] More such cases can be anticipated.

Meanwhile, the government has begun an educational effort. In mid-December 1992, an island-wide campaign was launched to promote awareness of wildlife conservation. Citizens were asked to sign cards endorsing the campaign's slogan "not to hunt, not to buy, not to eat, and not to keep wild animals." Cards and posters featured drawings of appealingly anthropomorphized members of endangered species, including a tiger and a rhinoceros.[55] The ROC has been trying to join the UN-administered Convention on International Trade in Endangered Species, better known as CITES, but action on its application was suspended after complaints from the PRC.[56]

Narcotics

Cognizant of the deleterious effect that opium had on nineteenth century China, the ROC government has had strict anti-narcotics laws from its inception. Nonetheless, the incidence of drug use seems to have increased in recent years. According to the investigation bureau of the Ministry of Justice's (MJIB) 1992 report on narcotics suppression, 988 cases involving 1,340 individuals were prosecuted in 1988, while 3,205 cases involving 4,991 individuals were prosecuted in 1991.[57] With the exception of two marijuana plantations that were discovered on the island, drugs are smuggled in rather than indigenous. Previously most opium came from Thailand via Hong Kong or Singapore, and marijuana from the Philippines. Recently, the mainland has become a major source of heroin. The incidence of cocaine use has been very small, though planners fear that this may change as closer trade ties are established with Latin American states.

Methods used by smugglers include sending packages into Taiwan through the mail or on fishing boats; concealing them in luggage, flower vases, and cans of cleaning detergents; and placing drugs in condoms, which are then swallowed or concealed in the smuggler's anus. A particularly ingenious method that was discovered in 1990 involved Thai heroin being placed inside the iron pipes of coconut shelling machines, and then welding the pipes shut. The heroin could neither be seen nor smelled, and would not have been discovered had not customs authorities received a tip from someone with inside information. MJIB puts the success rate of such smuggling techniques as very high, and the amount of drugs smuggled in through them as large.

ROC authorities have sought multinational cooperation to stop global drug trading. The MJIB exchanges narcotics-related information with a number of countries, including the United States, Thailand, Japan, Australia, South Korea, and Hong Kong. A number of cases have been solved in this way. For example, in 1992, it enabled the MJIB to arrest a British male, Malcolm Hughes, who was attempting to smuggle seven kilos of heroin into Taiwan from Thailand. The MJIB subsequently provided the U.S. Drug Enforcement Agency and the Royal Thai police with information, based on interrogation of Hughes and investigation of his case, that led to the drug trafficking ring he was operating on behalf of. In October 1993, the MJIB will host a seminar in Taipei to discuss data base exchanges and other methods of preventing drug smuggling, Representatives of eighteen countries will attend.[58]

Here again, progress in dealing with drug-related issues has been inhibited by the irregular diplomatic relations imposed on the ROC. The ROC has been able to make creative use of these problems to obtain more explicit international agreements. For example, when in June 1991, American officials uncovered the largest drug ring in U.S. history, five ROC citizens were among those arrested. However, American courts found it difficult to press the suit against the drug traffickers without the testimony of ROC customs personnel and MJIB officials. The U.S. request for testimony was rejected by the ROC, since the countries lacked a legal basis for regulating cooperation of this sort. Thus prodded, the American side agreed to draw up legislation to provide the legal basis for cooperation. In February 1993, such an agreement went into effect. The two sides agreed that law-enforcement officials would be invited to testify before courts of each other's country, and provided a framework for cooperative investigation and prosecution.[59] For similar reasons, work is also proceeding on a bilateral extradition treaty.[60]

The ROC was formerly a member of Interpol. The mainland announced that it would not join unless Taiwan was considered part of its delegation, which the island's government would not agree to. The position of the ROC within Interpol is somewhat difficult to define: it did not withdraw, but does not attend meetings. Yet the country continues to avail itself of Interpol's services. One observer characterizes this as using Interpol as a mailbox to pass messages back and forth.[61] Recently, there have been cooperative efforts between ROC and PRC law-enforcement authorities. Following the hijacking of a China Southern Airlines plane to Taiwan in April 1993, mainland Minister of Public Security Tao Siju announced that contacts had been made with the island's police to ascertain the details of the crime and arrange for repatriation.[62]

Human Rights and Democracy

The ROC, as a founding member of the United Nations, signed the Universal Declaration of Human Rights. Its national human rights organization was for many years headed by the late Dr. Han Lih-wu, an eminent statesman whose previous positions included minister of education, presidential adviser, and ambassador to several countries. Among his other activities, Dr. Han acceded to anti-Marcos Filipino dissident Benigno Aquino's request for help to allow him to return to Manila.

The major international focus of ROC international human rights and democracy efforts was until recently the communist countries, through the World Anti-Communist League (WACL) and Asian Peoples Anti-Communist League (APACL). A series of publications and yearly seminars drew attention to human rights violations and suggested redress. After the collapse of communist governments in Eastern Europe and the former Soviet Union, generous donations of food, medicine, and technical aid were granted to their successor states to ease the difficulties of adjusting to the post-communist era. World Vision of Taiwan, a local foundation established in 1964 to help the needy in poverty-stricken counties, carries out various humanitarian relief projects. In April 1993, it conducted a thirty-hour "Hunger Camp" in the plaza in front of Chiang Kai-shek Memorial Hall. Participants were asked to contribute the money they would have spent on meals to feed the needy; organizers raised about $4 million for their cause.[63]

Since the ROC is no longer a member of the United Nations, it has not been able to participate in UN-sponsored human rights meetings. It did not attend a meeting of forty-five Asian countries that was held in Bangkok March 29-April 2, 1993, to prepare for the second world conference on human rights. Nor was the ROC invited to attend the world in Vienna in June 1993.[64]

Domestically, Taiwan has undertaken impressive efforts to democratize and improve its own human rights situation. During the 1980s, a multiparty system took form; the emergency decrees ("martial law") were lifted; and various restrictions on the press and media were abolished. The elections for the Legislative Yuan held on December 19, 1992, were the first in over forty years in which all seats were contested.

In 1992 also the government cut its namelist of dissidents barred from returning to Taiwan from 280 to two.[65] These and other efforts received high marks in the U.S. State Department's Country Reports on Human Rights Practices for 1992.

However, taking note of that report, one of the island's independent newspapers pointed out three areas for improvement. First, people of mainland origin continue to exercise disproportionate influence at the highest level of party, government, and the military. Second, party and government are not clearly differentiated financially: Kuomintang (KMT)-owned enterprises receive public funds from administrative and security organizations. Finally, the KMT exercises undue influence over the electronic media.[66]

Conclusion

The ROC has been a responsible member of the global community. It has been responsive to international and individual-country concerns regarding trade issues, the environment, narcotics suppression, and democracy and human rights. Concerns remain in certain areas, most prominently on the issue of protection of intellectual property rights. The newly elected Legislative Yuan contains a much greater number of members who have been assertive with regard to independence and sovereignty issues than has heretofore been the case. While it is too early to assess the effect that this mindset will have on the solution of existing problems, it would appear that the new Legislative Yuan will be less compliant than its predecessors.[67]

The ROC has been significantly hindered in its effort to solve outstanding issues by the PRC's attempts to isolate it from normal diplomatic interchanges. The steps its government has undertaken to work around such hindrances are both creative and praiseworthy, but do not obviate the need for restoration of full diplomatic relations.[68]

Commentary

Fu-mei Chang Chen

The United States is Taiwan's most important trading partner. Under constant pressure to mitigate the large trade deficit in Taiwan's favor, the New Taiwan (NT) dollar's exchange rate with the U.S. dollar has rapidly appreciated, from 36:1 in mid-1986 to 25:1 in 1990. After holding steady at that rate for a couple of years, the NT dollar began to depreciate in July 1992, moving downward by 6 percent within eight months from 24.5:1 to 26:1. Ordinarily, such a change would stimulate Taiwan's export industries, but the even greater depreciation of the PRC's *renminbi* may have offset some of those potential gains. Now at the top of the U.S. priority watchlist, set up under Section 301 of the 1988 Trade Act, Taiwan is under the pall of threatened U.S. trade retaliation. If sanctions are imposed, Taiwan's export industries, particularly electronics, will be the hardest hit.[69]

Last year, Taiwan barely avoided Section 301 sanctions, but this year it may not be able to successfully defend itself. The International Intellectual Property Rights Union has charged Taiwanese copyright infringement with costing American businesses $669 million in losses. This serious problem, it would appear, is in part rooted in ROC government policy. For example, even today Taiwan's three television networks are entirely owned by the government and the KMT. Until the airwaves are opened to legal competition, illegal television stations will continue to air unauthorized copies of videotapes and movies.

The KMT regime faces another, institutional challenge. Since the December 1992 election awarded one-third of the seats in the Legislative Yuan to the opposition party and most of the newly elected KMT members have refused to toe the party line as they did earlier, the Legislative Yuan has become omnipotent and now has a mind of its own. The executive branch has found it difficult to act swiftly and decisively when negotiating with foreign governments, because it can no longer dictate the legislators' decisions. The newly formed ROC cabinet and the Legislative Yuan will have to learn to compromise and cooperate with each other if the government is to respond adequately to crises.

The ROC will also need to prepare for its upcoming review by the General Agreement on Tariffs and Trade (GATT) accession board. The next few months will be crucial.[70] The ROC was a charter member of GATT when that consortium was organized in 1948, but withdrew from it in 1950. After the PRC applied for admission to GATT in July 1986 and was granted observer status, the ROC sought to do likewise but was thwarted by PRC opposition. Because most GATT member states recognized the PRC, Taiwan could do very little until after the June 4, 1989, events in Tiananmen Square. When the ROC applied for accession in early 1990, the PRC's objection was somewhat muted by the U.S. Congress's effort to condition renewal of China's most-favored-nation (MFN) status on its willingness to allow Taiwan to apply for entry into the GATT.[71]

As Dreyer correctly notes, when the ROC was granted observer status in late September 1992, it was under Article 33, which deals with sovereign custom territories, not under Article 26, which applies to colonies such as Hong Kong and Macao, as the PRC had insisted. The ROC was officially listed as the "Separate Customs Territory of Taiwan, Penghu, Kinmen, and Matsu" (TPKM), but GATT yielded to intense PRC pressure in agreeing that the legal name TPKM would never be displayed or used. Instead, Taiwan will generally be referred to as "Chinese Taipei" (side by side with "Chinese Hong Kong" and "Chinese Macao"), with the PRC called simply "China." A special announcement by the council chairman acknowledged only one China, and many states asserted that the council should handle the PRC's accession ahead of Taiwan's. Mr. Wood, a GATT spokesman, declared that, due to its parallel with Hong Kong and Macao, Taiwan could establish only an Economic and Trade Office, not a Permanent Mission. These and other condescending remarks stirred up a public uproar in Taipei that dampened the excitement generated by the long-awaited initial approval. Some officials at the Ministry of Foreign Affairs also rebuked their counterparts at the Ministry of Economic Affairs (which was in charge of negotiations) for "leaping into a blind alley."[72] The two ministries apparently have not done a great job in coordinating their efforts.

The GATT application process and pressure by the opposition party, however, provided an impetus to privatize state-owned businesses. In 1953 the government had adopted privatization regulations as a means of facilitating land reform; in June 1991 those regulations were extensively revised by the Legislative Yuan. Even under the new rules, however, talk of "Transferring" state-owned enterprises to the private sector is a bit misleading, since the government intends in all cases to keep a 40 percent stake in them and remain the largest shareholder, thus retaining effective control of such firms. On paper, those companies will be private enterprises and thus exempt from parliamentary scrutiny; in reality, they will remain under government control. The inefficiency and waste so characteristic of public enterprises can hardly be eliminated when effective control remains in the same hands. The expedient of listing 51 percent of the stock of some twenty-two state-run enterprises often amounted to little more than clever scheme for raising capital from the uninformed public.[73]

In yet another effort to appease the U.S. government, in June 1992 a revised copyright law went into effect. The Taiwanese publishing industry immediately made the necessary adjustments: *China Times* signed deals with the *Los Angeles Times* and the magazines *Time* and *U.S. News and World Report*; and *United Daily* obtained authorization from the *New York Times* the *Washington Post*, *Newsweek*, and the *Star*. (In one case, the price of such permission climbed to $10,000 from the $2,500 negotiated a year earlier.) The notorious past practice of freeloading of articles and photos has been eradicated, but only with respect to English-language press. Japanese, French, and German publications have become Taiwan's favorite sources for pirated information.[74]

ROC investors had begun to pour money into mainland China long before 1987, when the government lifted its official ban on visits to the mainland. Businessmen were always far ahead of government policy, which had to take into consideration the political effects of contacts across the Taiwan Strait. About four or five years ago, the government actively encouraged Taiwanese businessmen to invest in Southeast Asia, but for various reasons the result was not satisfactory. Understandably, ROC entrepreneurs preferred mainland China, where they felt at ease and costs were low. Despite the ROC's exhortation to "leave the roots in Taiwan" (*ken liu T'ai-wan*) in order to prevent a "hollowing out" of the island's manufacturing sector, over the past few years there has been an apparent exodus of businesses headed primarily for the PRC, and emigration has, on average, exceeded an estimated 50,000 persons per year.[75]

The Taiwanese have almost always preferred to emigrate to the United States. Since 1982, Taiwan has enjoyed its own quota of 20,000 people per year, equal to that granted to the PRC. The U.S. government has also tried to attract new immigrants through a special investment arrangement, but so far there have been few Taiwanese takers. In the past decade, the presence of Taiwanese businesses has begun to make itself felt in this country. The investment of Y. C. Wang's Formosa Plastics in Texas is a good example. In 1990, Taiwan's computer kingpin, Acer, bought Silicon Valley's Altos for $97 million and tapped a top Chinese-American manager from IBM, Len Ying-wu Liu, to run it. Unfortunately, heavy losses forced Liu's resignation in April 1992. Taiwan's President Enterprises was a bit luckier in its American adventure: in acquiring Amos, the firm gained control of Girl Scout cookies, an institution as American as apple pie.[76]

Soon after General Hau Pei-ts'un became premier in 1990, he made the Six-Year Development Plan his pet project, despite criticism from three leading economics professors at National Taiwan University. Their opinion that the plan was poorly formulated was endorsed by another forty-eight economists. Although the government gave assurances that the national growth rate of 7 percent would continue and that per capita income would double in those six years,[77] the plan's proposed expenditure of an astronomical $300 billion frightened most people. The massive projects had indeed generated a great deal of interest in foreign countries eager to participate in the plan's bounty, but its future was called into question in December 1990 when Premier Hau abruptly announced that the Taipei I'lan Freeway had been cancelled. Hau was apparently infuriated by the environment-minded citizens of I'lan County who steadfastly refused to allow Formosa Plastics to build its Petroleum Cracking Plant No. 6 there, and wanted to teach them a lesson, so to speak.[78] Now that Premier Hau has stepped down, a reappraisal of the plan is probably in order.

Environmental Issues

Taiwan's economic miracle is internationally renowned. Not so well publicized, however, is the heavy price the people of Taiwan have paid—irreversible damage to the environment. In a show of concern for the environment, the Department of Health's Environmental Protection Bureau was elevated to ministerial rank in August 1987. In June 1991, Jaw Shau-kong, an unprecedentedly popular legislator from the Taipei district, was drafted as EPA chief, but the accumulated problems of 40 years were simply too mammoth for anyone to solve. A three-year program was instituted to teach people to sort their trash into three "aliens," color-coded recycling bins, but that effort failed when people learned to their disgust that, in the end, all trash was lumped indiscriminately. Alas, no more "aliens."

In 1991-92 the EPA spent eleven months surveying pollution problems among the top 500 industrial companies. The first scorecard, issued in August 1992, gave low marks to 57 percent of the 372 factories investigated, even when applying standards less stringent than those in the West.[79] Clearly, Taiwan has made only the most meager progress toward heightening environmental awareness and mobilizing the determination to ameliorate pollution.

The American environmentalist Sam LaBudde of the Earth Island Institute and Dr. Ros Reeve of the British Environmental Investigation Agency have recently charged that Taiwan allows rhinoceros horn to be imported. Another case of Taiwan's failure to protect endangered species surfaced last year. Half of the remaining 400 of the black-faced spoonbill, a migratory bird, fly from North Korea to Taiwan for the winter. Christopher Imboden, chairman of the International Council for Bird Protection, travelled to Tainan County to observe them and was appalled to find that twenty four birds had been injured by local hunters.[80] It has also been reported that "tiger whip" soup is sold for $325 per bowl in Taichung, The shop's owner indicated that the meat came from mainland China.[81]

On February 24, 1993, four animal-protection organizations held a press conference in Washington, D.C. to denounce the ROC for failing to protect wildlife. Claiming a combined membership of 16 million people, they pledged to boycott Taiwanese merchandise worldwide and threatened to campaign to block the ROC's accession to the GATT if Taiwan refuses to heed their protest.[82]

In June 1992, Mr. Jaw led a delegation of parliamentarians to the UN's Earth Summit in Rio de Janeiro. Several opposition leaders and environmental groups participated in their own delegation. Although the ROC is not a signatory to the 1987 Montreal Protocol, it pledged to control the use of ozone-depleting chlorofluorocarbons (CFCs) and, indeed, used 30 percent less in 1992 than the 10, 159 tons it consumed in 1986. Formosa Plastics, which had the capacity to produce 20,000 tons of CFCs, produced only 3,500 tons and imported another 3,500 tons. The ROC government hopes to reduce consumption by another 80 percent and eliminate CFC use altogether by the end of 1995.[83] Last November, another ROC delegation attended the fourth annual meeting of the Montreal Protocol in Copenhagen as an observer. Although the ROC intends to reduce and eventually eliminate CFC use, that program should be closely monitored by environmental organizations to ensure its enforcement. Too much—NT$200 billion—is at stake. Two Taiwanese-American scholars who have followed this issue carefully have informed me that smuggling of CFCs from Third World countries into Taiwan is quite serious.[84] Cheating and false product labels are not uncommon, either. If only for the sake of controlling CFCs, Taiwan should sign the 1987 Montreal Protocol and eventually join the UN.[85]

Narcotics

According to one legislator's report, in the first half of 1992 alone the Ministry of Justice's Investigation Bureau seized 230 kilos of heroin, double the total confiscated in the preceding six years. The 1991 statistics published by the Ministry of Justice in April 1992 show a net increase of 50 percent over the previous year in the number of narcotics cases prosecuted. Amphetamine smoking is an even more serious problem, with prosecutions jumping by 722 percent between 1990 and 1991.

A Bureau member was recently charged for his involvement with a group of physicians in the illegal sale and distribution of narcotics. Just two weeks before that case came to light, another two Bureau members and a businessman were accused of raping a secretary in a restaurant. These two scandals have seriously embarrassed the Bureau, and its chief may be cashiered for them. With money abundant in Taiwan, drug abuse is on the rise.[86]

Notes

1. *Ching-chi jih-pao* (Economy Daily) (Taipei), June 14, 1992, p. 1.

2. "Cultivating Comparative Advantage," *Free China Review* (hereafter, FCR) (Taipei), May 1991, p. 1.

3. Jennifer Chiu, "RSEA Park Safe Haven for Investors in Indonesia," *Free China Journal* (hereafter, FCJ) (Taipei), November 12, 1992, p. 5.

4. Cheng Chu-yuan, "A New Financial Power in the East," FCJ, November 20, 1992, p. 7.

5. As of mid-1993, per capita income was over $12,000.

6. Wyndham's most famous product is Girl Scout Cookies, which can fairly be described as being as American as apple pie, ROC ownership notwithstanding.

7. Philip Liu, "Investing in the Neighborhood," FCR, February 1993, p. 34.

8. *Central News Agency* (hereafter, CNA) (Taipei), February 13, 1993. See discussion of this issue in Harlan Jencks's chapter.

9. CNA, March 2, 1993, quoting Deputy Director-General T. H. Yeh.

10. The market for loans repayable on demand.

11. Philip Liu, "Opening the Door to Competition," FCR, September 1991, p. 36.

12. Dr. Raymond Chiang, financial consultant, personal interview, March 29, 1993.

13. Julia Leung, "Beijing Remains Silent as Japanese Banks Move Into Taiwan," *Asian Wall Street Journal Weekly* (New York), February 15, 1993, p. 7.

14. "Export-Import Bank Office Opening in Mexico Delayed," FCJ, February 5, 1993, p. 7.

15. The ROC joined GATT early in its existence, but subsequently withdrew because it did not wish to comply with certain regulations. When, some years later, the ROC sought to rejoin the organization, its application was blocked by pressure from the PRC. See also discussion in chapters by Samuel Kim and Ralph Clough.

16. The application process actually began in December 1987, when an interagency panel was set up in Taipei to plan the adjustments in economic structure that would be necessary for GATT membership, and to seek the support of GATT members.

17. Philip Liu, "Knocking At GATT's Door," FCR, October 1990, p. 40.

18. Allen Pun and Jennifer Chiu, "ROC Privatization Revs Its Motor," FCJ, January 1, 1993, p. 5.

19. Allen Pun, "GATT Entry Means Adjustments: Agricultural Sector Will Take Brunt of Trade Liberalization," FCJ, November 10, 1992, p. 2.

20. Ch'en Hsiu-lan, "Gradual Decontrol of Rice Imports Planned," *Chung-kuo shih-pao* (China Times) (Taipei), February 15, 1993, p. 1.

21. "GATT Observer Status Today, Member Tomorrow," FCJ, December 25, 1992, p. 8.

22. CNA, February 8, 1993.

23. CNA, October 28, 1992.

24. CNA, September 15, 1992. See Samuel Kim's chapter for a full discussion of Taiwan's efforts to enter international organizations.

25. CNA, May 11, 1993.

26. CNA, May 12, 1993.

27. Tammy Peng, "US Trade Sanctions Loom Over ROC," FCJ, February 16, 1993, p. 2; "US Group Cites Taiwan on Copyright Violations," China Broadcasting Corporation News Network (Taipei), February 13, 1993, in U.S. National Technical Information Service, *Foreign Broadcast Information Service: China* (FBIS-CHI), February 16, 1993, p. 67.

28. Laurie Underwood, "Survival of the Fittest," FCR, February 1993, pp. 36-40.

29. Author's conversation with Mr. Kenneth Allen of the USA-ROC Economic Council, March 31, 1993.

30. "Government To Seek Cooperation With Arbitration Groups," CNA, December 1, 1992.

31. Produced by Bill Moyers and the Center for Investigative Reporting, the film was shown on U.S. public television in 1990. Although still well worth seeing, much of the material on Taiwan is now outdated.

32. It is strongly suspected that Su Nan-ch'eng had concealed the fish in his pocket before jumping in. From a publicity point of view, however, the mayor had made his point: fish could again live in the river.

33. Philip Liu, "Getting Serious About Enforcement," FCR, May 1991, pp. 47-48.

34. David W. Chen, "Conservation For Kids," FCR, October 1990, pp. 46-53.

35. Rachel F. F. Lee, "`Igloo' Program Proves Unsuitable," FCJ, December 18, 1992, p. 4.

36. See chapter 14, "Environmental Protection," in *The Republic of China Yearbook, 1993*, (Taipei: Government Information Office), for a summary of recent efforts.

37. George Wehrfritz, "Hazardous Business: China Offers Taiwan Site for Taiwan Nuclear Waste," *Far Eastern Economic Review* (hereafter, FEER) (Hong Kong), March 25, 1993, p. 22.

38. Rachel F. F. Lee, "Taiwan Fortifying Environmental Protection," FCJ, June 5, 1992, p. 8.

39. North Korea was invited, but turned down the invitation.

40. *Yonhap* (Seoul), February 11, 1993, in U.S. National Technical Information Service (NTIS), *Foreign Broadcast Information Service: East Asia* (hereafter, FBIS-EAS), February 11, 1993, p. 1.

41. CNA, December 2, 1992.

42. Susan Yu, "ROC Delegation Reaches All Goals At CFC Meeting," FCJ, December 1, 1992, p. 2.

43. Philip Liu's, "The Rise and Fall Of Driftnet Fishing," FCR, July 1992, pp. 18-21, provides a superb summary of the complexities of this topic.

44. Purse seining is an alternate method of fishery involving towing and setting a large net, which can then be closed shut like a drawstring purse around the catch.

45. This writer visited fifteen states in Micronesia and the South Pacific during 1988 and 1989, in the course of two United States Information Agency-sponsored speaking tours. She found it a major topic of conversation in all states, and occasionally the *only* topic of conversation. Most interviewees had no knowledge of any arguments in favor of driftnetting, repeatedly stating that the "wall of death" represented an exploitative attack by outsiders on their way of life.

46. "Drift-Nets Face Extinction; ROC Complies With UN Call," FCJ, November 12, 1992, p. 4; Rachel F. F. Lee, "ROC Emphasizes Resolve To Meet Ban On Drift-Nets," FCJ, December 15, 1992, p. 4.

47. George Wehrfritz, "Gone Fishing: Rogue Trawlers May Be Dodging Official Driftnet Ban," FEER, February 25, 1993, p. 24; Julian Baum, "Nets Across the Strait: Driftnet Fishing Thrives Under Chinese Flag," FEER, July 8, 1993, pp. 22-23; CNA, July 15, 1993.

48. Laurie Underwood, "Conservation: On A Wing And A Prayer," FCR, May 1992, pp. 56-73, details these efforts with special emphasis on wild birds.

49. The Environmental Investigation Agency, Tusk Force, and the Shepherd's Foundation.

50. "Rhino Horn Charge Groundless," FCJ, November 20, 1992, p. 6.

51. CNA, November 18, 1992.

52. CNA, November 19, 1992.

53. CNA, November 19, 1992.

54. Diana Lin, "Police Nab Smugglers of Rhino Horns," FCJ, December 15, 1992, p. 4.

55. Diana Lin, "Wildlife Protection In Public Eye," FCJ, December 18, 1992, p. 4.

56. Rachel F. F. Lee, "Environmentalists Want Boycott: Official Says Threat `Ignores' Wildlife Protection Efforts," FCJ, March 2, 1993, p. 4.

57. Investigation Bureau, Ministry of Justice, Republic of China, *Report On Narcotics Suppression in the Republic of China: 1992*, p. 4. Unless otherwise noted, other data in this section are also derived from this report. The author is indebted to Mr. Leo Lee of the Coordination Council for North American Affairs in Washington, DC, for making this document available to her.

58. Ms. Cathy Chen, Coordination Council for North American Affairs, Washington DC, personal conversation, March 15, 1993.

59. CNA, February 26, 1993.

60. Information provided by Dr. Robert Sutter, director, Government Affairs Division, U.S. Library of Congress.

61. Dr. Ralph Clough of the School of Advanced International Studies, Johns Hopkins University.

62. *Xinhua* (Beijing), April 8, 1993, in FBIS-CHI, April 8, 1993, p. 14.

63. Diana Lin, "Local Fast To Help Feed Famished of the World," FCJ, February 23, 1993, p. 4.

64. "Bangkok To Host Preparatory Human Rights Meeting," *Bangkok Post*, February 24, 1993, p. 2, in FBIS-EAS, February 25, 1993, p. 2.

65. CNA, October 31, 1992.

66. Ts'ai Ts'ang-po, "Taiwan's Human Rights: Structural Problems Still Exist," *Tzu-li wan-pao* (Independent Evening News) (Taipei), January 15, 1993, p. 4.

67. Early indications that this may be the case can be found in Julian Baum's "No Way To Treat An Ally: US Pressures On Trade Irk Taipei Leaders," FEER, April 8, 1993, p. 21.

68. See full discussion of the PRC-Taiwan competition for international recognition in the chapter by Samuel Kim.

69. *Ts'ai-hsü yüeh-k'an* (Wealth Magazine), vol. 132, March 1, 1993, pp. 362-65 and 424-27.

70. *T'ien-hsia tsa-chih* (Commonwealth), no. 141, February 1, 1993, pp. 58-62 and 64-66; *Hsin hsin-wen* (The Journalist), no. 314, March 14-20, 1993.

71. *Kuo-chi jih-pao* (International Daily) (San Francisco, CA), July 17, 1990.

72. *Tzu-li chou-k'an* (Independence Weekly Post), no. 175, October 19, 1992, pp. 1-2.

73. Ch'en Shih-meng, et al., *Chieh-kou tang-kuo tzu-pen chu-i: lun T'ai-wan kuan-ying shih-yeh chih min-ying hua* (Disintegrating KMT-State Capitalism: A Closer Look at Privatizing Taiwan's State- and Party-Owned Enterprises), (Taipei: Ch'eng-she Taipei Society, 1991), pp. 217-40.

74. *Yüan-chien tsa-chih* (Global Views Monthly), no. 76, October 1992, pp. 112-15.

75. *Ts'ai-hsün yüeh-k'an*, vol. 127, October 1992, pp. 142-49.

76. *T'ien-hsia tsa-chih*, no. 139, December 1, 1992, pp. 28-33.

77. *Hsin hsin-wen*, no. 212, April 1-7, 1991, pp. 56-59; Ch'ü Hai-yüan, et al., in Lin Cheng-hung, ed., *Kai-ke ti hu-sheng* (Voices of Reform), (Taipei: Yün-ch'en wen-hua Publishing Co., 1991), pp. 424-28.

78. *Kai-ke ti hu-sheng*, pp. 449-52.

79. *T'ien-hsia tsa-chih*, no. 136 (September 1, 1992), pp. 172-178.

80. *Lin-ho-pao* (United Daily), November 30, 1992, p. 3.

81. *T'ai-wen t'ung-hsün* (Tai-Bun Thong-Sin) [Taiwanese Writing Forum], no. 18, March 1, 1993, p. 4.

82. The four organizations are: Earth Island Institute, Animal Welfare Institute, Environmental Investigation Agency, and the Humane Society of the United States/Humane Society International. *Tzu-li-chou-k'an*, no. 196, March 5, 1993, p. 10. I am grateful to Mr. Paul Ts'ai, a Washington-based reporter for the *Independence Post*, for providing me with the press release.

83. "Neng-teng chiu-teng, neng-chuan chiu-chuan?" *T'ien-hsia tsa-chih*, no. 136, September 1, 1993, pp. 90-93. This article describes the general attitude of Taiwanese CFC users as one of "wait until the last minute and make money while you can."

84. The two environmental specialists I consulted are Dr. Wu-nan Lin of the North America Taiwanese Professor's Association and Dr. James Chieh-mu Lee of Washington, DC. Dr. Lee has just published a book, *Huan-wo tzu-jan* (Return Nature to Us) (Taipei: Ch'ien-wei (Vanguard) Publishing House, 1992).

85. See *Li-fa-yüan king-pao* (Legislative Yüan Gazette), vol. 81, no. 68, pp. 95-97, October 28, 1992, for interpellation be legislator Liu Kuo-chao.

86. *Hsin hsin-wen*, no. 134, March 14-20, 1993, pp. 63-64.

5

Taiwan and the International System: The Challenge of Legitimation

Samuel S. Kim

China is willing to develop relations of friendship and cooperation with countries all over the world.... However, China is firm in its stand on major questions of principle such as Taiwan, Hong Kong, Tibet, and other issues relating to China's state sovereignty and the fundamental interests of the nation. China will never barter away its principles, and there is no room for concession in this respect. Any acts interfering in China's internal affairs would arouse strong reactions from the Chinese people.

—PRC Foreign Minister Qian Qichen[1]

Of all the guiding principles, the first is our one-China policy. We have made it very clear that there is only one China, the Republic of China. Of course, the mainland has a different view.

—ROC Foreign Minister
Frederick F. Chien[2]

Introduction

The status of the Republic of China (ROC) on Taiwan in the international system poses a paradox. On the one hand, Taiwan's "achievement status"—the so-called "Taiwan Miracle"—has become the envy of many developing countries. The basic indicators of Taiwan's economic progress with considerable social equity are impressive: per capita GNP of $10,215 in 1992 surpassing the $10,000 benchmark for passage into the exclusive club of rich countries (double that of Greece

145

or Portugal) and now projected to $20,669 by the year 2000;[3] the world's largest or second largest holder of foreign exchange reserves ($84 billion as of January 1993) and seventh largest aid donor; and one of the major trading and investment powers in the world. At the beginning of divided polity in 1950, the ROC and the People's Republic of China (PRC) had much the same per capita GNP (about $100), but today Taiwan's per capita income is about thirty times that of the mainland. On the other hand, Taiwan has become a virtual nonentity, an international orphan—or at best an odd entity with an array of misleading nomenclatures—in the statecentric world of nation-states and international organizations.

It is this glaring gap between economic and diplomatic statuses that reflects and affects the leitmotif of Taiwan's international relations. Bridging the international status gap has remained the central challenge of foreign policy. To what extent—and in what ways—has Taipei succeeded in meeting the challenge? How have the recent momentous changes in the international system influenced and shaped the rules of the game as they bear on Taipei's drive for international status? It is the main purpose of this chapter to address these questions as the central challenge of Taiwan's "flexible diplomacy." Inaugurated in 1988 with a change of leadership from Chiang Ching-kuo to Lee Teng-hui, this is diplomatic Darwinism—an omnidirectional and diversified strategy that has been adapted to realize three-fold objectives: 1) consolidating and strengthening existing diplomatic ties; 2) striving to develop functional ties with countries with no official diplomatic relations; and 3) participating (or attempting to participate) in international organizations and activities vital to Taiwan's national interests and legitimation.[4]

A full appreciation of the possibilities and limitations of flexible diplomacy, however, requires analyses of the interaction among domestic, regional (East Asian), and global processes. The study of Taiwan's foreign policy at this juncture in world history is complicated as Taipei's international status drive is belied and overlaid by Beijing's enormous demographic and geographic size and privileged position in the international system. There is a need for an analytical framework that would help us make sense of a great melange of national role conceptions and changing domestic and external situations.

Legitimation and Divided Polity

The notion of legitimacy may be used as a conceptual framework to examine the changes and the continuities of Taipei's foreign relations.

Since legitimacy is seldom employed in the study of foreign policy and international relations, the logic of this conceptual framework calls for an explanation.

Legitimacy is defined as "the foundation of such governmental power as is exercised both with a consciousness on the government's part that it has a right to govern and with some recognition by the governed of that right."[5] As such it functions as the ultimate maker and unmaker of any government. It is legitimacy that signifies the distinction between authority and raw power. Power becomes authority only to the extent that it can be upheld by the legitimating principles of the political system. Every political system, as Max Weber argued, "attempts to establish and to cultivate the belief in its legitimacy."[6] Legitimacy is established by compatibility of the values of those who rule and those who are ruled. Similarly, legitimacy eases the exercise of UN authority. It is the outer reach of Third World normative power and what animates critical social actors and movements outside the UN (e.g., nonstate actors and nongovernmental organizations) in their politics of thinking globally and acting locally. Above all, legitimacy is both the beginning and the end of the power of violence, as it strikes at the heart of power elites by withdrawing the consent, obedience, and cooperation of the people. Here then is the soft law of governance: the less the normative power (authority), the more coercive power (force) is required to keep the government afloat. Yet normative power without coercive power has a tenuous existence. (Joseph Stalin revealed the "realist" conception of power and legitimacy by dismissing the Pope's authority with the question "How many divisions does he have?")

The extent of legitimacy enjoyed by a political system is rarely self-evident and always open to debate. What cannot be disputed is that there is no government that commands absolute legitimacy because there is never absolute value compatibility at a given moment in time. Legitimacy is a relative, not an absolute, concept. There is no reason to assume that the political system has to be sustained by only one legitimating principle or only at one level of legitimation. Legitimacy is a dynamic, not a static, concept, evolving as the social and political situation changes.[7] As a relative, dynamic, and process-oriented concept, it is more appropriate to speak of "legitimation" rather than "legitimacy," although the two terms are often used interchangeably.[8]

The quest for legitimacy is an integral, if not always the most salient, part of any polity. As Weber observed, there is a seemingly universal need for rulers to cultivate the belief that their domination is a legitimate form of power. This need seems to have acquired salience in both traditional and contemporary Chinese politics. Historically, China was a civilizational state—or "a civilization pretending to be a state," as Lucian Pye put it[9]—sensitive to the rise and fall of the legitimating "Mandate of Heaven." The sheer size and societal, ethnonational, and demographic dimensions make socializing the popular belief and habit of compliance—to achieve stability with a minimum use of naked force—a normative imperative. Since most dynasties collapsed under the twin blows of *neiluan*, *waihuan* (internal disorder, external calamity), every government in Imperial China was faced with the continuing challenge of "remaking" the facts of its diplomatic practice validate its Mandate–of–Heaven claim to rule. Imperial China still "needed" external "barbarians" as the external reference group to validate its political identity as a universal civilizational state ruled by the Son of Heaven with a cosmic virtue. Such Sinocentric theory of political authority and legitimacy was developed by dynastic rulers over the centuries as the Chinese world order. As a set of norms, rules, and governing procedures, the Chinese world order was no more than a corollary of the Chinese image of domestic social order and thus really the externalization of its domestic orthodoxy. Indeed, there was no distinction between "legitimacy" and "orthodoxy" as the Confucian literati used the term *zhengtong* to mean both.

In our time the festering problem of national unification has forced the two Chinas into the zero-sum game of competitive legitimation and delegitimation. When PRC Foreign Minister Qian Qichen touts that "foreign policy is the extension of China's domestic policies,"[10] he is restating, wittingly or not, the longstanding tradition of acting out China's self–image in international relations. Even in the golden era of Sinocentric splendid isolationism, "China's external order was so closely related to her internal order that one could not long survive without the other."[11] The dynamics of legitimation challenge and response can be accepted as one crucial determinant to explain otherwise inexplicable diplomatic gyrations of both Chinas in the international system.

The concept of legitimation dovetails with the concept of national identity; they are closely related, even mutually enhancing, but not always and necessarily identical.[12] For a divided polity, however, the nexus between legitimation and identity crises seems closer, albeit still not completely identical (as is argued in this chapter). National identity is the characteristic collective behavior of the national system as a whole, in interaction with other subnational, national, and international systems, flowing from all shared attributes and symbols of a solidarity political group known as a "nation-state." Focused on systemic behavior, then, national identity may be defined not only in terms of what the state is (as represented by the myths, rituals, flag, constitution, and anthem that relate how the nation-state came to be and what it stands for)—as in the conventional definition—but also in terms of what the state does (via its role performance in domestic and foreign policy).[13]

Although the sources of legitimation-cum-national identity in our time are both internal and external, national identity theory postulates that domestic societal factors are generally more important than external systemic ones in the formation of national identity, whereas external systemic factors generally take precedence in determining the outcomes of national identity enactment. For a divided polity such as China's, the quest for national identity and the quest for international legitimation are substantially overlapping and mutually complementary, as the politics of competitive legitimation are contested in a distinct but changing international environment.

Legitimation via Diplomatic Recognition

In a sense, the Chinese civil war not so much ended in 1949 as it shifted from a military to political battleground—indeed the beginning of the politics of competitive legitimation of divided China. With the outbreak of the Korean War the two Chinas quickly locked themselves into the competing Cold War alliance systems in charting out separate paths in the nation-building and legitimacy-seeking process. The pursuit of legitimation became the central concern of both domestic and foreign policy of each of the two Chinas, and the politics of divided polity remained for at least two decades largely intractable and reunification attempts elusive owing to their clashing ideologies and claims for absolute legitimation. In this internecine zero-sum game each party came to view its own legitimation as dependent on the delegitimation of the other party. Seeking international legitimation via diplomatic recognition was a corollary of this highly competitive zero-sum game. The outbreak of the Korean War—and Beijing's intervention on behalf of its beleaguered ally in Pyongyang—was a God-send not only for Taipei's survival but also what seemed for many years an insurmountable edge in diplomatic recognition that American hegemony afforded for one of its frontline domino allies in the East Asian Cold War alliance system.

A changing correlation of diplomatic forces became evident in the annual voting on the question of Chinese representation at the 25th (1970) session of the UN General Assembly. For the first time, pro-PRC forces gained a 51 percent majority. The mid-1971 announcement of President Nixon's state visit to Beijing and China's entry into the United Nations in November in the wake of a 76 to 35 percent majority vote on the Albanian draft resolution opened a floodgate to a massive diplomatic switch from Taipei to Beijing as the number of countries extending diplomatic recognition to Beijing increased from five in 1970 to fifteen in 1971 to eighteen in 1972. Taipei's seemingly insurmountable head start in diplomatic recognition of the 1950s and 1960s had all but vanished in the early 1970s as Beijing recovered from the self-inflicted wounds of internal convulsions and diplomatic isolation during the Cultural Revolution and returned to the world diplomatic scene with a new, vigorous foreign policy. Taipei's greatest losses were incurred in 1970-1975 in the Third World, as Beijing established diplomatic relations with fifty-six countries (see Table 5.1 and Table 5.3). This proved to be a zero-sum game in the sense that, unlike the two Germanies (until 1990) and two Koreas (to this date), there is no dual recognition— Beijing's gain becomes *ipso facto* Taipei's loss.

Against this changing diplomatic backdrop the Taipei government came up with a new strategy of making the best of a worsening situation. What emerged in the wake of the lethal diplomatic blow at the United Nations in 1971 was "total diplomacy" (*zhongti waijiao*), which was designed to forge relations with other countries through political, economic, scientific, technological, cultural, and sports exchanges, "be they bilateral or multilateral, official or unofficial, direct or indirect, actual or implied."[14] Still, total diplomacy has had no visible effect in reversing Taipei's diplomatic isolation.

With the ascendancy of Lee Teng-hui as the first native Taiwanese president in 1988, total diplomacy gave way to "elastic diplomacy" or "flexible diplomacy" (*tanxing waijiao*). The major difference between total and flexible diplomacy is that the latter expresses greater adaptability to the logic of the international situation, implying that Taiwan is now willing to do just about anything—including giving up certain heretofore nonnegotiable preconditions for the establishment of official diplomatic relations—to enhance its international status and legitimation. Under the gathering momentum of flexible diplomacy, the Hallstein Doctrine (West Germany's demand in the 1950s and 1960s that any nation that wanted to have relations with it could not have diplomatic ties with East Germany) has fallen by the wayside. To answer Beijing's "one country, two systems" formula, Taipei came up with a "one country, two governments" formula, which, in diplomatic practice, would call for dual recognition. In a sense this was Taipei's belated attempt to

Table 5.1 Number of Countries Recognizing the PRC and ROC (1969-1992)

Year/End	PRC [a]	ROC [c]	UN Membership [d]
1969	49	67	126
1970	54 (+5)	67	127
1971	69 (+15)	54 (-13)	132
1972	87 (+18)	41 (-13)	132
1973	89 (+2)	37 (-4)	135
1974	96 (+7)	31 (-6)	138
1975	105 (+9)	27 (-4)	144
1976	109 (+4)	26 (-1)	147
1977	111 (+2)	23 (-3)	149
1978	113 (+4)	22 (-1)	151
1979	117 (+4)	22	152
1980	121 (+4)	22	154
1981	121	23 (+1)	157
1982	122 (+1)	23	157
1983	125 (+3)	24 (+1)	158
1984	126 (+1)	25 (+1)	159
1985	127 (+1)	23 (-2)	159
1986	127	23	159
1987	127	23	159
1988	130 (+3)	22 (-1)	159
1989	132 (+2)	23 (+1)	159
1990	136 (+4)	28 (+5)	160
1991	140 (+4)	29 (+1)	167
1992	154 (+14)[b]	29	179

Sources: (a) The PRC Ministry of Foreign Affairs, *Zhongguo waijiao gailan 1992* (Survey of Chinese Diplomacy 1992) (Beijing: Shijie zhishi chubanshe, 1992), pp. 481-487; (b) Liu Huaqiu, "China's Diplomatic Achievements in 1992," *Beijing Review,* vol. 35, no. 52 (December 28, 1992-January 3, 1993), p. 8.; (c) Department of Treaty and Legal Affairs, Ministry of Foreign Affairs, Republic of China; and (d) UN Press Release, ORG/1156 January 19, 1993.

emulate the international politics of divided Korea. In a frantic race for diplomatic recognition, it may be recalled, both Koreas abandoned in practice, if not in principle, the Hallstein Doctrine, thereby opening the way for dual recognition. Not a single country recognized both Seoul and Pyongyang in 1962; by mid-1976, however, some forty-nine countries had already done so without incurring diplomatic severance from either Korea. The politics of competitive legitimation of the two Koreas culminated in September 1991 when both Pyongyang and Seoul were admitted to the United Nations as the one hundred-sixtieth and one hundred-sixty first member states.

In establishing diplomatic relations with Grenada (which had already established relations with the PRC in October 1985) on July 20, 1989, the ROC signalled its willingness to live with dual recognition only to provoke Beijing's suspension of its diplomatic ties with Grenada on August 8, 1989. Taipei's diplomatic Darwinism means downplaying or at least putting in abeyance the myth of the ROC's sovereignty over all of China. What was once believed to be a necessary and legitimating myth, in fact, became self-delegitimating. And yet, Taipei could not make much headway largely due to Beijing's unyielding stand on the Hallstein Doctrine—the Beijing Formula—and its aggressive and omnidirectional quest for absolute legitimation.

As shown in Table 5.2, the Grenada precedent prevailed with the remaining seven other similar cases involving Liberia, Belize, Lesotho, Guinea-Bissau, Central African Republic, Nicaragua, and Niger.[15] The only brief exceptions to the Hallstein Doctrine or Beijing Formula occurred in 1989 when Grenada, Liberia, and Belize all recognized Taipei without breaking ties with Beijing, leading to short periods of dual recognition until Beijing severed relations and a forty-one day diplomatic tug-of-war between Beijing and Taipei in mid-1992 when Niger maintained dual recognition of both Chinese governments as a way of seeking the highest bidder in this diplomatic recognition/legitimation game. Not surprisingly, all nine small Third World countries that established or reestablished diplomatic ties with Taipei since President Lee took office and initiated flexible diplomacy in 1988 have received grants, loans, or pledges of foreign aid. The promise of aid was a decisive factor in enticing at least five of them to switch diplomatic recognition from Beijing to Taipei—Liberia, Guinea-Bissau, Belize, Grenada, and Niger. Although accused by Beijing of practicing "dollar diplomacy" (*jinqian waijiao*), Taipei's aid diplomacy is no different from Beijing's aid diplomacy of 1970-1971 (e.g., the PRC's economic aid increased from $13 million in 1969 to $728 million in 1970) as an integral part of its grand strategy of winning a UN seat.[16] It seems money talks in the diplomatic recognition game, at least in proportion to what the two Chinas have to offer to some cash-strapped African countries. Apparently, Beijing was either unable or unwilling to match the same bang for the buck in its flexible diplomacy, as Liberia had received $140 million in aid from Taiwan in 1988 while China had granted the African country only $20 million in aid over twelve years.[17]

For domestic legitimation the poor performance of flexible diplomacy in the recognition/legitimation race calls for some explanation. On March 19, 1993, Taipei's Ministry of Foreign Affairs released a fifty-

Table 5.2   States Having Diplomatic Relations with the ROC (as of the end of 1992)

Belize (R: 10/11/89)	Republic of Guinea-Bissau (R:5/26/90)
Central African Republic (R: 7/8/91)	Republic of Haiti
Commonwealth of the Bahamas	Republic of Honduras
Commonwealth of the Dominica	Republic of Liberia (R:10/9/89)
Dominican Republic	Republic of Malawi
Grenada (R: 7/20/89)	Republic of Nauru
The Holy See (Vatican City)	Republic of Panama
Kingdom of Swaziland	Republic of Paraguay
Kingdom of Tonga	Republic of South Africa
Lesotho (R: 4/5/90)	Saint Christopher and Nevis
Nicaragua (R: 11/6/90)	Saint Lucia
Niger (R: 6/19/92)	Saint Vincent and the Grenadines
Republic of Costa Rica	Solomon Islands
Republic of El Salvador	Tuvalu
Republic of Guatemala	

Source: Hungdah Chiu, "The International Legal Status of the Republic of China (Revised Version)," *Occasional Papers/Reprints Series in Contemporary Asian Studies*, no. 5, 1992, pp. 1-27; Shiru Chiang, deputy director, Public Affairs Division, Coordination Council for North American Affairs, Washington, DC. R=resumed diplomatic relationship that was broken.

page report designed to "improve the populace's understanding of Beijing's vicious attempt against the ROC behind its 'smiling offensives'," listing hundreds of cases of Peking's actions, such as "bribery, economic and trade incentives, political threats and military sales," in the two-year period between January 1991 and January 1993.[18]   Not surprisingly, however, the report skates over the untenable claim of Taiwan's own one-China principle—that offshore China, with less than one-fiftieth the population of mainland China still has *de jure*, if no longer *de facto*, sovereignty on all of China including Tibet and Mongolia—and as such a heavy burden to bear in this international recognition-cum-legitimation race.

Paradoxically, then, the Taiwan factor in Beijing's quest for absolute legitimation expands the limits of the possible and permissible in widening China's own official diplomatic network.   In some respects China has never been more at peace with its neighbors, especially Russia, Japan, Vietnam, and India, than it has been since 1991, as Beijing established or normalized official diplomatic relations with Indonesia, Singapore, Saudi Arabia, Israel, India, Vietnam, South Korea, and fifteen newly minted states from the ruins of the former Soviet Union.   The unusually swift recognition of twelve newly independent states in the wake of the collapse of the Soviet Union in December 1991 was prompted by the fear that Taiwan would jump the gun. The greatest leverage Beijing had in this connection was its veto power in the Security Council and the threat to use it in blocking the entry of any of these newly formed states into the world organization—no acceptance of the Beijing Formula, no UN entry.[19] There is also a sense in which such a *pro forma* establishment of diplomatic networking (154 countries at the end of 1992) is to make a virtue of necessity, bespeaking a deep anxiety about the viability of one sovereign, unified, multinational Chinese state amidst turbulent global politics and growing ethnonational conflicts in many trouble spots of the world. In at least one respect China is beyond comparison. No country in our times has talked as much about having "friends all over the world" and accomplished so little in developing enduring friendship with any of its neighbors, not even North Korea. China has no true friends or well-wishers among its regional powers—Japan, the United States, Russia, Korea, Vietnam, Indonesia, and India. At the same time, Taiwan is breaking away, Hong Kong is hard to control, Tibet wants an exit with voice, the Moslems in the Northwest are unhappy, and the Mongols would like to be independent. Hence, one thing seems obvious—China's determination to beef up its "comprehensive national strength" and to reassert itself as a regional superpower in East Asia as a way of shoring up its sagging domestic legitimacy and mobilizing its national identity dynamic.

Beijing's decision to recognize and establish full normalization with Seoul would seem to have ominous implications inasmuch as it seemed to signal Beijing's abandonment of the Hallstein Doctrine in the Korean peninsula and acceptance of the two Koreas as two separate and independent sovereign states. Actually, China's diplomatic maneuverability was greatly circumscribed, almost foreclosed, by Seoul's skillful *Nordpolitik* and Gorbachev's public declaration of support for Seoul's entry into the United Nations, leaving Beijing with a choice of going along with this diplomatic *fait accompli* or casting a solo veto.[20] In any case, Beijing's sudden decision to recognize Seoul is a reminder that Taipei's flexible diplomacy is no match for Beijing's own "flexible diplomacy"—staying firm in principle but flexible in practice (*yuanze de jianding xing, celüi de linghuo xing*). It also underlines another example of the maxi-mini strategy of making a virtue out of necessity. Foreign Minister Qian Qichen is reported to have used the metaphor of "downing four birds with one stone"—in favor of full normalization with Seoul—in his report to the CCP's central foreign affairs group, saying that such a preemptive strike (the Seoul card) would at once and the same time further isolate Taiwan diplomatically, strengthen Beijing's growing economic cooperation with Seoul (read more trade surplus and direct foreign investment and technology transfer), diminish Pyongyang's seemingly endless requests for more material, military, and political support, and give more bargaining leverage to defuse the mounting "Super 301" pressure from the United States to demand negotiations on unfair trade practices.[21] Furthermore, the Seoul connection is another way of demonstrating the indispensability of the China factor in the reshaping of a new regional order in Northeast Asia.

The two Chinas' flexible diplomacy battle in the international diplomatic recognition/legitimation race illustrates the limits of the possible and the permissible in Beijing's official international relations. In every case of a state setting up diplomatic relations with Taipei, Beijing has severed ties. In the intermediate case of "official but not diplomatic" consular ties, as in the case of Latvia, Beijing "suspended" diplomatic ties.[22] In countries such as Bolivia where Taiwan representative offices now use the official name of the ROC, Beijing has taken no retaliation, and in the unusual case of Vanuatu, Beijing actually rewarded the government after it "officially recognized" Taiwan.[23] High-level official visits to Taiwan have generated protests from Beijing, but only in the case of repeated trips by Philippine cabinet secretaries has the PRC taken action, rotating its ambassador home a year early. While no industrialized nation has yet to match the daring of Fiji and other small Third World states that have dispatched prime ministers and foreign ministers to Taiwan, the ratcheting up the level of Western visitors to the ministerial level will likely continue. What all of this reveals is the marginality of small and weak Third World states that ironically enables them to get away more easily with a greater volume and intensity of interactions with Taiwan than industrialized states like France and Great Britain.

Table 5.2 highlights the extent of Taiwan's diplomatic isolation in the international system. Practically all of the twenty-nine states currently maintaining official diplomatic relations with the ROC are small Third World countries, dubbed "tiny friends" in the Taiwan press, mostly in Africa and Latin America, that the average person in the streets of Beijing or Taipei could hardly recognize. With the loss of Seoul in 1992, Taiwan has no official diplomatic ties with any East Asian country, the most important region to both Beijing and Taipei economically, politically, and militarily. In a sense, then, Tables 5.2-5.3 represent the sum total of what Taipei's aid diplomacy has been able to sustain or accomplish. They suggest as well that there is no room to accommodate Taiwan's "one country, two governments" formula in the statecentric international system—not even in the wake of the Tiananmen massacre, which Lucian Pye has aptly characterized as "the universally acknowledged code word for repression in the search for legitimacy."[24] By abandoning the Hallstein Doctrine without giving up or changing its national identity (one-China principle), Taiwan's flexible diplomacy was supposed to transform its previous zero-sum lose-lose strategy into a new win-win strategy. The outcome, at least in this domain, indicates otherwise.

Table 5.3   A Chronicle of Diplomatic Relations with the ROC, 1971-1992

Year	Countries Breaking Ties with the ROC	Total	Countries Establishing or Reestablishing Ties with the ROC	Total
1971	Austria, Belgium, Cameroon, Chile, Ecuador, Iran, Kuwait, Lebanon, Mexico, Peru, Sierra Leone, Turkey	12		
1972	Argentina, Australia, Chad, Luxembourg, Madagascar, Maldives, Malta, New Zealand, Rwanda, Senegal, Togo	11	Tonga	1
1973	Bahrain, Spain, Upper Volta, Zaire	4		
1974	Botswana, Brazil, Gabon, the Gambia, Malaysia, Niger, Venezuela	7		
1975	Philippines, Portugal, Thailand, Samoa, Vietnam	5		
1976	Central African Republic	1	South Africa	1
1977	Barbados, Jordan, Liberia	3		
1978	Libya	1		
1979	United States of America	1	Tuvalu	1
1980	Colombia	1	Nauru	1

Table 5.3   (continued)

Year	Countries Breaking Ties with the ROC	Total	Countries Establishing or Reestablishing Ties with the ROC	Total
1981			St. Vincent and the Grenadines	2
1983	Ivory Coast, Lesotho	2	Dominica, Solomon Islands, St. Christopher and Nevis	3
1984			St. Lucia	1
1985	Bolivia, Nicaragua	2		
1988	Uruguay	1		
1989			Bahamas, Belize, Grenada, Liberia	4
1990	Saudi Arabia	1	Lesotho, Nicaragua, Guinea-Bissau	3
1991			Central African Republic	1
1992	South Korea	1	Niger	1
Total		53		18

Sources: Hung-mao Tien, *The Great Transition: Political and Social Change in the Republic of China*, (Stanford, CA: Hoover Institution Press, 1989), Table 9.1, p. 223, for the period 1971-1988; author's compilation of data from various sources including the sources listed in Table 5.1 for the period 1989-1992 and the ROC Ministry of Foreign Affairs, *Waijiao baogaoshu: Duiwai guanxi yu waijiao xingzheng* (Foreign Affairs White Paper: External Relations and Diplomatic Administration) (Taipei: The Ministry of Foreign Affairs, 1992).

Legitimation via International Organization

From its inception the United Nations has performed a dual physician/priest role in the making and legitimation of new states. While the world organization's effectiveness was closely keyed to superpower cooperation in world politics, the membership issue was dislodged in 1955 from the entanglement of East-West conflict when the Soviet Union and the United States reached an informal agreement not to veto membership applications of their respective allied states. As a result, sixteen countries entered the UN in 1955. The year 1960 was a culmination of the second big wave: the entry of seventeen newly independent Third World states, having now achieved a numerical majority in the General Assembly, quickly set in motion global normative politics or what is also called "the global politics of collective legitimation and delegitimation." With the end of the Cold War, the collapse of the second (socialist) world, and the outbreak of state-making wars in trouble spots around the world, the Security Council and General Assembly have suddenly been catapulted to preside over the third big wave—the biggest membership surge in the shortest span of time in UN history—as twenty newly minted states entered the world organization in the just ten months between September 17, 1991, and July 31, 1992. With the admission of Eritrea (a breakaway state from Ethiopia) and the Principality of Monaco on May 28, 1993, UN membership ballooned from 159 to 183 in twenty months.[25] Perhaps the most notable aspect of the post-Cold War wave in membership expansion is the entry of divided and/or breakaway states. There is little doubt that UN membership has come to be viewed as the imprimatur of international recognition and legitimation—a national identity badge, as it were—that no self-respecting country, especially divided or breakaway ones, could do without.

Viewed in this light, the PRC's entry into the world body, especially taking up China's seat as one of the Five Permanent Members (Perm Five) of the Security Council, proved to be a diplomatic disaster of global proportions for Taiwan and the beginning of the end of Taiwan's status as an independent sovereign state in the world of international organizations. International organization, for classification purposes, is the generic term referring to both international inter-governmental organizations (IGOs), the exclusive domain for "sovereignty-bound" state actors, and international nongovernmental organizations (INGOs), the inclusive domain for "sovereignty-free" nonstate actors and social and professional movements and organizations in the economic, social, cultural, humanitarian, and technical fields.[26] As shown in Table 5.4, Taiwan's INGO membership status has actually registered a four-fold increase since 1971. It is in the world of IGOs—popularly referred to as "international organizations"—where the respective international statuses of the two Chinas were dramatically reversed in the past twenty-two years.

Taiwan's relatively high level of representation in the world of INGOs is the result both of its own concerted drive under the banner of "total diplomacy" and "flexible diplomacy," and of China's own flexible policy adopted since the late 1970s to tolerate coexistence with Taiwan in INGOs under certain conditions. The two-Chinas problem was resolved in a compromise package—what came to be known as the Olympic Formula—when the full International Olympic Committee (IOC) decided that the title of China's Olympic Committee would be accepted as the "Chinese Olympic Committee" and that Taiwan should also stay in the IOC as the "Chinese Taipei Olympic Committee." A similar compromise was worked out at the International Council of Scientific Unions (ICSU) in September 1982—known as the ICSU Formula—that made it possible for China and Taiwan to enjoy the same membership status and rights. The Olympic Formula and the ICSU Formula soon became a precedent for other INGOs to follow. Taipei "won" this INGO membership battle by having its national identity preemptively misappropriated under the rubric of "China" or "Chinese" as a provincial entity ("Chinese Taipei" or "Taipei, China"). To regard these social and professional individuals and organizations as "sovereignty-free" nonstate actors distinct from and independent of the state is an overstatement as Chinese nongovernmental organizations serve in their semiofficial capacity as extended arms of the state, bridging agents of functional cooperation in the field of science and technology between the Chinese state and the world of INGOs. In a sense, then, the Olympic/ICSU Formula that brought about dual membership of both Chinas in so many INGOs testifies to the successful monument of both Chinas being firm in principle but flexible in practice. As such it may be more aptly characterized as a triumph of "functionalism-cum-federalism" with Chinese characteristics.[27]

The kind of flexibility shown in the INGO membership contest does not hold in the world of IGOs. Apparently, Beijing regarded its much-heralded entry into the United Nations in late 1971 as just the beginning of the zero-sum game of legitimation and delegitimation as far as the IGOs were concerned. Beijing immediately jumped the gun on the politics of national identity and competitive legitimation by advancing several rather surprising demands: 1) that it be identified simply as "China," not the "People's Republic of China"; 2) that references to the Republic of China or even "Taiwan" should be deleted from all UN documents, reports, and studies (even today "Taiwan" is not included in the World Bank's annual *World Development Report* and the UNDP's annual, *Human Development Report*; and the IMF's *Direction of Trade Statistics Yearbook*); 3) that the fifty-one Chinese international civil servants in the UN Secretariat (who were carrying ROC passports) should continue their work according to their conscience; and 4) China be allowed to work as a Group of One in the global group politics such as the UNCTAD (and of course decline the invitation from the Third World to join its global developmental caucus, Group of 77, and its geopolitical caucus, the Non-Aligned Movement (NAM)).[28]

The impact of China's entry into the world organization in 1971 is

Table 5.4 Participation of Selected Countries in International Organizations, 1960-1992

Country	1960	1966	1977	1984	1986	1987	1989	1992
China	**2**	**1**	**21**	**29**	**32**	**35**	**37**	**44**
	30	58	71	355	403	504	677	865
Hong Kong	**0**	**2**	**4**	**7**	**7**	**9**	**12**	**11**
	93	164	312	564	640	640	769	884
Taiwan	**22**	**39**	**10**	**6**	**6**	**6**	**6**	**7**
	108	182	239	429	419	464	554	695
India	**41**	**57**	**65**	**58**	**58**	**58**	**60**	**61**
	391	531	733	1067	1016	1156	1309	1428
Japan	**42**	**53**	**71**	**60**	**58**	**60**	**58**	**61**
	412	636	878	1296	1222	1420	1583	1749
France	**90**	**100**	**104**	**93**	**67**	**81**	**83**	**88**
	886	1168	1457	2227	1704	2264	2598	2879
UK	**76**	**90**	**91**	**79**	**63**	**72**	**71**	**70**
	742	1039	1380	2021	1607	2091	2416	2681
USA	**59**	**68**	**78**	**65**	**33**	**59**	**64**	**66**
	612	847	1106	1593	804	1579	1933	2127
USSR	**29**	**37**	**43**	**73**	**69**	**69**	**61**	**48**
	179	295	433	668	649	714	806	1074
Global	**154**			**365**	**369**	**311**	**300**	**286**
	1255			4615	4649	4235	4621	4696

Sources: Adapted from Union of International Association, *Yearbook of International Organizations 1985/86*, 3rd ed. vol. 2, (Munchen: K.G. Saur, 1985), pp. 1479, and 1481-83; *Yearbook of International Organizations 1986/87*, 4th ed., vol. 2, (Munchen: K. G. Saur, 1986), Tables 2 and 3; *Yearbook of International Organizations 1988/89*, 6th ed. vol. 2 (Munchen: K. G. Saur, 1988), Tables 2 and 3; *Yearbook of International Organizations 1989/90*, 7th ed., vol. 2, (Munchen: K. G. Saur, 1989), Tables 2 and 3; and *Yearbook of International Organizations 1992/1993*, 10th ed., vol. 2, (Munchen: K. G. Saur, 1992), pp. 1613-15. IGO figures are **bolded** throughout the table; INGO figures are in roman type.

evident in Table 5.4, as Beijing's IGO membership increased from one to forty-four while Taipei's IGO membership decreased from thirty-nine to seven in the period 1966-1992. Against this backdrop, two IGOs—the International Criminal Police Organization (Interpol) and the Asian Development Bank (ADB)—were confronted with the old question of Chinese representation when Beijing applied for membership with several preconditions in the ADB in February 1983 and Interpol in May 1984. Faced with Beijing's "conditional" application for membership (e.g., the name of the ROC had to be changed to "Taiwan, China," references to the ROC had to be exorcised from the organization's records and the ROC flag banned and the ROC's extant full membership had to be downgraded and appended to China's full membership), Interpol held separate ballots—the first two relating to China's admission and the third to its attached preconditions of entry. China failed to get the necessary two-thirds majority vote in the first ballot and succeeded in the second ballot with seventy-two and twenty-seven against. The third ballot on the preconditions was a forty-eight to forty-eight split. Despite such rather mixed results, China was admitted as a member, whereupon Taipei walked out in protest, thus mooting the controversy but placing Taiwan's legal status in limbo.

In the ADB case, unlike Interpol or any other IGO, Taipei enjoyed strong comparative advantages when in 1983 Beijing applied for membership with the precondition of Taiwan's expulsion: it was a founding member state in good standing; it was a capital guarantor rather than a borrower (and hence ADB member states were not too eager to reduce the available capital pool by welcoming what could become the ADB's largest borrower); and it enjoyed full support of the United States (the Reagan administration threatened to withhold its funding to the Bank if Taiwan's position was adversely affected). Moreover, as a regional intergovernmental organization with no links to the United Nations, the issue of the sole Chinese seat does not apply here. Beijing argued that Taipei took advantage of Beijing's exclusion from its rightful UN seat to become a member of the ADB. In the 1984 and 1985 annual meetings of the ADB's Board of Governors, China's application was taken off the agenda because of the unresolved nomenclature issue. In the end, without Taipei's approval over the name change, Beijing and the ADB reached a compromise in the form of a five-point memorandum of understanding on November 26, 1985, stating that the "People's Republic of China is the single legitimate representative of China" and that Taiwan could remain in the ADB under the new designation of "Taipei, China."[29] China in the end had to bend its "principled and nonnegotiable stand" to the Olympic Formula to finally achieve its admission on March 10, 1986, as the forty-seventh member of the ADB under its full name "People's Republic of China." What is important to note is China's softening of its previous rejectionist stand on co-membership, dual membership, or separate membership in any IGO. For Beijing, however, the ADB case is an exception that proves its own zero-sum rules of the legitimation game.[30]

Unlike the Interpol case, Taipei responded here by trying to outperform Beijing's style of being firm in principle but flexible in application. Taiwan's official response came in the form of three "nons"—nonacceptance, nonwithdrawal, and nonparticipation. Yet Taiwan's rejectionist stand on the name change too was progressively modified when, after two years of absence, it returned to the annual meeting held in Manila in 1988 under the name "Taipei, China." Growing pressure from the general public and opinion leaders in Taiwan was one of the major reasons the Taipei government gave up its "nonacceptance" and "nonparticipation" principles. In May 1989, for the first time, an ROC governmental representative—Finance Minister Shirley Kuo—came to Beijing to attend the annual meeting of the ADB. This is a significant departure from its longstanding "Three Nos" policy (no contact, no negotiation, and no conciliation). To a certain extent, the two Chinas' flexible diplomacy battle in the ADB membership race signalled a shift from the zero-sum game of representation to the mixed-sum game of nomenclature.[31] In the zero-sum game of representation, each IGO was asked to choose between the two competing governments with an almost predictable consequence—Taipei either withdrew or was expelled. In the new mixed-sum game of names, however, Beijing's status is rarely questioned or threatened. Only the status of the ROC is at stake. But this game of names is of greater importance to Taipei because it can be a positive-sum game with the possibility of more than one winner. The stage was thus set for the game of names to be played out with competing flexibility and zeal. Would it be "Taipei" or "Taiwan," before or after "China," with or without a comma or hyphen or parenthesis? For instance, Taipei, faced with a preemptive misappropriation of its official national identity, raised a counterproposal, offering to accept the "Taipei, China" designation only if the PRC accepted the designation "Beijing, China" in the ADB. Indeed, the challenge of Taiwan's flexible diplomacy in the world of international organizations has become clear and simple enough: how to raise the island's diplomatic stature to a level commensurate with its economic prowess, starting with international economic institutions where it enjoys comparative advantage but extending, by installments, to other IGOs, including the United Nations.

Post-Tiananmen China's search for international legitimation seems to have only emboldened Taipei's own quest for international legitimation via international organizations even as some international economic organizations became more accommodating to dual membership of both China and Taiwan. After intensive behind-the-scenes negotiations the twelve-member Asia-Pacific Economic Cooperation (APEC) announced August 28, 1991, that all three Chinese applicants—Beijing as the "People's Republic of China," Taipei as

"Chinese-Taipei," and Hong Kong as "Hong Kong"—would be accepted for membership with "equal, full-fledged status" as important economic regional entities regardless of sovereignty or territorial issues.[32] Accepting such an externally appropriated national identity as "Chinese-Taipei" is said to reflect the new spirit of pragmatism in Taipei, an indication that the government feels the name can be flexible as long as the ROC's membership status remains substantive and on an equal footing.

And yet, the obsession with its official national identity is a millstone around the neck of its flexible diplomacy. On January 1, 1990, the Taipei government redefined its national identity as a mere economic entity, a separate customs territory when it applied for membership in the General Agreement on Tariffs and Trade (GATT) as the "Separate Customs Territory of Taiwan, Penghu, Kinmen and Matsu." Thanks to the collapse of bipartisan consensus on China in American domestic politics and the strains in Sino-Americans relations over a range of issues (human rights abuse, arms sales and proliferation, and trading practices), the Bush administration, in June 1991, informed the Congress that the United States would support Taiwan's entry into the 106-member world trade body. This was followed by a similar pledge of support by the European Community member states. Yet Taipei rejected a proposal by leading members of the GATT for a name change—"Chinese Taipei"—because the suggested change does not correctly express "our national identity." This provoked vehement opposition from the local press. As *China Post* (Taipei) editorialized, "What's in the name anyway?" When the official title, ROC, cannot be used in any international organization, the editorial noted, what does it matter, even if "Chinese Taipei" is added, especially in view of the fact that this is the name Taiwan accepted in other international organizations such as the ADB?[33]

There simply is no logic in fact and practice for the government's opposition except that it expresses national identity angst. When Taiwan was granted on September 29, 1992, "observer status" in GATT as "Chinese Taipei," nobody seemed concerned about the name change as the whole island was celebrating this "great victory" in the international legitimation race. In October 1992, the GATT set up a working party for Taiwan's application. As a result, there are now expectations that Taipei would gain its membership in the not-too-distant future, hopefully in late 1993, even possibly before Beijing's entry.[34]

In 1992, then, one of Taiwan's top foreign policy objectives moved close to reality. Taiwan's full-fledged membership in the ADB and

APEC was a major boost, symbolizing and structuring Taiwan's status as an important East Asian economic power and opening up a new pathway of developing economic ties with the East Asian states on a regional governmental level that the absence of bilateral diplomatic relations denied. Now that per capita GNP surpassed the benchmark of $10,000 Taiwan has quietly launched a campaign to secure a seat in the Paris-based twenty-four-member "richman's club"—the Organization for Economic Cooperation and Development (OECD)—as another way of enhancing its international legitimation.[35]

Debate on Taiwan's UN membership was rekindled in 1991, in part catalyzed by the momentous changes in the United Nations—especially the entry of the two Koreas as two separate but equal member states and a dozen breakaway states. But the specific terms and contents of the debate were shaped by the national identity dynamics of domestic politics. Popular frustration over Taiwan's indeterminate status in the international system erupted, making the UN option a hotly contested domestic/foreign policy issue. In June 1991, the Legislative Yuan (Parliament) approved the draft resolution submitted by eighty-six lawmakers that the government should seek to rejoin the United Nations at an appropriate time under the name of the ROC, even as Premier Hau Pei-tsun stood firm on the one-China principle. The opposition Democratic Progressive Party (DDP) adopted the UN entry under the name "Republic of Taiwan" as their main foreign policy issue. On September 30, the Taiwan Television Enterprise sponsored the first-ever one-on-one live television debate pitting ROC Vice Foreign Minister John Chang against DPP legislator Hsieh Chang-ting (who led a group of followers to New York in September to seek support of the UN Security Council members for Taiwan's UN membership). In a challenge to Chang, Hsieh reminded some five million television viewers that it was "the Republic of China" that was kicked out of the United Nations in 1971, not Taiwan. A public opinion survey jointly conducted by the Taiwan Television Company and the *United Daily News* in September showed a sixty-one to fifteen majority of the people in favor of the country's bid for UN membership while, on a separate question, 41 percent thought the time was not ripe.[36]

Against this backdrop, the ROC government began to show the first signs of internal disagreement on the issue, with Premier Hau taking a hard line while the Ministry of Foreign Affairs took a more ambiguous soft line that the ROC would apply for readmission to the UN only under its official name and at an appropriate time. In 1992 bipartisan support for Taiwan's UN option gained broader support, though it still seemed more as a symbolic than a practical proposal given Beijing's ability to veto any such application through its permanent membership in the Security Council.

With the coming of the new premier, Lien Chan, in early 1993, what Beijing sees as the "creeping officiality" of Taiwan's flexible diplomacy has taken another great leap forward, as Lien in the course of his confirmation hearings told lawmakers that he supported dual recognition of China and Taiwan and Taiwan's return to the UN. On April 9, 1993, President Lee Teng-hui crossed the Rubicon in announcing to the Legislative Yuan that he intended to work toward placing the issue of the ROC's UN membership on the agenda of the world body within the next three years.[37] The announcement took many foreign policy observers and analysts by surprise as it seemed to signal the beginning of a new phase of Taipei's flexible diplomacy. On April 21, 1993, Foreign Minister Frederick Chien announced that the ROC will formally apply to rejoin the UN by September 1995, the first time that the government has set a specific time frame for the long-debated bid to rejoin the world body.[38]

In less than two years (from June 1991 to April 1993), the dynamics of Taiwan's domestic politics have changed to such an extent as to make the government's evasive line on UN membership untenable. In finally taking up the UN reentry option as top priority, Taipei too is trying to kill several birds with one stone. At the official level, the ROC's Foreign Ministry advances its case for UN membership on several grounds: (1) that the ROC's standing in global GNP, per capita income, trade, and foreign aid ranking fully satisfies the membership criteria specified in Article 4 of the UN Charter ("peace-loving states," ability and willingness to carry out international obligations) and as such Taiwan's exclusion is in contravention of the principle of universality and human rights encoded in the Charter; (2) that UN General Assembly Resolution 2758 (XXVI) of October 25, 1971, merely replaced one form of inequity with another, because the PRC could not represent the people on Taiwan any more than the ROC could represent the people of the mainland; and (3) that Taipei's UN membership, as made evident in the two Germanies' and two Koreas' presence in the world body, would not jeopardize the chance for national reunification.[39]

And yet the real motivation seems to lie in the quest for deeper legitimation. More than any other foreign policy decision, the 1993 UN reentry decision is a way of demonstrating that the government is responsive to *vox populi* while at the same time attempting to co-opt or neuter the DPP. Furthermore, the decision seems well-designed to perform a bridging function in helping Taiwan's multiple identities—regional, national, and global—coexist and be mutually complementary.

Strategically, too, the UN option as a long-term goal forces Beijing to siphon off its limited political and diplomatic capital in the pursuit of absolute international legitimation. As President Lee told reporters in his May 20, 1993, press conference, it took Beijing twenty-two years to gain UN admission but "I do not think it will take 22 years [for Taiwan] to get in."[40] It is precisely this fear that excites Beijing's "searching" behavior in the United Nations. In December 1988 Beijing submitted a memorandum to the UN Security Council warning member states of the clear and continuing danger of "creeping officiality" flowing from Taiwan's flexible diplomacy.[41] With the recent and unexpected revival of Taiwan's diplomatic campaign to reenter the United Nations, Beijing's veto power is repeatedly mentioned as the sword/shield that defends and protects the integrity of People's China as the only legitimate Chinese government in the world organization.

Legitimation via Functional Interdependence

One important aspect of multifaceted flexible diplomacy is complex and growing interdependence with the global political economy—"substantive relations" in Taiwan's diplomatic language. Just as Maoist China was forced to take the autocentric self-reliance path of development after the withdrawal of Soviet aid and personnel in mid-1960, Taiwan in the wake of America's derecognition was forced to adopt "compensatory diplomacy" in the form of various semiofficial devices and formulas to maintain its substantive economic and cultural relations with many countries that have already switched their diplomatic recognition to Beijing. The overall emphasis and direction of Taiwan's international relations shifted from seeking diplomatic breakthroughs to simultaneously upgrading cross-Strait relations and improving international relations.[42] With foreign trade accounting for about 80 percent of GDP, Taiwan's international economic relations are the lifeblood of regime survival and a critical source of performance-based legitimation. This explains the ease and speed with which the Taipei government quickly changed the national identity of its export products to "Made in Taiwan." The loss of such anti-communist allies as Saudi Arabia and South Korea in a post-communist world signals the irrelevance of ideology as a factor in the diplomatic recognition/legitimation game. The importance of performance-based legitimation through economic development and modernization has been magnified in the competitive legitimation politics of divided China.

The external shock of diplomatic isolation seemed to have worked as a powerful catalyst for disciplined economic work at home, as evident in the rising curves for foreign trade and surplus, first rather slowly in the 1970s and then rapidly in the 1980s. Taiwan's external relations increasingly are driven and overlaid by sovereignty-free actors who operate unhampered by the absence of official diplomatic ties. Japan's derecognition in 1972 engendered the "Japanese formula" to replace the ROC Embassy in Tokyo with the nominally private Association of East Asian Relations as a way of maintaining economic and cultural relations. The Japanese formula served as a precedent for the Philippines to emulate when Manila decided in 1975 to switch its diplomatic recognition to Beijing. America's derecognition in 1979 came as the single greatest blow, setting in motion agonizing debate on Taiwan's national identity. But here too behavioral Darwinism quickly intervened as the ROC government replaced its embassy and consulate-generals in the United States with the nondescript "Coordination Council for North American Affairs" (CCNAA) with its main office in Washington, DC, and branch offices in twelve major American cities.[43] That this nonofficial CCNAA has the largest number of Taiwanese diplomatic personnel abroad (about 200), seconded by several governmental ministries and commissions at home, speaks directly to the pivotal importance of the United States both as a market (accounting for over 30 percent of Taiwan's exports and a substantial portion of Taiwan's trade surplus) and as a *de facto*, if not *de jure*, guardian of island China's security.

Although Taiwan in a formal sense remains largely isolated in the statecentric world, substantive relations with major trading partners have improved dramatically in the past two years with the first visits by cabinet-level officials from several West European countries in more than twenty years, a steady stream of visitors from the Soviet Union and Eastern Europe in 1991, and the first visits by cabinet-level officials from Germany and the United States in 1992 (i.e., German Economics Minister Juergen Moellemann's official state visit followed by U.S. Trade Representative Carla Hills's visit). The improved prospects for substantive relations with major Western states, in particular France and the United States, have resulted from the diminution of Beijing's international reputation and legitimation, as well as from Taiwan's economic clout in the post-Cold War setting. Western competition for a slice of Taiwan's grandiose $303 billion infrastructure plan has become the continuation of legitimation politics by another means and name. After having established formal diplomatic ties with Beijing as the only way to gain UN membership, the newly independent Baltic states too turned to Taipei for aid, trade, and investment.

In Africa and Latin America, Taiwan's flexible diplomacy is and becomes "aid diplomacy" *par excellence*. President Lee's flexible diplomacy soon found its institutional anchor in the International Economic Cooperation Development Fund (IECDF), which was set up in October 1988 with a five-year goal of allocating US$1.1 billion in grants, soft loans, technical assistance, and other forms of assistance to "friendly" Third World countries, whether they have diplomatic relations with Taipei or not. Some 433 Chinese aid experts are currently at work in thirty-three developing countries, mostly in Africa and Latin America.[44] All eight countries that resumed official diplomatic relations with Taipei since 1989 (see Table 5.2) have received grants, loans, or pledges of aid in varying sums ranging from $50 million (Guinea-Bissau) to $140 million (Liberia). In the period 1988-1992 Taiwan offered more than $100 million in humanitarian disaster relief to fifty-four countries, including $30 million to Russia, $14 million to Ukraine, and $1 million to Belarus.[45]

Taiwan's Third World aid diplomacy seems designed to play a greater role in Third World development and debt relief as a way of projecting its new national identity/role as a rich industrialized and democratizing country; to consolidate existing diplomatic ties so as to prevent any more diplomatic defection; to win new friends in the face of determined efforts by Beijing to isolate it diplomatically; and to demonstrate to the domestic audience that Taiwan is no longer an orphan in the international community. Taiwan's aid diplomacy has also secured or strengthened commercial ties with countries that already maintain formal diplomatic relations with Beijing, including Mexico and the Philippines. In October 1992 the Taipei government decided to extend economic aid to Vietnam, Belarus, and South Africa, offering each a loan of $8 million to $15 million.

At the same time, Taiwan's flexible diplomacy as applied to the mainland seems rather complex and confusing. Taipei's economic interdependence widens and deepens unchecked, making offshore China's economic future increasingly dependent on investment and trade with China even as the government gradually shifts by fits and starts away from the one-China unification principles and policies of the conservative wing of the ruling Kuomintang (KMT) party to the dual-recognition principle. As already noted above, the "one-China" principle has been translated into the "one state, two governments" formula under the gathering momentum of flexible diplomacy. But the so-called "China fever" in Taiwan has little to do with a desire for unification. It is driven by the economic logic of going "upmarket" in Taiwan's entanglement in the global economy—that Taiwan would now have to turn to the mainland in search of cheap labor, profitable investments, consumer markets, and even a site for polluting industries. Indeed, Taiwan can be said to have positioned itself as the logical, or even pivotal, force in the political economy of "Greater China," also dubbed "Chinese Productivity Triangle" of Hong Kong, southern mainland China, and Taiwan. (See also discussion of this topic in chapters by Harry Harding and Ralph Clough.)

Taiwan's indirect trade with the mainland via Hong Kong—almost all of which is in Taiwan's favor—increased from $1 billion in 1986 to $3.5 billion in 1990 to $5.8 billion in 1991 and to $7 billion in 1992. The best guesses for Taiwan's investment in the mainland, mostly in southern coastal provinces, is about US$5 billion, and still growing rapidly. That Hong Kong and Taiwan have already emerged respectively as the first and second largest holders of China's "foreign" direct investment (FDI) speaks to the extent to which the power of shared culture and language coupled with the power of proximity fuels China's modernization drive. This kind of capital export and model projection to the mainland also help Taiwan's regime legitimation as there seems virtually little domestic opposition to the growing networks of functional interdependence. The logic of Beijing's open-door policy toward Taiwan seems equally compelling—the more Taiwan's capital and trade flow to the mainland, the more capital and jobs fuel China's modernization drive, the more the future of Taiwan's economic prosperity is dependent on the mainland, the less appeal for the independence movement, the greater the foundation for national unification. Given the size disparity, in Beijing's reasoning, China will be the ultimate winner in this game.

The politics of competitive legitimation and national identity mobilization are also played out in "External Diaspora China" to win the minds and hearts of some 29.2 million overseas Chinese—ethnic Chinese living outside China—who are most heavily concentrated in Southeast Asia (23.3 million). Taiwan's investment in Southeast Asia was estimated at more than US$10 billion in 1991 (about $5 billion in Malaysia, $3.4 billion in Thailand, and $2.8 billion in Indonesia) and is still growing rapidly.[46] This is also another arena where Taiwanese/Chinese entrepreneurs exploit synergistically the full weight of their shared culture, language, ethnic identity, money, and geographical proximity (Taiwan has already emerged as Vietnam's largest foreign investor). The Chinese national identity connection is clearly evident in these Southeast Asian countries from Indonesia to Malaysia to Thailand to Vietnam. (See also discussion in Erland Heginbotham's chapter.)

Legitimation via Democratization

Perhaps in no country in the world is the divide between domestic and foreign policies as blurred as in Taiwan. This is so only partly because of its size—more importantly because the government's foreign policy and mainland policy are so substantially overlapping as to make them the two sides of the same dialectical scissor. Consequently, domestic and international legitimation are mutually complementary. Indeed, this quest for legitimation has remained one of the most powerful motivating forces for the transformation of island China from a highly authoritarian newly industrializing country (NIC) to a newly democratizing country (NDC). The failure of Taipei's internationally based legitimation required it to replenish its supply of legitimacy by seeking deeper legitimation via democratization at home. This in turn fed back on Taiwan's *de facto* independence that has been taking place in recent years, very much to the detriment of PRC interests in its quest for national reunification.[47]

The roots of Taiwan's democratization can be traced back to the development of civil society in the 1970s. In the latter half of the 1980s, however, democratizing changes came to island China in multiple forms and fronts (e.g., the lifting of martial law, the legalization of opposition parties, the institutionalization of open, competitive elections, and the rejuvenation of legislative bodies) at a dizzying speed. What started in mid-1987 on the political scene as little more than the lonely liberal cry in the authoritarian wildness—when after thirty-eight years martial law was gingerly lifted—came true in just half a decade. By mid-1993, Taiwan seemed to have completed the transition to a full-fledged two-party system.

How can we explain such a remarkable democratizing process in an authoritarian island China? It is beyond the scope of this essay to fully discuss and evaluate competing theories of democracy. At first glance, however, Taiwanese democratization seems to validate the "economic wealth" theory that Seymour Martin Lipset advanced several decades ago. The "more well-to-do a nation," Lipset postulated, "the greater the chances that it will sustain democracy."[48] Barrington Moore has reformu-lated the theory more succinctly: "No bourgeois, no democracy."[49] The theory is based on the assumption that a growing economic prosperity means a growing middle class, which in turn means a growing intolerance of political oppression and political impotence. If this theory seems *prima facie* validated in South Korea and Taiwan, it does not seem to hold with other NICs, most notably Singapore.

A more plausible explanation lies in the dynamics of the politics of competitive legitimation of divided polity. Once martial law was lifted, democratization was allowed to take its course, or at least the government was deterred from suppressing it, to mitigate the delegitimation that the ROC's international diplomatic isolation vaunts to domestic and international audiences. Here enters another factor explaining the wave of democratization that has swept much of the Third World in the 1980s—the global communication and transparency revolution. For the first time in more than half a century, Taiwan is demolishing (with considerable help from China's own self-delegitimizing behavior) the harsh truth that has so long belied and overshadowed its own pursuit of domestic and international legitimation—namely, the political culture of the KMT and the CCP seemed immutably encoded by the same Leninist party-state structures and processes, the same intolerance of political liberalism, the same traditional cult of statism and gerontocracy, and the same traditional fear of *neiluan*. The legitimation factor assumed greater saliency with the ascendancy of Lee Teng-hui, who, as a native born and bred Taiwanese, had to seek a new source of legitimacy as president. In short, the synergistic interplay of four factors—the growing economic prosperity and middle class; the legitimation factor of divided polity; the global transparency revolution; and the new leadership—has speedily reflected and telescoped the Taiwanese democratization process. One of the least intended but most significant consequences of democratization has been to fuel the drive toward greater Taiwanization. Only a few years ago, calling for independence was considered sedition, punishable by seven years' imprisonment. With the lifting of so many bans and the repeal of the "emergency" laws in recent years, people have felt freer than ever to speak out, including advocacy of independence even as exiled independence movement leaders returned home to join the politics of the national identity dynamic. By August 1991, Taiwan's opposition DPP was emboldened enough to put forward a draft constitution for the "Republic of Taiwan." When the government threatened to prosecute the DDP for illegally advocating independence, the liberal wing of the ruling KMT quickly intervened to avert a legitimation disaster that would inevitably flow from governmental oppression. Faced with the clear and present danger of suppression and spurred by the rise of newly independent states from the ruins of a disintegrating Soviet Union, the DPP threatened to take their independence/legitimation struggle to the UN in New York and the U.S. Congress in Washington. The DPP performed rather poorly in Taiwan's 1991 second National Assembly election, winning only 23.9 percent, against 71.2 percent for the ruling KMT. The broader point is that the 1991 election was another big step forward in the democratization and Taiwanization process as the new National Assembly would no longer be made up mostly of gerontocrats (dubbed "old thieves" in the local press) who purported to represent districts in mainland China.

The democratization and Taiwanization process took another big step forward on December 19, 1992, when a pivotal election brought about the total renewal and revitalization of the most important legislative body, the Legislative Yuan.[50] In 1992 for the first time all legislators were elected directly by the voters on Taiwan. The results can only be characterized as remarkable losses for the ruling KMT (53.02 percent of the vote)—as anything less than 60 percent of the total vote is generally regarded as a crushing humiliation by Taiwan's standards—and major advances for the DPP (31.68 percent of the vote). This hotly contested election reflected and effected a three-way division among politicians and the voting public on the question of Taiwan's national identity: a majority of native Taiwanese KMT (the liberal wing) advocated a two-China policy; a minority pro-China conservative wing of the KMT (the New KMT Alliance) pushed for unification; and the opposition DPP stood firm on Taiwan's independence. The poor showing of the KMT in this pivotal election led to the resignation of the conservative mainlander Premier Hau Pei-tsun and the ascendancy of the first Taiwanese premier of the country, Lien Chan. For the first time, both the president and the prime minister are Taiwanese. The trend is clear enough—political power has effectively shifted from the KMT Central Standing Committee to the legislative bodies, and the conservative pro-China KMT forces are steadily losing their legitimacy in Taiwan's democratization-cum-Taiwanization process.

Paradoxically, Taiwan's march away from the mainland toward its own national identity as a newly enriched and newly democratizing country is now touted as a revolution of another kind, even a model for other Chinese communities to emulate. "It is worth noting," as Foreign Minister Frederick F. Chien writes, "that the R.O.C is the first Chinese-dominated society to practice pluralistic party politics....prosperity and democratization have been achieved without bloodshed and without overturning the existing socioeconomic order."[51] It is also reported that this peaceful democratic revolution in Taiwan is making mainland Chinese hearts grow fonder, a kind of "Taiwan fever" or "the China fever reversed" as it were, as more and more Chinese intellectuals on the mainland see in Taiwan a possible modelling pathway of how a repressive government based on Chinese culture can transform itself into a multiparty democratic system.[52]

In the past several years the ROC government has adopted various policy measures to enhance its legitimacy. All three stated objectives of the Six-Year Development Plan with investment capital of $303 billion (and some 779 infrastructural projects) are closely keyed to broadening the bases of legitimation. The first objective of improving the national well-being and quality of life is a long overdue response to come to grips with the ecological crisis belied by the rising per capita income and the growing popular demand to upgrade the quality of life on the island. The second objective of developing Taiwan into an international finance and transportation center is an adaptive Darwinian response to the changing realities of the global political economy—that Taiwan's competitiveness for labor-intensive products in the world market is rapidly disappearing and that Taiwan has no choice but to move up to knowledge-intensive goods and services for economic growth and prosperity. And the third objective of improving substantive relations with the West is another way of seeking international legitimation through economic leverage. About $100 of the $303 billion budget is reported to have been set aside for an international bidding war among Taiwan's major trade partners. Immediately after Premier Hau announced the plan in the summer of 1991, for instance, the American Chamber of Commerce in Taipei sent a letter to President Bush calling on him to lift a ban on visits by cabinet-level officials to Taiwan.[53] Surely, it is no accident that one Western nation after another was setting aside the ban for official cabinet-level visits to Taipei in wake of the plan. Taipei cannot compete with Beijing in an international bidding war to host the 2000 Olympic Games, to be sure, but the plan seems to have become the functional equivalent of a "coming-of-age" party that Taiwan is asking its major trade partners to join. It is a status drive par excellence as much as it is envisioned and designed to lift an international orphan into a fully developed country by 1996, to be situated in the ranks of developed nations.

In another surprising move the government released on February 22,

1992, its first official report on the "2/28" tragedy, Taiwan's Tiananmen massacre that took place on February 22, 1947, when the KMT soldiers killed between 18,000 to 28,000 native Taiwanese. Public discussion of the so-called "2/28 incident" remained taboo until a few years ago. However, President Lee Teng-hui ordered an independent report on the massacre, obviously as a way of seeking deeper legitimation. The unprecedented official report, written by a government research team commissioned by President Lee in 1990, avoids pointing its finger at the KMT leader, Chiang Kai-shek, blaming instead several of his top officials for the reprisals that went on for months. The larger point is that the government has finally brought its biggest skeleton out of the closet as a way of pacifying more than four decades of resentment over the 2/28 tragedy that has plagued relations between native-born Taiwanese and Chinese mainlanders, while the ROC Cabinet council joined local authorities in planning to erect memorials to commemorate the dead. "In 5,000 years of writing history, this is the first time that the Government hasn't interfered in the process," said Marvin C. H. Ho, president of the Taipei Language Institute and a member of the commission that issued the report.[54]

As a way of making defense and foreign policies a bit more transparent, democratic, and accountable, the Taipei government issued its first-ever "National Defense White Paper" on February 17, 1992. The demonstration of an assertive China so ready to engage in a clash of arms to claim the disputed Spratly islands and thus to assert its jurisdiction over sea space and related resources became a matter of acute security concern in East Asia and served as the proximate catalyst for releasing the defense white paper. But the white paper is another reminder that the democratization and relegitimation process is constantly expanding the limits of the possible and the permissible in Taiwan's domestic and foreign policy debate. The defense white paper now prognosticates seven, not three, plausible scenarios of a possible PRC military invasion: 1) should Taiwan advance toward independence; 2) should insurrection occur in Taiwan; 3) should foreign powers interfere in Chinese/Taiwanese domestic problems; 4) should Taiwan go nuclear; 5) should the PRC government feel threatened by Taiwan's active promotion of "peaceful evolution" in the mainland; 6) should the ROC government persist too long in refusing to negotiate the unification issue; and 7) should the ROC military force weaken.[55] In late December 1992 (although not actually released until January 21, 1993) the government also published—at the request of the Legislature's Foreign Affairs Committee and Overseas Affairs Committee in March 1992—its first-ever white paper on foreign policy to drive home the two central points of flexible diplomacy: 1) that the PRC is no longer a matter of concern in Taipei's pursuit of substantive international relations based on the "one China, two political entities" principle (i.e., the dual-recognition formula) and 2) that the UN reentry option remains one of the highest priorities in foreign relations.[56] Thus, the Taipei government is making its defense and foreign policies more transparent and accessible to the public as democracy takes root on island China.

Conclusion

Until the mid-1980s, most analysts and observers offered a rather pessimistic prognostication for the future of Taiwan, committing in the process the fallacy of premature specificity on the question of Taiwan's national identity and legitimation. Conventional wisdom generally proceeded from the premise of the old KMT party line/myth that the ROC is the sole government of China had to be sustained at any cost for it constitutes *raison d'état*, indeed the only basis of legitimacy. Without sustaining this myth that the mainland can still be recaptured, the foundation of the KMT's authority and power would simply collapse. This line of analysis has been belied by recent developments as sketched and analyzed in this chapter. What went wrong in scholarly analysis of Taiwan's international relations? Of course, certain unexpected changes in the international system in recent years account for part of the explanation for miscarried prognostication. More fundamental is the narrow and static conceptions of national identity and legitimation that many of us inherited and carried along in our analysis of Taiwan's role in the international system and that can be characterized as drawing a direct one-to-one causality between national identity and legitimation crises.

The widely perceived notion that Taiwan, like a compulsive overachiever who impresses everybody but himself, is nonetheless gripped by an acute and insoluble national identity crisis is only partially true. Taiwan's national identity is one of inclusion/exclusion, fitting the classic definition offered by Sidney Verba: National identity refers to the "set of individuals who fall within the decision-making scope of the state.... If some members of the populace do not consider themselves as appropriately falling within the domain of the government or, conversely, feel that some other group not within that domain falls within it, one can talk of an identity problem."[57] In terms of Verba's conception of national identity, Taiwan's struggle in the international system can be seen as an ongoing negotiating process to enhance physical and psychological well-being, in the course of which the self attempts to secure an identity that others do not bestow, while others attempt to bestow an identity the self does not wish to embrace. Still, it is remarkable testimonial to the dialectics of firm/flexible diplomacy that the government accepted, albeit haltingly and reluctantly, an imposed identity from the ADB, GATT, and APEC without generating an identity/legitimation crisis at home.

There are several explanations for this paradox. First of all, the national identity dynamic has to be seen and analyzed from a more flexible and contextual premise as the interplay between primordial and situational factors. If the primordial claim cannot be rejected in toto because identity in the classical inclusive sense cannot be changed completely, easily, or frequently, the situational factors do change and change rather frequently and unpredictably. Whatever may be the deeply encoded self-identity, the enactment of such identity is largely time and situation specific. In the case of Taiwan, as in the cases of Chinese people in Hong Kong, Southeast Asia, and North America, the interplay between primordial/ethnocentric and time/situational factors has brought about the coexistence of multiple identities—regional, state-national, and global. Increasingly, national identity is not a credible or meaningful option open to people in Taiwan because the Chinese nation-state is not the only or even the most experienced reality in their psychocultural consciousness and historical time. The much-envied economic success made it possible for a growing number of people in Taiwan to fuse local/regional and cosmopolitan/world identities while finessing the issue of Chinese national identity.[58] In short, people in Taiwan have chosen and altered their identity options to meet or redefine their current needs in light of changing temporal and situational factors. Like their compatriots in Southeast Asia, Taiwanese Chinese seem to be experiencing the simultaneous coexistence of regional, national, and world identities, and these multiple identities are mutually reinforcing.[59]

At the official government level, Beijing's attempt to impose its conception of national identity through the "one country, two systems" formula served as the catalyst for Taiwan's own reunification formulas (e.g., President Lee's "one country, two governments" formula—in effect, the "one nation, two states" formula—and Premier Hau's "one country, two regions" formula), all of which is still totally unacceptable to Beijing.[60] As noted in this chapter, every attempt of Taiwan to enter or reenter international organizations encounters Beijing's unit veto or, where this is not possible, Beijing's misappropriation of Taiwan's national identity as a subordinate Chinese local or provincial government. Even since the Beijing carnage of 1989, Taiwan finds itself unable to gain much in diplomatic recognition or enhanced national identity from the self-inflicted international isolation of its old communist foe, partly because of its own anachronistic pretensions—its claim, for instance, to rule both Mongolia and Tibet. By its own reckoning, the Republic of China is the second-largest country in the world, with Tibet and the Mongolia constituting nearly 42 percent of its more than 11.4 million square kilometers.[61]

At the same time, the quest for national identity and legitimation, when blocked in one dimension, compensates in another. Taiwan's increasingly flexible and heroic management of its national identity-cum-legitimation problems must be seen in this more synthetic sense of national identity. That is, Taiwan's national identity crisis in terms of what the state *is* substantially mitigated by what the state actually *does* in terms of alternative sources of legitimation. The Taipei government continues to argue, albeit with less normative energy and conviction, that the name "Taiwan" would play into the hands of the independence movement even as the Ministry of Economic Affairs and private business groups are funding a major global public relations campaign to identify export products as "Made in Taiwan" and the Ministry of Foreign Affairs is working hard to "upgrade" the titles of its semiofficial offices around the world so that they could more easily and correctly be recognized as belonging to Taiwan. The new preferred name that the Ministry of Foreign Affairs is pushing is "Taipei Economic and Cultural Office." The Japanese government accepted this name change in 1992.

There is little doubt that the government gradually shifted its main source of legitimation from the claim to represent all of China to the performance-based claim to have brought about economic power and prosperity for the people. Recently, such a claim has been further buttressed by the democratization process in Taiwan and by the self-delegitimating behavior of the party-state in the mainland. With the total retirement of the "old thieves," the reconstitution of the newly empowered Legislative Yuan through direct popular election, and the ascendancy of a native-born president and premier, the Taipei government for the first time has a credible claim to legitimacy based on the fact that it now represents the people of Taiwan, not old districts in the mainland lost to the Chinese communists during the Civil War.

For a long time state sovereignty, like self-reliance, served as an essential legitimizing principle for any newly independent state. In an age of global communication and interdependence, however, the symbolic trappings of state sovereignty (flag, anthem, diplomatic recognition, membership in international organizations, etc.) no longer bring power and plenty. Almost everywhere today—except, of course, in those few remaining oppressed nations still trapped in occupied territories and multinational empires (e.g., Palestinians and Tibetans)—state sovereignty is either in voluntary retreat or in a permeated situation. Economically, virtually every state today has a shared or compromised sovereignty. "Every industrial country, including Japan," as the *Economist* put it, "has more of its economy under the control of foreign firms than a decade ago."[62] With borderless information, money, and companies moving as freely and as fast as modern electronic impulses and in constant global search for the best returns comes steady slippage of state sovereignty on business and financial matters. Taiwan should not feel too badly for having lost its symbolic sovereignty and its name reappropriated in the international community, for there are people in at least 100 member states of the United Nations who would gladly swap their state sovereignty for Taiwan's economic growth with equity and democratization.

Of course, the principle of state sovereignty still remains the most powerful international barrier to external military aggression, as was most vividly demonstrated in the recent Gulf War. Indeed, this type of threat to sovereignty is becoming increasingly rare and quixotic not only because of the steady diminution in the utility of military power for all but purely defensive purposes but also because territory in much of the world has lost the paramount political and economic value it once had. Ironically, in the Taiwan case, it would be a precipitous claim to state sovereignty as an independent state of Taiwan that would provoke Beijing's resort to the use of military force. Herein lies the challenge of Taiwan's flexible diplomacy in the international system—trying to act as an independent sovereign member state in substance if not in official recognition and name. Despite the *pro forma* protestations, the Taipei government has in a way outperformed Beijing's own style of being firm in principle but flexible in practice, as shown in the preceding analysis. The principal outcome of Taipei's flexible diplomacy in recent years has been to diversify its relationship among a broader array of international actors, thereby expanding its policy options while skating over the issue of national identity. Taiwan finds itself engaged in a much denser and diversified web of complex global economic interdependence.

Predicting the future of any divided polity has always been hazardous and never more so than the present Grotian moment—as amply attested to by the sudden German reunification and the equally surprising entry of the two Koreas into the United Nations—even as the international system itself is undergoing a dramatic and long-term transformation. Given the size and proximity factor, the shape of things to come in Taiwan may depend, to a significant extent, on Beijing's unification policy, which in turn is being impacted upon and shaped by a host of domestic and external factors. Today, more than ever before—this is suggested as one plausible scenario extrapolated from the recent developments in both Chinas—the concept of one China seems like a myth that papers over growing economic, political, and identity disparities and tensions between mainland and island China. The two Chinas' reunification drive under various and varying formulas resembles a Taoist paradox: doing less and less is really achieving more and more. To hold together different parts of a whole, one must let them go.

Commentary

Charlotte Ku

International Legitimation in the Late Twentieth Century

Samuel Kim offers a comprehensive survey of relevant factors that, in the late twentieth century, contribute to status and legitimation in the international system. Two factors that are emerging as key to assessments of legitimacy are economic success and internal democratization; and based on these factors, the case for Taiwan's international status and legitimacy seems incontrovertible. As Kim indicates in his chapter, Taiwan's per capita income is about 30 times that of mainland China. The end of martial law and the free elections held in December 1992 indicate movement towards democratization in Taiwan.

Yet, as Kim's analysis shows, Taiwan has not regained the international status it commanded in 1949 when its per capita income was roughly equal to that of the mainland and it was governed by martial law. This is the case because the diplomatic recognition game played by the two entities claiming to represent all of China has developed into a zero-sum game where, as Kim points out, "each party has come to view its own legitimation as dependent on the delegitimation of the other." The meeting in late April 1993 of representatives of the two governments in Singapore may signal the lowering of the official stakes. Still, the official rhetoric—on both sides of the Taiwan Strait—remains that of one China.[63]

Why has the mainland attained the international recognition and status that Taiwan can also claim? The answer here is an objective one. There seems little question that Taiwan is a fully viable state in its own right, with the requisite factors of territory, population, government, and substantial independence of action. The difficulty arises in its claim to represent the government of all China. Where the facts diverge so widely from the claim, the claim becomes difficult to support. China's size—both in territory and in population—and its own increasing economic strength, plus a willingness to take part in international institutions and obligations, make Taiwan's claim even more untenable. But is it in the interest of the two entities, the region, and the international system to deny Taiwan status and legitimacy? The answer is clearly no, and Taiwan's flexible diplomacy and the mainland's pragmatism have made it possible for Taiwan to maintain and expand active international relations.

As countries moved in the 1970s to establish diplomatic ties with the People's Republic of China, Taiwan replaced its embassies and consulates with trade offices, cultural offices, and other carefully named entities such as the Coordination Council for North American Affairs, which maintains Taiwan's interests in the United States and issues visas for travel to Taiwan. Through these devices, Taiwan has managed to conduct its business and maintain its relations with countries that established formal ties with the PRC. Flexibility in relations between the two has also made possible the increase in individual and business contacts and relations across the Taiwan Strait. The management of issues like the repatriation of criminals, smuggling, and inheritance have also forged semiofficial links between the two governments. At the same time, President Lee Teng-hui has noted that: "We must be very patient in forging rapprochement with the mainland."[64]

But operating informally "within the family" is quite different from Taiwan representing China on the international level—in international organizations, for example. At this level, Beijing remains no less vigilant or insistent that it alone represents China—all of China, including Taiwan. Where organizations have chosen to provide a role for Taiwan, they have done so at Beijing's sufferance.

At the level of intergovernmental organizations like the United Nations, Taiwan not only lost the Chinese seat on the Security Council and in the General Assembly, but China moved to erase all trace of

Taiwan's former membership. This position on the part of Beijing softened in the case of membership in the Asian Development Bank where both the People's Republic of China and Taiwan, under the name of Taipei, China, participate as members. The incentive to find a workable formula for Taiwan to stay in the bank was great, given the financial resources that Taipei brought to it. As a potential borrower, China had incentive to accept Taiwan's continued membership in the bank and the capital that Taiwan contributed. Where incentives exist for China to accept Taiwan's participation in intergovernmental organizations and Taiwan is willing to join using a name other than the Republic of China, there appears to be movement on both sides away from the earlier zero-sum perceptions of legitimation and delegitimation.

The entry process into organizations like GATT makes it possible to calculate in advance the relative loss or gain for each side in the international legitimation game, since conditions for entry are spelled out in advance for each applicant—in Article XXXIII of the General Agreement on Tariffs and Trade, for example. These pre-entry negotiations provide an opportunity to define the precise scope of the entity's competence and obligation within a larger framework and make it possible to avoid the question of representation of China all together. The representation question has also been avoided in approaches like the one taken by Asia-Pacific Economic Cooperation, where three Chinese entities are members: Beijing (as the People's Republic of China), Taipei (as Chinese Taipei), and Hong Kong (as Hong Kong). Assuming no fundamental change in the positions of either Beijing or Taipei to represent China, the availability of these processes to lower the stakes in the legitimation game may provide a means to accommodate the needs of China, Taiwan, and the international community.

Domestic Politics as a Factor in the Quest for International Legitimation

As Kim points out, the dynamics of the quest for legitimation occur at different levels. Each of the entities must contend with external and internal forces. The history of the late Ch'ing dynasty and the pre-1949 years of the Republic of China show that external acceptance cannot create legitimacy for a government in the absence of internal support. For China, the need for external recognition and acceptance has increased in the post-Tiananmen Square period as the Chinese government seeks to bolster its internal legitimacy. If the ability of a recognized authority to govern effectively diverges too much from reality (as was the case in the two periods cited above), dependence on external acceptance and status can become a liability.

Although Beijing is still very much an effective government, it cannot ignore the implications of its internal politics on its international status. China is aware of this interplay. Beijing released dissidents associated with the spring 1989 democracy movement at critical points in the U.S. debate on renewal of China's most-favored-nation status, and loosened restrictions imposed on the press to enhance its chance of hosting the Olympic Games. The steady emergence since World War II of an international human rights regime has made it possible for other countries and groups to raise questions in international institutions about the treatment of individuals—including the nationals of third countries. This increased transparency in contemporary international relations makes the accountability of governments to those they govern a relevant factor in determining legitimacy and status in the international system.

Driven by the newly discovered possibilities of economic prosperity, segments of China are exerting pressure on the government to continue its opening in the economic area. Since Beijing is pursuing a policy of economic development, and with bilateral trade between Taiwan and the mainland now worth $7.4 billion, it would seem difficult to resist this pressure, even if it means closer relations with Taiwan. Taiwan's economic strength serves as a magnet that has moderated Beijing's campaign to delegitimize Taiwan. The view among the new mainland entrepreneurs is that politics should not stand in the way of market forces and economic development. Taiwan's needs for cheaper labor and new markets also create incentives for it to pursue economic relations with the mainland.

In contrast to the incentive for the mainland to overlook the question of Taiwan's political status, economic prosperity and development have produced frustration within Taiwan at its indeterminate political status despite its highly touted economic power. This frustration has recently taken the form of heightened domestic interest and political pressure for Taiwan to rejoin the United Nations—either as the Republic of China or the Republic of Taiwan. Political liberalization in Taiwan has provided a platform for this debate, which is increasingly pushing "one China" advocates into a conservative wing of the KMT. This turn of events has provoked several responses from the Beijing government, one of which was a March 15, 1993, statement by Premier Li Peng, who said: "We are resolutely opposed to any form of two China's [sic] or one China and one Taiwan; and we will take all necessary drastic measures to stop any activities aimed at making Taiwan independent and splitting the mother-land."

The irony is that while internal pressures on the mainland may be inducing a softening in Beijing's stance on Taiwan, and internal pressures in Taiwan may be moving it away from pursuing its claim to represent all China, this divergence may actually raise rather than lower the stakes in the legitimation game by introducing independence for Taiwan as an option. The growing strength of the Democratic Progressive Party in Taiwan may serve as a barometer for emerging political sentiment. According to one analysis of the DPP's 31 percent popular vote in the December 1992 Legislative Yuan election, "Name recognition and constituent services garnered the most votes, while domestic concerns for stability, competent government, and improved social services were the dominant issues, though 'independence' issues were scarcely below the surface."[65] Whatever the reasons, the change from 71 percent of the popular vote for the KMT versus 23 percent for the DPP in 1991 to 53 percent for the KMT and 31 percent for the DPP in 1992, indicates that change is afoot in Taiwan. The KMT is further weakened by its own internal factionalization.

Chinese National Identity and Territorial Reunification

On October 1, 1949, when Mao Tse-tung stepped onto the Gate of Heavenly Peace to proclaim the People's Republic of China, not only did it end decades of civil war, but it also initiated China's program of reunification and of regaining the status that it lost as a result of military weakness in the nineteenth century. This led the People's Republic to a concerted program of recreating China's territorial reach to that of the Ch'ing dynasty at the height of its power. The program included efforts to draw back into Chinese control Outer Mongolia, Manchuria, Tibet, and Hong Kong.

In the case of Tibet, the government of the People's Republic demonstrated that it would not hesitate to use force to achieve its purposes when it crushed a rebellion against Chinese communist rule in the 1950s. While the world community expressed outrage in the United Nations, it did little to reverse the action. Frequent skirmishes between the armies of China and the Soviet Union in the 1960s along the Mongolian and Manchurian frontiers made war between the two communist countries seem possible. The points of friction were the gradual cession, through treaty or other international agreements, of territory to Russia that China felt belonged to it. In the case of Hong Kong, reunification will be achieved peacefully by an agreement concluded with the United Kingdom in 1984 that will return control of the territory to China in 1997. However, the present transition from British to Chinese rule, with Beijing making plain that it wishes to have as few competing sources of power and authority in the governing of the territory as possible, have made these last years of British rule contentious ones.

This record demonstrates the seriousness with which China pursues its program of national reunification. It is a program that has contributed to the internal legitimation of the Chinese communist government, and that may force mainland action should Taiwan decide to declare its independence. Rumblings of Chinese intentions were heard in the shelling of Taiwan's offshore islands of Quemoy and Matsu in the 1950s.

Although Taiwan had been historically colonized by Portugal and Japan, its post-1949 government under the Kuomintang at least kept the island under Chinese rule. The difficult question is whether China can accept Taiwan as an independent entity, even if under the rule of a Chinese/Taiwanese population. The question is further complicated by uncertainty whether the international community is willing to allow China to intervene in the future political development of Taiwan. Given the great strides made towards democratization in Taiwan since the lifting of martial law in 1987, China may find its arguments that the future of the island is an internal matter weakened by strong and public statements from the people of Taiwan that their free choice is for independence. The suppression by military force of this expression of self-determination by an educated and prosperous population may well result in calls for an international response. However, as the effort to frame an international response to the situation in Bosnia demonstrates, the international community responds slowly, if at all.

What might induce caution on the part of the PRC is a functioning regional framework, which makes any military action taken by China against Taiwan subject to regional review and response. U.S. participation will likely be required to forge a common purpose of regional stability out of the disparate interests represented by the countries of the Pacific region. Genuine stability in the region will be hard to achieve until the relationship between China and Taiwan is clarified and made manageable. The present challenge is to channel the various political forces inside and outside China and Taiwan to that end.

Notes

I would like to thank the participants of the April 15, 1993, session of the Taiwan Study Group held at The Gaston Sigur Center of East Asian Studies, The George Washington University, Washington, DC, for their helpful oral comments and suggestions on an earlier draft of this chapter. I would especially like to thank Thomas Bernstein, Ralph Clough, Charlotte Ku, Andrew Nathan, and Robert Sutter for their helpful written comments and suggestions for revision, without implicating them in any particular argument or position adopted in the study.

1. Qian's answer to a reporter's question about a year-end's assessment of the Chinese foreign policy of 1992, as reported by *Xinhua* (New China News Agency) in Foreign Broadcast Information Service: Daily Report: China (hereafter cited as FBIS-China), December 29, 1992, p. 2.

2. "A Pragmatic Vision: Interview by Yvonne Yuan," *Free China Review*, vol. 43, no. 2, February 1993, p. 16.

3. In the most recent (1993) annual report based on 1991 figures, the World Bank uses a four-fold topology based on 1991 figures for categorizing the nation-states (and their economies): 1) low-income, $635 or less; 2) lower-middle-income, $636-$2,555; 3) upper-middle-income, $2,556-$7,910; and 4) high-income, $7,911 or more. For obvious reasons, Taiwan is treated as a nonentity, not even as an economy for classification purposes, hence it is excluded from this and other reports. See World Bank, *World Development Report 1993: Investing in Health*, (New York, NY: Oxford University Press, 1993), pp. 326-27.

4. Foreign Minister Frederick Chien's speech at Harvard University as excerpted in *Free China Journal*, November 26, 1991, p. 7. Also see discussion of "flexible diplomacy" in other chapters of this book, especially those by Jencks, Dreyer, and Gold.

5. Dolf Sternberger, "Legitimacy," in the *International Encyclopedia of the Social Sciences*, vol. 9, (New York, NY: Free Press, 1968), pp. 244-48; quote at p. 244.

6. Max Weber, *Economy and Society*, vol. I, Guenther Roth and Claus Wittich, eds., (Berkeley, CA: University of California Press, 1978), p. 213.

7. Max Weber has become an almost mandatory point of departure for any contemporary discussion of legitimacy. But Weber's three ideal types of legitimate authority—traditional, charismatic, and rational-legal—have provided an overly static and compartmentalized conception of legitimacy. Dankwart Rustow offers useful reformulations of Weber's theory: 1) political stability = legitimacy of institutions + personal legitimacy of rulers; and 2) political legitimacy = traditional legitimacy + rational/legal legitimacy + charismatic legitimacy. See Dankwart A. Rustow, *A World of Nations: Problems of Political Modernization*, (Washington, DC: The Brookings Institution, 1967), p. 157.

8. The literature on legitimacy or legitimation is too voluminous to cite, but a sample of useful works includes the following: William Connolly, ed., *Legitimacy and the State*, (New York, NY: New York University Press, 1984); Jürgen Habermas, *Legitimation Crisis*, trans. by Thomas McCarthy, (Boston, MA: Beacon Press, 1975); John H. Herz, "Legitimacy: Can We Retrieve It?" *Comparative Politics*, vol. 10, no. 3, April 1978, pp. 317-43; Lucian W. Pye, "The Legitimacy Crisis," in Leonard

Binder, et al., *Crises and Sequences in Political Development*, (Princeton, NJ: Princeton University Press, 1971), pp. 135-58; T. H. Rigby and Ferenc Feher, eds., *Political Legitimation in Communist States*, (New York, NY: St. Martin's Press, 1982); Rustow, *A World of Nations*; Frederick C. Teiwes, *Leadership, Legitimacy and Conflict in China: From a Charismatic Mao to the Politics of Succession*, (Armonk, NY: M. E. Sharpe, Inc., 1984); and Weber, *Economy and Society*.

9. Lucian W. Pye, "China: Erratic State, Frustrated Society," *Foreign Affairs*, vol. 69, no. 4, Fall 1990, p. 58.

10. "Qian Qichen on the World Situation," *Beijing Review*, vol. 33, no. 3, January 15-21, 1990, p. 16.

11. John K. Fairbank, "A Preliminary Framework," in John K. Fairbank, ed., *The Chinese World Order: Traditional China's Foreign Relations*, (Cambridge, MA: Harvard University Press, 1968), p. 3.

12. In this connection, Jürgen Habermas argues that legitimation crisis "is directly an identity crisis." Legitimation crisis defines the limit beyond which a system can no longer resolve its problems without giving up or altering its political identity. Lucian Pye also sees a close connection between the problems of identity and legitimacy. In a similar vein, John Herz defines legitimacy in terms of "internal (or regime) legitimacy" and "external (group) legitimacy," relating "to a basic need that human beings want units such as nation-states to satisfy: to give them a feeling of `belonging,' of identity with the group." See Habermas, *Legitimation Crisis*, pp. 2-4, 46, 48, 69, and 74-75; Pye, "The Legitimacy Crisis," pp. 135, 137, and 153; and Herz, "Legitimacy," p. 318.

13. For a synthetic formulation of national identity theory along this line, see Lowell Dittmer and Samuel S. Kim, "In Search of a Theory of National Identity," in Lowell Dittmer and Samuel S. Kim, eds., *China's Quest for National Identity*, (Ithaca, NY: Cornell University Press, 1993), pp. 1-31. For an application of such synthetic theory of national identity in the Chinese case, see various contributions in this volume including Samuel S. Kim and Lowell Dittmer, "Whither China's Quest for National Identity?" pp. 237-90.

14. The premier's oral report to the First Meeting of the 52nd Session of the First Legislative Yuan, September 25, 1973, cited in Byron S. J. Weng, "Taiwan's International Status," *The China Quarterly*, no. 99, September 1984, p. 465.

15. See Hungdah Chiu, "The International Legal Status of the Republic of China (Revised Version)," in *Occasional Papers/Reprints Series in Contemporary Asian Studies*, no. 5, 1992, pp. 16-18.

16. For details, see Samuel S. Kim, *China, the United Nations, and World Order*, (Princeton, NJ: Princeton University Press, 1979), pp. 102-4.

17. Hong Kong AFP in English, in FBIS-China, October 16, 1989, p. 64.

18. Taipei CNA in English in FBIS-China, March 22, 1993, p. 78.

19. Latvian Foreign Minister Janis Jurkans specifically mentioned this point during his visit to Taipei in December 1991. See James L. Tyson, "Taiwan, Besting China, Sets Up Ties to Baltics," *Christian Science Monitor*, December 27, 1991, p. 8; *Free China Journal*, January 31, 1992, p. 1.

20. For further analysis of the great power politics on the Korean UN membership question, see Samuel S. Kim, "The Long Road to the Two Koreas' UN

Membership," *Hokaku Semina* (Jurisprudential Seminar) (Tokyo), Special Issue on "The New Era of the United Nations: The First Step of Reform," vol. 36, no. 11, November 1991, pp. 65-71 (in Japanese).

21. See Tokyo KYODO in English, in FBIS-China, September 15, 1992, p. 12.

22. Latvia permitted the ROC to set up a consulate general in Riga, as a result of which the PRC suspended diplomatic relations.

23. On September 24, 1992, Vanuatu Foreign Minister Serge Vohor signed a joint communiqué with ROC Foreign Minister Frederick Chien whereby each side "officially recognized" the other. The next day, back in Vanuatu, PRC Vice Foreign Minister Wang Wendong reportedly stated the PRC did not object to "trade ties" between Vanuatu and Taiwan and a few days later signed a $3.6 million interest-free loan agreement with Vanuatu Prime Minister Maxime Carlot. See CNA September 24, 1992, in FBIS-China, September 1992, p. 67; and Radio Australia (Melbourne), September 30, 1992, in FBIS-EAS, October 2, 1992, p. 42.

24. Pye, "China: Erratic State, Frustrated Society," p. 61.

25. See UN Press Release, "United Nations Member States," ORG/1162, May 28, 1993.

26. The post-World War II structural transformation of world politics has come about through the replacement of the state system with a bifurcated system, James Rosenau argues, in which a new multicentric world coexists and competes with the old statecentric world. As a way of transcending statist thinking about world politics in a period of rapid and turbulent change and of not giving any unwarranted preeminence to the state system, Rosenau rejects the term "nonstate actor," as it "creates a residual category for all collectivities other than states, implying that they occupy subordinate statuses in the ranks of postinternational politics." Accordingly, Rosenau uses the terms "sovereignty-bound actors" and "sovereignty-free actors" with the former referring to what is normally called state actors and the latter referring to what is normally called nonstate actors. See James N. Rosenau, *Turbulence in World Politics: A Theory of Change and Continuity*, (Princeton, NJ: Princeton University Press, 1990), p. 36.

27. For a comprehensive and standard work on China and INGOs with detailed discussion on the making of the Olympic and ICSU Formulas, see Gerald Chan, *China and International Organizations: Participation in Non-Governmental Organizations Since 1971*, (New York, NY: Oxford University Press, 1989).

28. For detailed analysis, see Kim, *China, the United Nations, and World Order*, pp. 97-177.

29. See Cheng-yi Lin, "Taipei's ADB Policy and Its Implications for Taiwan's External Relations," in Yun-han Chu, ed., *The Role of Taiwan in International Economic Organizations*, (Taipei: Institute for National Policy Research, 1990), pp. 63-78, and Peter Yu, "On Taipei's Rejoining the Asian Development Bank (ADB) Subsequent to Beijing's Entry: One Country, Two Seats?" *Asian Affairs: An American Review*, vol. 17, no. 1, Spring 1990, pp. 4-5.

30. For the PRC statement to the effect that the ADB case is a special and exceptional case that "cannot be regarded as a model universally applicable to other intergovernmental, international organizations," see *Renmin Ribao* (People's Daily), overseas ed., December 20, 1988, p. 1.

31. For a more detailed analysis along this line, see Byron S. J. Weng, "Divided China and the Question of Membership in International Economic Organizations," in Chu, *The Role of Taiwan in International Economic Organizations*, pp. 27-62.

32. The compromise on bringing three Chinese entities into the APEC also included an understanding that "Chinese-Taipei" would be represented by its economic minister rather than its foreign minister.

33. "What's in the Name?", *China Post* (Taipei), August 18, 1992, p. 4.

34. Beijing's entry into the GATT got unexpectedly stalled in the final phase of bilateral Sino-American negotiations on the accession protocol with the major sticking points centering on China's reluctance to comply with Western demands for a more explicit trade and pricing system and for an anti-dumping safeguard system to protect against major surges in Chinese exports. This latest development considerably enhances the prospects of Taipei's entry before Beijing. See *The Economist*, March 6, 1993, pp. 35-36 and Lincoln Kaye, "Slow Boat for China: Peking's Application to Join GATT Appears Stalled," *Far Eastern Economic Review*, March 11, 1993, pp. 56-57.

35. Tammy C. Peng, "After GATT, OECD Next Challenge Confronting ROC," *Free China Journal*, February 2, 1993, p. 2.

36. Taipei CNA in English, in FBIS-China, September 23, 1991, p. 69.

37. *Zhongyang ribao* (Central Daily) (Taipei), April 10, 1993, p. 1.

38. Taipei CNA (in English), April 22, 1993, in FBIS-China, April 22, 1993, p. 39.

39. See the pamphlet *Zhonghua minguo canyu Lianheguo* (The ROC Participates in the United Nations), issued by the ROC Foreign Ministry in May 1993.

40. For a complete text of the press conference, see FBIS-China, May 21, 1993, pp. 70-79; quote at p. 72.

41. UN Doc. S/20355, December 28, 1988.

42. For a cogent analysis along this line, see Chi Su, "The International Relations of the Republic of China During the 1990s," paper presented at the 22nd Sino-American Conference on Contemporary China, Center for Strategic and International Studies, Washington, DC, June 21-22, 1993.

43. For a list of the ROC's semiofficial missions abroad, see Appendix II in Chiu, "The International Legal Status of the Republic of China," pp. 28-32.

44. See the ROC Ministry of Foreign Affairs, *Waijiao baogaoshu: Duiwai guanxi yu waijiao xingzheng* (Foreign Affairs White Paper: External Relations and Diplomatic Administration), (Taipei: Ministry of Foreign Affairs, 1992), pp. 314-15. Although the publication date is December 1992, this first-ever white paper on foreign policy was not released until late February 1993.

45. *Waijiao baogaoshu*, pp. 328-32.

46. For details see "Taiwan on the Move: Survey," *The Economist* (London), October 10, 1992, pp. 1-18 (inset), and "The Overseas Chinese," *The Economist*, July 18, 1992, pp. 21-24.

47. I owe this point to Andrew Nathan.

48. Seymour Martin Lipset, "Some Social Requisites of Democracy: Economic Development and Political Legitimacy," *American Political Science Review*, vol. 53, 1959, p. 75.

49. Barrington Moore, Jr., *Social Origins of Dictatorship and Democracy*, (Boston, MA: Beacon Press, 1966), p. 418.

50. See Andrew J. Nathan, "The Legislative Yuan Elections in Taiwan: Consequences of the Electoral System," *Asian Survey*, vol. 33, no. 4, April 1993, pp. 424-38.

51. Frederick F. Chien, "A View From Taipei," *Foreign Affairs*, vol. 70, no. 5, Winter 1991/92, p. 96.

52. Nicholas D. Kristof, "Taiwan's Parties Test Limits of New Freedom," *New York Times*, December 17, 1992, p. A19.

53. Sheryl WuDunn, "Taiwan Sets Plan To Rebuild Nation: $300 Billion Project Draws Bids From Around World," *New York Times*, October 27, 1991, pp. 1, and 14.

54. Cited in Nicholas D. Kristof, "The Horror of 2-28: Taiwan Rips Open the Past," *New York Times*, April 3, 1992, p. A4.

55. The ROC Ministry of Defense, *Guofang baogaoshu* (National Defense White Paper), (Taipei: Liming wenhua shiye gufen yuxian gongsi, 1992), p. 42.

56. *Waijiao baogaoshu*, op. cit.

57. Sidney Verba, "Sequences and Development," in Binder, *Crises and Sequences in Political Development*, p. 299.

58. For a thoroughgoing analysis along this line for coastal China embracing Hong Kong, Guangdong, and Taiwan, see Lynn White and Li Cheng, "China Coast Identities: Regional, National, Global," in Dittmer and Kim, *China's Quest for National Identity*, pp. 154-93.

59. In June 1989, Taiwan's independent Public Opinion Research Foundation asked, "What do you think will be [the] future relations between Taiwan and the mainland in 10 years?" The responses were as follows: 18.6 percent said Taiwan would reunify with China, 5.1 percent felt Taiwan would enter into a confederation, 1.2 percent predicted Taiwan would be independent, 22.3 percent did not see a change in Taiwan-mainland relations. The most common response, however, was "I don't know," which 36.5 percent checked off. See Carl Murphy, "The Knotty Question of China's Reunification," *Asian Wall Street Weekly*, vol. 11, August 7, 1989, p. 14.

60. For Beijing's total rejection, see *Renmin ribao*, overseas ed., May 3, 1990, p. 5.

61. According to Wu Hau-peng, chairman of the Taiwan's Mongolian and Tibetan Affairs Commission; see Lincoln Kaye, "China's Minorities Problems Are No Help to the KMT," *Far Eastern Economic Review*, May 17, 1990, p. 22.

62. "The Myth of Economic Sovereignty," *The Economist*, June 23, 1990, p. 67.

63. See Nicholas D. Kristof, "China and Taiwan Have First Talks," *New York Times*, April 28, 1993, p. A8.

64. Nicholas D. Kristof, "After Four Decades of Bitterness, China and Taiwan Plan to Meet," *New York Times*, April 12, 1993, p. A5.

65. "United States and China at a Crossroads," Atlantic Council Policy Paper, February 1993, p. 30.

6

Domestic Roots of Taiwan's Influence in World Affairs

Thomas B. Gold

Other chapters in this book examine some of Taiwan's activities in the international arena. It is clear that in spite of the fact that fewer than thirty countries recognize the Republic of China (ROC) as a sovereign nation, through channels such as quasi-governmental organizations, businesses, citizens groups, and individuals, Taiwan has become a global player. This chapter shifts the focus away from the world scene to Taiwan itself, addressing social, political, and economic sources for its external impact. Although I will separate them for analytical purposes, in reality they are closely interrelated, and create a climate or environment for domestic and foreign actors.

As I will argue, some elements of this environment serve to increase Taiwan's influence on the world stage, while others are limiting or eroding it.

Taiwan's Global Influence

The other chapters in this book cover Taiwan's role in several global systems. There is no need to go through them again except in list form: economic (import, export, investment, lending, competition, intellectual property violation, employment, investment site, source of tourists); political (lobbyist, aid provider, supporter or destroyer of particular political figures, intimidation of ROC citizens in other countries, stalwart anti-communist); cultural (repository of Chinese traditional art, creator and marketer of popular culture); criminal (drug trafficking, smuggling illegal emigrants from mainland China); educational (trainer, sender of students, research and development, funder of scholarly research and symposia); environmental; security; and normative (anti-communism, model of economic development and political democratization, philanthropy).

Taiwan's role is more substantial in some arenas—economic in particular—than others. Not enjoying diplomatic ties with most of the rest of the world, Taiwan has settled for so-called substantive relations as a substitute. To ensure its survival as a separate entity, the government has aggressively promoted multifarious ties between Taiwanese organizations, of a quasi-governmental or private nature, and counterpart groups abroad. Some countries or regions, such as the United States, the People's Republic of China (PRC), Japan, and East Asia, figure more prominently in Taiwan's external relations than others.

Does playing a "role" translate into "influence"? By "influence," I mean inducing other actors to consider Taiwan's position and possible response when making decisions. "Actors" include governments, even those that do not have diplomatic relations with the ROC, as well as nongovernmental actors. The decisions they make need not be of earthshaking importance; the idea is that the decision-makers consciously take into consideration the needs, wants, requests, or demands of Taiwanese actors while reaching a decision. Although hard to measure accurately, evidence of "influence" can be detected without much difficulty. In the case of Taiwan, because so few countries acknowledge the existence of a legitimate national government there, and risk incurring sanctions from the PRC if they deal with Taiwan in sensitive ways, we can fairly assume that virtually any dealing with Taiwanese actors, especially in public and for the record, proves that some actor in Taiwan has enough clout to compel another country's actors to engage in some form of intercourse.

Other chapters persuasively demonstrate that other actors in fact not only consider Taiwan's response, but actively consult with it, including meeting governmental officials as well as private representatives. They have dispatched former or sitting state leaders and chairs of organizations, acquiesced in the ROC's demands to establish quasi-consular offices, and supported Taiwan's membership in international organizations, even those comprising only sovereign states. Some of these actions are primarily symbolic—for instance, U.S. Trade Representative Carla Hills's visit in 1992, but in Chinese politics, symbols count for a great deal and must not be denigrated.

While official state-to-state influence has declined since the early

1970s, nonofficial influence (some of which is clearly state-sponsored but managed "privately") has increased dramatically. This is due to the ROC's declining international political fortunes and need to employ indirect channels to maintain contacts, as well as changes within Taiwan itself, the subject of the rest of this chapter.

Domestic Roots

In this section, I will examine relevant changes in Taiwan's social, political, and economic structures, and suggest ways in which these impact Taiwan's influence in world affairs.

Social Roots

By any measure, Taiwan's society has undergone a revolutionary structural change over the past four decades under Nationalist rule. In 1991, nearly 60 percent of the population age 6 and above had completed secondary school, with 11.5 percent receiving higher education. The illiteracy rate was below 7 percent.[1] Employment in the primary sector plummeted from 56 percent in 1952 to 12.9 percent in 1991, although even here, since most of Taiwan's farmers engage in farming only on a part-time basis, these figures probably overstate the real numbers. Over 30 percent of the labor force work in manufacturing, and 47 percent are in the tertiary sector.[2] The number of hospital beds per 10,000 persons rose from 22 as recently as 1980 to 45 in 1991, and the number of health personnel per 10,000 persons rose from 23.8 in 1980 to 47 in 1991.[3] Life expectancy for males is 71.5 years, for females it is 76.75. As part of a natural demographic transition, Taiwan's population increase rate declined to 1.05 percent in 1991—it had been as high as 3.67 percent in 1955.[4] The proportion of the population under 15 years of age declined from a high of 46.0 percent in 1962 to only 26.3 percent in 1991. In 1991, the proportion aged 15-24 was 18 percent.[5] Although this age group's relative share of the total population has shrunk noticeably, the rise of a consumer culture and improved material standard of living have made it an active and significant participant in the market.

A frequently remarked-upon aspect of Taiwan's economic growth has been the relatively equitable way in which the fruits have been distributed.[6] Although this has worsened somewhat in the past decade, Taiwan's achievements in this area cannot be denied. All told, Taiwan now possesses a sizeable middle class. This is a slippery term to define,[7] but in terms of income distribution, self-definition, and consumption patterns, there is a noticeable homogenization and one does not see the glaring inequalities so common in most of the rest of the world. This helped Taiwan avoid the devastating class warfare so common in much of the rest of the developing world. With a savings rate still approaching 30 percent and an official per capita income above US$10,000,[8] Taiwan's people can afford a material standard of living comparable to that in much of the developed world. This includes purchasing extremely upscale automobiles, electrical appliances, and designer clothing, travelling abroad,[9] and cultivating an appreciation for art and music.

While consumerism is rampant, Taiwan's people have become increasingly interested in quality of life issues.[10] Many wealthy individuals have established foundations and think tanks to support a variety of philanthropic causes and engage in policy-related research. A prime example is Chang Yung-fa of Evergreen, who set up the National Policy Research Institute, which undertakes a variety of high-profile studies, publications, and conferences. Regarding the concern for quality of life and the consequences of rapid industrialization, of special import is the environmental cleanup and protection movement, which culminated in the establishment of the cabinet-level Environmental Protection Agency in 1987.[11] Popular concern with the environment has been a major impetus behind the significant investment—approximately US$10.7 billion—in the cleanup and protection of the environment in the Six-Year National Development Plan, entailing imports of equipment, technology, and consultants.[12]

Public concern over the environment is part of a larger trend of the emergence of civil society in Taiwan.[13] By "civil society," I mean the realm between unorganized society and the state, comprising associations that enjoy autonomy to establish themselves, determine their boundaries and membership, administer their own affairs, and engage in relationships with other similar associations at home and abroad. With increased speed at the end of the 1980s, citizens in Taiwan autonomously organized groups to address a wide range of issues, such as the environment, nuclear power, consumer protection, women, labor, human rights, and so on. This is a radical departure from the previous corporatist system where the Kuomintang (KMT), in Leninist fashion, either organized or co-opted all such associations and prohibited the autonomous formation of competing bodies. Civil society has become so active now that citizens' groups demand to be heard by the government before major or minor decisions are made. This has impacted the ability of the government to formulate and implement policies. Activists have established links with comparable organizations abroad. Not all of the organizations in civil society are oriented toward political activism; others, such as the Rotary, Jaycees, Lions, and Bar Association, perform other social and professional functions.

The dismantling of the authoritarian system has freed many concerned citizens to organize around issues large and small. At the same time, other elements in society have taken advantage of the restraints on the instruments of repression to violate the law. From a reputation as an extremely orderly and safe society, Taiwan in the 1980s witnessed a severe deterioration in social order. In addition to increased gang activities, individuals engaged in crime as well. Serious crimes, once almost unheard of, also registered a noticeable rise. At the turn of the 1990s, there was a frightening upsurge in kidnappings. Some of the targets were family members of rich businessmen, but others appeared to be random, with the perpetrators hoping they had abducted someone from a family rich enough to meet hefty ransom demands.

In 1990, in response, the new premier, General Hau Pei-tsun, promised to crack down on crime. While there were many arrests, criminal gangs spread their activities abroad, as far away as North America and Europe, disrupting social order there as well. This was sometimes done in collaboration with elements of the Hong Kong underworld that were also moving offshore in anticipation of a crackdown after the colony reverts to Chinese sovereignty in 1997.[14]

Many of Taiwan's richer residents decided that the decline in social order had made life unbearable on the island. This psychology, combined with a search for new investment outlets, the strength of the New Taiwan dollar, the fear of an eventual communist takeover, and the extremely competitive admissions competition for higher education, pushed them to move their households abroad. In addition to setting up businesses,[15] they have invaded property markets, buying expensive real estate with cash, thereby dramatically inflating the cost of housing in certain areas, such as California.[16] This resettlement has resulted in a significant rise of Chinese professionals and students in North American schools at all levels. The students and parents bring over the extraordinarily competitive, test-driven education mindset from Taiwan that often catapults them to the top of their schools, breeding resentment from less achievement-oriented classmates.

Over the course of the 1980s, the divisions between Taiwanese and mainlanders that had been largely suppressed came back to the surface, first in the form of a call for "self-determination," then in the open advocacy of Taiwan's independence. In the cultural realm as well there was a conscious effort to elaborate a distinct Taiwanese identity, which included use of the local dialect.[17] This effectively excluded many mainlander adults and increased their sense of alienation. As they began to age, and as the PRC opened people-to-people contacts with the outside world, many of them reestablished links with their relatives on the mainland. In 1987 in particular, old soldiers, many of whom had been wrenched from their families and taken to Taiwan against their will, demonstrated to be permitted to return to their native places. President Chiang Ching-kuo granted official permission for this in November of that year.

These changes in social structure, standard of living, organization, and values have had varied repercussions abroad. Many top-of-the-line retailers, such as Rolls Royce and Jaguar, Christian Dior and Gucci, have opened outlets to sell into this market, as have less exclusive companies such as Watsons, Seven Eleven, McDonalds, and Domino's Pizza. Real estate promoters from the United States flock to Taiwan to market commercial as well as residential properties. Flush with cash, many Taiwanese are able to indulge a traditional taste for rare and exotic things, such as rhinoceros horns and tiger parts. This has drawn the attention of activists trying to protect endangered species from many countries and international agencies.

National airlines in Western Europe have set up subsidiaries to fly directly to Taiwan to bring tourists. Foreign airlines are hiring Mandarin-, and sometimes Taiwanese-speaking flight attendants. Tourist facilities in many countries are printing materials in Chinese and reorganizing some of their facilities to be more enticing to free-spending Taiwanese tourists. They are aggressively promoting themselves in Taiwan. Some Las Vegas resorts arrange special programs for Taiwanese during the Christmas season when their American business falls off. They provide a range of special services to accommodate Taiwanese high rollers. Cultural products from Taiwan have risen in quality to satisfy local aficionados, and some have attracted the attention of foreign consumers and distributors. This is most prevalent among Chinese communities in Southeast Asia and mainland China. Young mainlanders are particularly attracted to Taiwan's youth-oriented life style, spending time in game parlors, karaoke bars, and coffee shops, while purchasing Taiwanese popular music cassettes. They are creating a new model of what it means to be a "modern" Chinese. International organizations of all sorts are admitting their Taiwanese counterparts and regularly hold regional or global conferences on the island.

Taiwan's private and state-sponsored philanthropists have attracted a great deal of attention from cash-strapped foreign universities and think tanks. The Chiang Ching-kuo Foundation has become the largest single funder of research on China. American institutions, for example, are aggressively seeking out illustrious and well-heeled, or well-connected alumni in Taiwan to pitch for support. Scholars, including many with no prior experience with Taiwan, have begun to conduct research about the island. The number of conferences and publications about Taiwan, often with financial support from various Taiwan organizations, has increased dramatically.

These examples show the way in which a range of international actors have come to include Taiwan in their planning and tailor some of their activities to the demands of the Taiwanese market.

Political Roots

In the late 1980s, Taiwan's internal political activities began to have international repercussions after a long stretch of near-irrelevance. This came about for several intertwined reasons addressed in this section: the changing way in which the KMT regime legitimizes its rule to its citizenry; the transition to new leaders in the party and state; and the emergence of civil society pressing demands on the state.

During the most intense phase of the Cold War in the 1950s and 1960s, the mainlander-dominated KMT party/state established and maintained Leninist-type control over political life. It did not tolerate dissent, dealing ruthlessly with its critics at home and abroad through a vast, global security network.[18] It controlled government appointments, maintained a political commissar system in the armed forces, monopolized the media and educational systems, and manipulated elections held for sub-national offices. It institutionalized its hard authoritarianism in the form of the Provisional Amendments for the Period of Mobilization of the Suppression of Communist Rebellion, which gave legal authority to martial law. It legitimated these actions in terms of its prominent role on the front lines in the global struggle against communism and the necessity of marshalling all resources to recover the mainland. Its major American backer made very few demands on the regime to soften its control, despite the regime's claim to be "Free China." The KMT was also on record as intent on building an electoral democracy based on the writings of Dr. Sun Yat-sen.

As the economy took off beginning in the late 1960s, the regime took few measures to soften its authoritarian control. Its first reaction to the international diplomatic setbacks it began to incur from the early 1970s was to clamp down hard on internal dissent.[19] It claimed that in the threatening international environment, where its erstwhile allies were shifting their ties from Taipei to Beijing, it was even more crucial to maintain "stability." For most of the 1970s and 1980s, Taiwan's influence on world affairs was negligible. In fact, except for staunch anti-communist allies such as South Korea, South Africa, Paraguay, and Saudi Arabia, other countries derided the ROC for its stubborn refusal to deal with the PRC, which was beginning to enter the world stage as a reformer.

During the 1970s, a transition within the KMT and state began with the rise of Chiang Ching-kuo.[20] Technocrats began to replace ideologues, civilians took over from military men. Chiang, who became premier in 1972 as his father's health declined, recognized the necessity of focusing on the economy. This was because continued economic growth became the basis for the KMT's appeals for legitimacy at home. The rest of the world no longer took the ROC's trumpeting of anti-communism terribly seriously, thereby undercutting a pillar of the regime's claim to its own people of the need for tight control. In addition, Chiang Ching-kuo began to promote Taiwanese in the party and state, as it became clear that the aging mainlander KMT elite could not reproduce itself: its own children emigrated in large numbers and the new successors did not have the same priorities.

The new elite concentrated its energies on improving Taiwan's economy. Clearly, it accepted the reality that Taiwan, or the Republic of China, was not a great power, but a small entity. It had to scale down its pretensions to global importance and adjust to the reality of being an economic powerhouse with virtually no international political clout.

As shown in the discussion of social change, beginning in the late 1970s then gathering steam in the mid-1980s, citizens in Taiwan began to organize outside party control, initiating the creation of civil society. They started by pressing issues of consumer and environmental protection, which were not intrinsically political. However, in the context of the regime's previous consistent record of stamping out autonomous organizations, these activities naturally assumed political significance. At the same time, dissidents became more organized and vocal, in particular demanding the lifting of prohibitions against forming new political parties.

A confluence of several trends decidedly pushed Taiwan's liberalization and democratization onto the fast track: relentless pressure by the opposition, new blood in the Legislative Yuan—both KMT and oppositionists—who raised fundamental questions about the nature of Taiwan's political system; Chiang Ching-kuo's decisions to engage in dialogue with the opposition and abandon suppression; criticism by foreigners, especially members of the U.S. Congress, who had good contacts with the opposition and with activist dissidents from Taiwan residing in the United States.

By the early 1990s, the domestic political system in Taiwan had undergone fundamental change. It passed from a one-party, statist, militarized, hard authoritarianism to a soft authoritarianism,[21] and is now maturing into a multi-party electoral democracy. Many previously unthinkable changes have become commonplace: non-suppression of the newly established Democratic Progressive Party (DPP) despite clear violation of the rigidly enforced prohibition against new political parties (1986); the termination of martial law (1987); permission to travel to the mainland (1987); a Taiwanese president (1988); new laws removing the ban on new political parties, new civic organizations, and new newspapers and the length of newspapers (1989); public advocacy of Taiwan's Independence (1989); removal of the temporary Provisional Amendments for the Period of Mobilization of the Suppression of Communist Rebellion ("Temporary Provisions"), which gave legal authority to martial law (1991); mandated retirement of those members of the National Assembly, Legislative Yuan, and Control Yuan who had been elected in 1946-1947, and would not have had to stand for reelection until the regime recovered the mainland (1991); popular election of a new National Assembly (1991); popular election of a new Legislative Yuan (1992); a Taiwanese premier (1993); and compensation for and a memorial commemorating victims of the February 28, 1947, Massacre (1993).[22]

The transition in the KMT and state has continued. The Legislative Yuan election at the end of 1992 in particular brought in a cohort of well-educated, ambitious, election-oriented, and media-savvy politicians attuned to the demands of their constituents. Nearly one-third of the legislators are members of the DPP, and the KMT itself is seriously split. Its center comprises mostly Taiwanese technocrats advocating flexible diplomacy as a way for the ROC, under almost any name, to re-enter formal international life.[23] The 1992 election brought forth a New KMT Alliance, comprising mainlanders opposed to what they see as trends towards money politics and open advocacy of permanent separation from the mainland.[24] The DPP feels it lacks equal access to the media, so it often engages in excessive action as a way of drawing attention to itself.

This adds up to a situation where Taiwan has become bogged down in the politics of posturing and negotiation. Decisions that would have been easy to make and implement before, such as agreeing to buy U.S. F-16 fighter jets or building a nuclear power plant, now become subject to torturous debate. Government officials undergo pointed interpellation as much to score points and attract attention for politicians as to investigate policies seriously. Politicians seek opportunities to embarrass each other and derail pet projects. The priorities of former Premier Hau Pei-tsun's (1990-1993) Six Year Plan for National Development are being revised, and instances of corruption are being alleged on some projects. In 1993, the DPP and reformist KMT members allied against the KMT center to push passage of a so-called Sunshine Law, forcing government officials to disclose their financial assets. All of these political battles raise questions among foreigners interested in doing business in Taiwan, as to its stability and reliability.

These issues of continued democratization are important and attract the attention of foreign scholars and activists. They have impacted theoretical discussions of democratic transitions from authoritarianism. But the subject with the most potential for influence outside the island is the extremely sensitive matter of Taiwan's identity. It surfaced under various guises—self-determination, independence, one China, one Taiwan—in the elections of 1989, 1991, and 1992. It is written into the DPP's party platform.

Proponents of both sides have sought support from foreign public opinion, and lobbied foreign politicians. They have mobilized organizations of Taiwanese abroad. Many Taiwanese scholars abroad have returned to Taiwan to participate in politics, both directly, such as Fu-mei Chang Chen (National Assembly) and Parris Chang (Legislative Yuan), or through policy-oriented think tanks, such as Hung-mao Tien (Institute for National Policy Research) and Ying-mao Kau (Twenty-first Century Foundation). Long-time exiled advocates of Taiwan's independence, such as Peng Ming-min and George Chang, have also plunged into Taiwan's political life.

Widespread frustration with Taiwan's near nonexistence on the global stage, fanned by the DPP, has compelled the KMT to change its position on national identity and permit a public debate on this once taboo subject. President Lee Teng-hui's policy of flexible or substantive diplomacy is one response—accepting a variety of names for Taiwan to enable it to enter or remain in international organizations. One striking example is GATT, where Taiwan calls itself the Customs Area of Taiwan, Penghu, Quemoy, and Matsu.

Posing a potentially difficult decision for other countries is the ROC

Foreign Ministry's determination, bowing to opposition pressure, to seek some form of participation in the United Nations. It is using the vague Chinese term *canyu*, which means participate, rather than *jiaru* (enter) or *chongfan* (return to), but still faces an uphill battle.

The PRC is determined to prevent Taiwan's formal independence or emergence on the world scene with the acknowledgement by other countries that Taiwan is a sovereign nation. Some politicians in Taiwan use Taiwan's independence as a rhetorical device to push for increased *glasnost* throughout the once-closed political system, but others are quite determined to advance a formal declaration of independence, believing the PRC's threats to be mere bluffs. Should they gain the upper hand, the PRC would be forced to take some decisive action, and other countries, the United States in particular, would be compelled to take a public stance. To date, the United States and other countries have been able to get away with declarations supporting one China, while strengthening all forms of substantive ties with Taiwan. They have even granted consular powers to various "private" organizations from both sides. Should advocates of Taiwan's independence force the issue, a number of cozy arrangements might suffer.

Once proactive and hegemonic, the KMT has become reactive and defensive. Initiatives come from the DPP and non-mainstream KMT members. The KMT now bases its claims to legitimacy on its past record of economic development (though many quality-of-lifers criticize the costs) and the argument that only it has the organization, maturity, and stature to lead Taiwan through this difficult phase of generational transition, economic transformation, democratization, and reemergence on the world stage.

Because of domestic weakness, the KMT desperately needs some international victories, and that means something more significant than diplomatic relations with Belize. That is why it is aggressively pursuing membership in GATT, participation in the UN, and some way to engage in the OECD, World Bank, and International Monetary Fund. The KMT is now playing to a highly politicized domestic electorate, which is actively considering voting it out of office.[25]

Economic Roots

The strength of Taiwan's economy has been the primary reason it has been able to maintain some influence in world affairs in the face of continuous diplomatic setbacks. It has been able to use economic clout, primarily in the form of enormous foreign reserve holdings, to exact some political benefits, symbolic and substantive, in the form of visits by high-level officials to the island, upgraded representation, participation in international organizations, and purchase of advanced defense material.

Taiwan's economic structure has changed dramatically in a very short time and is increasingly resembling that of a mature developed economy.[26] The economy faces many challenges in order to adapt to the new domestic and external environment, and, as in the past, the state is taking the lead in trying to address them.

At the end of the 1980s, Taiwan was no longer competitive in the types of activities—labor-intensive, low value-added export goods enjoying almost untrammelled access to the American market—that had brought forth the miracle.

Abundant, low-cost, disciplined labor was key to this strategy, but by the period in question there was a severe shortage of labor (the official unemployment rate hovers around 1.5 percent); wages had skyrocketed (from an average manufacturing wage of NT$13,987 in 1986 to NT$24,571 at the end of 1991);[27] many local workers shunned dirty and dangerous jobs; and a new militancy spread throughout the workforce. Workers began to flood into Taiwan illegally from elsewhere in Asia, including mainland China. Realizing the necessity of hiring this cheaper labor in order to maintain production and finish ambitious infrastructural projects, in 1991 the government promulgated regulations on labor imports. This involved negotiations with governments of sending countries such as the Philippines, Thailand, Indonesia, Malaysia, and Vietnam. By mid-1993, the numbers of legally imported workers were already in the tens of thousands.[28]

In addition to the soaring cost of labor, land prices likewise rose to absurd heights. Much of this can be tied to policy changes in 1987. Prior to that year, the ROC government had exercised extremely tight control over access to foreign exchange. This grew out of the lesson of the civil war, when uncontrolled inflation contributed to the KMT's defeat. However, by the 1980s, the years of successful exports had filled the coffers to overflowing. The government feared too much money could stimulate inflation. In addition, its major market, the United States, in a protectionist mood, was pressuring the ROC to relax controls over the New Taiwan dollar, arguing that the currency was seriously undervalued, and thus exacerbating the severe trade deficit. The state thus loosened controls over foreign exchange.

This had several consequences. A great deal of "hot money" from abroad flowed into Taiwan to speculate on the currency. The NT dollar rose from about 35 to one U.S. dollar in 1986, to 28 a year later, and is around 25 now. Cash rich punters also put their money into the stock market, land, real estate, and underground investment houses, all of which took off. The Taipei Stock Exchange index reached 12,683 in early 1990 before crashing to around 2,500 in October.[29] A two-bedroom apartment in Taiwan cost US$200,000.[30] Government regulators cracked down on illegal investment houses, but prices for land and rent stayed high. In addition to raising the prices of key factors of production, so many people got so rich so quickly without physical exertion, that it became declassé to engage in actual labor. In the minds of many local and foreign investors, the work ethic suffered a serious blow.[31]

Although many people lost a great deal of money in the crash of 1990, a lot still remained searching for new outlets. Some of this went into consumption, fueling the import of luxury goods and the opening of upscale outlets, as discussed earlier. This gigantic accumulation of cash also stimulated much of the outward investment into Southeast Asia and then the Chinese mainland: people searching for new ways to make money, as well as businessmen no longer able to make a profit in labor-intensive manufacturing in Taiwan.[32]

The government was not entirely unhappy to see some of this money go abroad, as it dampened inflation somewhat. The bureaucracies in charge of the economy hoped to use the nonviability of labor-intensive manufacturing and the reserves of capital to induce investors into new sectors that would help upgrade the entire industrial structure. This was not a new strategy, but by 1990 the environment was more conducive to implementing it.

Enter new Premier Hau Pei-tsun. He backed the Council for Economic Planning and Development (CEPD) in its formulation of the Six-Year National Development Plan (1991-1996).[33] Estimated to cost in excess of US$300 billion, it is a comprehensive plan linking 775 projects in the economy, infrastructure, public construction, education, culture, medicine, the environment, and social development. It would solve many severe infrastructural bottlenecks, as well as channel investment monies into new sectors.[34] Many of these projects were already underway; the plan attempts to give them coherence and coordination. The plan got off to a slow start, and the newly seated Legislative Yuan was attacking the spending priorities. The authorities are already backing away from anticipating completion within six years;[35] nonetheless, in an age of global recession, news of money to be spent suddenly raised Taiwan's attractiveness in the global business and political communities. There was a parade of businessmen as well as ministerial-level officials from countries that had scrupulously avoided contact with Taiwan for decades. Taiwan's media gave them extensive coverage as a way for the KMT in particular to regain some domestic prestige for its ability to bring Taiwan back to international prominence.

The government has selected ten key industries for special incentives, all of which can expect to draw foreign investment and imports. These are: telecommunications, information, consumer electronics, precision machinery and automation, high end material, semi-conductors, medicine and health, specialty chemicals and pharmaceuticals, aerospace, and pollution control. Some are new; most are designed to upgrade industries in which Taiwan already has experience and expertise.

Exactly how much of the $300 billion will be available for foreign exporters, consultants, engineers, and builders, among others, is not clear. Approximately 30 percent of the expenditures needs to go for land alone; not surprisingly, land prices have taken off again.[36] The selection of aerospace as a priority sector sparked particular interest in the depressed global airline manufacturing sector.

For several years, Taiwan's foreign exchange holdings have been in excess of US$80 billion, ranking first or second in the world. Not surprisingly, many foreigners have hoped to tap into these reserves. But Taiwan's tightly regulated financial sector, including the state-dominated banking industry, prevented direct participation by foreigners. Again, trends in the past few years have brought changes. When Britain and China announced their agreement in 1984 regarding the return of Hong Kong to Chinese sovereignty in 1997, many officials in Taiwan sensed an opportunity to siphon off much of Hong Kong's financial sector to the island. In January 1990, the ROC applied to join GATT, which entailed dismantling many of the barriers to foreign participation in the financial sector. As more opposition figures joined the Legislative Yuan, they began to demand that the KMT-dominated government loosen its control over the financial sector and privatize many of the two dozen or so enterprises it owned, some of which are among the island's largest.[37]

The state permitted foreign securities houses to engage in joint ventures with local brokers in 1989, and the following year let foreign securities firms open branches on the island. This opened the way for local residents to invest directly in foreign financial markets, while letting foreign institutional investors invest directly in the Taiwan stock market. There are also several mutual funds that trade in Taiwan stocks now listed on foreign exchanges. Foreign insurance companies have expanded their scope of operation by investing in Taiwan's real estate and securities markets.[38] The state has permitted the opening of new private banks, adding liveliness and competition to the moribund "pawnshop" banking sector.

In addition to private interest in tapping in to Taiwan's cash reserves, several international organizations, governmental and nongovernmental, have also scrambled to find ways to bring Taiwan and its money into their activities. As noted several times, the ROC's new-found willingness to compromise on the use of its name has greatly facilitated this. In the region, Taiwan is a member of the Pacific Economic Cooperation Conference, the Pacific Basin Economic Council, and the Asian Pacific Economic Cooperation.

Although its GNP growth rate has slowed measurably from the takeoff period, Taiwan's maturing economy still has a major impact on world affairs—as importer and exporter and investment site—although the opportunities have changed. Most significant has been Taiwan's emergence as a source of investment capital, a major player in the Asia-Pacific region, including mainland China. Investment decisions in Taipei now involve consequences for the economic and political health of many regimes with which it does not have formal ties.

Conclusion: Status and Prospects of Domestic Sources

Taiwan's rapidly growing economy has been the foundation of its influence on world affairs since its diplomatic status deteriorated starting in the early 1970s. The state's ability to channel the entrepreneurial talents of its people and guide Taiwan into the global economy made it a source of exports and a popular location for foreign investment. The state utilized economic ties to substitute for formal diplomatic linkages. As this chapter has shown, changes within Taiwan, many of which are themselves the result of shifts in the global system, are impacting the nature of Taiwan's influence abroad. Some are conducive to expanding influence, some, however, will limit it.

Clearly, the accumulation of huge amounts of foreign exchange and the government's ambitious Development Plan have increased Taiwan's external influence: as a purchaser, investor, lender, and spender. Business people, government officials, academics, and international organizations have all come to Taiwan to find ways to establish a claim on some of this money.

The new associations in civil society have raised Taiwan's profile abroad, especially when they are able to join international organizations.

However, there are other countervailing trends, which may impair

Taiwan's ability to increase its influence. As discussed above, the economic miracle resulted in social structural changes, which have also impacted the political system. It adds up to the fact that Taiwan's business climate has changed fundamentally, and this may have deleterious consequences for Taiwan's own future, to say nothing of its impact abroad. The rise of civil society, protest movements, crime, weakened work ethic, contentious legislatures at all levels, and reduced power and efficacy of the dominant party have made Taiwan unattractive as an investment site for local and foreign investors. Foreign interests come to Taiwan now almost parasitically—seeking money and willing to take some political risks to do so. But they are not putting much back that will fuel further growth. Should Taiwan's economy not be able to grow, should the hollowing out of industry continue (especially to the mainland), should social and political unrest continue to frighten investors away, then it may only be a matter of time before the funds that give it clout now will have dwindled significantly. In a normative sense, democracy is positive and Taiwan's political transition has attracted much-deserved attention, especially among many former communist countries seeking a model in the post-Cold War era. But democracy is also messy and inefficient, and the things that made Taiwan attractive to investors in the past that involved closing their eyes to violations of human rights are intolerable in the new environment.

The 1990s will witness continued efforts to restructure the state to reflect more accurately Taiwan's *de facto* independence and lack of interest in recovering the mainland. With a wide range of social groups relentlessly pressing their interests and the immature political institutions and politicians unable to process these demands and unwilling to yield, Taiwan could be facing paralysis or chaos. This might invite forceful action by the PRC. These sorts of domestic circumstances would surely have a global impact, but it is doubtful whether any other countries, surely not the United Nations, would come to Taiwan's aid.

Commentary

Hung-mao Tien

Thomas Gold provides a brief but penetrating summary of the social changes as well as the political and economic developments of the Republic of China (ROC) on Taiwan in recent years. He gives a causal analysis of how these developments shape Taiwan's influence in world affairs. Gold describes such influence as "increasing," referring to the nonofficial arena. One could argue, however, that Taiwan's influence in world affairs has actually decreased with respect to a whole array of diplomatic and other state-sponsored activities (e.g., sending agricultural teams to Africa) that took place before Taiwan's expulsion from the United Nations in 1971 and its subsequent diplomatic misfortunes between the early 1970s and mid-1980s. Gold describes Taiwan's increasing influence despite its diplomatic eclipse. Conceptually, this is a very interesting case: a rise in Taiwan's unofficial influence despite the regime's declining legitimacy in the world community.

According to Gold, Taiwan has become a global player in eleven ways: as importer, exporter, competitor, investor, employer, funds provider, tourist, source of criminals, lobbyists, regional (Asia-Pacific) operations center, and active member of the world's cultural community. At least eight of these roles of influence can be attributed to Taiwan's success in trade and other economic activities. Gold, however, goes beyond economic variables. He analyzes the changes in Taiwan's social structure that gave rise to an affluent middle class (broadly defined), consumerism, a civil society, philanthropic activism, social reorientation, and the politicization of the subethnic division between the Taiwanese and mainlanders. Some of these social changes, strictly speaking, have little to do with Taiwan's influence abroad. But the emergence of a large middle class in an increasingly pluralistic environment does contribute significantly to the growth of Taiwan's influence. Many of the several thousand "secondary groups" actively promote transnational activities that enhance Taiwan's visibility. Rotary clubs and the Lions International in Taiwan, for instance, are very active in fostering sister relations with their counterparts in Japan, the United States, South Korea, and other Asia-Pacific countries. Private foundations, corporations, and professional groups sponsor many international meetings in Taipei. For example, the Y. F. Chang Foundation's Institute for National Policy Research cosponsored (with the Asia Society and the *Asian Wall Street Journal*) a large international conference in Taipei in May 1992. About 1,200 persons from the corporate community, 400 of them from foreign countries, attended the conference. It also featured an array of twenty-eight speakers that included such foreign dignitaries as former President Giscard d'Estaing of France, Singapore's deputy premier, the president of the Asian Development Bank, Malaysia's trade minister, and a former MITI minister of Japan. The Taipei Bar Association hosted the Inter-Pacific Bar Association annual conference on May 3-5, 1993. About 500 legal professionals from the region participated in the event. Rotary

International will hold a worldwide conference in Taipei in 1994. These are nongovernmental activities that put Taiwan "on the world stage."

Gold also provides an informative account of political democratization in Taiwan since 1986, when the first genuine opposition party—the Democratic Progressive Party (DPP)—was formed. Democratization puts the ROC in clear contrast with the PRC's authoritarian political system and helps improve Taiwan's image abroad. Yet, to what extent does a democratic ROC enhance its acceptability in the world community, particularly among industrialized democracies? In recent years Taiwan has accomplished much in strengthening nondiplomatic ties with many nations. It is not clear whether democratic transformation, rather than other factors, has been crucial in fostering closer foreign relations and elevating Taipei's international standing. These are important issues that require careful analysis in order to assess fully the impact of democratic transformation at home on foreign influence.

Moreover, the democratic transition brings about a new sense of national identity based on feelings of common destiny that widely shared among Taiwan's 20 million residents. Thus, the world community must decide whether, or even how to accept Taiwan either as a full fledged independent state or an ROC no longer having jurisdictional ties with the mainland. As political power increasingly shift from mainlanders to the Taiwanese, "the Taiwanizing state" is inclined to seek entry into the official international community with a fresh identity, as Gold acknowledges.

The development of a competitive party system also propels additional transnational activism. Both the KMT and the DPP are bent on promoting "party diplomacy." They join international party organizations and seek bilateral relations with foreign political parties of similar ideological outlook. In 1989 the KMT became a member of the Pacific Democratic Union (PDU); three years later, it entered the International Democratic Union (IDU). The KMT also maintains standing relations with the Republican Party of the United States, the British Conservative Party, the German Christian Democratic Union, and Japan's Liberal Democratic Party. On the other hand, the DPP is promoting friendly ties with the U.S. Democratic Party, Japan's Socialist Party, Korean opposition parties, and some European liberals and social democrats. In 1988 it participated in the annual conference of Liberal International (LI) and achieved "observer status" in 1993. The DPP plans to join the LI as a member in 1995.

Finally, changes in the economic structure also foster a variety of greater external ties. Taiwan is using its large financial resources to enhance its international influence. Taipei's minister of economic affairs is officially welcomed by cabinet ministers, chief executives of government, and even heads of state when he travels to countries with which Taiwan does not maintain diplomatic relations. On several occasions during 1990-1992, the former minister Vincent C. Siew (Hsiao Wan-chang) enjoyed such courtesies on his visits to Brazil, Mexico, the Philippines, Malaysia, Indonesia, Australia, Germany, and Japan. Many government officials from countries without diplomatic relations with the ROC have also visited Taiwan. Tom Gold is right: the parade of ranking foreign officials in Taipei is attracted by the much—publicized US$300 billion initially earmarked for the Six-Year National Development Plan (1991-1996).

In short, Taiwan's influence in world affairs is indeed considerable despite its limited diplomatic ties (with only twenty-nine states) and lack of membership in significant international organizations, except the Asian Development Bank and Asia-Pacific Economic Cooperation. It has "substantive relations" (nondiplomatic) with 120 countries and unofficial representation in fifty-five. Taiwan has a large number of transnational ties and activities. These accomplishments have been possible mostly by virtue of Taiwan's economic prosperity and success in trade that have accumulated a range of US$80 billion to $90 billion in foreign exchange reserves in recent years.

These economic factors plus domestic development of social pluralism and political democratization inject much needed vitality into the ROC's external relations. The domestic roots of influence also gradually extend beyond the Taiwan Strait into the mainland, particularly its coastal provinces. Taiwanese residents made 4.5 million cross-Strait visits by the end of 1992 and ROC businessmen have invested over US$10 billion in the mainland. Trade flourished to $7 billion in 1992. Taiwan's lifestyle and folk music are admired and gaining popularity in many mainland provinces and cities.

A new sense of self-esteem has emerged among Taiwan's 20 million residents. They are demanding more recognition from the international community as well as the PRC government. Domestic pressure is rising that urges the ROC government to seek entry into international governmental organizations. Obtaining membership in the UN General Assembly ranks as the highest in priority. There is also widespread sentiment to join the GATT, World Bank, IMF, and OECD.

In the foreseeable future, the domestic push for active participation in world affairs and, more importantly, for formal acceptance of Taiwan as a sovereign state, regardless of national title, will continue to enhance its global influence. The ROC government and the people in general, irrespective of partisan orientation, share a rare consensus that Taiwan's available resources must be mobilized to enhance the country's international influence. It is perceived to be a matter of survival.

Notes

I would especially like to thank Hung-mao Tien for his comments on an earlier draft of this chapter.

1. Council for Economic Planning and Development, *Taiwan Statistical Data Book, 1992*, (hereafter, TSDB 1992), p. 9.

2. Ibid, p. 18.

3. Ibid, p. 280.

4. Ibid, p. 7.

5. Ibid, p. 13.

6. John C. H. Fei, Gustav Ranis, and Shirley W. Y. Kuo, *Growth With Equity: The Taiwan Case*, (New York, NY: Oxford University Press, 1979). This goes for the gap between rural and urban incomes and life styles as well, something very rare in the developing world. See Alden Speare, Jr., "Taiwan's Rural Populace: Brought in or Left Out of the Economic Miracle?" in Denis Fred Simon and Michael Y. M. Kau, eds., *Taiwan: Beyond the Economic Miracle*, (Armonk, NY: M. E. Sharpe, 1992), pp. 211-33. Income is not the same as total wealth, and in this aspect, the gap between the top and bottom quintiles is larger: 16.8 times. The main reason is the skyrocketing price of real estate. When that variable is factored out, the difference shrinks to 10 times. This is still much better than most of the rest of the world. "Real estate divides rich from poor," *Free China Journal*, (hereafter, FCJ), June 4, 1993, p. 4.

7. For some discussion on this, see Hsin-Huang Michael Hsiao, "The Middle Classes in Taiwan: Origins, Formation and Significance," in Hsin-huang Michael Hsiao, Wei-Yuan Cheng, and Hou-sheng Chan, eds., *Taiwan: A Newly Industrialized State* (Taipei: Department of Sociology, National Taiwan University, 1989), pp. 151-65; and Jia-you Sheu, "The Class Structure in Taiwan and Its Changes," pp. 117-149, in the same volume.

8. This figure is approached with great skepticism due to severe under-reporting of income and the large underground economy. Seeing the level of consumption in Taiwan makes it hard to believe anyone could enjoy such material comforts on only $10,000 annually.

9. In 1991, Taiwan was the world's second largest spender on international tourism in terms of percentage of GNP, right behind Austria. It was twelfth in terms of absolute amount. (FCJ, May 21, 1993, p. 1.)

10. See two series of articles in the very influential journal, *Tianxia* (Commonwealth): "*Shenghuo Pinzhire*" (Quality of life fever), vol. 141, February 1, 1993, pp. 20-38; and "*Zixingdi Taiwan*" (Self-reflecting Taiwan), vol. 145, June 1, 1993, pp. 20-50.

11. Jack F. Williams, "Environmentalism in Taiwan," in Simon and Kau, eds., *Taiwan: Beyond the Economic Miracle*, pp. 187-210. On the environmental protection movement as an example of a social movement, see Zhang Maugui, *Shehui Yundong yu Zhengzhi Zhuanhua* (Social movements and political transformation), (Taipei: Guojia Zhengce Yanjiuziliao Zhongxin, 1989), pp. 51-58. For a detailed case study of popular protest related to the environment, see James Reardon-Anderson, *Pollution, Politics and Foreign Investment in Taiwan: The Lukang Rebellion*, (Armonk NY: M. E. Sharpe, 1992).

12. Paula L. Green, "US Firms Hope to Grab Big Piece of Taiwan Pie," *Journal of Commerce*, May 3, 1993, p. 1A.

13. Thomas B. Gold, "Civil Society and Taiwan's Quest for Identity," Stevan Harrell and Huang Chun-chieh, eds., *Culture Change in Postwar Taiwan*, (forthcoming); Hsin-Huang Michael Hsiao, "Emerging Social Movements and the Rise of a Demanding Civil Society in Taiwan," *The Australian Journal of Chinese Affairs*, vol. 24, July 1990, pp. 163-79.

14. In addition to other forms of illegal activities, gang participation was suspected in the appearance of a veritable armada of mainland Chinese (many on Taiwan-registry ships) trying to enter the United States illegally in 1992 and 1993. (Pamela Burdman, "How Gangsters Cash In On Human Smuggling," *San Francisco Chronicle*, April 28, 1993, pp. A1, A8.)

15. Diversification of risk, including geographically, is a long-time family strategy among Chinese. See Susan Greenhalgh, "Networks and their Nodes: Urban Society on Taiwan," *China Quarterly*, no. 99, September 1984, pp. 529-52.

16. Although they suffer in translation, two puns have been coined to characterize these split families: "*taikongren*" (astronaut) reflects the shuttling back and forth by the father between the United States and Taiwan; with other tones, it can mean "someone whose home in Taiwan is empty;" and "*neizaimei*" (internal beauty) where the pun is "wife is in America" (*neiren zai Meiguo*).

17. Gold, "Civil Society and Taiwan's Quest for Identity." On changing Taiwanese-mainlander relations in the 1980s, see Marshall Johnson, "Classification, Power, and Markets: Waning of the Ethnic Division of Labor," in Simon and Kau, eds., *Taiwan: Beyond the Economic Miracle*, pp. 69-97.

18. For three critical portraits of the domestic political scene during this period, see George Kerr, *Formosa Betrayed*, (Boston, MA: Houghton-Mifflin, 1965); Douglas Mendel, *The Politics of Formosan Nationalism*, (Berkeley, CA: University of California Press, 1970); and Peng Ming-min, *A Taste of Freedom*, (New York, NY: Holt, Reinhart, Winston, 1972). On the squelching of criticism abroad, in particular the Henry Liu murder in California in 1984, see David E. Kaplan, *Fires of the Dragon*, (New York, NY: Atheneum, 1992).

19. Mab Huang, *Intellectual Ferment for Political Reforms in Taiwan, 1971-73*, (Ann Arbor, MI: Center for Chinese Studies, University of Michigan, 1976).

20. For more on this, see Li Cheng and Lynn White, "Elite Transformation and Modern Change in Mainland China and Taiwan: Empirical Data and the Theory of Technocracy," *China Quarterly*, no. 121, 1990, pp. 1-35.

21. The terms are from Edwin A. Winckler, "Institutionalization and Participation on Taiwan: From Hard to Soft Authoritarianism," *China Quarterly*, vol. 99, September 1984, pp. 482-99. Useful for understanding this process in a theoretical and comparative sense is Guillermo O'Donnell and Philippe C. Schmitter, *Transitions from Authoritarian Rule: Tentative Conclusions about Uncertain Democracies*, (Baltimore, MD, and London: The Johns Hopkins University Press, 1986).

22. For overviews, see Yun-han Chu, *Crafting Democracy in Taiwan*, (Taipei: Institute for National Policy Research, 1992); Stephen Haggard and Tun-jen Cheng, eds., *Political Change in Taiwan*, (Boulder, CO: Lynne Rienner, 1992); Hung-mao Tien, *The Great Transition*, and "Taiwan's Evolution Toward Democracy: A Historical Perspective," in Simon and Kau, pp. 3-23.

23. Nearly three-fourths of the party's membership is Taiwanese.

24. In August 1993, on the eve of the KMT's 14th Party Congress, the New KMT Alliance formally established the New Party. Prominent members included former cabinet officials elected to the Legislative Yuan in 1992, Jaw Shao-kang and Wang Chien-shien. Business groups with mainland investments have also made inroads into the Legislative Yuan. See Tan Shuzhen, "*Yizhi Dalu Jingmao Bingtuan Gongjinle Lifayuan*" (A mainland economic and trade corps advances in to the Legislative Yuan), *Xinxinwen* (The Journalist), vol. 303, December 27, 1992, pp. 74-6.

25. Nearly one-fourth of those surveyed considered the DPP capable of governing, although 46 percent said they did not. ("24% of Taiwan residents feel DPP able to govern," FCJ, June 1, 1993, p. 2.)

26. I analyzed the evolution into import substitution, export orientation, and then vertically integrated export orientation up to the mid-1980s, in *State and Society in the Taiwan Miracle*, (Armonk, NY: M. E. Sharpe, 1986).

27. TSDB 1992, p. 20. The Council of Labor Affairs raised the minimum monthly wage to NT$11,040 in August of 1991. The average wage overall in 1990 was NT$24,340, up from $21,176 the year before. *ROC Yearbook 1991-92*, (Taipei: Kwang Hwa Publishing Company, 1991), p. 259. The Council predicted the minimum wage would rise again, to NT$13,080 in 1993. This is a 5.7 percent rise on top of a 12 percent rise in 1992. (FCJ, June 24, 1993, p. 4). (The exchange rate in 1992 was about US$1 = NT$25.)

28. "Vietnamese workers join ROC's labor list," FCJ, July 9, 1993, p. 4.

29. *ROC Yearbook, 1991-92*, p. 196. In March 1993 it reached 5,000.

30. "Rebuilding a Tiger: Who'll Get the Lion's Share?" *Business Week*, March 25, 1991, p. 46.

31. For views of Taiwan big businesses towards the problems of workers, youth, and the work ethic, see "*Daqiye Luanshi Qiusheng*" (Big enterprises seek life in a chaotic market), *Tianxia*, vol. 144, May 1, 1993, pp. 20-67.

32. The mainland replaced Southeast Asia in 1993 as the favored location for outward investment. The rush to the mainland shows no sign of abating; in fact, the capital outflow for the first five months of 1993 grew 700 percent. There was also a trend away from labor-intensive manufactured goods into technology-intensive electronics. ("Mainland top investment spot," FCJ, June 15, 1993, p. 3.)

33. The more conservative Ministry of Finance has been much less sanguine about the plan, especially as it will involve floating NT$400-plus billion in government bonds annually at a time of record government budget deficits. See Julia Leung and Jeremy Mark, "Taiwan Spending Plan is Clouded by Disputes," *Asian Wall Street Journal Weekly*, April 20, 1992, p. 1.

34. As noted in the discussion on social structure, it also addresses issues of the environment, education, and welfare raised by elements in civil society. Hau, who had a long career in the military, wanted to demonstrate that he was a hands-on politician, so the plan has domestic political significance as well.

35. Diao Manfeng, "Guojian Jingmeng" (The National development plan is startled from a dream), *Tianxia*, vol. 144, May 1, 1993, pp. 68-74. In July 1993, the government scaled the plan's cost by 22 percent and the number of projects to 634. Julian Baum, *Far Eastern Economic Review*, July 15, 1993, pp. 60-61.

36. Speech by Ying Price, senior commercial officer, American Institute in Taiwan, Los Angeles, March 16, 1992.

37. Jeremy Mark and Julia Leung, "KMT's Blend of Business And Politics Draws Fire," *The Asian Wall Street Journal*, December 2, 1992, p. 1.

38. *ROC Yearbook, 1991-92*, pp. 195-96.

7

Taiwan-PRC Relations

Ralph N. Clough

The relationship between Taiwan and mainland China is an odd mix of cooperation and contention. Basically, the relationship is contentious, because the two governments disagree on crucial points: Taiwan's identity, the method and timing of bringing about Taiwan's unification with the China mainland, and the channel to be used for negotiations between the two sides. Moreover, the People's Republic of China (PRC) threatens Taiwan with the use of military force if the government should declare Taiwan *de jure* independent of China and the Republic of China (ROC) maintains a strong and costly force of its own to deter Beijing from resorting to forceful reunification. In addition, the ROC strives to strengthen its position in the international community, while the PRC tries to enforce limits on its status.

Samuel Kim's chapter shows how successfully the PRC has excluded the ROC from intergovernmental organizations and has prevented most nations from having diplomatic relations with the ROC. Yet he and the other authors also point out how successful the ROC has been in achieving status in the world community, not through the traditional method of gaining diplomatic recognition, but through acquiring economic power at a period in history when the meaning of state sovereignty

There is not a commentary following this chapter because Hungdah Chiu, who was the discussant for Ralph Clough's paper, was appointed minister without portfolio to the prime minister's cabinet in the Republic of China and was unable to continue as a member of the study group.

is undergoing change. As Kim says, "economically, virtually every state today has a shared or compromised sovereignty" and Taiwan is enmeshed increasingly in a complex global web of economic interdependence.

Both governments assert that there is but one China and that Taiwan and China should eventually be unified. The PRC wants Taiwan integrated with China as a "special administrative region," subordinate to the central government in Beijing like Hong Kong after 1997, but with a greater degree of autonomy. It refers to this arrangement as "one country, two systems." It proposes negotiations on reunification between the Chinese Communist Party (CCP) and the Kuomintang (KMT) on an equal basis. The ROC rejects party-to-party negotiations as incompatible with Taiwan's democratic political system. It proposes instead negotiations between the two governments on an equal basis, but only when the PRC has dropped its threat of force and stops interfering with the ROC's efforts to improve its international status. The ROC refers to the current situation as "one country, two areas, two political entities" or, more simply, as "one country, two governments." It has adopted "National Unification Guidelines" consisting of three phases. In the first phase people-to-people relations are stressed; in the second phase direct communication and transportation across the Strait will occur and official contacts will begin; in the third phase negotiations on reunification will take place. The ROC has not specified what form the reunification of Taiwan with the mainland will take, leaving that to be negotiated.[1]

People-to-People Cooperation

Taipei and Beijing have made no significant progress in narrowing the differences in their views on unification. Nevertheless, since 1987 their contention on basic issues has been accompanied by expanding areas of people-to-people cooperation. Once the ROC lifted the ban on travel to the mainland in 1987, a flood of visitors made the trip—over 4 million visits by the end of 1992. Many of these travellers visited their poorer relatives to whom they brought substantial gifts in the form of goods or hard currency. Fewer persons have travelled from the mainland to Taiwan, perhaps 50,000, but ROC restrictions have gradually been eased. The bulk of those going to the mainland went to visit family members, to sightsee, or to do business, but other visitors included media representatives, politicians, scientists, academics, athletes, legislators, and officials. The PRC welcomed the visitors from Taiwan and urged the ROC to relax further the restrictions on travel from the mainland to

Taiwan. In general, both governments see the travel as improving understanding and easing tension across the Strait.

The outstanding area of cooperation has been in two-way trade and investment on the mainland by Taiwan's entrepreneurs. Two-way trade reached $7.4 billion in 1992 and investment exceeded $6 billion.[2] Trade and investment have been growing rapidly, for they bring economic benefits to both sides, as well as profits to the individuals and companies involved. Taiwan has been transferring to the mainland the bulk of its labor-intensive industries, such as those producing footwear, toys, umbrellas, Christmas ornaments, and many other inexpensive consumer products. Rising wages have made the production of these goods in Taiwan noncompetitive on the world market. Land and labor costs are much lower on the mainland and familiarity with the Chinese language and customs makes the mainland the ideal place to transfer labor-intensive industries, even though ROC policy requires that trade, travel, and investment be indirect, usually through Hong Kong. For Taiwan's small and medium-sized companies, the investment is relatively small and the profits for selling the products in hard currency markets are good. The PRC benefits from the capital investment, the jobs provided, the managerial skills, and market expertise of Taiwan's entrepreneurs and a share in the returns from hard currency sales.

The PRC has offered a variety of inducements to encourage Taiwan's investors, including the establishment of special zones exclusively for their use. It also has opened its internal market to goods manufactured by Taiwan-invested factories, holding out the allure of China's huge market to potential investors. Those responding have increasingly included large Taiwanese firms, such as Far Eastern, a textile manufacturer, and President Enterprises, a food and beverage producer. Investment projects now include not only consumer goods, but basic metals and machinery, electrical engineering, and transportation.[3] The ROC government has approved plans by the China External Trade Development Council (CETRA) to assist Taiwan's entrepreneurs in exploiting the growing mainland market. A recent survey by the director general of Budget, Accounting and Statistics indicated that 72 percent of the companies planning overseas investment in the next two years intend to invest in mainland China.[4]

The ROC, while appreciating the economic benefits of trade and investment in the PRC, is concerned that too much of a particular industry might be transferred to the mainland, thus "hollowing out" the industry in Taiwan, or that certain industries might become too dependent on mainland sources or markets. ROC authorities also oppose the transfer of high technology from Taiwan to the mainland. They fear that too close an economic embrace by Beijing would restrict Taipei's maneuvering room. They are aware, however, that their ability to constrain Taiwan's profit-seeking, free-wheeling entrepreneurs from indirect investment in the mainland is limited.

In addition to the economic benefits that both sides hope to gain from cross-Strait trade and investment, each has long-term political objectives, where contention rather than cooperation becomes the predominant characteristic. The PRC hopes to create a dense network of economic links that will give it political leverage in Taiwan and diminish the risk that the island might declare its independence. For its part, the ROC hopes that contributions to the economic modernization of the mainland by Taiwan's entrepreneurs will keep low the risk of armed conflict, strengthen Beijing's commitment to an expanding market economy, and promote the gradual formation of a middle-class pluralistic society in which concepts of democracy could take root as they have in Taiwan. Mainland visits by certain influential individuals have been especially important in giving impetus to advances in economic, scientific, and technical cooperation between the two sides of the Strait. One such visit was by former Economics Minister Chao Yao-tung, a national policy adviser to President Lee Teng-hui, who spent twenty-five days on the mainland in 1992 as a member of a delegation from the private Chunghua Institute of Economic Research. Chao met with President Yang Shangkun and other senior PRC officials. On his return he expressed the conviction that economic reform on the mainland was irreversible and urged Taiwanese investors to shift their attention from light industries to heavy and high technology industries.

Another high-level visitor in 1992 was Wu Ta-you, the 85-year-old president of the Academia Sinica. During a twenty-six-day visit, Wu attended three international scientific conferences, conferred with many mainland scientists, and met with President Yang Shangkun, CCP General Secretary Jiang Zemin, and Premier Li Peng. Back in Taiwan, Wu pointed to the advanced levels reached by mainland scientists in certain areas and stressed the need for developing scientific and technological cooperation between Taiwan and the mainland. During 1992 and 1993 two groups of distinguished mainland scientists, invited by Wu, visited Taiwan. The ROC minister of economic affairs announced the allocation of $3,850,000 for fiscal year 1993-1994 to facilitate bilateral exchanges of science and technology and the introduction into Taiwan of mainland industrial know-how.[5] In April 1993 geologists from the PRC arrived in Taipei to attend the Past Global Changes Workshop. This was the first group of scientists from mainland China to attend an international conference in Taiwan.[6]

An area in which cooperation surprisingly predominated over contention was in the repatriation of illegal immigrants into Taiwan from the mainland. Taiwan's high wages and shortage of labor inevitably attracted job-seekers from Fujian who spoke Taiwanese and thus could readily meld into the local population. For a substantial fee, fishing boats would drop job-seekers on deserted beaches in the middle of the night. Soon the Taiwan police were apprehending hundreds of illegal immigrants. At first they were sent back on confiscated fishing boats, but two accidents in 1990 resulting in the deaths of scores of persons being repatriated caused the Red Cross societies of the two sides to reach agreement on a regularized repatriation method, whereby mainland vessels operated by the Beijing Red Cross society would pick up repatriates brought from Taiwan to Matsu by the ROC navy.

Repatriation did not always run smoothly, however. In April 1993, allegedly because the PRC had not completed a new ship it was building to conduct repatriations, more than 2,000 illegal immigrants had piled up in Taiwan's overcrowded detention centers, some of them having been held for more than a year.

Fisheries is another area in which cooperation between the two sides of the Strait has developed. Work on Taiwan's many fishing boats is hard and dangerous and the pay is low. Consequently, a severe shortage of labor emerged. As early as December 1990, according to the chairman of the Council on Agriculture, Yu Yu-hsien, 3,000 mainland fishermen were already working illegally on Taiwanese boats.[7] The council subsequently issued regulations allowing fishing boat owners to hire foreign fishermen (including those from mainland China) to make up not over one-third of a boat's crew. In January 1993 the quota was raised to one-half of the crew.[8] Governor Jia Qinglin of Fujian Province said that in 1992 4,000 fishermen from the province were working on Taiwan ships.[9]

In August 1990 a private group from Taiwan, the China Fisheries Association, visited fisheries in seven mainland cities to discuss possible cooperation with fisheries officials. The delegation noted that although mainland techniques in distant fisheries were inferior to those used by fishing boats from Taiwan, the PRC's stronger international position would be an advantage to Taiwanese companies cooperating with those on the mainland.[10] An example of this form of cooperation was the Dalian Ocean Fishing Company, a joint venture with a Taiwanese company that dispatched two trawlers to Latin America in early 1992 to fish for squid, to be returned to Dalian for processing.[11] In December 1992 a seminar on cooperative development of seafood breeding was held in Beijing, attended by nineteen experts and entrepreneurs from Taiwan.[12]

Cooperation in the exchange of media representatives has encountered obstacles, initially because of the reluctance of the ROC to admit to Taiwan any member of the CCP. (Most PRC journalists are, or are assumed to be, members of the CCP.) Hundreds of journalists and TV reporters from Taiwan visited the mainland from 1989 on, but no journalist from the mainland visited Taiwan until August 1991. Since then the restrictions on the admission of CCP members have been relaxed and a few mainland media representatives have visited Taiwan, but the flow continues to be heavily one-sided. Official control of the press in the PRC contrasts sharply with the virtual freedom of the press in Taiwan, making cooperation in this area particularly difficult. Neither side permits the free circulation of newspapers and journals published on the other side of the Strait. Technological advances, however, have greatly increased the flow of information across the Strait by radio and by TV tuned in through satellite dishes, diminishing the ability of governments to control the flow.

Sports, cultural, and academic exchanges have steadily increased. In general, the growth of people-to-people interchange has been constrained by the ROC's fear of being overwhelmed by its huge neighbor. Hence, the flow of people and goods to the mainland, which imposes few restrictions, has been much larger than the reverse flow. The PRC complains about ROC restrictions and presses for the establishment of direct communication, transportation, trade, and investment from Taiwan to the mainland rather than indirectly through Hong Kong. The ROC demands, first, that the PRC recognize the ROC as an equal political entity, drop the threat to use force, and stop interfering with the ROC's efforts to improve its status in the international community.

A Channel for "Unofficial" Negotiations

The growing people-to-people interaction between Taiwan and the PRC inevitably produced incidents of disagreement, friction, and misunderstanding that were difficult to resolve in the absence of official contacts at any level. In order to deal with such matters without breaching its "three no's" policy (no official contact, negotiation, or compromise), the ROC in March 1991 created an ostensibly private organization, the Straits Exchange Foundation (SEF), to negotiate with PRC officials. SEF is specifically prohibited from engaging in talks with PRC officials on political questions such as the definition of "one China" or the establishment of direct communication and transportation links. Koo Chen-fu, a prominent Taiwanese businessman and member of the KMT Central Committee, was appointed chairman. In December 1991 the PRC created a counterpart organization, the Association for Relations Across the Taiwan Straits(ARATS), headed by Wang Daohan, a former mayor of Shanghai.

SEF and ARATS have established a useful channel for communication between the two sides, but have had difficulty in resolving practical problems. For example, several meetings beginning in March 1992 between SEF and ARATS for the purpose of agreeing on methods of authenticating documents such as marriage certificates issued by officials of the other side failed to make progress because the two parties could not agree on how to spell out that their negotiations were being conducted within the framework of "one China." The ROC feared that treating document authentication as a domestic matter would strengthen the PRC view that the ROC was a local government, while the PRC wanted to avoid any implication that authentication of documents by the PRC and ROC was comparable to similar services performed by consular officers in foreign countries. Not until April 1993 was agreement reached on this issue, in preparation for the first meeting between Koo and Wang, held in Singapore in late April 1993.

The Koo-Wang meeting attracted international attention because it was the highest level meeting ever held between the two sides. Even though the meeting was billed as "unofficial" and its agenda was limited to the discussion of functional, nonpolitical issues, the prominent status of the two principals in their respective political parties gave it symbolic importance. Koo and Wang signed the two agreements initialed earlier by the two vice-chairmen in Beijing: on verification of official documents and on the handling of registered mail. They agreed that working-level meetings of SEF and ARATS would be held every three months and a meeting of the secretary-generals every six months. They also signed a joint statement specifying issues on which further discussions would be held, including repatriation of illegal immigrants, joint efforts to suppress smuggling and piracy, fishing disputes, protection of intellectual property, and contact and assistance between the judicial and legal entities of the two sides. They agreed to have further discussions on problems of Taiwan investors on the mainland, on strengthening exploration and exchanges on energy and resources, and on promoting press, technology, scientific, and cultural exchanges.

The Koo-Wang talks demonstrated that the two sides could set aside political differences and make progress in resolving practical problems that hindered the expansion of people-to-people relations. The negotiations made no progress on Koo's proposal for an investment guarantee agreement to protect Taiwanese investors because Wang countered that Taiwan should first permit direct trade and investment. Despite the restriction of the agenda to nonpolitical topics, each side claimed political gains in the continuing struggle over Taiwan's identity in the international community. Taipei stressed the acceptance by the PRC of the equal status of the two delegations, while Beijing portrayed the meeting as an important advance along the road to the reunification of China.

Effect of Taiwan's International Activities on ROC/PRC Cooperation

Taiwan's activities in the international arena affect both cooperation and contention between the ROC and the PRC. The two governments do not cooperate directly—that form of cooperation has been reserved by the ROC for the second phase of the unification guidelines, after direct contacts between officials of the two governments become possible and direct communication and transportation links have been established. But the activities of the government, companies, private institutions, and people of Taiwan in the international arena, particularly in terms of economic relations, strengthen Taiwan's ability to cooperate with the PRC through people-to-people relationships.

Taiwan's growing economic activities in the world, as discussed in Erland Heginbotham's chapter, have greatly enhanced Taiwan's ability to conduct people-to-people economic cooperation with the mainland in the form of trade and investment. Participation in world trade on a large scale has created a class of experienced entrepreneurs willing and able to invest on the mainland. As rising wage costs have forced the transfer of labor-intensive industry to mainland China and Southeast Asia, capital investment in Taiwan has been shifted increasingly to higher technology and service industries, often in cooperation with foreign multinational firms. More is being expended on research and development in order to compete more effectively in the highly competitive advanced technology sectors of the world market, such as the computer industry.

The ROC restricts the transfer of advanced technology to the PRC, but pressure to reduce the restrictions has been increasing and the government has been compelled gradually to expand the list of permitted investments. Thus, the PRC will benefit from the rising technological skills of Taiwan manufacturers, although the government probably will continue to block the transfer to the mainland of the most advanced technology, as well as very large investments, such as Formosa Plastics' proposed $8 billion petrochemical complex.

The PRC recognizes that economic growth in Taiwan can make a significant contribution to economic growth on the mainland. Consequently, it has not attempted to interfere directly with the expansion of Taiwan's economic relations with the rest of the world. There was a time when the PRC sought to prevent foreign companies from doing business both in Taiwan and on the mainland. But that time is long past. Today, foreign companies with operations in both places serve the PRC interest in building economic bonds between Taiwan and the mainland. For example, AT&T recently signed a large contract for modernizing telephone facilities in the PRC. At about the same time, the company announced a decision to invest in a modem design center in Taiwan, adding to the microelectronics center and the integrated circuits design center that it had already established on the island.[13] Some American companies have hired specialists from Taiwan to assist in their operations in the PRC. Many large American companies belong to both the USA-ROC Economic Council and the United States-China Business Council, showing that the PRC is no longer opposed to companies' operating on both sides of the Strait.

Another way in which cooperation between Taiwan and mainland China benefits from Taiwan's growing role in the international community is through the participation of experts and professionals from Taiwan and the PRC in international nongovernmental organizations (INGOs), as discussed in Kim's chapter. The problem of nomenclature has not proved to be a serious obstacle as it has in international governmental organizations (IGOs), for individuals and organizations in Taiwan belong to some 700 INGOs. Subjects dealt with in such organizations range from science and technology, engineering, electronics, agriculture, forestry, fisheries, mining and energy, business and finance, and ecological protection to sports, education, tourism, culture, and art.[14] Specialists from Taiwan and the PRC also attend a great variety of international conferences each year, including some in mainland China and a small but increasing number in Taiwan. The contacts between individuals through these channels make an important contribution to cooperation between the two sides of the Strait.

Contention over the ROC's International Activities

While the PRC declares that it has no objection to Taiwan's *unofficial* international relations and does not interfere directly with the expansion of such relations, it does interfere indirectly in many ways by attempting to restrict Taiwan's *official* relations. International travel and economic relations cannot be conducted without the participation of governments. The passage of people and goods across national borders is subject to governmental regulation and to a variety of government-to-government agreements. Lacking diplomatic relations with most countries, the ROC has had to resort to ostensibly unofficial agreements with organizations in other countries that have served as surrogates for the government itself. The leading example is the American Institute in Taiwan (AIT), established by the Taiwan Relations Act of 1979, that has concluded more than fifty agreements with its counterpart, the Coordination Council for North American Affairs (CCNAA).[15]

The ROC could undoubtedly play a more effective role in international affairs if it had normal diplomatic relations. Its ability and willingness to cooperate effectively with the PRC in economic and other relations would be correspondingly enhanced. But PRC leaders no doubt would consider this a marginal increase over Taiwan's current ability and willingness to cooperate and not worth paying the price of tolerating "two Chinas" or "one China, one Taiwan" in the international community, even temporarily as occurred with the two Germanies before their unification. The PRC has demonstrated its power to enforce a "Hallstein doctrine," a power that West Germany lacked. Hence, it maintains a rigid and uncompromising opposition to the establishment of diplomatic or consular relations between the ROC and any state.

Between the establishment of diplomatic or consular relations with Taiwan, which the PRC punishes by suspending its own diplomatic relations with the offending state, and the conduct of unofficial trade, travel, sports, and cultural exchanges, which the PRC tolerates, there is a broad gray area within which the PRC and the ROC contend. ROC diplomats strive to upgrade Taiwan's interactions with other governments so they take on a brighter aura of officiality—the "creeping officiality" that the PRC warned against in its memorandum to the UN Security Council of December 1988.[16]

Upgrading consists in some countries of agreeing to the use of the official name, "Republic of China" for the ROC's representative office. Sixteen countries have accepted this nomenclature, despite the PRC's protests. In most countries, however, Taiwan's representation goes by the name of "Taipei Economic and Cultural Office." Another form of upgrading is expanding the size and functions of the thirty-seven representative offices maintained in Taiwan by foreign countries and assigning high-level professional diplomats to head them. Still another is persuading governments to send high-level officials to visit Taiwan and to receive senior ROC officials in other countries. During the past several years, cabinet ministers from France, Germany, Australia, Italy, the Netherlands, and other countries visited Taiwan. In December 1992 U.S. Trade Representative Carla Hills, the first U.S. cabinet-level official to visit Taiwan since 1978, met with ROC officials to discuss trade issues.

Economic officials from Taiwan frequently travel to other countries and even the foreign minister, whose travel the PRC considers to be more political, makes tours abroad. In a visit to Indonesia in February 1993, Foreign Minister Frederick Chien met with President Suharto. But in a subsequent "private" trip to Japan, the first by a ROC foreign minister since 1972, he met only Diet members. Such was the sensitivity of the Japanese government to possible PRC protests that it announced publicly that no government officials would meet with Chien.[17]

The PRC has vigorously opposed the establishment of air services between Taiwan and other countries, declaring that the opening of air services to Taiwan by any airline company, including private ones, of a country having diplomatic relations with the PRC constitutes a political issue involving China's sovereignty.[18] PRC protests succeeded in delaying for a year the establishment of air services between Taiwan and Vietnam, but flights began in September 1992. Since Taiwan had become the leading investor in Vietnam, air services between the two places were too important to allow Beijing to stand in the way. PRC protests also failed to prevent the establishment during the past two years of air services between Taiwan and Canada, Australia, and the United Kingdom. In order to conclude air agreements in the face of PRC protests, the ROC often agrees that air services will be provided by unofficial airline companies, such as EVA Air or Mandarin Airlines, a subsidiary of the ROC's official carrier, China Airlines.

The PRC is most hostile to the supply of weapons to Taiwan, as discussed in Harlan Jencks's chapter. It regards arms sales as inherently government-to-government transactions, though they may be presented as sales by private firms. It denounced vehemently the sale of 150 F-16s approved by the Bush administration in September 1992, but has not yet retaliated in any concrete way. It did, however, force the French government to close its Guangzhou Consulate General in retaliation for the sale to Taiwan of sixty *Mirage*-2000 fighter aircraft in November 1992 and may also have excluded French companies from bidding on certain government contracts.

These few examples suggest that as Taiwan's economic importance grows, the effect of PRC protests on Taiwan's trading partners declines. With respect to *de jure* recognition, formal diplomatic and consular relations, and entry into the United Nations, the PRC can appeal to well-established principles of international law, as well as its ability to break relations or employ the veto to prevent governments from granting the ROC the status it would like to have in the international community. But with respect to the gray area, no firmly established rules exist as to how to treat a government in the ROC's position. Whether a government responds to PRC pressures to limit its official relationships with Taiwan is essentially a political decision. It depends on the relative value a country attaches to its relationship with the PRC and Taiwan and that country's judgment as to the costs and benefits of taking an action that the PRC is likely to oppose.

Many of the actions taken by a country to upgrade its relations with Taiwan are minor in themselves and unlikely to provoke a reaction from Beijing that significantly damages that country's relations with the PRC. Nevertheless, cumulatively and collectively, the upgrading of relations by those countries that have important relations with Taiwan (including the world's leading industrial nations) bring their relations closer to the official level, though they may be cloaked in unofficial nomenclature. This "creeping officiality" that the PRC complains of is difficult for the PRC to prevent. PRC officials and propagandists rail against the successes of the ROC's "pragmatic diplomacy" (also known as "flexible diplomacy") in strengthening Taiwan's substantive relations around the world, but PRC leverage in this area, either against Taiwan itself or against the country upgrading relations with Taiwan, is relatively weak. The more countries that, for example, send cabinet ministers to Taiwan, the more other countries are likely to follow their example, creating a trend that Beijing seems powerless to halt.

Taiwan-United States Relations

Taiwan's most important international relationship since 1950 has been its relationship with the United States. Richard Bush's chapter discusses the implications of Taiwan's role in international affairs for U.S. policy. Comments here will be restricted to the interaction of U.S.-Taiwan relations and the evolving Taiwan-mainland China relationship.

Since 1950 Taiwan has relied on the United States for its security against the PRC's threat of military force to reunify Taiwan with mainland China. Even though the mutual defense treaty was abrogated by the United States in 1979, the Taiwan Relations Act commits the United States to supply defensive weapons to Taiwan and declares that any effort to determine the future of Taiwan by other than peaceful means would be of grave concern to the United States. Restrictions on U.S. arms sales to Taiwan agreed to between the United States and the PRC in August 1982 have not prevented the United States from supplying weapons needed for a strong defense of Taiwan, as demonstrated by President Bush's approval of the F-16 sale in September 1992. Although Beijing denounced the U.S. sale as a violation of the 1982 joint communiqué, it did not criticize Taiwan's authorities for having bought the weapons. The sale seems to have had no significant adverse effect on the continuing expansion of people-to-people relations between Taiwan and mainland China. On the contrary, Taiwan's demonstrated ability to acquire advanced weapons contributes to a feeling of confidence on the part of the authorities there that helps them work toward a sustainable state of peaceful coexistence with their giant neighbor.

Economic relations between the United States and Taiwan, the United States and the PRC, and Taiwan and the PRC affect each other. Since the mid-1960s the United States has been Taiwan's most important export market, in 1984 taking 49 percent of Taiwan's exports. By 1991, however, the U.S. share had fallen to 29 percent.[19] An important reason for the change was that Taiwan's manufacturers of labor-intensive products had shifted much of their production to mainland China, causing a sizeable increase in Taiwan's exports to the mainland of machinery, components, and raw materials for industrial use. The manufactured products formerly shipped from Taiwan to the United States were now shipped from mainland China, causing a sharp decline in Taiwan's trade surplus with the United States and contributing to the rapid increase in the U.S. trade deficit with the PRC.[20] The growth in this triangular trade would be checked or even reversed if President Clinton were to refuse to extend the most-favored-nation status of the PRC's exports.

Domestic Politics and Cross-Strait Relations

Domestic politics in Taiwan have not only affected Taiwan's role in international affairs, as discussed in Thomas Gold's chapter, but have also had an impact on Taiwan-mainland China relations. The contest between the ruling KMT and the chief opposition party, the DPP, is basically a struggle for power, in which the DPP made important gains in the December 1992 Legislative Yuan election. The DPP, whose members are almost all Taiwanese, bases its opposition to the KMT on the ground that the KMT is a mainlander-dominated party that came from the mainland, took over the island in 1945, and ruled it autocratically for decades, favoring the interests of mainlanders over those of the Taiwanese. Moreover, the professed goal of the KMT is the reunification of Taiwan with mainland China, which would perpetuate control of the island by the China mainland. The DPP's slogan is "Taiwan for the Taiwanese" and in its party platform of 1991 it adopted a provision to submit to a popular referendum the establishment of an independent Republic of Taiwan.

The political power struggle in Taiwan is less clear-cut, however, than DPP propaganda would make it appear. First, the KMT is no longer simply a "mainlander" party. Since 1988, the party chairman (and president of the ROC) has been Lee Teng-hui, a Taiwanese. Seventy percent of the membership and a majority of the central standing committee are Taiwanese. More than two-thirds of the KMT legislators elected in 1992 are Taiwanese. Thus, even though mainlanders continue to wield influence in the KMT disproportionate to their numbers in the general population, that influence is declining and the KMT today is far from being a "mainlander" party.

Second, the difference between the KMT and the DPP over unification versus independence is less clear-cut than it appears. The DPP advocates a formal declaration of independence in the hope of winning international recognition and membership in intergovernmental organizations as a new state. The KMT rejects the DPP approach as risking triggering PRC use of force against Taiwan and unlikely to win international recognition. It proposes instead to maintain and strengthen Taiwan's current status as a *de facto* independent state while seeking to establish a lasting condition of peaceful coexistence with the PRC. The KMT envisions the unification of Taiwan with the mainland only as a long-term goal, with the manner and form of unification unspecified. The fundamentally conservative Taiwan electorate so far has favored the cautious and time-tested policy of the KMT rather than the dramatic but risky DPP proposal. A public opinion poll taken in early May 1993 shows only 23.7 percent of the respondents favoring Taiwan independence and 54.3 percent against it.[21] Although this poll shows a significant rise in pro-independence sentiment compared to previous polls, opposition remains strong.

DPP spokesmen express concern that KMT policy will lead to early negotiations with the PRC on unification. When denied representation in the Koo-Wang talks, they sent a delegation to Singapore to caution SEF negotiators not to go beyond the specified narrow agenda on functional issues and to counter treatment of the talks by elements of the world press as the beginning of negotiations on unification. DPP leaders have demanded a share in the determination of policy toward the mainland, both through the creation of a mainland affairs committee in the Legislative Yuan and through representation in the government's Mainland Affairs Council and the unofficial Straits Exchange Foundation. There is little doubt that the DPP will acquire increased influence on mainland policy. The KMT itself is split on mainland policy, with a significant minority advocating a forthright "one China, one Taiwan" position, rather than the government's more ambiguous "one country, two governments" or "one country, two areas."

PRC authorities follow closely domestic politics in Taiwan, showing particular concern when calls for Taiwan's independence grow louder. From time to time they repeat their warning that a declaration of independence would provoke a military response by the mainland. They cultivate Taiwanese businessmen with a stake in their investments on the mainland, many of whom share the PRC's desire for the early establishment of direct transportation links across the Strait. Some of these Taiwanese businessmen may be in a position to influence DPP leaders toward moderation on the Taiwan independence issue through granting or threatening to withhold financial backing of the party.

The "Three Links" and the ROC's International Position

The contention between Taipei and Beijing over the ROC's international status has had little direct effect on the expansion of people-to-people relations between Taiwan and mainland China. Indirectly, of course, it has had a significant retarding effect. ROC authorities place limitations on the interaction, in part because of the PRC's hostile behavior toward the ROC in the international arena. ROC authorities also have sought to create a direct linkage by conditioning the establishment of the "three links" (direct mail, trade, and air and shipping services) on the PRC's willingness to end its interference with the ROC's moves to improve its international status.

Direct mail, air, and shipping services across the Taiwan Strait would obviously facilitate trade and travel, thus bringing economic benefits to both sides. Many Taiwanese businessmen have urged the government to agree to the three links, especially the opening of air travel across the Strait. But the ROC contends that direct links would require official contacts between the two sides and talks between the two governments on the basis of equality. Ma Ying-jeou, the former vice chairman of the MAC, now minister of justice, said: "When Peking is ready not to deny Taipei's existence as a political entity, not to use force to settle bilateral disputes, and not to interfere with Taipei's conduct of external relations under the one-China principle, direct links may be established."[22]

The PRC insists that accepting the ROC's conditions would amount to acquiescing in "two Chinas" or "one China, one Taiwan." It has declared again and again that it will never agree to such a status for Taiwan. PRC authorities obviously rely on growing pressures on the ROC government from Taiwan's entrepreneurs to bring about the establishment of the three links without making the political concessions in the international arena that the ROC demands.

Conclusion

The fundamental dispute between Taipei and Beijing is over the status of Taiwan in the international community; this dispute colors the whole range of their relationship. The PRC presses for unification under the "one country, two systems" formula. PRC leaders recognize that unification at best will likely be a long-term, step-by-step process. In the meantime, their prime concern is that Taiwan's authorities maintain the one-China principle and the goal of unification, resisting domestic pressures for a formal declaration of independence. PRC authorities promote people-to-people relations across the Strait, both for the economic gains involved and in order to tie Taiwan more firmly to the mainland by an ever-denser web of relationships. They would like to institute direct contacts between official agencies on the two sides of the Strait, partly in order to resolve problems arising in people-to-people relations; but, faced with the ROC's rejection of official contacts, they have agreed to handle such problems through the quasi-official SEF and ARATS mechanisms. They oppose the ROC's efforts to upgrade its international status through "pragmatic diplomacy" because they fear that Lee Teng-hui's efforts to secure greater "wiggle room" for Taiwan in the international community is a disguised method of moving gradually to eventual formal independence.

Lee Teng-hui's primary goals are to preserve Taiwan's security and prosperity. Security requires the maintenance of a strong defense force, which, in turn, requires access to foreign suppliers of advanced weapons. Security also requires a degree of control over the expansion of people-to-people relations so that Taiwan is not overwhelmed by the sheer massiveness of the mainland and the PRC is prevented from acquiring substantial leverage in Taiwan's domestic politics. Maintenance of Taiwan's prosperity requires the ability to transfer the island's sunset industries to the mainland and to exploit the opening mainland market, but at the same time it also requires sufficient government controls to avert economic overdependence on the mainland and the hollowing out of industry in Taiwan itself.

Preserving Taiwan's security also requires avoiding unnecessary provocation of the PRC—including keeping the door open for the eventual reunification of Taiwan with mainland China. Primary motivations for encouraging people-to-people interaction across the Strait and for entering into quasi-official talks with the PRC are to lower tensions between Taipei and Beijing and to work toward a stable status of peaceful coexistence between them. The establishment of the National Unification Council and the adoption of the National Unification Guidelines were signals to the PRC as well as to mainlanders within the KMT that Lee Teng-hui is committed to a long-term policy of eventual unification.

Active pursuit of "pragmatic diplomacy" has become an essential element of Lee's policy, both with respect to upgrading bilateral relations with foreign countries and reentering intergovernmental organizations. Any Taiwan leader today must be able to demonstrate, for domestic political reasons, that he is making progress in narrowing the gap between Taiwan's economic weight in the world and its formal international status. Unfortunately, the successes of the foreign ministry in steadily upgrading bilateral relationships with countries with which the ROC lacks diplomatic relations, despite their importance in enabling the ROC to conduct its foreign relations more effectively, do not make a strong impact on public opinion in Taipei. Public attention tends to be focused, not on these successive small victories over the PRC, but on those cases in which the ROC achieves (or fails to achieve) a breakthrough by establishing diplomatic relations with a country or by becoming a member of an intergovernmental organization. These are the areas in which PRC opposition is most effective.

The coming few years will see a sharpening of the ROC/PRC contest in the international arena. Taiwan has already made noticeable progress toward becoming a member of GATT. Responding to domestic political pressures, the ROC government has set up a task force on joining the United Nations. Foreign Minister Frederick Chien has said that efforts will concentrate first on becoming a member of international financial organizations, which, because of Taiwan's economic clout, are expected to be easier to join than the United Nations itself: the International Monetary Fund, the World Bank, the International Development Association and the International Finance Corporation.[23]

The PRC has indicated that it will oppose vigorously ROC attempts to join these UN-affiliated IGOs, but there have been private hints from scholars in institutes of international relations in Shanghai, said to be close to CCP General Secretary Jiang Zemin, that the PRC might be prepared to make some concessions regarding Taiwan's international position. What *quid pro quo* would be expected is not clear, but it is conceivable that a bargain might be struck involving a compromise on the name under which Taiwan entered the IGOs and some progress on the three links.

An intriguing arms-length exchange of views on the issue of the PRC's threat of force began in May 1992 with a proposal by Chiu Chin-yi (Cheyne Chiu) that the ROC and the PRC sign a nonaggression pact similar to the one signed between East and West Germany. At that time Chiu was spokesman of the president's office; later he became secretary-general of SEF. Chiu was attending a private conference and characterized his proposal as a "personal opinion," but commentators viewed it as a trial balloon.

On April 5, 1993, Wang Zhaoguo, head of the Taiwan affairs offices of both the State Council and the CCP Central Committee and also director of the party's united front department, received five legislators from Taiwan in his office in Beijing. He told them that as long as both sides maintained the one-China principle and gradually advanced toward peaceful unification, the PRC would not oppose a proposal to sign a peace agreement and end the hostile confrontation.[24] Wang's comments leave unanswered the obvious question as to whether the PRC would regard the agreement as between a central and provincial government or between two equal political entities. Nevertheless, his remarks suggest a feeler as to whether a pledge not to use force might be exchanged for a pledge not to declare formal independence.

Two processes are now underway between Taiwan and mainland China. One is the expansion of people-to-people relations. The other is the exploration by the two governments of ways in which their relationship might become more stable and regularized. Both sides recognize that the road ahead is long and that as they proceed each will be trying to maximize its gains and minimize its costs and risks. It is not, however, a zero-sum game; there will be scope for cooperation as well as contention. Taiwan's international status will continue to be the central issue between Taipei and Beijing. It will be affected by the domestic power struggle in Taiwan and perhaps also become an element in a power struggle in Beijing after Deng Xiaoping's death.

Despite the many uncertainties involving both world trends and domestic conditions on the mainland and in Taiwan, the following developments seem most probable in the remaining years until the end of the century:

- The economic integration of Taiwan, mainland China, and Hong Kong will advance much further.
- Taiwan will refrain from declaring formal independence.
- Taiwan will improve its international position significantly, becoming a member of GATT and possibly one of the international financial institutions.
- The PRC will continue to prevent Taiwan from having diplomatic relations with most countries and keep it out of most intergovernmental organizations.
- SEF and ARATS will have established offices on the other side of the Taiwan Strait; they will have devised ways of resolving many of the problems arising in people-to-people interaction, but the problem rooted in Taiwan's identity and political relationship to mainland China will not have been resolved.

Notes

1. Huang Kun-huei, *The Key Points and Content of the Guidelines for National Unification*, (Taipei: Mainland Affairs Council, December 1991).

2. Beijing, *Xinhua* broadcast, January 4, 1993, in *Foreign Broadcast Information Service, Daily Report, China*, (hereafter cited as *FBIS-China*), January 19, 1993. See also statement by Governor Samuel Hsieh of the Central Bank of China (Taipei) that net capital outflow from Taiwan to the mainland during 1991 and 1992 amounted to $6 billion. *Free China Journal*, March 26, 1993.

234

3. *Free China Journal*, March 12, 1993.

4. *Free China Journal*, March 9, 1993.

5. *FBIS-China*, April 19, 1993, p. 66.

6. *Free China Journal*, April 23, 1993.

7. *China Post*, December 5, 1990.

8. *China Post*, January 30, 1993.

9. *FBIS-China*, March 26, 1993, p. 99.

10. *Chung Kuo Shih Pao Chou Kan* (China Times Weekly), no. 290, September 15-21, 1990, pp. 12-13.

11. *FBIS-China*, February 24, 1992, p. 71.

12. *FBIS-China*, January 19, 1993, p. 71.

13. *Free China Journal*, March 26, 1993.

14. The *Republic of China Yearbook, 1989*, p. 760, lists the number of INGOs in each of twenty-one categories to which Taiwan belongs, a total of 728 INGOs.

15. Lori Fisler Damrosch, *The Taiwan Relations Act After Ten Years*, University of Maryland School of Law, Occasional Papers/Reprints Series in Contemporary Asian Studies, no. 4, 1990, (99), p. 22.

16. See Samuel Kim's chapter.

17. *China Post*, February 20, 1993.

18. *Free China Journal*, February 7, 1991.

19. *Taiwan Statistical Data Book 1992*, (Taipei: Council on Economic Planning and Development), p. 203.

20. Nicholas Kristoff, "China Is Making Asia's Goods and the U.S. is Buying," *New York Times*, March 21, 1993.

21. *China Post*, May 10, 1993.

22. "The Republic of China's Policy toward the China Mainland," Taipei: Institute of International Relations, *Issues and Studies*, vol. 28, no. 6, June 1992, p. 5.

23. *Free China Journal*, March 19, 1993.

24. *Chung Kuo Shih Pao Chou Kan*, no. 68, April 18-24, 1993, pp. 31-32.

8

Taiwan and Greater China

Harry Harding

The term "Greater China" is currently in vogue among both analysts and practitioners interested in Asian affairs. The phrase is controversial, for it has several contrasting connotations. To some observers, it denotes the emergence of a dynamic new marketplace, offering greater economic opportunity to Chinese and foreigners alike. To others, in contrast, it evokes the image of an aggressive China on the march, seeking to extend its sovereignty over territories and peoples it does not presently control. Notwithstanding the debate over the appropriateness of the term, "Greater China" undeniably provides a succinct and vivid way of characterizing the growing interaction among the members of what Joel Kotkin has called the global Chinese "tribe."[1] Whatever its shortcomings, it is likely to become a permanent part of the vocabulary for discussing contemporary international issues.

"Greater China" subsumes a much larger number of related concepts that have been recently introduced in both Chinese and English, ranging from a "Chinese Common Market" and a "South China Economic Circle" to a "Chinese Civilizational Community" and a "Chinese Federation." Some of these terms are attempts to describe an emerging reality in international affairs, whereas others are efforts to forecast or prescribe what might happen in the future. Some focus on the prospects for the political integration of various Chinese societies; others on the economic and cultural ties between them. Although the different concepts therefore have different meanings, they all refer to aspects of a common phenomenon: the construction or revival of economic, political, and cultural ties among dispersed Chinese communities around the world as the political barriers to their interaction fall.

Taiwan plays an important part in virtually all these formulas, whether descriptive or prescriptive. This is entirely appropriate, for Taiwan is a prime example of all the major dynamics of Greater China: the forces that produced a dispersed Chinese world, the political barriers that restricted contacts within it, the factors that have eroded those barriers and encouraged renewed interaction, and the remaining obstacles to the emergence of a fully integrated global Chinese community. As such, an understanding of Taiwan's relationship with the rest of the Chinese world—particularly mainland China—is essential to an analysis of the prospects for Greater China.

To begin with, the history of Taiwan illustrates the population movements that, over the last four hundred years, have produced a dispersed international Chinese community. Ethnic Chinese first settled in Taiwan in large numbers in the seventeenth century as they fled the mainland to avoid economic hardship and political turmoil at the end of the Ming dynasty and the beginning of the Qing. Migration continued through the nineteenth and twentieth centuries, as more Chinese sought to escape poverty, civil war, and communism. Some emigrated to North America, Southeast Asia, Australia, and other parts of the world, but several million moved to Taiwan. Today, virtually all of Taiwan's twenty million people trace their roots to these migrants from mainland China, even though only around 15-20 percent are related to those who first moved to the island after 1945.

Taiwan also exemplifies the gradual political disintegration of China since the end of the Ming dynasty. The island was a Japanese colony from 1895 to 1945, one of several areas along the Chinese periphery (parts of Siberia, Hong Kong, Macao, Mongolia, and Manchuria) that foreign imperial powers detached from the Qing dynasty and republican China. After 1945, Taiwan was occupied by the armies of Nationalist China, and became the Kuomintang's capital after it lost control of the mainland in 1949. More than any other territory, Taiwan is an instance of both of the processes—foreign colonialism and civil war—that created a divided China.

With the retreat of the nationalists to Taipei, and the establishment of a communist government in Beijing, the two largest parts of what once had been a unified country were isolated from one another. There was virtually no trade, no investment, no travel, no political dialogue, or cultural exchange in either direction. Contacts between residents of Taiwan and the mainland in third countries were minimal. Taiwan had somewhat more interaction with Hong Kong and Macao, but the desire of the British and Portuguese governments to avoid provoking Beijing meant that noneconomic linkages, both cultural and political, were kept to a minimum.[2] Taiwan's main ties to the rest of the Chinese world were through those sympathetic to either the Kuomintang or to the Taiwanese Independence Movement in Japan, Southeast Asia, and the West.

Since the late 1970s, the political barriers to interaction have begun to fall, and Taiwan's linkages with the rest of the Chinese world have increased exponentially. The most dramatic change, of course, has been in Taiwan's relations with mainland China, as evidenced by the explosion of economic ties, the expansion of cultural relations, and even the limited establishment of semiofficial political contacts across the Taiwan Strait. Since Taiwan has not yet permitted direct communication or transportation links with the mainland, however, most of these relationships are conducted through Hong Kong, meaning a great expansion in Hong Kong-Taiwan contacts as well. In addition, Taiwan's economic and cultural ties with overseas Chinese in North America and Southeast Asia have also been growing rapidly.

The explosion of Taiwan's contacts with other parts of the international Chinese community, especially with mainland China, illustrates the factors that are partially reintegrating what had been mutually isolated parts of Greater China. In essence, three forces are at work. Taiwan's desire for markets and for a lower-cost manufacturing base, and the mainland's quest for foreign capital and technology, are fostering commercial ties across the Taiwan Strait. Common history, language, and family ties are encouraging the revival of cultural exchanges among Taiwan, the mainland, and other Chinese communities, that in turn are greatly facilitated by modern transportation and telecommunications. The long-standing ideal of a politically integrated China is also sustaining discussion of the terms by which Taiwan and the mainland might be reunified, just as it is forcing the return of both Hong Kong and Macao to Chinese sovereignty by the end of this century.

Yet Taiwan also epitomizes a contradictory fact. Alongside the forces promoting greater unity are powerful factors that foster continued separation. Although Taiwan has a significant interest in promoting closer commercial ties with mainland China and Hong Kong, it does not want to lose its economic connections with the United States and the rest of Asia. Even though Taiwanese have strong historic and cultural ties with the mainland, they have also developed their own local traditions, evolved a separate identity, and speak a dialect that distinguishes them from most other Chinese. Also, despite the fact that many residents of Taiwan still hope for the eventual reunification of the island with the mainland, a significant minority favor formal independence for Taiwan, and a great majority oppose political reintegration under present circumstances. Consequently, the future of Taiwan's involvement in Greater China remains indeterminate, the product of a complex blend of centrifugal and centripetal forces.

The best way to explore Taiwan's role in Greater China is to organize the discussion around the three main aspects of the phenomenon: cultural, economic, and political. Each of these facets of Greater China has, at present, its own boundaries, its own centers of activity, and its own dynamics. As a result, each also has quite different prospects. In the pages that follow, we will see that Taiwan's involvement in a transnational Chinese economy is significantly more likely than its full incorporation into an integrated Cultural China,[3] which is more likely yet than Taiwan's inclusion in a unified Chinese state. In each case, however, Taiwan's integration with the rest of the Chinese world must still overcome significant obstacles.

Cultural Ties

Of all the obstacles to contacts across the Taiwan Strait, the barriers to cultural ties were among the first to fall. The easing of restrictions occurred first on the mainland, where the political liberalization associated with the post-Mao reforms of the early 1980s made it conceivable to permit a wider range of contacts with Chinese on Taiwan. Gradually, Taipei also changed its policies to permit its citizens to take advantage of these new opportunities. In 1981, it agreed to a formula that allowed its athletes to take part in international sporting events in third countries, along with representatives of the mainland. This formula was soon extended to include participation in meetings sponsored by nongovernmental organizations in third countries in fields other than athletics. In October 1987, Taipei allowed its citizens to visit the mainland for family reunions. The following year, it authorized participation in meetings arranged by international nongovernmental organizations in mainland China, as well as in third countries. In 1988-1989, Taipei also permitted indirect postal and telephone contacts between Taiwan and the mainland.

With political barriers reduced, and with modern transportation and telecommunications facilities at the disposal of those who wished to use them, cultural and humanitarian contacts across the Taiwan Strait increased rapidly. It is estimated that, by the end of 1992, a cumulative total of more than four million Taiwanese visits to the mainland had occurred, and some thirty-two thousand visits to Taiwan by residents of the People's Republic had taken place. The volume of mail has risen to the level of 24 million pieces per year. And the volume of telephone calls now exceeds 40,000 per day from the mainland to Taiwan alone.[4]

The common cultural background of Taiwanese and mainland societies was, of course, the principal factor stimulating the dismantling of barriers to cultural and humanitarian exchange. Families longed for reunion; Chinese on Taiwan wanted the opportunity to visit their native places; parents wished to show their children the great scenic historical sites on the mainland; intellectuals and scholars hoped to discuss common issues with their counterparts; and ordinary people sought to experience the popular culture produced on the other side of the Taiwan Strait. What gave the issue particular urgency and poignancy was the fact that, after almost forty years of division, long family separations were becoming increasingly painful. Indeed, the immediate cause of the change in Taipei's policy on the issue was the hijacking of a China Airlines cargo plane by its own pilot, out of a desire to see his aging father on the mainland before death precluded their reunion.

But there are other, less natural forces at work as well. Political leaders on both sides of the Taiwan Strait see the assertion of a common Chinese identity as an important factor contributing to eventual political reunification. On the mainland, this motive was evident in the long-standing incorporation of Taiwanese performing and literary arts in official cultural activity, as a way of symbolizing Taiwan's inclusion in a single Chinese society. On Taiwan, it was reflected in the nationalist government's equally prolonged insistence that, through its sponsorship of museums and traditional opera, it was preserving high Chinese culture against the communists' attempts to eradicate it. Since the mid-1980s, the revival of direct contacts across the Taiwan Strait was therefore encouraged by the two governments, partly on the grounds that cultural interaction would eventually promote political reunification.

Meanwhile, comparable ties have been growing between Taiwan and other parts of Greater China. Greater wealth and leisure time, the relaxation of restrictions on foreign travel, and more convenient international air transportation have promoted Taiwanese tourism overseas. In 1991, for example, almost one and a half million Taiwanese visited Hong Kong, nearly three quarters of a million visited the ASEAN countries, and more than 250,000 visited the United States.[5] Presumably a very large number of the visitors to Hong Kong did so *en route* to and from mainland China, and a sizeable proportion of the Taiwanese travelling to North America or Southeast Asia did so simply as tourists, just as they might visit Europe or Japan. Still, a significant percentage of Taiwanese travellers to these areas probably visited Chinese friends, saw relatives, or conducted business there, and thus can be said to be participating in the Greater China phenomenon.

The flows to Taiwan from other parts of the global Chinese community are even more difficult to measure. Around 225,000 Americans, 185,000 Southeast Asians, and 180,000 residents of Hong Kong visited Taiwan in 1991. But it is impossible to know how many of these did so as tourists, and how many were visiting friends, seeing relatives, or conducting business. It is equally difficult to know how many of those from North America and Southeast Asia were themselves of Chinese descent. Official Taiwanese statistics report that 225,000 overseas Chinese visited the island in 1991, representing 12 percent of total tourist arrivals. Judging from the small number of visitors from Southeast Asia classified as overseas Chinese, however, it is likely that many tourists reported as "foreigners" were actually of Chinese origin.[6]

Even more significant is the decision of ethnic Chinese to move back to Taiwan more permanently, after a period of study and residence overseas. Anecdotal evidence suggests that this "reverse brain drain" is now reaching significant proportions, as economic and political opportunities in Taiwan begin to match, or even exceed, those available in the United States and Canada. Chinese from abroad are playing an important role in the development of high-tech industry and advanced services in Taiwan.[7] Chinese scholars living in the United States, such as Ying-mao Kau and Hung-mao Tien, have been actively involved in the emergence of independent research institutions and foundations in Taiwan. In addition, both the ruling and the opposition parties have sought to recruit overseas Chinese to serve in prominent political positions: Hung-dah Chiu as a minister without portfolio in the Kuomintang government, and Parris Chang as a shadow foreign minister for the Democratic Progressive Party.

The exchange of ideas and the sharing of cultural products is as important as is the direct contact among people. Here, popular culture has led the way. Taiwanese popular music—mainly in Mandarin Chinese, but also some in *minnan* dialect—has been sweeping the mainland ever since the mid-1980s, when tape recordings of the popular singer Theresa Teng (Deng Lijun) first became the rage. To a much smaller degree, film and literature from Taiwan has also found audiences on the mainland. The flow of popular culture has been far less in the other direction, with the most prominent exception having been the revival of opportunities for Taiwanese to participate in folk religious activities along the Fujian coast.

Taiwan is also involved in the exchange of popular culture with other parts of Greater China, with modern technology again greatly facilitating the process. Video stores serving the Chinese communities in North America and Southeast Asia are stocked with tapes of movies produced on Taiwan. Taiwanese television programs appear regularly on Chinese-language cable channels in the United States. And Taiwanese songs, movies, music videos, and television programs are an important feature of the Chinese-language channel of Star TV, the satellite broadcasting service aimed at overseas Chinese in Hong Kong, Singapore, and other parts of Asia.

Contacts in the realm of high culture have also been growing, although not as dramatically. There are now regular dialogues between Taiwanese scholars and their mainland counterparts, primarily on the mainland and in third countries, but occasionally on Taiwan as well. There has also been some exchange of performing arts troupes and art exhibitions. But economics may be a problem. The products of popular culture can be directly broadcast by radio and television, both of which can reach to some degree across the Taiwan Strait, and by relatively inexpensive video and audio cassettes. Although the output of high culture can also be transmitted through books and film, much elite cultural exchange involves art exhibitions, stage performances, and participation in seminars and conferences, all of which are more expensive and more likely to require subsidies.

There are further obstacles to Taiwan's full integration into a single "Cultural China." The most immediate are the political barriers between Taiwan and the mainland, mostly imposed by Taipei, that remain in place despite the rapprochement of the last five to six years. Despite the importuning of its counterpart on the mainland, the Taiwan government has steadfastly refused to permit the establishment of direct mail, telecommunications, or transportation links across the Taiwan Strait. Given the sophistication of the modern international telecommunications system, this is not a significant obstacle to telephonic interaction, as phone calls can be instantly routed through intermediate switchboards. But the policy is a barrier to mail service, and a major inconvenience for travellers, all of whom must pass through a third port (usually Hong Kong, but often Tokyo) on their way from Taiwan to the mainland.

In addition, although the nationalist government has now eliminated all restrictions on travel to the mainland, except for high-ranking officials, it continues to limit the flow of visitors from the mainland to

Taiwan. Although Taipei has eliminated its earlier requirements that mainland residents have lived abroad for five years or that they renounce their membership in the Chinese Communist Party, other restrictions on short-term visits remain in force. Applicants for entry visas are still subject to scrutiny concerning their political affiliations and their possible desire to remain in Taiwan as "economic migrants."

The two sides maintain even stricter controls over long-term visitors. In the absence of official contacts between the two governments, neither Taipei nor Beijing will permit citizens from one side of the Taiwan Strait to establish residence in the other. Thus, although there have been short-term academic exchanges in both directions, there are no professors from Taiwan teaching at mainland universities, or students from mainland China studying in institutions of higher education on Taiwan. Similarly, although a small number of mainland journalists have visited Taiwan, and a much larger number of Taiwanese reporters regularly travel to the mainland on short-term visas, the news media from one society have not yet been allowed to establish standing bureaus in the other. The nationalist government permits a small number of mainlanders to work on Taiwanese fishing boats, but apparently not to establish residence on Taiwan itself. It is resisting demands from its own business community to import inexpensive labor from the mainland to work in the industrial and service sectors on Taiwan.

The two governments also control the exchange of cultural products. Books and periodicals from one society do not regularly appear in bookstores and newsstands in the other. The Taiwanese government limits the screening of mainland films and television programs, and even restricts the amount of time that mainland actors and actresses can appear on the screen in co-productions. Films and television programs produced on Taiwan do appear regularly in movie theaters and on television screens on the mainland, but those selected are more likely to deal with historical subjects than with contemporary ones.

In the end, however, cultural differences, rather than political barriers, may prove the principal obstacle to the inclusion of Taiwanese in an integrated Cultural China. Many Taiwanese intellectuals insist that the differences in historical experience, level of development, political system, and degree of exposure to the rest of the world have produced a significant divergence between Taiwanese and mainland culture. Moreover, despite the government's policy of encouraging all residents of Taiwan to regard themselves as Chinese, the process of political liberalization is permitting the resurgence of a sense of local Taiwanese identity, a renewed interest in Taiwanese history and culture, and a revived use of Taiwan dialect.

Thus, it should not be assumed that all citizens of Taiwan regard themselves as an integral part of a global Chinese culture. Indeed, to the most militant advocates of Taiwanese independence, appeals to a common Chinese culture at best are regarded as a veiled rationale for an unwanted political reunification with the mainland, and at worst are portrayed as a program of "cultural genocide" against Taiwanese. An even larger number of Taiwanese, less concerned with political issues, simply believe that Taiwan has now developed its own cultural identity, separate from that of the mainland. As one intellectual has put it, although the two cultures may come from the same root (*tonggen*), they are no longer of the same nature (*tongzhi*).[8] To the extent that these views become widespread, they will reduce, although not completely eliminate, Taiwan's interest in maintaining extensive cultural ties with non-Taiwanese, either on the mainland or elsewhere.

Data from recent public opinion polls conducted on Taiwan have shed some preliminary light on how far this process has gone. In 1992, a sample of residents of Taiwan was asked which of four ethnic labels they would apply to themselves: 23.7 percent described themselves as Taiwanese, 23.4 percent as Chinese, 30.7 percent as Taiwanese as well as Chinese (*wo shi Taiwanren ye shi Zhongguoren*), and 19.0 percent as Chinese as well as Taiwanese (*wo shi Zhongguoren ye shi Taiwanren*). These data suggest that a slight majority of 54.4 percent now see themselves primarily or exclusively as Taiwanese, compared with 42.4 percent who identify themselves primarily or exclusively as Chinese. Just as interesting, the same data reveal that residents of Taiwan are divided almost equally between those who portray themselves as incorporating two cultural identities, Chinese and Taiwanese (49.7 percent), and those who describe themselves as either one or the other (47.1 percent).[9]

Thus, although Taiwan's cultural ties with other Chinese are likely to grow, prospects for the full integration of Taiwan into a cultural Greater China are limited. The gradual improvement of political relations should permit the establishment of direct transportation and communications links across the Taiwan Strait, and thus further facilitate cultural contacts between Taiwan and the mainland. Similarly, progress on political issues may lead to the reduction of the remaining barriers both to short-term travel from the mainland to Taiwan, and to longer-term travel in both directions. Greater prosperity on Taiwan, and the growing ease of international travel and communication, will continue to promote contacts between Taiwanese residents and other members of the global Chinese community. But the remaining political and cultural differences will still obstruct the process, especially if the majority of Taiwan's people come to adopt a predominantly Taiwanese, as opposed to Chinese, identity.

The resurgence of Taiwanese culture raises another possibility. Could there emerge, at least in terms of popular culture, a "Greater Fujian" (or "Greater *Minnan* Cultural Area"), alongside the "Greater Guangdong" (or "Greater Cantonese Cultural Area") that is already developing to the south? It is conceivable that those on Taiwan who resist identification with all of mainland China might still be willing to identify with their relatives in Fujian, and there is little doubt that *minnan* popular culture on Taiwan would be of enormous appeal to the Fujianese. The notion of several different economic regions emerging along the Chinese coast, each with a different center, is already a familiar element in discussions of China's future. But the concept of a China divided into several subregions, rather than unified into a single macro-entity, could also apply to the cultural realm as well.

Economic Ties

The barriers to economic interactions across the Taiwan Strait began to fall at about the same time as did the obstacles to cultural relations. Again, mainland China was the first to act. In the late 1970s, as part of the post-Mao reform program, Beijing indicated its willingness to open its economy to the outside world, including Taiwan, by reforming the structure of its foreign trade apparatus and by creating opportunities for foreign direct investment. In 1979, Beijing established four special economic zones along the southeastern coast of China to attract foreign investment. One of these, Xiamen, was located directly opposite Taiwan, and was clearly intended to serve investors from the island. That same year, the central government also gave several provincial-level units greater autonomy over foreign trade and investment decisions. Again, by selecting Fujian as one of the provinces to receive such privileges,[10] Beijing was clearly signalling its intention to promote economic links with Taiwan.

Beijing also adopted other, more specific, measures to encourage trade and investment with Taiwan.[11] Initially, it exempted imports from Taiwan from customs duties, on the grounds that Taiwan was a part of China and should not be subject to the same tariffs imposed on foreign countries. Although this preferential policy on trade was soon reversed, it was replaced by special incentives (such as longer tax holidays) for Taiwanese investing in the special economic zones (May 1983), and then everywhere else on the mainland (July 1988).

Although it acted more slowly than Beijing, the Taiwan government also reduced the barriers to trade and investment with the mainland. Beginning in the early 1980s, it turned an increasingly tolerant eye toward the surge of Taiwanese exports to the mainland. Then, in 1987-1988, it formally authorized the import of commodities from the mainland and Taiwanese investment on the mainland. In each case, however, Taipei insisted that the economic relationships be conducted indirectly: that imports and exports trade pass through third ports, and that investment be conducted by subsidiaries or dummy corporations in third countries. Hong Kong quickly established itself as the principal intermediary for these new relationships. Although the nationalist government still insists on reviewing Taiwanese investment on the mainland, its regulations in this regard have become progressively more lenient. In August 1992, for example, Taipei decided that only investment projects valued at more than US$3 million would require prior approval, whereas those valued at less could simply be reported for the record.

These more facilitative and less restrictive policies have dramatically increased economic interaction across the Taiwan Strait, especially since the mid-1980s. Taiwan's exports to the mainland began to rise as early as 1979 as, under economic reform, mainland firms and trading companies gained greater authority to buy goods from Taiwan. In contrast, Taiwan's purchases from the mainland increased much more slowly, until the relaxation of Taipei's import restrictions in 1987. Thereafter, trade between Taiwan and the mainland has experienced explosive growth, rising from $2.7 billion in 1988 to $4.1 billion in 1990 and $7.4 billion in 1992. At present levels, the two-way trade represents around 4.5 percent of each economy's global trade. This makes each side a significant partner for the other, but not as important as either Japan or the United States.

Investment—almost exclusively Taiwanese investment in mainland China[12]—has also been increasing rapidly since 1987. The data are hard to come by, since so much of the investment is carried in Hong Kong's accounts, and so little has been formally and accurately reported to the nationalist government. By the end of 1992, Taiwan's Ministry of Economic Affairs announced that Taiwanese investment on the mainland had reached a cumulative total of $3.68 billion, but other estimates suggested a total of some $6.75 billion, if not higher.[13] Although initially concentrated in Fujian province, where people speak the same dialect as in Taiwan, Taiwanese investment has been moving south into Guangdong, and north into the Pudong area of Shanghai and other areas along the coast. The bulk of the investment has been small-scale factories producing light industrial products for export.

Even if the official figures understate the actual level of Taiwan's foreign direct investment, they still reveal an important trend: that mainland China is gaining a growing share of Taiwan's outbound investment. Before 1991, the Taiwan government did not even report how much investment it had approved in the mainland. In 1991, it authorized $175 million in investment in the mainland, or about 10 percent of the total approvals for the year. In 1992, the Taiwan government approved $246 million in additional investment across the Taiwan Strait, representing more than 20 percent of the total investments approved.[14]

The growth of economic activity across the Taiwan Strait has been widely interpreted as the actualization of a "natural economic territory" linking Taiwan and the mainland.[15] And, indeed, powerful economic forces are stimulating these new commercial relationships. The mainland's interest is principally in gaining capital, technology, and managerial know-how from Taiwan, and in gaining access to Western markets through Taiwanese intermediaries. In this sense, Taiwan can serve as a center for growth for mainland China, much in the same way as Hong Kong has been doing.

Taiwan's interests are a bit more complex. First, Taiwanese entrepreneurs have been interested in relocating their manufacturing operations out of Taiwan, especially those that produce for export. As labor costs and land rents have risen, as the Taiwanese currency has appreciated, and as environmental policies have become more restrictive, it is no longer economically competitive to continue to manufacture labor-intensive exports on Taiwan. Taiwanese entrepreneurs have been looking to a variety of economies as alternative sites for production: the Caribbean and Mexico, to take advantage of preferential American tariff treatment given those countries, and Southeast Asia, especially the Philippines, to take advantage of geographic proximity. But mainland China has been a particularly attractive site, not only because of its economic advantages, but also because of the common language, family connections, and other ethnic ties that link it to Taiwan.[16]

A second motive has been to take advantage of the large and growing market on the mainland. The PRC offers to Taiwan—as it does to all traders and investors—the world's largest population, one of the largest gross national products, and one of the world's fastest growth rates. Some two hundred million people on the mainland are estimated to have an annual purchasing power equivalent to US$1,000. That subeconomy totals $200 billion, roughly equal to Taiwan's own gross national product. Even at official figures, which are likely to undercount mainland China's true economic activity, the PRC's GDP is now $420 billion. At 10 percent annual growth, mainland China is expanding at the rate of half a Hong Kong every year. Increasingly, therefore, Taiwanese entrepreneurs are looking to the mainland as a market, as well as a production platform.

Finally, in the last several years many on Taiwan have been touting the way in which economic interaction across the Taiwan Strait can gain a third advantage: attracting foreign multinational corporations to locate their regional operations and manufacturing centers on Taiwan, from which they can serve both the Taiwan and the mainland market. Although Taiwan does not have the geographical proximity or direct transportation links to the mainland that Hong Kong enjoys, proponents of this concept point out that Taiwan's local market is twice the size of Hong Kong's in aggregate terms, and is even larger in some specific sectors.[17]

Although economic factors are therefore one of the principal forces promoting commercial interaction between Taiwan and mainland China, they are not the only cause at work. Political factors are also involved on both sides. Paradoxically, the two governments are encouraging a common set of economic interactions for political reasons that are at least partially contradictory.

To begin with, there are those in each society—particularly in the mainland, but some on Taiwan as well—who believe that economic interaction can serve as the precondition for political reunification. Beijing has clearly been trying to use economics in this way. By placing three of its four special economic zones adjacent to Macao, Hong Kong, and Taiwan, it has attempted to blur the distinctions between these three territories and the mainland, so as to make reunification appear more feasible and less threatening. In the same way, by promoting trade and investment with Taiwan, Beijing has also wanted to create a situation in which Taiwan's economy is inexorably intertwined with the mainland. By giving the Taiwanese business community a large and growing stake in the mainland Chinese economy, Beijing is simultaneously attempting to forestall any movement toward independence, and to produce greater interest in eventual reunification.

Some on Taiwan think along similar lines. Like their counterparts on the mainland, they believe that economic interdependence is a crucial strategy for preventing independence and fostering reunification. Moreover, the advocates of reunification on Taiwan fully realize that the prospects for such a development are remote as long as the social and economic gaps between the two societies remain so wide. From their perspective, economic links across the Taiwan Strait can promote growth, improve living standards, foster marketization and privatization, and even stimulate movement toward political liberalization—all of which are necessary preconditions for political integration.

The paradox is that others on Taiwan reach the same policy conclusion from totally different premises. For them, economic interaction is a deterrent against forcible reunification in the short run, and very likely a substitute for any form of reunification over the longer term. Just as their counterparts on the mainland view economic ties as a way of dissuading Taiwan from declaring independence, so do these elements on Taiwan regard commercial links as a way of discouraging Beijing from using force against Taiwan. The use of coercion would threaten the economic viability of those mainland firms that rely on commercial relationships with Taiwan. At the same time, the strategy of enticing foreign multinationals to establish regional headquarters on Taiwan is also designed to put the economic interests of other countries at risk in such a situation as well.

The growth in Taiwan's investment and trade relations with the mainland has been accompanied by substantial increases in its economic ties with other parts of the international Chinese community. Even after excluding *entrepot* trade, Taiwan's two-way trade with Hong Kong amounted to nearly $10 billion in 1992, up from $3 billion in 1988 and $4.3 billion in 1990. Taiwan therefore conducted more trade with the six million people of Hong Kong than with the billion Chinese on the mainland.[18]

Investment relations between Taiwan and Hong Kong have also been growing. According to Taiwan's official accounts, Hong Kong invested around $130 million in Taiwan in 1991 and another $213 million in 1992, roughly equal to its level of investment in the late 1980s. Although Taiwan's investment in Hong Kong was somewhat lower, it rose dramatically over the same period, as Taiwan accumulated foreign exchange and as the restrictions on outward investment were relaxed. Approvals for Taiwanese investment in Hong Kong increased from only $8 million in 1988 to $200 million in 1991, before falling back to $55 million in 1992.[19] It is estimated that Taiwan has invested a cumulative total of $2 billion in Hong Kong, and that Hong Kong has invested some $1.5 billion in Taiwan.[20]

Taiwan's economic relations with Chinese entrepreneurs in Southeast Asia are another aspect of the Greater China phenomenon. Taiwan's trade with ASEAN totalled $14.2 billion in 1992, up from $7.0 billion in 1988 and $10.8 billion in 1990.[21] In Southeast Asia, Singapore is Taiwan's largest trading partner, accounting for about 30 percent of the island's trade with ASEAN. Malaysia is responsible for another 25 percent, followed by Indonesia and Thailand with about 15 percent each, and by the Philippines with 10 percent.

Investment links between Taiwan and Southeast Asia have also been on the rise. Taiwan's direct investment in the ASEAN economies grew from $60 million in 1988, to $700 million in 1991, before falling back to $290 million in 1992. Most of the island's investment has been directed at Malaysia, with lesser amounts flowing to Thailand, Indonesia, and the Philippines.[22] In the other direction, annual investment in Taiwan from Singapore—ASEAN's principal source of outward investment—was reported at approximately $17 million in 1988, $73 million in 1990, and $190 million in 1992. Investment from the Philippines has also been rising rapidly in recent years, even surpassing that from Singapore in 1990 and 1991.[23] On a cumulative basis, it is likely that Taiwan has invested around $2 billion in Southeast Asia, and that Singapore and the Philippines have together invested around $1 billion in Taiwan.[24]

Since economic data are organized by country, not by ethnicity, it is difficult to assess the extent to which Taiwan's economic relations with Southeast Asia have been conducted with Chinese counterparts. A rough estimate can be made by assessing the proportion of economic activity in each Southeast Asian country accounted for by ethnic Chinese, and then applying those same percentages to the trade and investment flows between Taiwan and Southeast Asia.[25] Such calculations suggest that in 1992 about $9.1 billion of Taiwan's $14.2 billion trade with ASEAN, and about $205 million of its $290 million annual investment there, were conducted with overseas Chinese entrepreneurs. This represented about 65-70 percent of the total trade and investment flows between Taiwan and ASEAN.

Taiwan is expanding its commercial activities with these overseas Chinese communities for a blend of economic and political reasons. The principal motivating factor, of course, is the search for profit. As the cost of labor and land on Taiwan rises, and as Taiwanese entrepreneurs look overseas for lower-cost production sites, they are attracted to many of the emerging economies of Southeast Asia, as well as to mainland

China. These investment flows are contributing to increasing prosperity in the region, which in turn is creating larger markets for Taiwanese goods in both Southeast Asia and Hong Kong.

The cultural factor reinforces these economic calculations. The overseas Chinese business community in Hong Kong and Southeast Asia is a natural partner for these commercial activities—not simply because they share a common ethnic background with Taiwanese entrepreneurs, but because of the leading, if not dominant, place they occupy in their local economies. It has been estimated that ethnic Chinese account for between 40 percent and 80 percent of private business activity in Southeast Asia, depending on the particular country, and for 90 percent of private business activity in Hong Kong.[26]

There are also political motives in play on Taiwan. In a reversal of the nineteenth century doctrine that "trade follows the flag," the government in Taipei has concluded that expanding Taiwan's commercial activities in Hong Kong and Southeast Asia will help improve the island's unofficial political standing in those areas, and therefore partially overcome the island's lack of formal diplomatic ties. This will prevent the mainland from isolating Taiwan in the international community.

The barriers to the further expansion of these economic activities are significantly lower than the obstacles to commercial ties across the Taiwan Strait. The absence of diplomatic relations between Taiwan and its trading partners is a barrier to business transactions, but not a crippling one. Many Southeast Asian governments worry that their ethnic Chinese entrepreneurs will invest more in mainland China than they will at home, but they do not appear to resent Taiwanese investment in their own economies. The Taiwan government initially warned that, after Hong Kong's reversion to Chinese sovereignty in 1997, it would impose the same controls on economic ties with Hong Kong as it did on economic relations with the mainland, but it has subsequently abandoned that position. Beijing, too, has pledged that the framework for economic relations between Taiwan and Hong Kong will remain unchanged. Thus, the limits to Taiwan's economic ties with Hong Kong and Southeast Asia are essentially those that stem from the business climate in those societies: the rate of growth, the level of corruption, and the degree of political instability.

Altogether, the data reported above suggest that Greater China now accounts for a significant, although not yet dominant, share of Taiwan's foreign economic activity. In 1992, Taiwan conducted $7.4 billion in trade with the mainland, $10.0 billion with Hong Kong, and an estimated $9.1 billion in trade with overseas Chinese entrepreneurs in the ASEAN countries. The total, $26.5 billion, constituted 17.3 percent of Taiwan's global trade for the year, as compared with $39.3 billion (25.6 percent) with the United States and $30.7 billion (20.0 percent) with Japan.

The share of Taiwan's outward direct investment going to Greater China is significantly larger. Looking again at 1992, approved Taiwanese investments amounted to $246 in the mainland, $55 million in Hong Kong, and an estimated $205 million with Chinese partners in ASEAN.[27] This suggests that about 45 percent of Taiwan's outward foreign investment was destined for Greater China that year, as compared with 17 percent to the United States and less than one percent to Japan.

Greater China also plays a significant role in Taiwan's inbound investment picture. According to the official figures—which probably understate the proportion of incoming investment provided by ethnic Chinese—21 percent of the $1.8 billion in inbound foreign investment in 1992 was provided by overseas Chinese. If the rest of the investment coming from Hong Kong and Singapore is added to this total, the proportion rises to 35 percent. In contrast, 29 percent of approved investments came from Japan, while only 15 percent came from the United States.[28]

The increase in Taiwan's economic ties with other Chinese communities has led to growing discussion of institutionalizing the process by creating some kind of "Chinese Economic Community." Interest in such a concept has been evident in Taiwan, as well as in Hong Kong, on the mainland, and among overseas Chinese. Taiwanese analysts have presented several different variants on this theme since the early 1990s. Some foresee an economic region that would include mainland China, Taiwan, Hong Kong, and Singapore; others predict that the process of economic integration will be limited, at least in the middle run, to Taiwan, Hong Kong, Guangdong, Fujian, and perhaps other parts of southern China. Some propose the creation of a full-fledged common market, characterized by the absence of any form of barrier to trade or to the mobility of the factors of production; others argue for a more informal process of economic coordination and cooperation. And, as noted above, some analysts view economic integration as a stepping stone to political unification, while others regard it as an alternative to an integrated political community.[29] In general, these variations parallel the range of views developed elsewhere.[30]

The idea of a Chinese economic community has occasionally received official endorsement in Taipei, at least as a long-range goal.[31] And yet, as compared with their counterparts in Hong Kong and mainland China, Taiwanese analysts tend to be more skeptical about both the feasibility and desirability of the concept, at least insofar as it would involve the fuller integration of Taiwan and the mainland. This accurately reflects the fact that there the nationalist government still maintains significant barriers on commercial relations across the Taiwan Strait. As of today, there is still no direct transportation, no direct communication, no lending from Taiwan to the mainland, no foreign investment from the mainland to Taiwan, and no long-term residence possible in either direction. There is no investment treaty, no consular protection, and no diplomatic representation to protect the interests of one side in the other. It would be as if Washington and Ottawa were thinking of creating the North American Free Trade Area even before they had established diplomatic relations with each other.

The speed with which these barriers can be reduced or eliminated remains uncertain. Taipei has set three conditions for permitting the establishment of direct transportation and communication links across the Taiwan Strait: Beijing must acknowledge Taiwan as an equal political entity, facilitate its participation in the international community, and renounce the use of force against the island. Although there have been some promising replies from Beijing on at least two of these three points, Taipei does not regard its conditions to have been met. Moreover, since these preconditions are also limiting political dialogue between the two sides, advocates of Taiwanese independence are insisting that the nationalist government adhere to them strictly, so as to delay any discussion of political issues as long as possible. Public opinion polls on Taiwan also reveal considerable concern that extensive mainland involvement in the island's economy—as distinct from Taiwanese participation in economic activities on the mainland—would pose a threat to Taiwanese security.[32]

In addition, there are a number of other obstacles that economic integration between Taiwan and the mainland must overcome. These include the imperfections in the mainland's business climate that discourage potential traders and investors from any other society: inadequate infrastructure, increasing corruption, an incomplete legal system, a cumbersome bureaucracy, extensive administrative interference in economic operations, wide fluctuations in the rate of economic growth, periodic restrictions on the availability of foreign exchange and working capital, and the potential for political and social unrest. In Taiwan's case, there is the additional concern that, having encouraged the growth of economic ties across the Taiwan Strait, the communists will then manipulate those linkages for political ends.

Even if these barriers were removed, the result would be to create a normal institutional infrastructure for trade and investment, such as that which presently exists between the United States and the People's Republic, rather than a particularly favorable relationship. If the concept of a Chinese economic community is to be taken literally, it would involve further steps, which would not be easy to achieve: the elimination of all tariff and non-tariff barriers to trade; the removal of restrictions on the flow of labor, technology, and capital across the Taiwan Strait; fully convertible currencies; and the coordination of monetary, fiscal, and social welfare policies. While not totally inconceivable in the case of Taiwan and mainland China,[33] such developments would obviously require much time and effort.

Finally, it is highly unlikely that Taiwan would be interested in forming a Chinese economic community if it were to imply an exclusive economic bloc, especially if it raised barriers to trade with others. Entrepreneurs in Taiwan will want to maintain their commercial relations with other trading and investment partners in Japan, North America, and Europe. Some in Taiwan are already talking of a free trade agreement with the United States, or a common market linking them with Japan and the other three Asian NICs, as either an alternative or a supplement to a closer economic relationship with mainland China.[34]

On balance, one can forecast growing trade and investment across the Taiwan Strait, especially if direct transportation links can be established and if an investment protection agreement can be reached. Taiwan's growing economic interaction with the mainland, especially the southeastern provinces, will transform what is now "Greater Hong Kong" (Hong Kong plus Guangdong) into "Greater South China" (Hong Kong and Taiwan, plus Guangdong, Fujian, and Hainan). Over time, the boundaries of Greater South China will spread northward and westward on the mainland, incorporating a greater portion of the territory of the People's Republic. Although Hong Kong will probably remain the financial and commercial capital of Greater South China, Taipei will assume a greater role on both dimensions, and may take the lead in the promotion of capital- and technology-intensive industry. It will be difficult, however, to codify these relations into a formal economic arrangement linking Taiwan to Hong Kong and the mainland, let alone to Southeast Asia.

Political Ties

Of all the potential forms a Greater China might take, the creation of a reunified China—or even the establishment of official political ties across the Taiwan Strait—faces the greatest obstacles. Although the reunification of Hong Kong with mainland China is now a certainty, the prospects for the reunification of Taiwan with the mainland remain dim.

In theory, of course, both the communist government in Beijing and the nationalist government of Taiwan uphold the objective of a unified China, which would incorporate not only China proper, but also Xinjiang, Tibet, and Manchuria, which are already under Beijing's control, as well as Hong Kong and Macao, which will be returned to Chinese sovereignty toward the end of the century. The status of Outer Mongolia in such a vision remains more ambiguous. The nationalist government has, since 1949, considered Mongolia to be part of China, but now seems to be softening its position and is acknowledging the Mongolian Republic to be a sovereign independent state. Conversely, the communist government has, over the same period, recognized Mongolia as independent, but a surprising number of younger Chinese still seem to regard it as naturally part of Greater China.

Taiwan's place in a unified China has also had its own ambiguities—far more than either the nationalist or communist government is willing officially to admit. In 1936, none other than Mao Zedong told Edgar Snow that, in his opinion, both Taiwan and Korea should become independent states after they ceased being colonies of Japan.[35] And, in 1947, the Taiwanese uprising of February 28 could be interpreted as a demand for independence from both Japan and China, similar to the abortive declaration of a Taiwanese Republic when the island was transferred from China to Japan in 1895. By 1949, however, both the nationalist and the communist governments were fully committed to the idea of one China that included both Taiwan and the mainland. Their principal difference was over which government should be recognized as having legitimate authority over that single political entity.

For the next four decades, the two rival governments endeavored to defend the principle of one China, even as, year after year, the reality was that there were two. The communist government advocated the "liberation" of Taiwan from nationalist rule, and periodically threatened the use of military force to help bring that about. On two occasions in the 1950s—1954-1955 and again in 1958—the communists attacked offshore islands held by Taiwan, in the hopes that a successful assault would so weaken the nationalists as to prompt their collapse. When it became clear that the threat of military force against Taiwan was only solidifying Taipei's alliance with Washington, and that the successful seizure of the offshore islands would only serve more clearly to separate

Taiwan from the mainland, Beijing changed its strategy. From the early 1960s onward, its one China policy was reflected less in its strategy toward Taiwan than in its strategy toward the rest of the world: its insistence that those wishing to establish diplomatic relations with Beijing must break official ties with Taipei, but also that they acknowledge or agree that Taiwan was part of China.

For its part, the nationalist government also kept the idea of one China alive. Rather than depicting themselves as an independent government ruling a separate nation-state, the nationalists portrayed themselves as the legitimate government of all China, temporarily in exile on Taiwan, that was rebuilding its strength so as to regain its rightful position on the mainland. Domestic propaganda constantly stressed the long-term goal of *guangfu dalu*: recovering the mainland. School textbooks contained ambitious maps, not only showing the routes that the eventual invasion would take, but also suggesting that the boundaries of nationalist China would ultimately include not just the existing People's Republic, but Outer Mongolia and large portions of Siberia and Central Asia as well.[36] Like its counterpart on the mainland, the nationalist government steadfastly refused to accept dual recognition from foreign countries. Like Beijing, Taipei realized the importance of the offshore islands as a symbol of a reunified China, and refused considerable American pressure in the latter half of the 1950s to abandon them. Following the precedent established by the February 28 Incident, the nationalist government also vigorously suppressed any advocacy of Taiwanese independence.

Although still committed to the principle of a single, reunified China, in recent years both Beijing and Taipei have moderated their positions on the mechanism of reunification. As in the economic and cultural realms, Beijing was the first to make adjustments. In 1979, it began to suggest that it would primarily use peaceful means, rather than force, to obtain the reunification of Taiwan with the mainland. It offered to negotiate reunification either with the government of Taiwan as a local authority, or with the Nationalist Party as a political party with equal standing to the communists. Although it never renounced the use of force, it listed, with increasing specificity, the limited conditions under which it would use military pressure against Taiwan. It also offered to open direct trade, mail, and transportation links (the so-called *santong*) with Taiwan as an intermediate step to improve relations. Then, in the mid-1980s, Chinese leaders made clear that the concept of "one country, two systems" being developed for Hong Kong would apply to Taiwan as well, perhaps with even more generous terms.[37]

For some time, the nationalists on Taiwan rejected all these overtures from Beijing. Chiang Ching-kuo's response to the normalization of Sino-American relations in early 1979, and to the early communist overtures that accompanied it, was to declare that Taipei would never enter into negotiations or compromises with Beijing.[38] By 1981, this initial reaction had been codified into the so-called "three nos" formula: no contacts, no negotiations, and no compromise with Beijing. Taiwan refused to enter into discussions with the mainland authorities, either as a local government or as a political party. It also rejected the formula of "one country, two systems," insisting instead that China should be reunified under a single system, that guided by Sun Yat-sen's "Three Principles of the People."[39]

In the late 1980s, however, Taiwan's position began to moderate—in part to accompany the relaxation of constraints on economic and cultural interactions across the Taiwan Strait. In 1987, the secretary-general of the Kuomintang, Lee Huan, significantly modified the nationalists' "one country, one system" approach. Lee still insisted that Beijing's concept of "one country, two systems" was unrealistic, and that reunification could occur only if there were thoroughgoing political and economic liberalization on the mainland. But he went on to say that the nationalists did not necessarily intend to supplant the communists on the mainland.[40] Two years later, Taiwan sent its finance minister, Shirley Kuo, to Beijing to participate in the annual meeting of the Asian Development Bank. Together, these steps implied, for the first time, a willingness to acknowledge the communists as an equal political entity. Lee Teng-hui made this position explicit in May 1991 when he formally accepted the reality that China was ruled by two governments, and that the nationalists' jurisdiction extended only to Taiwan, the Pescadores, and the offshore islands.

In 1991, the Kuomintang put forward its own formula for reunification, the National Unification Guidelines, as a counter to the communists' concept of "one country, two systems." The nationalists' formula envisioned three stages: the first, in which there could be indirect and unofficial contacts across the Taiwan Strait; the second, in which the two sides could establish direct transportation links and open official contacts; and the third, in which the two parties would negotiate the terms of formal reunification. With the relaxation of the barriers to economic and cultural ties in 1986-1988, the relationship between the two sides was said already to be in the first stage. The transition to the second stage would occur when Beijing agreed to acknowledge Taiwan as an equal political entity, much as Taiwan had already done with the

People's Republic; when the mainland took a more forthcoming position toward Taiwan's participation in international intergovernmental organizations; and when Beijing renounced the use of force against Taiwan.[41]

Under this formula, Taiwan announced the creation of the Straits Exchange Foundation (SEF) as the nominally unofficial entity designated to engage in dialogue with the mainland. After some hesitation, Beijing created the Association for Relations Across the Taiwan Strait (ARATS) as the counterpart for the SEF. Preliminary meetings were held by the staff of the two organizations, followed by a meeting of the heads of the two organizations in Singapore in April 1993. This constituted the first acknowledged direct political dialogue between the two sides since 1949. And, if the reunification of Taiwan with the mainland should ever occur, the meeting would doubtless be seen as the first step in that process.

Whatever the symbolic importance of the Singapore conference as a breakthrough in the political relationships across the Taiwan Strait, it simultaneously illustrated the enormous barriers to the incorporation of Taiwan and the mainland into a reunified China. At Taipei's insistence, the meeting dealt exclusively with relatively technical issues involving economic and humanitarian exchange. An effort by Wang Daohan, chairman of the mainland's ARATS, to discuss the terms for the establishment of direct transportation links between Taiwan and the mainland was rebuffed by his Taiwanese counterpart as premature. Taipei made no public effort to explore indirect signals coming simultaneously from Beijing that mainland China might be prepared to meet some of Taiwan's conditions for opening air and shipping services between the two sides.

The key barrier to political integration is that, despite the commitment of the nationalists to the idea of eventual reunification, very few on Taiwan are willing to accept the mainland's formula of "one country, two systems" as the method for attaining that objective. One of the basic elements of that formula—that Taiwan would become a local jurisdiction under Beijing's sovereignty—makes it highly unpopular on Taiwan. To a degree, the unacceptability of the formula is related to the uncertainties surrounding Hong Kong's reversion to Chinese sovereignty on similar terms. It is conceivable that, if the transition in Hong Kong proceeds smoothly and successfully, a larger proportion of Taiwan's population might be willing to take another and more favorable look at the "one country, two systems" formula. Pending greater confidence about the future of Hong Kong, however, the mainland's proposal has virtually no support on Taiwan. One recent survey on the island, for example, found that only 6 percent of the respondents endorsed the formula of "one country, two systems."[42]

Nor have Taiwanese officials or scholars devoted much attention to developing a detailed alternative formula for reunification. The official position has variously been that China should be reunified under the existing republican constitution, under Sun Yat-sen's "Three Principles of the People" (the *sanmin zhuyi*), or at least under a single democratic capitalist system. A few Taiwanese scholars have discussed a federal solution for reunification, but this formula has attracted much less attention on Taiwan than it has on the mainland, in Hong Kong, and among Chinese overseas. Instead, Taiwanese analysts and political leaders have focused primarily on the problem of expanding Taiwan's role in the international community before a final solution to the Taiwan question can be found. Their heated discussions of concepts such as "one country, two governments" or "one country, two regions" are concerned more with reaching an interim *modus vivendi* with mainland China than with finding the ultimate formula for reunification.

Moreover, setting aside the specific formula for reunification, there is also the problem that a substantial number of people on Taiwan would vastly prefer the present situation to reunification with a communist China. Although most of the recent public opinion surveys indicate the percentage of Taiwanese supporting a formal declaration of independence hovering around only 10-15 percent,[43] they also show that a much higher percentage, around 45 percent, would prefer to preserve their *de facto* independence from the mainland.[44] In contrast, only 10 percent expressed the willingness to see Taiwan united with a mainland that was still governed by the present communist system.[45]

Not only does public opinion therefore resist any rapid movement toward reunification, but it also obstructs any effort by Taipei even to begin an extensive political dialogue with Beijing. A significant proportion of the Taiwanese public worries that its government is about to embark down a slippery slope: if it begins semiofficial discussions with Beijing, it will soon be lured into an official negotiation; if it starts discussing technical issues relating to economic and cultural exchange, it will soon be forced to discuss the reopening of direct transportation and communication links across the Taiwan Strait; and if it agrees to discuss the opening of the *santong*, it will soon be drawn into discussions of formal reunification. A poll conducted in May 1993 gives graphic evidence of such fears: more than 60 percent of those surveyed worried that the future of Taiwan was going to be decided by a small number of politicians rather than by the people of Taiwan, while only 37 percent were confident that those politicians would be able to safeguard Taiwan's interests in their discussions with Beijing.[46]

Thus, despite the signs of flexibility in each side's negotiating position, and despite the rapid expansion of economic and cultural ties across the Taiwan Strait, the prospects for incorporating Taiwan into a reunified China are virtually nil for the foreseeable future. The political dialogue between the two sides will continue, but is likely to be slow and halting.

Over the longer term, of course, the range of possibilities broadens. One of the most important barriers to political dialogue with the mainland is the widespread view on Taiwan that, despite the political reforms of the past decade, the Kuomintang cannot be trusted to negotiate the island's future with the communists on the mainland. This barrier could be reduced or removed under either of two circumstances: if there is further reform of the Kuomintang such that it gains greater legitimacy in addressing or handling this issue, or if the Democratic Progressive Party should come to power in Taiwan in the next election. Under either circumstance, the government in Taipei might enjoy greater flexibility in conducting dialogue with Beijing than it does today.

In addition, political dialogue would also be facilitated by further changes of policy in mainland China. As noted above, the Kuomintang has set three conditions for moving from the first to the second stage of cross-Strait relations that would include the opening of formal political dialogue with the mainland. It is unlikely that Beijing can fully meet all three of those conditions. But if it can show flexibility on most of them—renouncing the use of force unless Taiwan declares independence, accepting the seating of both Chinas in international organizations, or acknowledging Taiwan to be an equal political entity within the rubric of a single China—then Taipei would be more likely to move to a higher level of political dialogue with Beijing.

Still, upgrading official dialogue is far from agreeing on the terms for reunification. The merger of Taiwan and the mainland under a single sovereign government remains highly unlikely, unless there is massive political and economic change on the mainland. Perhaps the most that could reasonably be expected is that, after further economic and political liberalization on the mainland, and assuming the smooth return of Hong Kong to Chinese sovereignty, there were created some kind of loose federation in which Taiwan retained full domestic autonomy as well as substantial international representation.

One last possibility deserves brief consideration: the political unification of Taiwan not with the mainland as a whole, but with a much smaller fragment of Chinese territory following the disintegration of the present People's Republic. Assuming that Fujian would be the most likely candidate for such a merger, this scenario would involve the creation of a political "Greater Taiwan," supplementing the "Greater Fujian" mentioned in the earlier discussion of cultural ties.

Albeit conceivable, this scenario, too, has a relatively low probability. To begin with, although greater than they seemed a few years ago, the chances of the geographic disintegration of mainland China, along the lines of what has occurred in the former Soviet Union and Yugoslavia, remain remote. At this point, the vitality of the Chinese economy and the viability of the Chinese government are such that the preservation of a single national entity—even though one that may be corrupt, decentralized, and unstable—remains a much more probable outcome than is systemic collapse. Moreover, even if China should disintegrate regionally, Taiwan would be more likely to remain aloof, or even to declare independence, than to involve itself in the mainland's problems by pursuing unification with Fujian.

Conclusion

Taiwan thus illustrates many of the integrative factors that are working toward the creation of a Greater China. To begin with, there are enormous economic complementarities across the Taiwan Strait. Taiwan can provide advanced technology, managerial experience, entrepreneurial talent, financial capital, and extensive connections with international markets. The mainland can contribute vast pools of relatively inexpensive but diligent labor, low-cost land, raw materials, and even, to a degree, a comparative advantage in heavy industry and lower-end technology. Given its location and infrastructure, Hong Kong will continue to play a key intermediary role in this process. Similar complementarities link Taiwan to the developing economies of Southeast Asia, especially Malaysia, Thailand, Vietnam, and the Philippines.

These economic complementarities are reinforced by the cultural ties between Taiwan and other parts of the international Chinese community. Except for a small number of aborigines of Malay descent, all Taiwanese trace their roots to mainland China. Common culture, common language, and common family ties are facilitating Taiwan's economic relationships with mainland China, Southeast Asia, and, to a degree, with North America. They are also providing a powerful stimulus for various cultural exchanges, ranging from family reunions to intellectual dialogue.

Part of the common culture that Taiwan shares with the rest of the global Chinese community is a commitment to the reunification of China after periods of division. This serves as a third integrative factor working toward the creation of a Greater China. Both the communist government in Beijing and the nationalist government in Taipei are at least nominally committed to the eventual merger of Taiwan and the mainland into a single Chinese state. In the last several years, both sides have put forward more flexible formulas, in which reunification could occur in ways short of one party imposing full sovereignty over the other.

But this list of integrative factors constitutes only one side of the ledger. There also exist both barriers to the realization of a Greater China, and powerful disintegrative forces that challenge the entire concept. The principal obstacle, of course, is the gap in economic and political conditions across the Taiwan Strait. Political mistrust makes rapid reunification impossible, obstructs direct commercial ties, and even complicates cultural exchanges. The difference between the level of economic performance and the structure of economic institutions on the two sides also serves as a daunting independent barrier to the elimination of restrictions on trade, investment, and the flow of the factors of production, as implied by the concept of a Chinese economic community.

Even if these barriers could be reduced or removed, other powerful factors would discourage the creation of Greater China. Perhaps the strongest of these centrifugal forces are the ones pulling Taiwan away from the Chinese heartland. These include the demand for complete political autonomy, if not full independence. They also include the complementary quest for a distinctive cultural identity—a separate language, a unique culture, and a sense of history distinct from that of China proper.

There are also forces that pull Taiwan in other directions. Many on the island wish to preserve their commercial ties with the United States and Japan and to expand them with Europe and Russia, rather than becoming solely dependent on economic relationships with other Chinese societies. A smaller, but still significant, number will regard themselves as part of a cosmopolitan community of international elites, rather than simply as part of a separate Chinese cultural sphere. To be sure, economic and cultural relationships should not be defined in zero-sum terms, in which trade and investment with mainland China prevents commercial ties with the United States, or where cultural exchange with Hong Kong precludes that with Europe. To a degree, however, Taiwan's desire for diversity in its economic and cultural relationships will deter the creation of a formal Chinese economic community or even the development of Cultural China.

There is no one single forecast, then, for Taiwan's place in a Greater China. The prospects differ with the issue at stake. It is likely that the economic relations between Taiwan and the rest of the transnational Chinese economy, including Hong Kong and the Chinese entrepreneurs of Southeast Asia and North America, will continue to grow quantitatively and deepen qualitatively in the years to come. Many of the remaining political and administrative barriers to these relations should also fall. In particular, Taiwan will become an important part of a "Greater South China," whose boundaries will gradually extend to include more of mainland China as well as Hong Kong. But this transnational grouping will not become an exclusive economic bloc, uninterested in maintaining its ties with other economies. Instead, for both economic and political reasons, Taiwan will insist on preserving access to markets, technology, and capital in other parts of the world. Nor will Taipei be eager to see Greater South China transformed into a formal free trade area or economic community, as opposed to an informal network of commercial relationships.

The prospects for a single Cultural China are somewhat more problematic. The flow of people and messages across the Taiwan Strait will certainly continue and expand, as economic relations increase and as political obstacles recede. Taipei will become an important popular cultural center, both for Fujian and for the rest of the mainland. Elite exchanges with other Chinese cultural centers, including those on the mainland, will also continue, although they will be more susceptible to remaining political barriers than will the flow of popular culture. On balance, however, Taiwan is unlikely to identify itself solely with a Cultural China. The people of Taiwan will also increasingly establish their own identity as Taiwanese, and many of them will wish to create and maintain an additional identity as cosmopolitan citizens of the global community.

The probability of Taiwan's inclusion in a politically reunified China is lowest of all. Unlike Hong Kong, whose fate was determined by the expiration of the lease of the New Territories in 1997, there is no deadline forcing Taiwan to return to Chinese sovereignty. Under present circumstances, a very small percentage of Taiwan's population would choose to accept the mainland's formula of "one country, two systems," or indeed to reunify with the mainland under any terms. The prospects for an independent Taiwan are therefore as great, if not greater, as the chances for a truly reunified China. If political reunification ever occurs, it is likely to be nominal, involving a confederal system rather than an unitary one. Indeed, it is increasingly likely that the unity of China will be expressed in economic and cultural interaction, rather than in political integration.

Given the uncertain prospects for the emergence of Greater China, and for Taiwan's involvement in it, the implications for the United States and the rest of the world need to be drawn with considerable care. Like any new commercial relationship, the development of economic ties between Taiwan and other Chinese communities has the potential both to divert existing trade and investment flows and to create new ones. Thus far, the relocation of economic activity within Greater China has already had a significant impact on the United States. In response to rising costs at home, Taiwanese manufacturers have moved their factories from Taiwan to mainland China and parts of Southeast Asia. This means that goods that used to be exported to the United States from Taiwan are now being exported from mainland China, so that Taiwan's surplus with the United States declines, the PRC's rises, and the resulting political burden shifts from Taipei to Beijing.[47] The extent to which investment decisions made on Taiwan are contributing to the American trade deficit with mainland China is not yet adequately appreciated in the United States.

Over the longer term, the danger is that the development of some form of Chinese economic community would mean that mainland China would import its advanced technology from Taiwan, thus diverting exports from the United States. Although theoretically possible, this outcome remains highly implausible. Since the technological gap between Taiwan and the United States is not likely to narrow completely, the United States should always have a comparative advantage over Taiwan in exporting advanced equipment to mainland China. Moreover, as mainland China itself modernizes, its need for that advanced equipment will increase.

Indeed, the emergence of a dynamic Greater China is likely, on balance, to generate significant new opportunities for American trade and investment. The decline of barriers among the various Chinese economies will create a more unified market that is already attracting American investment. And, as this transnational Chinese economy grows, it will be able to absorb more imports from other countries and, increasingly, generate savings that can be invested elsewhere. Although a portion of the resulting trade and investment is certain to flow among the Chinese economies, it is unlikely that their integration will be so tight and exclusive that their growth will be at the expense of other economic systems. Rather, it will produce commercial opportunities for the rest of the world as well.

Taiwan's involvement in a global Cultural China will also have implications for the United States, albeit largely indirect. Taiwan is an active participant in a growing network of linkages among Chinese all over the world. As these contacts grow, it is likely that overseas Chinese in the United States, including those whose families have lived in America for several generations, will develop a more active interest in issues involving China, and become a more visible and powerful force in the formation of American policy toward China. Given the political divisions within the global Chinese community, however, Chinese-Americans will not speak with a single voice. Rather, some will support accommodative relations with the People's Republic, others will favor expanding political ties with Taiwan, and still others will be active proponents of Taiwanese independence.

Another aspect of the emergence of a global Cultural China is the transnational dialogue among Chinese intellectuals about what it means to be Chinese in the modern era. One important element in that conversation is a debate over the degree to which modern Chinese political systems can become fully democratic, or whether, as neo-Confucian societies, they should be expected to retain semi-authoritarian features for the sake of economic dynamism and social stability. The debate over this issue is pitting intellectuals in Singapore and mainland China, where the authoritarian tendencies are strongest, against intellectuals in Hong Kong, Taiwan, and the United States, who tend to favor democratization. The evolution of that discussion will be strongly influenced in large part on the future of the emerging democratic institutions on Taiwan, and the ability of Taiwanese intellectuals to make the case for democratization in other parts of Greater China. The outcome of the debate will determine the extent to which modern Confucian culture—one of the principal participants in what Samuel Huntington has called the coming "clash of civilizations"—will converge with, or diverge from, Western political values.[48]

Finally, the possibility of the reunification of China will also affect American interests. Of these, the most immediate involve the way in which the process takes place. Although most Americans would not oppose, in principle, the incorporation of Taiwan into a single Chinese state, they would strenuously object if it occurred through coercion. This is arguably the most basic and enduring American interest in Taiwan, and has been embodied in law through the Taiwan Relations Act.[49] Thus, the unprovoked use of force by the mainland against

Taiwan would almost certainly trigger a sharp American response, possibly including the deployment of U.S. military power to assist in the island's defense.

By whatever process it occurred, the full reunification of China would have fundamental implications for the rest of the Asia-Pacific region, and for the global balance of power as well. The economic, technological, and military resources presently controlled by Taiwan and Hong Kong would be added to those controlled by the People's Republic. It has already become commonplace to point out that, if put together, the foreign exchange reserves of Taiwan and the People's Republic would dwarf those of any other country, that the combined global trade of the three Chinese economies approaches that of Japan, and that the military apparatus of Taiwan would make a major addition to the armed forces of the mainland.[50]

And yet, political integration is unlikely to proceed far enough for these calculations to be relevant. Adding up the resources of the three Chinese societies makes sense analytically only if they are at the disposal of a single political will that can allocate the combined foreign exchange reserves, deploy the joint armed forces, or regulate the massive foreign trade volumes. A loose confederation, the only formula that is likely to bring Taiwan and the mainland together peacefully, will not create such a single political will. As a result, although both Taiwan and mainland China will be important players in regional and global affairs, they will continue to act independently, rather than in unison.

Commentary

David M. Lampton

One of Harding's core conclusions, to which I would tentatively subscribe, is that increasing cultural, economic, and political interaction between Taiwan and the People's Republic of China (PRC) does not necessarily lead to the emergence of an integrated ("Greater China") entity that will purposefully and coherently act as a unit in the international system or become a trading bloc.[51] Nor will the increasing interaction of the PRC and Taiwan necessarily culminate in their political reunification. Indeed, the future could quite conceivably witness increased degrees of economic, cultural, and political interaction among the PRC, Taiwan, and Hong Kong at the same time that Taiwan enjoys progressively greater degrees of political autonomy in the international system (a topic to which I shall return).

I would add to the analysis that produced these broad conclusions in two areas. First, a concept such as "Greater China" is developed to help us understand, or deal with, a particular aspect of current reality or evaluate future possibilities. Some observers have used the increase of economic, cultural, and other interaction in "Greater China" as a device to explain why their preferred outcome of a reunified China (or Chinese Commonwealth) is likely and why "Greater China," in their view, is destined to become a powerful, unitary global actor. Harding performs a service by arguing that unification is by no means the only conceivable (or even most likely) outcome and "Greater China" as a unitary, powerful global actor may not be the most likely result.

The concept of "Greater China," and Taiwan's role in it, however, also have an analytic utility that Harding does not address in any depth and that, from my perspective, is a major reason why the concept has attracted attention in the United States. The idea of "Greater China" has a utility found less in predicting the future than helping us deal with the present. The increased economic interaction among Taiwan, Hong Kong, and the PRC (and sometimes the Chinese diaspora more broadly) has implications for the public and private sector policies of the United States. For the U.S. government, the implication (or an implication) is that one cannot adopt policies (e.g., tariff policies, technology transfer policies, or sanctions) aimed at one portion of "Greater China" without considering the effects on the other parts—"Greater China" simply is the geographic expression of economic interdependence.

For the private sector, the concept helps identify appropriate business strategies—one can foster economic relations with one part of "Greater China" (e.g., Taiwan) in order to provide a springboard for economic penetration of other portions (e.g., the mainland). A good example would be the behavior of the American shoe industry and the thought that some high-tech firms (such as McDonnell Douglas Corporation) have given to integrated production and marketing processes that span Taiwan, Hong Kong, and China's mainland.

The second point I would make is that the Taiwanese government, by 1992, was using the "Greater China" concept (though it dislikes the term) in a much more purposeful (and strategic) manner than some of Harding's analysis suggests to me. I believe that the Taiwanese government is using the increased cultural, economic, and political interaction in "Greater China" (particularly between Taiwan and the mainland) to create a web of positive incentives for, and constraints on, Beijing that will induce the PRC to accept Taiwan's drive for more international breathing space, identity, dignity, and autonomy.

Lee Teng-hui has offset every recent move toward facilitating economic, cultural, and political contact with the mainland by an equal and opposite move that is designed to give Taiwan more "space" to operate in the international system. A good example would be the coupling of the announcements of the April 1993 Singapore talks between the Association for Relations Across the Straits (ARATS) and the Straits Exchange Foundation (SEF) with the statement that Taipei would increase its efforts to join a broad range of international organizations, including the United Nations. This obviously is a sophisticated strategy in which one reassures Beijing of presumed long-term intentions to reunify at the same time one reassures the Taiwan populace that this is not going to happen in any foreseeable future. At a minimum, it buys time for generational succession in both societies to occur.

In short, while I agree that initially Taiwan was in a reactive mode to the PRC in the late-1970s and throughout the 1980s, I think that the Taiwanese government has a much more purposeful and activist concept now, that it is taking the initiative, that its purpose is to gain more international autonomy, and that, in considerable measure, it is Beijing that seems to be at a bit of a loss as how to proceed. While the Democratic Progressive Party (DPP) is not at all sure that the Kuomintang (KMT)-run government has such an objective, my sense is that there is rather widespread agreement within the KMT that this is the basic strategy to pursue, even as there are intra-party disputes over how best to implement it.

Implications

One of the strong implications of Harding's analysis is, *first*, that the combined factors of rising Taiwanese cultural self-identity, political pluralism on the island (giving increased voice to calls for independence), and still diverging per capita income levels between Taiwan and the mainland could quite conceivably produce increasing calls (on Taiwan) for some kind of formalized political separation between Taiwan and the mainland—albeit perhaps with some face-saving fig-leaf of a "unified

China" at an abstract level. "One country, two governments" is one expression of this impulse.

Some of the possible contingencies raise challenges for American policy. Most basically, the United States has not come to terms with a latent problem in the formula for normalization of relations with the PRC worked out in the 1970s because "Chinese on both sides of the Taiwan Strait" have thus far formally adhered to a "one China" concept. American policy has been "peaceful resolution" while "acknowledging" their "one China" concept. If this suddenly were to change by Taiwan unilaterally jettisoning the "one China" formula, Americans immediately would face the contradiction between the "gravitational pull" for them of the principle of "self-determination" and the dangers of the endless subdivision of national communities, with the painful vision of the Balkans staring us in the face. We immediately would be caught in the seeming contradiction of our past acknowledgement of one China, Americans' partiality toward self-determination, the not fully defined obligations that exist under the 1979 Taiwan Relations Act, and our complex economic and security interests.

This raises the core policy issue that I pose, but to which I have no answer. Should the United States send any further messages to the various parties on Taiwan (and the PRC) as to how Washington will react under various contingencies? Would such messages be credible, given the contingent nature of our political system? Or, does the absence of a clear policy offer the best guarantee that both Taiwan and Beijing will be prudent? Is uncertainty about a possible American reaction a sobering deterrent to both sides and, therefore, is it best to maintain as much ambiguity as possible? Or, does ambiguity feed illusion, particularly on Taiwan, where various new political groupings might attach undue weight to some of the rhetoric they hear in Washington from time to time?

Second, does the succession process on the mainland and on Taiwan offer hope of avoiding that kind of conundrum? The question is simply this. What do we know about the salience that the emerging leaders in Beijing, and younger Chinese on the mainland more generally, attach to Taiwan, particularly unification with the island? My sense, based on only the sketchiest anecdotal data, is that younger Chinese on the mainland, by and large, attach less importance to Taiwan's international status than their elders seemingly have and that, therefore, they may prove more flexible in the future.

As for the generational succession on Taiwan, I get the sense that younger leaders both within the KMT and outside the party see their political, economic, and social futures on Taiwan, a Taiwan that need not maintain a fiction of "one China" indefinitely. I get a sense of a generation of emerging leaders in Taiwan that is waiting for its elders to pass from the scene, waiting for the older generation on the mainland to depart, and that this is a generation that believes that the world is evolving in a direction that will be more supportive of aspirations for self-determination.

My preliminary hypothesis is, therefore, that succession in the PRC may produce more flexibility on the mainland, but that the emerging leadership on Taiwan is likely to test with increasing vigor the limits of the mainland's flexibility. If Harding's analysis could deal with how succession processes on both the mainland and Taiwan might influence the evolving mainland-Taiwan relationship, that obviously would be a major contribution.

Third, what are likely to be the dimensions of the "Greater China" in which Taiwan is a major player—is it likely only to be South China? In cultural terms, because of the family, dialect, and cultural ties that literally straddle the Taiwan Strait, the "cultural Greater China" involving Taiwan is likely to remain most evident in South China. Moreover, it is true that economic ties will enjoy an advantage in areas where these cultural links are strongest. Having said this, however, I believe that Taiwanese investment is spreading across the face of the PRC very rapidly, more rapidly than I sense from Harding's analysis, though he notes that such spread is occurring.

There is anecdotal evidence that Taiwanese investment is moving quite rapidly into the Shanghai area and there is somewhat more fragmentary evidence that Taiwanese investors are expanding with rapidity into China's heartland in search of lower wage rates. For instance, manual labor costs along China's coast can be up to ten times as high as in the heartland. The same economic dynamic that attracted Taiwanese industry from the island to the mainland will now attract Taiwanese-invested labor-intensive industries from China's coast to the PRC's vast, labor-surplus interior. It is very important that we obtain data about the quantity and distribution of Taiwanese investment in the PRC and its rate of growth in the interior.

Fourth, Harding makes two interrelated points about Taiwan's (and the PRC's) desire to diversify trade partners (to include North America, Japan, Southeast Asia, and Europe) and not simply tie itself exclusively to a Chinese economic bloc. I agree with this, though it is important to note that Taiwanese (and, for that matter, mainland) officials seem to have a greater fear of economic dependence on Japan than they do of the economic embrace of each other.

Further, with respect to Taiwan's desire not to become dependent on any closed Asian or Chinese trading bloc, I would simply add that developments in the global system could conceivably drive them in this direction, whether this is their preferred course or not. To a considerable extent, developments in this regard will depend on the degree to which the rest of the global trading system remains open or develops into regional trading blocs. The current problems of the GATT discussions are worrisome and Chinese in Hong Kong, Taiwan, and the mainland are concerned about what the North American Free Trade Agreement might portend as well. But, all things considered, both the PRC and Taiwan have an enormous interest in diversifying their trading relationships and not signing onto the notion of a Chinese economic trading bloc, unless events force them to do so.

Notes

I wish to acknowledge, with gratitude, the invaluable research assistance provided me by Scott Kennedy of The Brookings Institution.

1. Joel Kotkin, *Tribes: How Race, Religion, and Ethnicity Determine Success in the New Global Economy*, (New York, NY: Random House, 1992).

2. One of the exceptions to this generalization was the community of Rennie's Mill, whose citizens enthusiastically flew the flag of the Republic of China from their homes. Otherwise, Taiwan and the Kuomintang had virtually no visible presence in Hong Kong.

3. The term "Cultural China" is drawn from Tu Wei-ming, "Cultural China: The Periphery as Center," *Daedalus*, vol. 120, no. 2, 1991, pp. 1-32.

4. The data on Taiwanese travel to the mainland are drawn from Chong-pin Lin, "Beijing and Taipei: Interactions in the Post-Tiananmen Period," in *China Quarterly*, forthcoming; and *Renmin ribao* (overseas edition), January 29, 1993, p. 5. The figures on mainland travel to Taiwan are from *Jiushi niandai* (Hong Kong), February 1993, p. 20. The data on mail and telephone calls are from *Renmin ribao* (overseas edition), February 16, 1993, p. 5.

5. *Statistical Abstract of Transportation and Communications,* (Taipei: Ministry of Transportation and Communication, Republic of China, various years). The figures for ASEAN do not include Brunei.

6. *Monthly Statistics of the Republic of China,* (Taipei: Directorate-General of Budget, Accounting, and Statistics, Executive Yuan, Republic of China, various issues). For example, of the nearly 63,000 Singaporeans visiting Taiwan in 1991, less than one thousand, or only 1.6 percent, were reported as "overseas Chinese," when 75 percent of Singapore's total population is of Chinese descent.

7. See Laurence Zuckerman, "Return of the Natives," *Asian Wall Street Journal,* May 24, 1993, p. 9.

8. Shen Qingsong, "Tongqing de liaojie, duibi de zijue" (Sympathetic understanding, different consciousness), *Ershiyi shiji* (Hong Kong), no. 4, April 1991, pp. 9-11. As one young Taiwanese civil servant has been quoted as saying, "Sure, I'm interested in the mainland. But I don't belong to it and it doesn't belong to me." *The Guardian,* June 22, 1992.

9. "Taiwan diqu shehui bianqian jiben diaocha jihua dierqi disanci diaocha jihua zhixing baogao" (Report on the third survey in the second period of the basic program for polling on social change in the Taiwan region), (Taipei: Institute of Ethnology, Academia Sinica, December 1992). I thank Michael Hsiao of the Institute of Ethnology for sharing these data with me.

10. The other provinces were Guangdong, Beijing, Shanghai, and Tianjin.

11. The following paragraph is based upon Lai To Lee, *The Reunification of China: PRC-Taiwan Relations in Flux,* (New York, NY: Praeger, 1991), pp. 118-31; and *Business Asia,* February 3, 1992.

12. There has been some speculation that, of the cumulative total of $1.2 billion that Hong Kong has invested in Taiwan, a small fraction represents hidden investment by mainland Chinese firms.

13. The official figure is from Central News Agency, March 22, 1993, in *Foreign Broadcast Information Service Daily Report: China,* March 22, 1993, p. 78.

14. *Free China Journal,* January 19, 1993, p. 3.

15. The term is most closely associated with Robert Scalapino. See his *The Last Leninists: The Uncertain Future of Asia's Communist States,* (Washington, DC: Center for Strategic and International Studies, 1992), p. 20.

16. It is commonly presumed that a common culture has facilitated the development of economic relations between Taiwan and mainland China, as well as between the PRC and Hong Kong. Such an argument is implicit, for example, in the title of an important short study by Yun-Wing Sung: "Non-Institutional Economic Integration Via Cultural Affinity: The Case of Mainland China, Taiwan and Hong Kong," Occasional Paper, no. 13, (Shatin: Hong Kong Institute of Asia-Pacific Studies, Chinese University of Hong Kong, 1992). Some express more skeptical views, however. George Liu, general manager of a venture capital firm, Taiwanvest, argues that, "for Taiwan companies, going to [mainland] China is not going home; it's a different country, very much a cross-border venture. Only the language and the skin color are the same. It's a totally different system." *Business Taiwan,* February 28, 1993.

17. On the general concept, see *Business Taiwan,* March 8, 1993. Microsoft has already established its regional headquarters in Taiwan rather than in Hong Kong; one factor in its decision was the fact that annual sales of personal computers in Taiwan are almost five times higher than in Hong Kong. *Business International,* February 22, 1993.

18. These figures represent the sum of Hong Kong's domestic exports to Taiwan, plus Hong Kong's imports from Taiwan, minus Hong Kong's re-exports that originated in Taiwan. They are derived from various Hong Kong Government sources, especially the *Hong Kong Annual Digest of Statistics,* (Hong Kong: Census

and Statistics Department, Hong Kong government, various years), and monthly reports from the Census and Statistics Department.

19. *Statistics on Overseas Chinese and Foreign Investment, Technical Cooperation, Outward Investment, [and] Outward Technical Cooperation,* (Taipei: Investment Commission, Ministry of Economic Affairs, Republic of China, December 1992). These statistics, the best available, measure only investments approved by the Taiwan government, not commitments or actual flows.

20. Hong Kong's cumulative investment in Taiwan has been obtained by totaling the investment approvals contained in *Statistics on Overseas Chinese and Foreign Investment.* The estimate of Taiwan's cumulative investment in Hong Kong is from *Business Asia,* February 3, 1992.

21. *1993 Foreign Trade Development of the Republic of China,* (Taipei: Bureau of Foreign Trade, Ministry of Economic Affairs, Republic of China, 1993).

22. Taiwanese entrepreneurs have also been investing in Vietnam, but their activities are not yet included in Taiwan's official statistics.

23. *Statistics on Overseas Chinese and Foreign Investment.* As with Taiwan's investment in mainland China, much higher estimates of Taiwanese investments in Southeast Asia can be found in unofficial sources. See, for example, "Taipei's Offshore Empire," *Far Eastern Economic Review,* March 18, 1993, pp. 44-45. For an explanation as to why the official statistics undercount actual outbound investment, see Zao Xiaoheng, "Taiwan duiwai zhijie tats de gawking j Teuton" (The situation and special characteristics of Taiwan's foreign direct investment), *Taiwan yanjiu* (Beijing), no. 1, March 20, 1993, pp. 62-67.

24. These are very crude estimates, derived simply by adding the official annual investment approvals.

25. See Linda Y. C. Lim, "The New Ascendence of Chinese Business in Southeast Asia: Political, Cultural, Economic and Business Implications" (Ann Arbor, MI: University of Michigan, March 1991). The ratios apply only to private business activity, and exclude the state sector and foreign enterprises.

26. According to Linda Lim of the University of Michigan, ethnic Chinese account for 40 percent of private business activity in the Philippines, 50 percent in Singapore, 65 percent in Malaysia, and 80 percent in both Thailand and the Indonesia. Lim, "The New Ascendence of Chinese."

27. See *Statistics on Overseas Chinese and Foreign Investment.* Again, these figures represent only investments reported to, and approved by, the Taiwan government, rather than investments actually made. And the level of Taiwan's investment with overseas Chinese partners in ASEAN is based on assumptions concerning the role of ethnic Chinese in Southeast Asian economies that may not be accurate. Nonetheless, the data do strongly suggest the basic conclusion drawn here: that Taiwan's investment relations with Greater China are substantial, and Greater China is a more important investment partner for Taiwan than it is a trading partner.

28. *Statistics on Overseas Chinese and Foreign Investment.* However, the proportion of inbound investment coming from overseas Chinese is much lower now than it was in the past. In the years 1952 to 1961, for example, fully 38 percent of Taiwan's incoming investment was from overseas Chinese. See Zhuang Guotu, "Luelun Taiwan dangju yinjin qiaozi de cuoshi he chengxiao" (A brief discussion of the measures taken by the Taiwan authorities to attract overseas Chinese capital and

their results), *Taiwan yanjiu* (Beijing), no. 1, March 20, 1993, pp. 48-54 and 35.

29. For a representative selection of Taiwanese writings on a Chinese Economic Community, see Gao Xijun [Charng Kao], "Zhongguoren ruhe miandui jingji bilei? Jianli `yazhou huaren gongtong shichang' de tantao" (How should Chinese confront economic blocs? Probing the construction of an "Asian Chinese Common Market"), *Yuanjian* (Taipei), October 15, 1988, pp. 101-105; Xu Donghai, "`Da zhongguo jingji gongtongti' shexiang yu pinggu" (A critique of the idea of a "Greater China Economic Commonwealth"), *Gongdang wenti yanjiu* (Taipei), vol. 16, no. 1, January 1990, pp. 73-78; Fu Dongchang, "Xianggang, taiwan, dalu jingji tonghe de qianjing" (The prospects for economic unification between Hong Kong, Taiwan, and the Mainland), *Shibao zhoukan* (Taipei), January 5-11, 1992, pp. 15-22; An-chia Wu, "The Political Implications of the `Coordination of Chinese Economic Systems,'" *Issues and Studies*, vol. 28, no. 4, April 1992, pp. 1-9; Charng Kao, "A `Greater China Economic Sphere': Reality and Prospects," *Issues and Studies*, vol. 28, no. 11, November 1992, pp. 49-64; and Ricky Tung, "Economic Interaction Between Taiwan and South China's Fukien and Kwangtung Provinces," *Issues and Studies*, vol. 29, no. 7, July 1993, pp. 26-42.

30. For a review of the different formulas for a transnational Chinese economy, see Harry Harding, "Greater China: Themes, Variations, and Reservations," in *China Quarterly*, forthcoming.

31. One of the most authoritative endorsements of the concept came from Taiwan's minister of economic affairs, Vincent Siew, who said in November 1991 that the creation of a "Greater China Common Market" was a "long-term goal worthy of efforts by the Chinese on both sides of the Taiwan Straits and in Hong Kong." Central News Agency, November 4, 1991.

32. For example, nearly half of those surveyed in 1990 felt that permitting mainlanders to live or work on Taiwan would jeopardize the island's security. In contrast, only about 22 percent believed it would be dangerous to permit Taiwanese to live or work on the mainland. See "Taiwan diqu shehui yixiang diaocha diyici ji dierci budingqi diaocha zhixing baogao" (Report of the first and second occasional polls on social trends in the Taiwan region), (Taipei: Zhongshan Humanities and Social Sciences Institute, Academia Sinica, December 1990). Once again, I am grateful to Michael Hsiao for making these data available.

33. Yun-Wing Sung argues that such steps are impossible in the case of Hong Kong and mainland China. Since Hong Kong is a free port, the elimination of all barriers to trade between Hong Kong and the mainland would imply that all the mainland become a free port as well. Sung, "Non-Institutional Economic Integration," p. 38.

34. InterPress Service, January 30, 1992.

35. Edgar Snow, *Red Star Over China,* (New York, NY: Grove Press, 1961), p. 96.

36. The maps divided Siberia and Central Asia into new Chinese provinces, with such poetic names as Perpetual Peace (*yong'an*) and Eternal Tranquility (*yongning*). I am grateful to Stephen Uhalley, Jr., for bringing these maps to my attention. See his "`Greater China': What's In a Name?," paper presented to the Regional Seminar on "Greater China" sponsored by the Center for Chinese Studies of the University of California, Berkeley, California, February 26-27, 1993.

37. The most authoritative statement of mainland policy is contained in "The Taiwan Question and the Reunification of China," a white paper issued by the Taiwan Affairs Office and the Information Office of the State Council, relayed by Xinhua News Agency, August 31, 1993, in *Foreign Broadcast Information Service Daily Report: China*, September 1, 1993, pp. 43-51.

38. Lee, *Reunification of China*, p. 38.

39. In 1982, in a slightly less rigid version of this formula, Premier Sun Yun-suan noted that there could be an improvement of Taiwan-mainland relations, including even the initiation of dialogue between the two sides, if the economic and political system of the People's Republic began to converge with that of Taiwan.

40. Lee, *Reunification of China*, p. 47.

41. For the text of the guidelines, see *Free China Journal*, March 11, 1991, p. 1.

42. *China Times* poll of September 1, 1993, as reported in *Free China Journal*, September 3, 1993, p. 1.

43. See, for example, *Free China Journal*, September 3, 1993, citing *China Times* polls of April 28 and September 1. A few polls have attained different results, however. One, released in May 1993, showed that the percentage of people supporting a formal declaration of independence had risen in just seven months from the usual level of about 15 percent to nearly one-quarter of the population. See *Japan Economic Newswire*, May 10, 1993. One other poll, taken in late 1992, obtained a similar result, but only by positing that peaceful relations with the mainland could be guaranteed in the course of independence. "Taiwan diqu shehui bianqian jiben diaocha jihua dierqi disanci diaocha jihua zhixing baogao" (Report of the third survey in the second period of the basic program for polling on social change in the Taiwan region), (Taipei: Institute of Ethnology, Academia Sinica, December 1992). These polling data from the Academia Sinica were also provided by Michael Hsiao.

44. *China Times* polls of April 28 and September 1, 1993, as reported in *Free China Journal*, September 3, 1993, p. 1.

45. "Taiwan diqu shehui yixiang diaocha [minguo] 80-nian 8-yue dingqi diaocha baogao" (Report of the regular August 1991 poll on social trends in the Taiwan region), (Taipei: Zhongshan Social Sciences and Humanities Institute, June 1992); and *China Times* polls of April 28 and September 1, 1993, as reported in *Free China Journal*, September 3, 1993, p. 1.

46. Japan Economic Newswire, May 10, 1993.

47. I first made this point in "The US and Greater China," *China Business Review*, vol. 19, no. 3, May-June 1992, pp. 18-22.

48. Samuel P. Huntington, "The Clash of Civilizations?" *Foreign Affairs*, vol. 72, no. 3, Summer 1993, pp. 22-49.

49. See Harry Harding, "The Legacy of the Decade for Later Years: An American Perspective," in Harry Harding and Yuan Ming, eds., *Sino-American Relations, 1945-1955: A Joint Reassessment of a Critical Decade*, (Wilmington, DE: Scholarly Resources, 1989), esp. pp. 325-26.

50. For one of the best examples in the economic sphere, see the discussion of the "Chinese Economic Area" in *Global Economic Prospects and the Developing Countries, 1993*, (Washington, DC: World Bank, 1993), pp. 66-67.

51. The views expressed in this commentary are the author's own and are not to be construed as those of the National Committee on United States-China Relations, its members, or its contributors.

9

Taiwan's International Role: Implications for U.S. Policy

Richard Bush

Introduction

Half a century after the Cairo Conference, the relationship between the People's Republic of China (PRC) and Taiwan remains the most obvious case of post-World War II unfinished business. The division of Vietnam was ended when the North Vietnamese army overran the South in 1975 and Hanoi arbitrarily incorporated the Saigon regime into the Socialist Republic of Vietnam one year later. Germany moved toward unity in the early 1970s with the general recognition of two states within one German nation. The collapse of the German Democratic Republic two decades later paved the way for the peaceful recreation of a united Germany on terms set by the Bonn government and the West. On the Korean peninsula, the existence of two states has been accepted. Whether, when, and how the two may combine into one is unclear, yet time does not seem to be on the side of the isolated and renegade North. In Taiwan's case, however, neither does the island have the generally recognized status of a sovereign state, nor is the nature of its ultimate relationship with the PRC at all defined. This case of unresolved sovereignty—the one that was first de-linked from the U.S.-Soviet conflict as a result of Richard Nixon's 1971-1972 opening to China—is ironically the most up for grabs.

Because of the U.S. involvement in the Chinese civil war and its dominant position in Asia, every shift in the relationship of the PRC-Taiwan nexus with the international community has had implications for U.S. policy toward Taiwan. That was true when the

PRC was founded, when both the Korean and Vietnam Wars began, when the Sino-Soviet dispute became extremely dangerous in the late 1960s, when the PRC moved toward strategic alignment with the West in the late 1970s, and now with the collapse of the Soviet Union.

From Taiwan's perspective, the most fundamental change in its place in the international system came with the announcement of the normalization of U.S.-PRC relations in 1978. That the island has maintained and enhanced its *de facto* independence since then is all the more impressive in view of the power asymmetries between it and the mainland, the Kuomintang's (KMT's) past fixation (both internally and externally) on the myth that it was the government of all of China, and the jeopardy that Washington placed it in after 1971 when President Richard Nixon announced the U.S. opening to Beijing. For its own survival, Taiwan has sought to carve out a unique place in the international system. U.S. policy has tended to muddle quietly through the problems that Taiwan's new role has created, believing that the less said the better. Yet silence may be a luxury that Washington can no longer afford.

This chapter attempts to sort through the implications of Taiwan's emergent, post-Cold War place in the international order for U.S. foreign policy. It begins with a recapitulation of Taiwan's present role in the international system and a summary of U.S. policy over the last decade, and then addresses the topic at hand.

Recapitulating the Interpretive Framework

Figure 9.1 recapitulates, with some elaboration, the interpretive framework of this volume. The basic argument is that domestic forces have prompted an evolution of Taiwan's role in the international system along four dimensions: security, political, socioeconomic, and cultural. The expansion of Taiwan's role, in turn, has consequences for the integration of the Chinese cultural world, for the specific relationship between Taiwan and the mainland, and for U.S. policy.

Implicit in this schema are several elaborations on the discussion so far. First of all, Taiwan's participation in the global arms market, as described in the chapter by Harlan Jencks, is only one element of its larger role in the larger *international security system*. This was probably the arena in which the PRC's emergence in the 1970s most degraded Taiwan's importance. Formerly part of the array of alliances created to deter Chinese expansionism, Taiwan became irrelevant to the U.S.-PRC-

Figure 9.1   Taiwan's International Role: Sources and Consequences

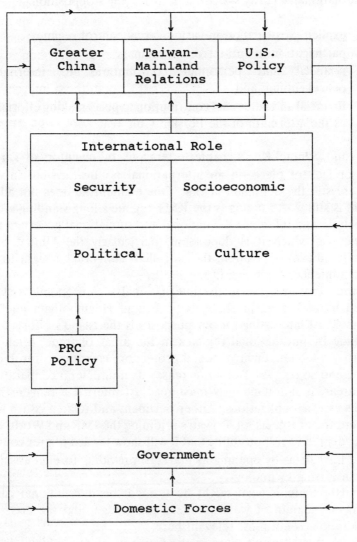

→   causation

Japan-ASEAN alignment against the Soviet Union. It was not until there emerged a buyer's market for arms that Taiwan was freed from some past constraints.

It is also worth noting the ways in which Taiwan might participate in the international security system, absent Beijing's opposition:

- explicit participation in various arms control regimes;
- participation in anti-terrorism regimes;
- financial and personnel contributions to international peacekeeping; and
- financial and personnel contribution to peacemaking efforts, such as the aftermath of the Persian Gulf War.

Second, Samuel Kim's chapter offers a useful inventory of Taiwan's place—or lack of place—in an international political system in which states are still the dominant actors. One element he does not address but that is still worth noting is the KMT regime's long-standing attempt to penetrate and influence the national and subnational governments of countries on which it is dependent, particularly the United States. Taiwan's political opposition, the so-called "*dang-wai,*" sought to have similar influence, beginning in the 1980s.

Third, Taiwan's role in the international socioeconomic system is covered by and large in chapters by Erland Heginbotham and June Dreyer. Most interesting for our purposes is the island's efforts to join and abide by international regimes in the areas of trade, intellectual property protection, environmental protection, narcotics control, crime control, and so on. As Taiwan increases its multilateral cooperation in these areas, it simultaneously must readjust internal arrangements to meet its external obligations. Other pertinent and related issues in this arena are the prospects for Taiwan's rejoining the IMF and World Bank, and the degree of responsibility that it will show toward poorer countries beyond East Asia—by opening its markets, providing foreign assistance, and transferring technology.

Fourth, there is what might be termed the international cultural system, the domain of values, beliefs, knowledge, and the arts. Two considerations seem most relevant here.

The first is Taiwan's place in the Chinese cultural milieu. In what way is Taiwan the carrier of the core values of Chinese civilization, as KMT ideological guardians have claimed? Is it merely a provincial variant of modern Chinese culture as defined by mandarins on the mainland? Or is its deviation from the Sinic norm great enough to merit recognition as a national ethos all its own, as Taiwanese nationalists assert? To the extent that the island mixes the great Confucian tradition, local folkways, and Western modernism, is the whole both relatively coherent and greater than the sum of the parts? This chapter does not go beyond Harry Harding's discussion of these profound questions, except to note that because the essence of Chineseness today is so muddled, no answer may be possible.

The second issue is Taiwan's place in the world-historical struggle between the fundamental political value-sets of collectivism on the one hand and individualism on the other. The first three decades of Kuomintang rule suggested a bias in favor of collectivism that was anti-communist in ideology, but a mix of Leninism and fascism in organization. The last decade has seen a striking trend in the direction of liberal order that has allowed the island to catch the wave of democratization that began in Latin America, spread to East Asia, and moved later to Eastern Europe and the Soviet Union. Taiwan's remarkable movement along the political-cultural spectrum has made it a model of sorts for a number of authoritarian countries. Its demonstration effect has a particularly strong impact on the Chinese cultural world, so far belying the cynical view that Sinic peoples are culture-bound to authoritarian regimes,

Fifth, as the discussion in other chapters makes clear, other factors are at play in the causal chain as follows:

- The relationship between political, economic, social, and cultural forces within Taiwan, on the one hand, and the island's international role, on the other, is mediated to a greater or lesser extent by the choices made by the government on Taiwan. Indeed, one of the most significant developments of the past decade has been the degree to which the government has permitted such mediation to take place. Although societal forces have a direct and growing impact on the larger system, the government—and who controls the government—remains extremely important;

- The policies and actions of the PRC affect all other elements of the equation: public opinion on Taiwan; government choices on Taiwan; the scope of Taiwan's international role; cross-Strait relations; the degree of integration of Greater China; and U.S.

policy. For example, changes in the PRC's military force structure may have an impact on Taiwan's perception of its security, on its arms acquisition, on the U.S. response, and so on;

- U.S. policy may effect every link in the causal chain; and
- The evolution of Taiwan's international role and its relationship with the mainland play back into Taiwan, affecting political, economic, and social forces on the island.

Taipei's Changing External Strategy

Taiwan's changing strategy may be clarified in terms of the analytical framework elaborated above. Built into the discussion is the use of the concept of "role" in its sociological sense, that is, a set of norms that govern the action of the occupant of the role.[1]

In the wake of its 1949 military defeat, the KMT regime conducted a diplomatic battle with its communist rival over who was the rightful "China" incumbent of a variety of international roles. At least in form, Taipei accepted the customary norms of existing international systems. It continued to propagate the appropriate myths that it was the legitimate government of all of China (even as it suppressed claims from within its subject population that the Republic of China (ROC) was not the rightful sovereign of the only territory it controlled). That effort was successful until the PRC was seen as a critical element in the international balance of power and, with its own myth-making, was able to secure broad agreement that it was the rightful government of China and as such was entitled to represent China in international organizations, to the exclusion of the ROC.

Taipei certainly has not abandoned the contest with Beijing, but since the mid-1980s it has sought to improve the terms on which it competes. It has sought to identify and occupy all available niches in the international system that the PRC will allow, and will change internal arrangements to make them consistent with rules of the global regime in question. The rigid commitment of the past to the "Republic of China" name has been abandoned and terminological flexibility is seen as an acceptable price of entry. While not formally abandoning the claim that it is the government of China, the KMT government's medium-term goal is to be recognized as a separate state (or nation/country, two governments). In instances like GATT, it has taken advantage of the opportunity of non-state entries for substantive participation on a par with states.

Taiwan has thus sought to expand its international role by accepting what might be called second-order norms—that is, the norms of international institutions. Its strategy of institutional insinuation and adjustment of the internal rules of the game has been most successful in the soft-power arenas of economics and culture. The PRC has responded by asserting the first-order norm that states are the only qualified members of the international community; Taiwan may not participate by definition since it is not a state. Beijing undoubtedly fears that Taiwan will acquire statehood incrementally, and its resistance has been most effective in the formal political arena. It is ironic indeed that the more conservative KMT regime should now be taking the more radical stance; that the CCP regime, which was originally intent on the transformation of the international system, should now use traditional norms to defend its position; and that the forces for Taiwan's independence, who are usually seen as radical, are actually making claims within that same traditional frame of reference.

U.S. Taiwan Policy in the 1980s

In assessing the implications of Taiwan's changing international role for U.S. policy, it is first necessary to specify what that policy has been. Policy can be a set of outcomes that a government defines and seeks to achieve with rhetoric, resources, and the application of leverage. It is often, on the other hand, a set of outcomes that a government hopes will occur but that, because of the circumstances, it chooses not to declare; for which it does not overtly commit resources; and concerning which it applies leverage only for the purposes of removing obstacles.

This latter, more Daoist approach to policy characterizes the approach that the United States has taken towards Taiwan since the announcement of the normalization of U.S.-PRC relations in 1978. Caught between the PRC belief that Washington should not have a policy toward a part of China of which it was the sole legal government, and the suspicions of conservatives in Congress that the KMT might be sold out once again, executive branch policymakers engaged in "stealth" diplomacy.

It is still possible to detect the signature of U.S. policy by looking carefully at Washington's various words and deeds concerning Taiwan over the past decade. Policy, moreover, is not just what the executive branch does and says; it should include actions that Congress takes on its own initiative.

Policy Declarations

Successive administrations have said relatively little publicly about Taiwan and its relationship to the PRC, yet the words enunciated are significant. First of all, in late 1978 the U.S. executive branch, at the same time that it recognized the PRC as the sole legal government of China, only acknowledged "the Chinese position" that Taiwan is a part of China.[2]

Second, at the time of normalization and on numerous occasions since, successive administrations have stated the expectation that the future of Taiwan will be resolved peacefully by the parties concerned.

Third, in the spring of 1979, the U.S. Congress passed and President Carter signed the Taiwan Relations Act, which among other things included:

- a commitment to provide arms to Taiwan to ensure that it had a sufficient self-defense capability; and
- a policy statement that hostile action by the PRC against Taiwan would be regarded as a matter of grave concern to the United States, in response to which the president and Congress would consult and take appropriate action.

Fourth, in August 1982 the Reagan administration identified several outcomes that it would not promote: two Chinas; one China, one Taiwan; or an independent Taiwan. (There is, however, a difference between promoting an outcome that would not otherwise occur and accepting an outcome that emerged from the dynamics of the situation.)

Fifth, also in the summer of 1982, the Reagan administration reportedly informed the Taipei government of the "six nos"—six steps it had not or would not take:

- setting a date for ending arms sales;
- holding prior consultations with Beijing on arms sales to Taiwan;
- playing any mediation role between Taipei and Beijing;
- revising the Taiwan Relations Act;
- altering its position regarding the sovereignty over Taiwan; and

- exerting pressure on Taiwan to enter into negotiations with the PRC.

Policy Actions

Among the many steps that Washington has taken in the last fourteen years, seven seem to be the most significant.

First of all, in 1979 the United States, with the cooperation of the government on Taiwan, created a web of institutional channels that were unofficial in their form but effective in their substance.

Second, as a result of a 1981 congressional initiative, Taiwan-born people were given a 20,000 annual quota of immigration visas separate from that of the PRC. As a result, the kinship ties that link many communities in the United States with cities, towns, and villages all over Taiwan continued to grow in number and density, and the Taiwanese-American community's impact on American politics expanded.

Third, where possible, the United States has sought to work behind the scenes to help preserve Taiwan's presence in international organizations, most notably the Asian Development Bank. Having staunched the erosion of Taiwan's formal international presence, the island's political leaders now seek to expand that presence.

Fourth, the United States has put pressure on Taiwan to open its markets to American products and services, and to facilitate an appreciation in the value of the New Taiwan dollar. As a result, the structural transformation of the island's domestic economy was accelerated and its integration with the international economy—especially with the mainland and Southeast Asia—has increased, as Erland Heginbotham's chapter elaborates.

Fifth, the United States has assisted Taiwan's armed forces in maintaining an adequate deterrent against military action by the PRC. True, the Reagan administration reduced American flexibility in U.S.-Taiwan security cooperation by virtue of the limitations to which it agreed in the August 1982 Communiqué. Soon thereafter, however, it began a program of transferring defense technology to Taiwan so that the island's weapons capabilities could be modernized indigenously. This effort has been very expensive, but it has been successful in many areas. The confidence of leaders of the armed forces in their ability to make the mainland pay a high price for any attempted aggression deepened. (The U.S. contribution to Taiwan's defense was racheted up with the decision to sell F-16s in September 1992.)

Sixth, the United States has kept its word on the "six nos." On a number of occasions, high-level PRC officials have asked their American counterparts to facilitate the reunification of Taiwan and the mainland. Beyond favoring the creation of a peaceful environment across the Strait, the consistent American reply has been negative. In the U.S. view, the key obstacle to any reassociation is the mistrust that Taiwan feels toward Beijing, an obstacle that only Beijing can remove. The firm U.S. stance, which the United States took vis-à-vis Beijing—that Washington would not be the mid-wife of reunification—may have contributed to the reduction of tensions that occurred between the mainland and Taiwan after 1987.

Seventh, the U.S. Congress focused attention on the political and human rights situation on Taiwan. This was done through hearings, efforts to enact non-binding resolutions calling for positive change, private appeals to KMT leaders, and so on. These actions were reinforced by the executive branch's private diplomacy. In addition, the Congress took action in 1981 to deter the KMT regime's long-standing practice of enforcing its political orthodoxy in the United States. (It should be noted that members of Congress have generally shied away from the issue of Taiwan's legal status.)

U.S. support for democratization and human rights was, to be sure, not the determining factor in the liberalizing process that began in the fall of 1986. More important were the actions of progressive individuals inside the Kuomintang and the challenge to authoritarian rule by the *dang wai*. Yet because KMT leaders took seriously both the domestic ideals of their party and their international reputation, external pressure was hardly trivial.

This policy approach was solidified during the first Reagan administration in the wake of the uncertainty created by the August 1982 Communiqué. It was facilitated by Chiang Ching-kuo's determination to undertake political liberalization, by the decline of the Soviet Union, and by Beijing's bloody suppression of the opposition movement of 1989. There were some side benefits as well. First of all, U.S. policy toward Taiwan for the first time was not simply a function of American policy towards the PRC. As the PRC loomed smaller in the U.S. strategic calculus, Taiwan could be increasingly addressed on its own terms and for its own sake. Second, the policies begun by the Reagan administration and political liberalization on the island fostered broad support for the island in the Congress among liberals and conservatives alike.

Although Washington's primary purpose concerning Taiwan was avoidance of bad outcomes, and although not all the beneficial effects of

U.S. policy were expected or intended, management of policy since normalization must be considered a success. Through a skillful balancing of U.S. interests on both sides of the Taiwan Strait, Washington was able to maintain productive relations with both. On the one hand, it did not jeopardize the geopolitical benefits that flowed from the relationship with the PRC by acting in ways that suggested that its objective was making Taiwan's separateness permanent. On the other hand, the United States helped facilitate a situation in which Taiwan did not have to make fundamental choices about its future in international isolation and under PRC duress, or make decisions that ignored the wishes of the people on Taiwan.

Taiwan's New External Strategy: Evolution of Equilibrium

The initiatives begun by Chiang Ching-kuo and continued by Lee Teng-hui—democratization on the island, the opening of cross-Strait relations, and incremental expansion of the civilian international role—in theory posed no fundamental problem for U.S. policy. It seemed, to a considerable extent, to be an optimal situation. Washington could continue to balance its interests with both sides of the Strait at low cost. The role of Congress receded as conservatives apparently raised no questions about Taipei's opening to Beijing and liberals declined to support the DPP's flirting with independence. To the extent that increased contacts and integration across the Taiwan Strait reduced tensions, they were consistent with Washington's hope for a peaceful solution.[3] Moreover, Taipei was prepared to play the primary part in expanding its international role, expecting Washington to provide modest support, if any. In addition, the United States could sometimes use Taiwan's desire for increased international status—entry into GATT, for example—to secure more concessions from the PRC.

Reinforcing the more flexible balance of U.S. policy objectives was the equilibrium that Taiwan's leaders engineered between pressures on the island for self-determination, released by political liberalization, and the demands for increased contacts with the mainland. The Lee Teng-hui center of the Kuomintang tacked between the apparent goals of independence and reunification, keeping the right wing of the KMT, the PRC, and the DPP guessing about its intentions. Elastic diplomacy unnerved KMT mainlanders and Beijing, and cross-Strait openings worried Taiwanese nationalists. When calls by the DPP for independence grew too loud (as they did in the 1991 National Assembly election campaign) the PRC responded with threats to use force, both strengthening the political position of the Kuomintang center and increasing Taiwanese mistrust of the communist leaders. When pressure built for overtures toward the mainland, public opinion on the island acted as a rein.

With some manipulation by the center, the tension between the two opposing tendencies had a stabilizing effect. Each of the various players in this game lacked sufficient power or will to secured its preferred option. Each was willing to tolerate certain outcomes for the present but opposed certain other options and moved to block them. The only option that enjoyed all-round mutual tolerance was the status quo. For each actor, it provided less benefit than the outcome it desired but was sufficiently better than the alternative it feared.

For all its Newtonian beauty, this was still a dynamic situation. It could spin out of control and force upon the United States choices that it preferred not to make. Preservation of this advantageous status quo in fact rested on several assumptions, most of which were outside U.S. control.

First of all, maintaining a balance between reunification and independence tendencies was more likely if the Taiwanese core of the KMT retained the lion's share of political power. If the center could not hold, it would not necessarily precipitate a crisis with the mainland, but it would increase the odds and require a different set of conflict management techniques.

Second, the Taiwanese wing of the KMT and the DPP had to have certain fundamental interests in common and so coordinate their actions. If the DPP saw no incentive to exercise restraint when its KMT cousins asked it to, then greater instability might result.

Third, Lee Teng-hui could remain the master of events only if both the PRC and the DPP did not run out of objectives. The reason the two forces were prepared to stay in the game was that it offered something to each to win.

Fourth, public opinion on Taiwan had to remain satisfied with the incremental expansion of Taiwan's international role, particularly with respect to the political arena. If, on the other hand, the DPP was able to convince the public that the KMT had been unwilling to seize opportunities that existed or had been inept in taking them, then the ruling party's hold on power would be further jeopardized.

Fifth, if the PRC in fact intended to use force in the event of a declaration of independence by Taiwan, its threats to do so had to remain credible in the eyes of the people on Taiwan. As a corollary, the people on Taiwan had to believe that a declaration of independence would not receive international support. If neither condition or both were no longer true, a principal obstacle to the DPP's winning power would be removed.

Sixth, the United States and the PRC had to have some level of mutually beneficial relations. If they did not, then the price that Beijing perceived it would pay for action against Taiwan would not decline and the imperative that Washington felt to come to Taiwan's defense would only grow.

Sources of Disequilibrium

Despite these dangers, the picture at the beginning of the 1990s was quite favorable. On three key issues—Taiwan's civilian international role, Taiwan's global arms acquisitions, and cross-Strait relations—there existed patterns of mutual adjustment that met at least the minimum interests of the parties concerned. For U.S. policymakers, managing relations with the island was not a burden and could be allocated a relatively low level of attention as U.S.-PRC relations became politicized after Tiananmen. Yet two developments have threatened to disturb the equilibrium: the collapse of the Soviet Union and politics on Taiwan.

Collapse of the Soviet Union

A key consequence of the end of the USSR was the emergence of a buyer's market for international arms, as Harlan Jencks's chapter comprehensively elaborates. The coin of geopolitical competition quickly took on more of the character of a commodity, and Taiwan suddenly had an opportunity to broaden its international role beyond the soft arenas of economics, society, and culture. Bargain-basement prices for advanced systems and the fact that the PRC itself decided to acquire power-projection capability on the cheap worked together to reduce the power of the constraints on weapons sales to Taiwan that Beijing had erected in the early 1980s. The PRC's purchase of Russian Su-27s created a sufficient reason—compounded by the imperatives of electoral politics in Texas—for the Bush administration to agree to sell 150 F-16s to Taiwan in September 1992, in spite of the pledges made in the August 1982 Communiqué as Beijing understood them.

This new security dimension of Taiwan's international role has introduced a new significant factor into the context of U.S. policy.

However successful Lee Teng-hui's balancing of reunification and independence objectives is, a new vicious circle may be in formation. The PRC's acquisition of a weapons system that threatens the security of Taiwan, plus the need for American arms manufacturers to compete in all available markets, will fuel pressures for the Clinton administration to permit the transfer of a countervailing system to Taiwan. The United States might face a choice between relations with China and the security of Taiwan.[4]

Beijing has reasons, of course, not to force a deterioration in the U.S. relationship over the arms sales issue. Yet there is presumably a limit to the offense it is willing to take, and a limit to which civilian officials can restrain generals and others from achieving the long-sought objective of a militarily powerful nation. For its part, the military on Taiwan will be tempted to seek modern equipment in the current buyer's market whether or not there is a specific mainland capability to defend against. Furthermore, opposition politicians will be all too ready to criticize the government's unwillingness to get the best possible system at the lowest price—as they have already done in the F-16 sale.

Politics on Taiwan

In addition to the arms sales conundrum, Lee Teng-hui's balancing act was becoming more difficult. Some of the preconditions for playing this double game seem to be weakening. Politics on Taiwan, including the politics of the island's international role, is increasing the chances that the United States might have to make a fundamental choice between Beijing and Taipei.

First of all, the KMT's continued hold on power is more in doubt than at any time since the late 1940s. Of the three principal forces in the island's electoral politics, the Taiwanese KMT lost the most in the 1992 Legislative Yuan elections. Whipsawed by the DPP's appeals for "one China, one Taiwan" on the one hand and the mainlander KMT's organizational advantages on the other, Lee Teng-hui's supporters in the legislature hold around seventy seats, less than the eighty-two-seat majority. Strains are growing between the party center and the New Alliance KMT, and unless Lee can maintain confidence in his middle-of-the-road strategy, political momentum will increasingly shift to the DPP.

Second, with the departure of Hau Pei-tsun, the DPP may be less inclined to cooperate with the Taiwanese within the ruling party. The tactical caution and willingness to work with President Lee, fostered by fear of a conservative crackdown in the late 1980s and early 1990s, seems to have dissipated. If the DPP no longer needs to cooperate with the KMT center, it will have been freed to become a real opposition party whose primary goal is gaining power.

Third, Taiwan's public tolerance for incremental expansion of the island's international role—and for making the domestic adjustments needed to satisfy global norms—may be less than circumstances would seem to require. Since the entry of the two Koreas into the United Nations, the opposition has pushed the government to secure membership for the island in the organization sooner rather than later, disdaining both the PRC's opposition and the better chances of success that may lie with an indirect route. The KMT may need to provoke PRC opposition in order to prove its commitment to expanding Taiwan's status in the international political system; whether voters will blame Beijing is another question. Similarly, domestic interest groups and their defenders in the Legislative Yuan have resisted the concessions that Taiwan will have to make to meet the standards for GATT membership and to avoid U.S. sanctions for violations of intellectual property rights.

Fourth, Taiwanese fear of a mainland attack in the event of a declaration of independence may be declining. This is suggested implicitly by polls, which show a near doubling of the population that favors independence. Some oppositionists have fed such attitudes by challenging the KMT assertion that independence would invite an invasion or blockade, or they have simply dismissed PRC threats and the issue of reunification as unimportant. An example of the latter stance was provided in a recent talk in Washington by George Chang, president of the World Formosans for Independence:

> The fundamental dynamic of the Taiwan-China confrontation is the inherent instability. The conflicting claims of Communist China and the KMT automatically create tension and uncertainty in the area....Taiwan independence provides an answer to these uncertainties. An independent Taiwan would immediately abolish all Chinese territorial claims to the island and its surrounding parcels of land, eliminating all reasons for tension between the two peoples.[5]

Built into the current situation on Taiwan, therefore, is the danger of miscalculation should the DPP take power or appear that it is about to. Compounding the danger further is the likelihood that Beijing would overreact to the possibility that its objective on national unification might be permanently frustrated. Compounding it still further is the likely DPP disbelief, evidence to the contrary notwithstanding, that the United

States would not recognize the new government and come to its aid if it is attacked.

Near-Term U.S. Responses

The danger for the United States in these developments is that the mutual adjustment that has so far been possible—on issues such as arms sales to Taiwan, Taiwan's civilian international role, and cross-Strait relations—cannot be sustained. In one of two ways, Taiwan and PRC policies over the next few years will require Washington to face choices that jeopardize its finely balanced sets of competing interests. On the one hand, the vector of the KMT government's quest for a better civilian and security international role will interact to America's detriment with the vector of Beijing's desire to build a modern military and preserve Chinese sovereignty. On the other hand, Lee Teng-hui's effort to improve Taiwan's international status would ultimately fail to satisfy public opinion on the island. The DPP would come to power and alter the vector of policy in a way that would make a clash with the PRC more certain. In either case, adjustment would give way to confrontation.

Options

The United States appears to have five basic options with respect to Taiwan. The first is a passive tilt toward Lee Teng-hui—quiet and indirect association with an effort to balance the tendencies of reunification and independence. This, in essence, would be a continuation of the current policy approach, which implicitly favors the center of Taiwan's political system, occupied by Lee Teng-hui. It would include the following elements:

- reemphasizing the importance of a peaceful process;
- expressing no preference regarding ultimate outcomes, constituting a tacit acceptance of the island's dynamic status quo;
- reaffirming the August 1982 Communiqué while continuing flexible yet quiet implementation of its commitments;
- softly endorsing increased contact between the island and the mainland; and
- endorsing (but not actively promoting) an international civilian role for Taiwan that is acceptable to both Beijing and Taipei.

The second option is an active tilt toward the DPP and the goal of self-determination for the people of Taiwan. Such an approach, grounded in anti-PRC assumptions, would include these elements:

- an explicit rejection of Beijing's claim that Taiwan is a part of China;
- a declared willingness to accept the outcome of some type of act of self-determination by the people of the island;
- active promotion of Taiwan's membership in a variety of international organizations;
- abandonment of the commitments made in the August 1982 Communiqué; and
- a willingness to sell whatever military equipment Taiwan might need, and, if necessary, help the island defend itself if it were attacked.

The third option is an active tilt toward the PRC and against the idea of an independent Taiwan. This policy, which would be premised on the importance of relations with China, would include:

- an explicit statement that some sort of formal association between the island and the mainland under Beijing's sovereignty was in the interest of the United States, and that a unilateral declaration of independence was not;
- rigid enforcement of the terms of the August 1982 Communiqué;
- pressure on the government in Taipei to negotiate with Beijing on the best terms it could get;
- distancing the United States from the DPP and its objectives; and
- opposition at the margin to a more robust international civilian role for Taiwan.

The fourth option is active support of the center of Taiwan's political system, currently occupied by Lee Teng-hui. This approach favors the current dynamic status quo, as in the first option, but takes deliberate steps, in view of the center's perceived weakness, to help maintain it. U.S. actions would be directed at whichever actor threatened to upset the balance. Although the beneficiary of this policy right now would be helpful to Lee Teng-hui, weighing in on the side of a moderate DPP leadership would conceptually not be ruled out. Depending on the circumstances, such a policy might include:

- enunciation of either or both of two corollaries to the traditional U.S. principle of peaceful resolution. The first corollary would be that a resolution of the Taiwan question that does not take into account the views of the people on Taiwan is unacceptable because it is likely to prompt disorders on the island. The second would be that actions that provoke or are likely to provoke a violent response from the PRC are as unacceptable as violence itself and, depending on the circumstances, are unlikely to be supported by the United States;
- private statements to all leaders of the DPP of what they might and might not expect if, in the event they gain power, they proceed down the road toward independence; and
- active assistance of government efforts to secure a broader international role (particularly in the global political system), in order to forestall demands by Taiwan's public for independence.

The fifth option is to distance the United States from the dynamic Taiwan situation and to forego efforts to affect the outcome. The premise of such an approach would be that the United States no longer had a significant national interest in Taiwan's political and security future, both for its own sake and for its linkage to U.S.-China relations. The United States might continue to sell arms to the island, guided by commercial, not foreign policy, considerations. Trade would continue as before but Taiwan would be left to make its own arrangements vis-à-vis Beijing and the international community, and be responsible for the consequences.

Considerations

A number of considerations govern the choice of which option to pursue. First of all, the people on Taiwan probably have the best claim of any currently stateless people to some form of sovereign status. Not only is the island a going concern politically, economically, socially, and culturally, and not only is its military capable of mounting a credible defense of the territory under its control, but, in addition, the government of the island has for the most part been picked on a representative basis by the people of Taiwan. Only the presidency, the provincial governorship, and the mayoralties of Taipei are the major offices not filled by direct elections. If one accepts popular sovereignty as a legitimate basis of statehood (as opposed to the principle that existing states must sanction the creation of new ones), then Taiwan is already a state.

Second, Americans would probably instinctively be inclined to support a claim for self-determination by the people on Taiwan. Our own revolution, after all, was fought to defend the right and necessity of one people to "dissolve the bands which have connected them with another." Ever since, the United States has been associated with the principle of self-determination, and the burden of proof tends to be placed on those who would deny for reasons of realpolitik a people's desire for nationhood. With a social system that is closer than the PRC's to our own, Taiwan in extremis would command the sympathy of the American people, and the David-and-Goliath nature of any struggle would only heighten it.

Third, despite the American affinity for self-determination, the Taiwan question is symptomatic of an emergent international phenomenon, which may be beyond the capacity of that simple principle to accommodate. As the constraints of the Cold War are removed, peoples all over the world who previously had little hope of realizing their aspirations for a separate identity are now asserting themselves. For the United States, the line between supporting human rights and democracy on the one hand, and self-determination on the other, is becoming increasingly blurred. Little consideration has been given to formulating general guidelines for responding to peoples who through democratic means assert their nationhood. Policy concerning this problem may ultimately have to be devised on a case-by-case basis. Although the United States may intervene militarily to support the cause of some self-determination movements, this does not mean that we would intervene to support all. The DPP, therefore, cannot assume that the United States would definitely support a drive to independence that provoked a vigorous military response by China.[6]

Fourth, it is not clear why Taiwan's claim to statehood—within or without the Chinese nation—will be in greater jeopardy later than it is now. Indeed, it is difficult to see the risks of deferring a final decision on Taiwan's international status until after the generational succession in the PRC is more advanced, particularly if a gradual expansion of Taiwan's international role is possible. Nor is it clear why the achievement of statehood for Taiwan without Taiwanese nationhood as a medium-term objective would not be a victory for the DPP or would necessarily rule out nationhood later on.

The only serious problem with a pragmatic and patient approach by Taiwan might be that the PRC's military build-up would degrade Taiwan's qualitative deterrent edge, and so limit its medium-term freedom of political maneuver. That, some might claim, would argue for forcing the issue now rather than waiting, particularly if Taiwan were unable to compensate for an increase in PRC capabilities. Which argument is more valid would depend in part on a technical assessment of how fast the PRC is acquiring and deploying the weapons most threatening to Taiwan, relative to political change on the mainland. If Beijing's acquisitions do not have immediate consequences for force structure that is relevant to the island's security, Taiwan may have more breathing room. By and large, however, it appears that time is on Taiwan's side in terms of choosing a course that is commensurate with its interests and the wishes of its people.

Fifth, simply because the dynamics of Taiwan's situation create the possibility of fundamental dilemmas for U.S. policy does not mean that they will occur. The scenario that currently creates the most anxiety for U.S. policymakers—the DPP gaining power and, driven by its radical wing, making a unilateral declaration of independence—may never occur. The KMT still has considerable strength, and Taiwan's electorate possesses a strong pragmatic streak. Even if the DPP were to win power, its more moderate wing might dominate policymaking and abandon the rhetorical stance it had taken for the sake of gaining power. A DPP government might even work out its own accommodation with Beijing. On the other side of the coin, it may be too early to judge the military impact of the PRC's arms acquisitions. They may be less threatening to Taiwan in the medium term than some suggest, particularly if the PRC is purchasing a limited number of copies of each system with the intent of developing and producing clones in China's military industrial complex. Consequently, the United States need not act right now as if the island and the mainland are doomed to an arms race and as if the DPP is destined to declare independence. U.S. actions designed to head off the worse case may make a manageable situation more unstable than otherwise would have been the case.

Sixth, although U.S. policy in the last decade has been able to address Taiwan for its own sake, there is an irreducible degree to which it is inextricably linked to the U.S. relationship with China. That is because the PRC insists that is be so (or, more precisely, will only tolerate a certain level of autonomy to the U.S.-Taiwan relationship). To the extent, therefore, that Washington retains an interest in good relations with Beijing, there are limits to which it may associate itself with trends on Taiwan that the PRC opposes. Even if U.S.-China relations were to deteriorate to the point that there were few common interests left, it may still be in Taiwan's interest for the United States to avoid provoking China to take actions against the island that could otherwise be avoided. Obviously, PRC tolerance will vary from time to time, and political forces on Taiwan are right to test the limits of tolerance. Yet because favorable U.S.-China relations have, in fact, been good for Taiwan, reckless initiatives may turn out to be doubly counterproductive.

Seventh, it is not always easy to gauge the level of political support in the United States for policies other than quiet endorsement of the status quo on Taiwan. As indicated above, there would probably be widespread opposition in Congress and the country to a tilt in U.S. policy towards the PRC. Also problematic is a tilt in favor of the DPP, particularly if the issue of military intervention came into play. The departure of Stephen Solarz from Congress has deprived the DPP of its most active ally and potential advocate in Washington policy circles, and public support for the use of military force is a case-by-case proposition. It is not clear, moreover, whether more conservative members of Congress will transfer the support they provided to KMT mainlanders to KMT Taiwanese, to say nothing of a DPP government should one come to power. Finally, there has been a generational change in Congress, the consequences of which for Taiwan are difficult to measure.[7]

On balance, the dynamic Taiwan situation seems to call for a basic continuity of American policy over the next couple of years, albeit in the knowledge that changes that might undermine U.S. interests could come very quickly and require a timely response. Lee Teng-hui's middle-of-the-road approach is congruent with the multiplicity of American interests, and these are likely to be served as long as the KMT's mainstream remains in power. Lee's government's efforts to secure a broader international role is legitimate given Taiwan's developmental accomplishments, and should be supported at the margins. Yet in any specific case, responsibility for creating the international consensus in Taiwan's favor lies with Taipei. Putting the onus on Beijing to justify to the world why Taiwan should be excluded from global institutions will probably be more successful than having Washington bear the burden of explaining to Beijing why the island should be included. In the security field, although the United States retains a responsibility for the island, the threat that China poses should be evaluated objectively and in the context of Taiwan's overall relationship with the mainland. If the United States is to transfer defense systems to Taiwan that put its relationship with China at a grave risk, it should be in response to PRC acquisitions that indisputably put Taiwan in danger. Concerning the DPP, because it will not have an electoral chance to come to power until 1995, there remains an opportunity to pursue a focused and expanded dialogue with all elements of the party to facilitate a better understanding of U.S. interests. (Enhancing Beijing's understanding of the meaning of developments on Taiwan will promote stability as well.) At all times, U.S. officials should be on guard in case changes occur that dictate a more activist American approach.

Beyond the Short Term

Each of the elements in the analytical chain of this study has been treated more or less as constants, which makes sense at any particular point in time. Yet each factor may be treated as a variable with the potential to create radically different implications for U.S. policy. Still other questions deserve some speculation, among them the following:

- Regarding governmental control on Taiwan, what if the DPP in fact won power and moved to assert Taiwan's *de jure* independence?
- Concerning the international economic system, will a GATT-based or GATT-like structure continue?
- Concerning the international political system, do alternatives exist to one of the fundamental norms of the post-Westphalia system, that new states only emerge by virtue of the agreement of existing states?
- Concerning the international security system, are there circumstances under which Taiwan might again become a geopolitical partner of sufficient value to set aside the constraints that have operated on it for the past twenty-two years?
- What is the future of the PRC? Will a successor leadership be willing and able to hold the country together and sustain the current view of the scope of the Chinese state?

Obviously, these are only a few of the significant changes in the current situation that should have an impact on Taiwan's international role and its implications. Limited answers are offered to some of the questions, while scenarios are elaborated for others.

If the DPP won power and pursued the independence route, and if some sort of PRC military action was likely, the United States would initially find itself in a dilemma. Should it support the principle of self-determination or seek to preserve the status quo? The resolution of that dilemma is almost impossible to predict, since it would depend on the degree of public and congressional support that existed for the Taiwanese cause. There is a decent chance, however, that the United States would weigh in on the side of peace and regional stability, and engage in an intensive effort to get the DPP to back off. This is made more likely because Taiwan's options are probably not foreclosed by a strategy of patience. Although Washington would have a leading role in the effort to persuade a DPP government to step back from the brink, it would probably not be alone. Most governments in East Asia that have their own relationships with Beijing and their own deep interests in regional stability could be counted upon to weigh in on the side of caution. Although an adverse outcome may not be ruled out, neither is it a certainty.

On the global economic system, Taiwan's interests seem to lie with a continuation of a GATT or GATT-like structure. It has benefitted from relatively open access to the U.S. market in the past, and its diversification of export markets in the future will be facilitated by membership in GATT. The internal reforms it will have to make to secure access will only make its economy more efficient. However, the decline of an open trading system on either a global or Asia-Pacific basis would work to the island's economic and political disadvantage. It has been in the economic arena, after all, that Taiwan has been most able to expand its international role. In a more mercantilist system, moreover, Taiwan might have to make a fundamental choice as to which larger economy it would align with, the United States and the PRC being the most obvious partners.

Regarding the international political system, there is a new fluidity emerging in the concept of statehood. Just as there are peoples or entities that are claiming the right to separate status on grounds related to the principle of popular sovereignty, there are also existing states that lack the capacity to govern themselves, such as Somalia. Increasingly, the international community is having to face the claims of the former and the needs of the latter, and create the bases in international law as it goes along.[8] As suggested above, Taiwan probably has as good a claim as any entity for statehood. In cases like Cambodia and Somalia, the international community has basically taken on the role of guardian of the people of the country concerned as the justification for various types of neo-colonial presence. Consequently, the international system is becoming more flexible at the very time that Taiwan is creating a unique international role. The main obstacle is political: the opposition of the PRC (which, not surprisingly, has questioned recent instances of humanitarian intervention on the grounds that they are a violation of "sovereignty").

It is too early to say how engaged the United States will be in post-Cold War Asia. Executive branch policymakers pledge that America will not walk away from the region, but an imbalance between commitments and declining resources may dictate otherwise. If the United States does withdraw, Taiwan will be among the former American clients most at risk, although the anxiety of current treaty partners would be considerable. The island would likely have to choose between finding another protector (Japan, perhaps?) or making peace with the PRC.

East Asia's Military Future

Related to the future role of the United States in East Asia is the prospect of a major shift in the regional balance of military power. The most intriguing scenario from Taiwan's point of view is the possible emergence of a militarily and economically robust PRC, which seeks to be the dominant power in the region and threatens not only Taiwan but others as well.

Such a development would not only present Taiwan with serious challenges concerning its own defense, with implications for U.S. arms sales policy (as discussed previously). Indeed, Taiwan would be the most obvious unresolved territorial issue in Beijing's eyes. But PRC hegemonism might also create pressures for all states in the region that felt threatened to join together in a formal or informal collective security structure. Because the acquisition of power projection capabilities is an important feature of the PRC's buildup, the island states of the region would share a common interest, along with Vietnam and perhaps Korea. Such an arrangement would be similar to the containment chain erected by the United States during the 1950s and 1960s, of which Taiwan was an important link, and would also recall Japan's colonial patronage of Taiwan in the first half of this century. The emergence of an anti-PRC alliance would presumably increase the incentives for an independent Taiwan.

What would be the role of the United States in this new regional power configuration? If the United States chose to remain in Asia, its first impulse probably would be to create circumstances to limit the growth of PRC power and encourage its acceptance of a multipolar order. If that did not work, Washington would presumably take the lead in organizing the collective security structure. If the United States chose not to be responsible for regional peace and security, its role would resemble the one it had in the early 1930s.

Other Futures for the PRC

The achievement of wealth and power with region-wide implications is not the only possible future for the PRC after the death of the current old guard. Another scenario suggests itself—that the new Beijing leadership will not have the organizational and political reach of even the current government. Obviously, the degree to which the power of the center might be degraded is impossible to predict. Clearly, the cohesion of the military would be a critical factor in determining the approach of this "new China" towards Taiwan. To the extent, however, that the central government is less able to enforce its claims vis-à-vis Taiwan, the stronger would be the island's bargaining power, and the more likely Beijing might be to concede statehood to Taipei in order to keep it in the Chinese nation. Conversely, the greater the scope of central authority, the more likely Taiwan might have the incentive to enter into some kind of commonwealth and the less likely it would be to move toward an independent Taiwan. The possibility of a more flexible approach towards Taiwan's status and its role in the world might be reinforced by a more cosmopolitan world view on the part of the new leadership, cultivated by a greater exposure to the outside world. Even if a narrow nationalism remained strong under this scenario, it could not be sustained without sufficient power, and the political imperative of maintaining economic growth, especially in south China, would probably rule out military adventurism. As for U.S. policy, the outcomes that might follow from a weakening of the PRC center would probably not necessitate continued avoidance of a choice between the mainland and Taiwan.

Conclusion

Taiwan's search for a new international role did not initially create problems for U.S. policy. It was, in a sense, an outcome of U.S. actions. In addition, the opening to the mainland with which Taipei balanced its pragmatic diplomacy worked to Washington's indirect benefit. Although it was recognized that the island's increasingly open politics held some peril for U.S. policy, it has been the unexpected—the collapse of the Soviet Union—that has created the most volatility.

Prospects for the future, and for U.S. policy, seem to depend on the time-frame. In the short term, the critical factor is whether the Kuomintang, and in particular its new Taiwanese center, can maintain its hold on power. If it loses power in the 1995 elections and before China's remaining elders die, demands for Taiwanese nationhood may provoke the crisis that the United States has worked assiduously to avoid. If, on the other hand, the KMT can stay in power until the communist gerontocracy passes from the scene, then the key variable determining Taiwan's future becomes political change in the PRC. Whether the new leadership will be passively introverted or aggressively extroverted; whether it will be as nationalistic as its predecessors, cannot be predicted, and a dangerous scenario cannot be ruled out. Yet even if that occurs, Taiwan will not be the only actor at risk and the United States is probably more likely to see its interests threatened. Regarding more benign scenarios, the consequences for Taiwan seem to be an international role more of its own choosing, and one that is commensurate with the accomplishments of the island's people. For the United States, that would be a satisfactory dividend from its past policy.

Commentary

Nancy Bernkopf Tucker

The author lays out with great precision the key factors that have shaped Washington's "stealth diplomacy"—advocacy of Taiwan's interests by indirection, including acknowledgment of the view that Taiwan is a part of China, observance of the Taiwan Relations Act, under which the United States continued to provide the means for Taiwan's defense, and refusal to play a mediating role to resolve differences between the players except to emphasize that resolution must come peacefully. Bush contends that preservation of an effective, low-key approach that appears neutral and involves a considerable element of benign neglect is contingent upon conditions in Taiwan remaining fundamentally unchanged.

But as Bush makes clear, the status quo cannot be preserved and the changing balance of power on the island will probably have serious consequences for the United States. Among the most destabilizing factors he mentions are the loss of control by the Kuomintang and the concomitant decline in the willingness of the Democratic Progressive Party to cooperate with it, the disenchantment of the public with a gradualistic approach to acquiring international status, and the ebbing fear of retribution by the People's Republic of China (PRC) accompanied by a conviction that the United States would come to the rescue if Beijing were to mount an attack.[9] These views promise to be increasingly provocative from the viewpoint of the Chinese communist leadership and, were they to be acted upon, could lead to a new Taiwan Strait crisis.

For the United States, which in the past 40 years has successfully pursued a modified two Chinas policy, the challenge is one of fundamental principle: the choice between respect for self-determination and sovereignty. Taiwan, more than most claimants, has a clear economic, political, social, and perhaps even cultural case for statehood and Americans believe staunchly in the concept of self-determination, articulated for them persuasively by Woodrow Wilson in the 1910s. It is hard to see how Washington could ignore or repudiate a decisive drive for independence. When Americans have rejected self-determination in the past it has been because people, Vietnamese for instance, opted to live under communist rulers. The people on Taiwan, however, are achieving a long-sought democratic order, promoted and, in part, financed by the United States.[10] Is it realistic to think that at the moment democracy is realized Washington could walk away?

Americans admittedly have turned their backs on Bosnia, but Taiwan is not Bosnia. For historical, geographic, and strategic reasons, including Taiwan's accessibility to the U.S. Navy, the pressures upon the government to do something would be intense and, as in the Persian Gulf War, the public might believe the prospects for victory irresistibly low-cost and bright. Whatever policymakers say ahead of time, in a military confrontation between China and Taiwan it seems unlikely that the United States could remain a spectator and allow Taiwan to be devastated, occupied, and swallowed.

The United States, after all, already behaves as though Taiwan is a separate state, and has done so almost consistently since 1949. Even after the Shanghai Communiqué and the normalization accord, Washington's policies continued to relate to Beijing and Taipei more or less as capitals of two distinct countries. The American Institute in Taiwan and the Coordination Council for North American Affairs, although informal representative organizations, have virtually all the attributes of embassies.

But Americans also have an historical reverence for sovereignty and have never been quick to support movements to disaggregate existing political entities. This is complemented by awareness of the dangerous backlash that Taiwan's independence would have, threatening both conflict in the Strait and an abrupt break in Sino-American relations. Thus the American government is caught between two dearly held principles that render an effective policy almost impossible to devise were the existing posture of noninvolvement no longer to suffice.

What Richard Bush does not emphasize adequately is the rising tide of nationalism in the post-Cold War world and the degree to which it is capturing imaginations in China and Taiwan. In other words, even were the communist government in Beijing to pass from the scene tomorrow, there is little to suggest that a new democratically inclined leadership would be more willing than the current rulers to accept self-determination for Taiwan. Witness the determination of liberal intellectuals today to keep Tibet and Taiwan firmly within the Chinese fold. Moreover, even with a democratic government in Beijing, it is not at all clear that the Taiwanese would willingly surrender their *de facto* independence and reunite with the mainland. Were they to be convinced that a democratic regime would not use force against them, the pressure for an instant declaration of independence would most likely escalate instantly. Of course, under such circumstances the implications for the United States might be far less disastrous, although Beijing would most likely be resentful and hold Washington partly responsible.

Another issue that ought to be emphasized is the hallowed tradition of nationalist Chinese manipulation of the United States. Although Taiwan is the far smaller and weaker entity, it invariably has found ways to assert its agenda and solicit behavior from Washington that served Taipei's interests—sometimes in direct contradiction to Washington's objectives.[11] The most notorious example would be the 1954 Mutual Defense Treaty, which John Foster Dulles did not want to sign, but which he was maneuvered into granting during the Taiwan Strait Crisis. He had avoided commitment for many months but, fearful of the risk of a major war in the Strait, he relented in exchange for Chiang Kai-shek's agreement not to veto the U.S. effort to resolve the crisis through intercession by the United Nations (UN).[12] Throughout the 1950s and until the mid-1960s, at a time of extreme Taiwan dependence upon the United States, economically and militarily, Washington found itself no more able to occasion action than it had been to forestall it. The United

States failed to cajole or coerce nationalist officials to cut their defense budget.[13]   Chiang and his associates refined and built upon their successful tactics, making management of the United States a key element in Taiwan's foreign policy.

In the 1990s, Taiwan utilized European willingness to explore expanded trade relations with Taiwan through visits by high-level government officials to compel Washington to violate its understandings with the PRC and send a cabinet-level official, Trade Representative Carla Hills, to Taipei. Similarly, Taipei saw negotiations with France to buy the Mirage aircraft as leverage, alongside U.S. security concerns and election politics in 1992, to convince Washington that it had to reverse its ban on sales of advanced fighter jets and provide Taiwan with the F-16.[14]   The Bush administration claimed that the PRC purchase of Russian SU-27 aircraft and general technological advances meant that the F-16 no longer qualified as an offensive weapon threatening to the PRC. However, its symbolic significance, as the plane denied to Taiwan by previous administrations because it was deemed too provocative, elevated its strategic importance and implied, as Harlan Jencks noted elsewhere in this volume, that constraints set by agreements between Washington and Beijing might be overlooked in sales of other sophisticated weapons.

Alongside security issues, the United States also confronted difficult economic questions, particularly Taiwan's membership in the General Agreement on Tariffs and Trade (GATT). Taipei wants to join and has come a long way toward meeting the requirements for adherence, much further than has the PRC, which presumes it will enter first. Taiwan managed to persuade President George Bush and members of Congress that it has a good case, and as a result the United States became the first major power to call for Taiwan's admission publicly. This the president did in exchange for votes in Congress in 1991 to support most-favored-nation treatment for Beijing.[15]   It is not, however, absolutely clear that Taiwan's entry into GATT serves U.S. interests nearly as well as a Taiwan on its best behavior, striving to get in, but still legally able to grant the United States trade preferences.

Overall the essay says little about economic frictions between the United States and Taiwan. American anxiety probably peaked in the late 1980s when the U.S.-Taiwan trade deficit rose eight-fold from a level of $2.3 billion in 1979 to some $19 billion in 1987. On a per capita basis this figure significantly exceeded even the U.S.-Japan imbalance. Aggravated by U.S. concern about Taiwan's excessive foreign exchange reserves and currency management, trade problems finally triggered a comprehensive tariff reduction program, revaluation of the New Taiwan dollar and relaxation of controls on foreign financial activities.[16] But despite reduction of the trade deficit, a series of tensions remain, including the costly matters of intellectual property right infringement—copyrights, patents, and trademarks.[17]

In the original paper written for the Taiwan workshop convened at the Sigur Center, the options proposed for U.S. policymakers were more limited than those explored in the revised essay published here. The current review of alternatives, being internally more consistent and covering the range of possible action more comprehensively, requires fewer comments. It may, nonetheless, be worth adding some further "considerations" to the list provided for evaluation of the Bush policy options.

First, the Taiwan lobby, which has been a powerful force protecting the interests of the nationalist Chinese in Washington for decades, has weakened, but by no means disappeared. Some argue that it has been the most effective foreign lobby excepting only that of the Israelis. Its continuing influence will narrow Washington's choices.

Second, the perils of a push for independence are obvious, but it may not be the only course that would be dangerous for Washington to support. Should the United States flatly oppose the movement favoring independence, it would hazard alienating a growing segment of the population on the island. One day it might put the United States in a very difficult situation vis-à-vis an independent government, should one materialize.

Third, if independence risks provoking a cataclysm, reunification also has the potential of yielding negative results for the United States. Already the growing economic integration of Taiwan and China has allowed Taiwanese businessmen to avoid reducing trade imbalances with the United States by shifting factory production to the mainland. Unity might also create a more self-assured, aggressive, and assertive Chinese foreign policy. Washington welcomed the reunification of Germany only to find German decisions on international affairs departing more sharply from American preferences (especially with regard to the breakup of Yugoslavia) than before.

Fourth, Bush has focused on a pro-independence force that approaches the matter prudently. But there are also those for whom this is an emotional issue, whose assessment of the probable outcome is not realistic, and whose limited experience in international relations creates false expectations. Recent demands, from members of the Kuomintang, that the government reopen the question of a Taiwan seat in the United

Nations, in the face of certain and belligerent opposition from Beijing, testifies to the power of delusions and demagoguery abroad in the land.[18] The risk that the explosive issue of independence will continue to gain momentum, as it has in the past year, must not be ignored.

Finally, though the essay advocates better education of both Chinas regarding the perils of precipitous action to resolve the reunification issue, it does not call strongly for education of the American electorate. Rarely does news about Taiwan receive much attention from the U.S. media and this apathy and ignorance could prove perilous if a rapid response to crisis conditions proved necessary. The American people over time have demonstrated considerable disinterest in Asia—they will not remedy the deficit on their own. There needs to be a greater effort by the administration to keep the American people informed about developments in this possibly volatile area.

The relationship between Taiwan and the United States has been an unusual one, extremely close and yet fraught with internecine turmoil and opportunities for larger regional destructiveness since the 1940s. Early on there was the constant threat that Chiang Kai-shek would involve the United States in a war with China. As late as the mid-1960s Chiang proposed paralleling a Kuomintang attack on the mainland with American military action in Vietnam to rid Asia of the communist menace.[19] The United States had insisted, beginning in the 1950s, that the nationalists abandon efforts to recover the mainland, but diametrically different views of Taiwan's interests and significance in Taipei and Washington produced repeated disputes over mainland recovery and a host of other political, economic, and military problems. In the cultural sphere, Taiwan wrestled with the implications of American influence, at times displaying reactions akin to Beijing's rejection of Western spiritual pollution.[20]

Nevertheless, when Cold War imperatives led Washington formally to abandon Taiwan in 1972 and 1978, the nationalists felt betrayed and accused the United States of renouncing principles of freedom and friendship vital to the continued existence of the Taipei government. Through provisions of the Taiwan Relations Act and the necessity of continued ties with the United States for the island's economy and defense, Taipei learned to live with the new reality. But now a new crisis looms in which it again becomes apparent that Taiwan's needs and the priorities of the United States are not only not identical, but may be fundamentally antithetical. Bush has wrestled with this truth and astutely clarified the problems and the possibilities—a solution remains disturbingly out of reach.

Notes

The views expressed in this chapter are those of the author alone, and not necessarily those of the U.S. Congress, the House Foreign Affairs Committee, or its members. The author expresses his appreciation to other members of the George Washington University Taiwan Study Group for their useful comments on a draft of this essay.

1. In the basic sociological understanding of the term, roles are the constituent element of a structure of social action. Each role is defined both by a particular status and by a set of norms (rights and obligations), which the incumbent of the role incurs and which govern its interaction between other roles in the structure. The operation of the structure has consequences (functions or dysfunctions) for the workings of the larger system of which the structure is a part. It is worth asking whether Taiwan's international behavior—or any international actor's, for that matter—is best explained on the basis of such a normative mode of analysis. A role-based framework may be more useful for explaining realms of behavior where norms are more clearly defined and broadly accepted. International politics, one might argue, is an arena in which norms are merely the rationalizing cloaks of contests for power.

2. The U.S. formulation concerning Taiwan's status at the time of normalization is, in my view, more significant than the one made in the 1972 Shanghai Communiqué. The normalization statement on Taiwan was connected with the recognition of the PRC as the sole legal government of China, and so represents something of a qualification of what the United States understands the term "China" to mean. Note that the United States made no such qualification concerning Tibet.

3. This linkage was drawn as early as March 1987 by Secretary of State George Shultz in a statement in Shanghai: "We support a continuing evolutionary process toward a peaceful resolution of the Taiwan issue. The pace, however, will be determined by the Chinese on either side of the Taiwan Strait, free of outside pressure. For our part, we have welcomed developments, including indirect trade and increasing human interchange, which have contributed to a relaxation of tensions in the Taiwan Strait. Our steadfast policy seeks to foster an environment in which such developments can continue to take place," *Department of State Bulletin*, May 1987, p. 11.

4. The forcing of a choice grew closer in July 1993 when the Senate Foreign Relations Committee, with the encouragement of U.S. arms exporters, approved an amendment to the Taiwan Relations Act that stated that the arms-sales provisions of the TRA "superseded" the relevant sections of the August 1982 Communiqué. This amendment was deliberately designed to end the "bucket," the requirement that the quantity of arms sales decline over time. The amendment, which was included in the State Department Authorization Bill for Fiscal Year 1994-1995, was opposed by the Clinton administration. Whether it will survive the House-Senate conference on the bill was unclear at the time that the final draft of this essay was completed.

5. George T. Chang, "Toward an Independent Taiwan," speech delivered to the U.S. Congress, May 21, 1993.

6. For recent discussions of the self-determination dilemma, see Amitai Etzioni, "The Evils of Self-Determination," *Foreign Policy*, vol. 89, Winter 1992-1993, pp. 21-35; and Robert Cullen, "Human Rights Quandary," *Foreign Affairs*, vol. 71, no. 5, Winter 1992-1993, pp. 78-88.

7. It is also worth noting that a policy other than the current one and opting out would require close attention and skillful management, with sustained high-level attention. In a policymaking environment where crises crowd out consideration of second- and third-order issues, it remains to be seen, however, how much attention a more activist Taiwan policy might get.

8. See, for example, Paul Johnson, "Colonialism's Back—And Not a Moment Too Soon," *The New York Times Magazine*, April 18, 1993.

9. The assertion that people in Taiwan fear mainland retribution less to some extent is contradicted by the nervousness developing in the Asian area regarding China's development of a blue water navy and its arms purchases from the former Soviet Union.

10. Neil H. Jacoby, *U.S. Aid to Taiwan*, (New York, NY: Praeger, 1966).

11. For an extended discussion of this problem see Nancy Bernkopf Tucker, *Taiwan, Hong Kong and the United States, 1945-1992*, (New York, NY: Twayne, 1994). See also Steve Chan, "The Mouse that Roared: Taiwan's Management of Trade Relations with the United States," *Comparative Political Studies*, vol. 20, October 1987, pp. 251-92.

12. Nancy Bernkopf Tucker, "John Foster Dulles and the Taiwan Roots of the `Two Chinas' Policy," in Richard H. Immerman, ed., *John Foster Dulles and the Diplomacy of the Cold War*, (Princeton, NJ: Princeton University Press, 1989), pp. 235-62.

13. 793.5/8-2351 Memo Perkins (CA) to Merchant (FE), Box 4219, Record Group 59: General Records of the Department of State, National Archives, Washington, DC, (hereafter RG 59, NA); 793.5MAP/8-1651 Memo Merchant to Rusk, Box 4221, RG 59, NA; Chase to Rankin, October 5, 1953, Box 11, folder: 501, Record Group 84: China Post Files, General Archives Division, Washington National Records Center; Annex III: "Countering the Chinese Communist Military Threat," in Communist China Long Range Study, June 1966, National Security File, Country File, China, Box 245, Lyndon Baines Johnson Library, Austin, Texas (hereafter LBJ).

14. Interview with former senior Taiwan official, July 1993.

15. Julian Baum, "A favour of sorts," *Far Eastern Economic Review*, August 8, 1991, p. 8.

16. *International Herald Tribune*, June 23, 1989, p. 15; Penelope Hartland-Thunberg, *China, Hong Kong, Taiwan and the World Trading System*, (New York, NY: St. Martin's Press, 1990), pp. 117-18; Christopher Marchand, "A win for Washington," *Far Eastern Economic Review*, April 6, 1989, p. 79.

17. In April 1992, for instance the United States trade representative cited Taiwan under provisions of Section 301 of the 1988 Trade Act. In computer software alone, Taiwan held the distinction of distributing roughly 90 percent of the fraudulent materials produced worldwide. Harriet King, "Microsoft Nails Some Pirates," *New York Times*, May 10, 1992, p. 7F.

18. Julian Baum, "In search of recognition," *Far Eastern Economic Review*, July 18, 1991, p. 26.

19. Memorandum of Conversation Rusk with Chiang, April 16, 1964, NSF, Country File China, vol. 4, Box 238, LBJ; Memo for the Record: Views of Ambassador Wright, May 12, 1964, James C. Thomson Papers, F: Far East: Taiwan 1958, 1962-1964, John F. Kennedy Library, Columbia Point, Boston, MA; Memo Jenkins to Rostow, March 7, 1967, NSF Country File China, Box 241, F: China Memos, vol. IX, 3/67-6/67, LBJ.

20. Warren Tozer, "Taiwan's Cultural Renaissance': A Preliminary View," *China Quarterly*, July/September, 1970.

About the Contributors

Richard Bush is a professional staff member of the Committee on Foreign Affairs of the U.S. House of Representatives with responsibility for East Asia. He is the author of *The Politics of Cotton Textiles in Kuomintang China* (1982).

Fu-mei Chang Chen is a research fellow at the Hoover Institution, Stanford University, and member of the National Assembly in Taiwan. She is also co-editor with Jerome Alan Cohen and R. Randle Edwards of *Essays on China's Legal Tradition* (1981).

Ralph N. Clough, a professorial lecturer at The Paul H. Nitze School of Advanced International Studies of the Johns Hopkins University in Washington, DC, is the author of *Reaching Across the Taiwan Strait: People to People Diplomacy* (1993).

June Teufel Dreyer is a professor in the Department of Political Science at the University of Miami in Coral Gables. She is the author of *China's Political System: Modernization and Tradition* (1993).

Thomas B. Gold is an associate professor in the Department of Sociology, and chair, Center for Chinese Studies, at the University of California, Berkeley. He is the author of *State and Society in the Taiwan Miracle* (1986).

Harry Harding is a senior fellow in the Foreign Policy Studies Program at The Brookings Institution in Washington, DC. His most recent book is *A Fragile Relationship: The United States and China Since 1972* (1992).

Erland Heginbotham is a senior fellow at the National Planning Association in Washington, DC, and director of Gateway Japan. He formerly served in the Foreign Service.

Harlan W. Jencks is a research associate with the Center for Chinese Studies of the University of California, Berkeley, and author of *From Muskets to Missiles: Politics and Professionalism in the Chinese Army, 1945-1981* (1982).

William R. Johnson is associate director of The Gaston Sigur Center for East Asian Studies of the Elliott School of International Affairs and program director of East Asian Studies at The George Washington University, Washington, DC.

Samuel S. Kim is a senior research scholar with the East Asian Institute of Columbia University in New York. His numerous publications include *China and the World 1994: Chinese Foreign Relations in the Post-Cold War Era,* 3rd ed. (1994) of which he is the editor.

Charlotte Ku is deputy executive director of the American Society of International Law in Washington, DC.

David M. Lampton is president of the National Committee on United States-China Relations in New York. He is also co-editor with Kenneth Lieberthal of *Bureaucracy, Politics, and Decision Making in Post-Mao China* (1992).

Ronald N. Montaperto is a senior fellow with the Institute for National Strategic Studies of the National Defense University in Washington, DC, and author of *Cooperative Engagement and Economic Security in the Asia-Pacific Region* (1993).

James Riedel is a professor of international economics with The Paul H. Nitze School of Advanced International Studies of the Johns Hopkins University in Washington, DC. He is also contributor and co-editor with C. Pearson of *The Direction of Trade Policy* (1990).

Robert G. Sutter is a senior specialist in international policy with the Congressional Research Service of the Library of Congress and adjunct professor at The Gaston Sigur Center for East Asian Studies, Elliott School of International Affairs, The George Washington University, Washington, DC. His numerous publications include *East Asia and the Pacific: Challenges for U.S. Policy* (1992).

Hung-mao Tien is a professor of political science at the University of Wisconsin, Milwaukee, and author of *The Great Transition: Political and Social Change in the Republic of China* (1989).

Nancy Bernkopf Tucker is on the faculty of the Department of History and the School of Foreign Service at Georgetown University. She has recently completed *Taiwan, Hong Kong and the United States, 1945-1992* for Twayne Press International History series at Macmillan Publishers.

About the Book

Traditionally, Taiwan has been viewed as the passive pawn of more aggressive powers, yet now it has begun to assert its voice in world affairs—especially through economic influence. This volume brings together leading scholars to examine the origins and implications of Taiwan's global role and the ramifications of its growing strength for such crucial policy issues as China's reunification and U.S. policy in East Asia.

Index